THE WAY TO KEEP HIM AND FIVE OTHER PLAYS

from Works (1786)

Arthur Murphy

The Way to Keep Him

five other plays by

ARTHUR MURPHY

edited by
John Pike Emery

NEW YORK UNIVERSITY PRESS

WASHINGTON SQUARE · NEW YORK

1956

Manufactured in the United States of America

To

My Wife

CONTENTS

PREFACE

BETWEEN 1756 and 1777, no English dramatist contributed to the repertoires of the regular London theaters, Drury Lane and Covent Garden, more stock plays of merit than did Arthur Murphy (1727-1805). Some well-known English and American critics have ranked his best comedies, *The Way to Keep Him* and particularly *Know Your Own Mind*, above the comedies of his contemporaries Oliver Goldsmith and Richard Brinsley Sheridan. The recent publication of two biographical and critical monographs (Howard H. Dunbar, *The Dramatic Career of Arthur Murphy*, New York, 1946; John P. Emery, *Arthur Murphy: An Eminent English Dramatist of the Eighteenth Century*, Philadelphia, 1946) has corroborated the interest in Murphy. The purpose of this edition is to make accessible his best farces and comedies. The above-mentioned earlier book of the editor answers any reader who has questions concerning the present choice of plays or who desires a full analysis of Murphy's sources. The editor believes that his own sustained enthusiasm during the many years of this undertaking will be duplicated by the interest of the reader. As the separate introductions to the six plays explain, the best and most authoritative text is in *The Works of Arthur Murphy* (1786). The editor has kept in mind the general reader, the undergraduate, and the specialist in providing the exegetical and textual footnotes.

The collated texts are in the following libraries: British Museum, Bryn Mawr College, Columbia University, Library of Congress, Harvard University, Haverford College, Henry E. Huntington Library, State University of Iowa, Library Company of Philadelphia, University of Pennsylvania, Princeton University, Temple Univer-

ix

sity, University of Wisconsin, and Yale University. Also, for personal courtesies and correspondence, the editor desires to thank members of these additional library staffs: Birmingham Reference Library (England), Bodleian Library, Boston Public Library, Brown University, University of California at Los Angeles, University Library of Cambridge, University of Chicago, Cornell University, Courtauld Institute of Art of the University of London, Folger Shakespeare Library, Frick Art Reference Library, Grosvenor Library (Buffalo), University of Illinois, Johns Hopkins University, City of Leicester Museum and Art Gallery, Metropolitan Museum of Art, University of Michigan, Newberry Library (Chicago), New York Public Library, University of North Carolina, Northwestern University, Peabody Institute (Baltimore), Philadelphia Bar Association Library, Philadelphia Free Library, Pierpont Morgan Library, Stanford University, University of Texas, University of Virginia, and University of Washington. This work was aided by a grant from the Committee on Research and Publication of Temple University. The editor desires to thank his colleague Dr. C. William Miller for bibliographical criticism and Dean Howard H. Dunbar of New York University for reading the complete manuscript and recommending several specific changes in the separate introductions and footnotes.

J. P. E.

January 26, 1956

THE APPRENTICE (1756)

ARTHUR MURPHY composed *The Apprentice*, a farce of two acts, in 1754. The characters of the first draft did not include the elder Wingate, who was added as a satire of the author's late maternal uncle, Jeffrey French, recommender of Edward Cocker's *Arithmetick*. With a prologue by David Garrick, spoken by Murphy himself, dressed in black, the play opened at Drury Lane Theatre January 2, 1756, with immediate success. Henry Woodward acted the role of Dick, the apprentice, and Richard Yates that of Wingate, his father. *The Apprentice* became an established piece in the repertoires of the London and provincial theaters and held the stage until at least the middle of the nineteenth century. John Bannister, who starred as Dick in 1778 and in later years, was outstanding in imitating various other actors as he spouted the apprentice's numerous dramatic quotations.

The Apprentice presents English life of the time. The farce humorously satirizes London apprentices who neglected business in order to rehearse plays at spouting clubs, which were havens for stage-struck amateur actors. The apprentice quotes from a play at every opportunity and imitates Romeo by mounting to his bride-to-be on a ladder rather than by the accessible staircase. In truth, the play in part checked the spouting craze of the day. With its steady incitement to laughter, *The Apprentice* is an admirable first creation.

Soon after the farce opened in January, 1756, the London bookseller Paul Vaillant paid Murphy £40 and published the first edition. Within three months appeared The Second Edition, with the prologue lengthened and appropriately altered by Henry Woodward, who delivered it regularly in place of Murphy. The third edition, in 1764, has the original prologue. The fourth edition, in 1769, gives an altered version of the prologue of The Second Edition. There is no evidence of the author's hand in the second, third, and fourth editions.

For *The Works of Arthur Murphy*, published in seven octavo volumes in 1786 by Thomas Cadell, Murphy revised *The Apprentice*. He expanded all the roles by longer and new speeches, particularly the part of Wingate, though he deleted a few lines. He introduced for Dick eleven additional quotations. There is one transposition of a few words of Wingate. In comparison with the original text, that of 1786 has more exact exposition; better clarity; superior, more precise, and more up-to-date diction; added illustrations and allusions; and inserted stage directions and greater logic for certain exits.

In this present edition of *The Apprentice*, the editor reproduces the text of 1786, with conservative modernizations in punctuation, capitalization, and spelling. Often, the eighteenth-century punctuation perfectly denotes the most effective theatrical pauses. The title page is from the first edition. The "Advertisement," "Prologue," "Dramatis Personae," and "Epilogue" are from the third or 1764 edition, which is better typographically than the first edition. The *Works* omit the "Advertisement" and include the prologue for Woodward, not Murphy. It is impossible to indicate the complete collation between the 1786 text and the earlier text, but the footnotes present significant alterations. In the separate editions only, some of the quotations of the spouters have footnotes referring to the dramatic sources. The editor rectifies a few of these footnotes, subjoins to all Murphy's original footnotes act, scene, and lines (even if the quotation is familiar), and points out the source for every quotation not previously annotated.

Texts Collated

Murphy, [Arthur], *The Apprentice*. London: Paul Vaillant, 1756. [Library Company of Philadelphia]

——, *The Apprentice*. [The Second Edition] London: P. Vaillant, 1756. [The designation "THE SECOND EDITION" appears on the leaf before the title page.] [Harvard University]

——, *The Apprentice*. London: P. Vaillant, 1764. [Bryn Mawr]

——, *The Apprentice*. London: P. Vaillant, 1769. [Library of Congress]

The Works of Arthur Murphy, II, 1-74. London: T. Cadell, 1786. [University of Pennsylvania; Copy of Editor]

THE
APPRENTICE.

A
FARCE,
IN TWO ACTS,
As it is Perform'd at the
THEATRE-ROYAL, in Drury-Lane.

By Mr. MURPHY.

LONDON.
Printed for PAUL VAILLANT, facing Southampton-street, in the Strand. 1756.

[Price One Shilling.]

ADVERTISEMENT

THERE was room to apprehend, before the representation of the following farce, that the subject might appear extravagant and merely ideal; but the real existence of it is displayed in such a lively and picturesque manner by the author of the prologue, and was at once so universally felt by the audience, that all necessity of saying anything farther on this head is now entirely superseded. What at present remains to be feared, is, that *The Apprentice* will not make so lively a figure in the closet as on the stage, where the parts in general were allowed to be well performed; where Simon was represented with a perfection of folly; where the skill of Mr. Yates exhibited the impotence of a mind whose ideas extend very little beyond the multiplication table, and whose passions are ever in a crazy conflict, unless when they all subside into a sordid love of gain; and where Mr. Woodward's admirable comic genius gave such a spirit to the whole that there is reason to think, whenever he relinquishes the part, the Apprentice may again elope from his friends without anyone's desiring him to return to his business.

The author has, however, endeavoured to render all its defects as excusable as he could; and he wishes no stronger criticism could be brought against him than the two following observations, which he thinks very singular and somewhat entertaining. "I can't," says one, "give my opinion of the piece till I have time to consider the depth of it."——"Po!" says another, "this is not all his own; I remember some of it in other plays."——In order to assist the former in his deep researches and to enable the latter to make good his charge of plagiarism, references are made to the several

9

plays [1] from which the distempered hero of the piece makes up
his motley but characteristic dialect. The intelligent reader, if he
think it worth his while to turn over these leaves, will be pleased
to remember that a parody does not always carry with it a burlesque on the lines alluded to. For (as it is judiciously remarked
in a note to Mr. Pope's *Dunciad*), "It is a common, but foolish,
mistake that a ludicrous parody of a grave and celebrated passage
is a ridicule of that passage. A ridicule indeed there is in every
parody; but where the image is transferred from one object to
another, there the ridicule falls not on the thing imitated, but imitating. Thus, for instance, when

Old Edward's armour beams on Cibber's breast, [2]

it is without doubt an object ridiculous enough; but then, I think,
it falls neither on old King Edward nor his armour, but on his
armour-bearer only."

But this is prefacing a farce as if it were a thing of moment;
I shall therefore dismiss it to the press without adding anything
farther except my grateful acknowledgments for the very favourable reception with which the public has honoured the trifling
scenes of

> Their most obliged
> And most obedient servant,
>
> ARTHUR MURPHY.

Tavistock-Row,
5th Jan. 1756.

----

[1] See editor's "Introduction."

[2] Murphy annotates: "A Line of Pope's, in a ludicrous Account of the
Coronation in Henry the VIIIth." Pope, *First Epistle of the Second Book
of Horace*, line 319. In Nov., 1727, Drury Lane added to *Henry VIII* a
pantomime of the Champion of the Coronation, with the armour of an
English king borrowed from the Tower. See R. H. Barker, *Mr. Cibber of
Drury Lane* (New York, 1939), pp. 140-141. The entire passage is quoted
from William Warburton's note on *The Dunciad* II.405.

PROLOGUE,

Written by Mr. Garrick,

And originally spoken by the Author, dress'd in Black.

Behold, a wonder for theatric story!
The culprit of this night appears before ye.
Before his judges dares these boards to tread,
"With all his imperfections on his head!" [3]
Prologues precede the piece——in mournful verse;
As undertakers——walk before the hearse;
Whose doleful march may strike the harden'd mind,
And wake its feelings——for the dead——behind.
Trickt out in black, thus actors try their art,
To melt that rock of rocks——the critic's heart.
No acted fears my vanity betray;
I am indeed——what others only play.
Thus far myself——the farce comes next in view;
Tho' many are its faults, at least 'tis new.
No smuggled, pilfer'd scenes from France we show,
'Tis English——English, Sirs!——from top to toe.
Tho' coarse my colours, and my hand unskill'd,
From real life my little cloth is fill'd.
My hero is a youth——by fate design'd
For culling simples——but whose stage-struck mind,
Nor fate could rule, nor his indentures bind.

---

[3] *Hamlet* I.v.79. The editor does not indicate all alterations in the quotations.

A place there is where such young Quixotes meet;
'Tis call'd the Spouting Club——a glorious treat!
Where 'prentic'd kings——alarm the gaping street!
There Brutus starts and stares by midnight taper; [4]
Who all the day enacts——a woollen draper.
There Hamlet's Ghost stalks forth with doubl'd fist,
Cries out with hollow voice——"List, list, O list!" [5]
And frightens Denmark's Prince——a young tobacconist.
The Spirit too, clear'd from his deadly white,
Rises——a haberdasher to the sight!
Not young attorneys——have this rage withstood,
But change their pens for truncheons, ink for blood;
And (strange reverse!)——die for their country's good.
Thro' all the town this folly you may trace;
Myself am witness——'tis a common case.
I've further proofs, could ye but think I wrong ye;
Look round——you'll find some spouting youths among ye.
To check these heroes, and their laurels crop,
To bring 'em back to reason——and their shop,
To raise an harmless laugh was all my aim,
And if I shun contempt——I seek not fame.
Indulge this firstling——let me but begin,
Nor nip me——in the buddings of my sin; [6]
Some hopes I cherish——in your smiles I read 'em;
Whate'er my faults——your candor can exceed 'em.

---

[4] *Julius Caesar* II.i; IV.iii.
[5] *Hamlet* I.v.22.
[6] *Ibid.* I.v.76.

DRAMATIS PERSONAE

Wingate, a passionate old man, particularly fond of money and figures, and involuntarily uneasy about his son, } Mr. Yates.

Dick, his son, bound to an apothecary, and fond of going on the stage, } Mr. Woodward.

Gargle, an apothecary,	Mr. Burton.
Charlotte, daughter to Gargle,	Miss Minors.
Simon, servant to Gargle,	Mr. H. Vaughan.
Scotchman,	Mr. Blakes.
Irishman,	Mr. Jefferson.
Catchpole, a bailiff,	Mr. Vaughan.

Spouting-Club, Watchmen, &c.

THE

APPRENTICE

ACT the FIRST
SCENE the FIRST

[Room in Wingate's London house]

Enter WINGATE *and* SIMON.

WINGATE. Hold your tongue, you blockhead; don't argue with me; don't think to impose upon me; I am convinced; I know it all; and if you imagine, varlet, that you are to trifle with me——what right have you to trifle with me?——You are in the plot, you scoundrel, and if you don't discover all——

SIMON. Dear heart, Sir, you won't give a body time.

WINGATE. Tell me all you know this moment, or——zookers! A whole month missing, and no account of him far or near!——It is too much for a father: a vile, ungrateful prodigal!——Plague and distraction! Where can the fellow be?——Look you, friend; don't you presume——

SIMON. Lord, Sir, you are so main passionate, you won't let a body speak.

WINGATE. Speak out then, and don't stand muttering.——What a lubberly fellow you are! (*Looks at him and laughs*)——Ha! ha! Such a scarecrow figure! Why don't you speak out, you blockhead?

14

SIMON. Mercy on us!——Your son to be sure is a fine young gentleman, and a sweet young gentleman; but lackaday, Sir, how should I know anything of him?

WINGATE. Prevaricating booby! With more evasions than if you were before a Middlesex justice!——Has not he been apprentice to your master, my friend Gargle——who by the bye is as great a fool as yourself——has not he been apprentice to him these three years? Have not you lived there all the time, and could you be so long in one house with my son and not know all his haunts and all his ways? And then, you vagabond, you rascal, what are you lurking about my doors for? What brings you hither so often?

SIMON. My master Gargle and I, Sir, have been so uneasy about him that I have been running all over the town ever since morning to enquire for him, everywhere, high and low; and so in my way, I thought I might as well call here.

WINGATE. A villain, to give his father all this trouble! And so you have not heard anything of him, friend?

SIMON. Not a word, Sir, as I hope for mercy.

WINGATE. You numskull! You booby! Why did not you tell me so at first?

SIMON. I told you as soon as you would hear me; and as sure as you are there, for all I know nothing, I believe I can guess what is come of him.

WINGATE. Ay!——Guess then, sirrah; tell me as you guess.

SIMON. As sure as anything, Master, the gypsies have gotten hold of him, and we shall have him come as thin as a rake, like the young girl in the city, with living upon nothing but crusts and water for six and twenty days.[7]

WINGATE. The gypsies have got hold of him!——Get out of the room, you blockhead, you driveller, you nonsensical——ha! ha! The gypsies got hold of him!——Here, you, Simon——

SIMON. Sir; anan——

---

[7] The notorious Elizabeth Canning claimed that she had lived for twenty-eight days in January, 1753, on crusts and water while confined in the house of Susannah Wells, where she was robbed by the gypsy Mary Squires.

WINGATE. Where are you going in such a hurry?——Let me see; wounds! What must be done?——I'll plague myself no more; let him go on his own way.——An absurd, ridiculous, a silly, empty-headed coxcomb! With his *Cassanders*,[8] and his *Cloppatras*, and his trumpery; with his romances, and his damn'd plays, and his *Odyssey Popes*, and a parcel of fellows not worth a groat! Wearing stone-buckles,[9] and cocking his hat: what right has he to wear stone-buckles and cock his hat? But I'll not put myself in a passion——death and fury! I never wear stone-buckles; never cock my hat. I think of nothing but the main chance; and——Simon, do you step, and tell my friend Gargle that I want to speak to him. And yet, I don't know, why should I send for him? A sly, slow, hesitating, pedantic blockhead!——I send for such a fellow! A pestle-and-mortar, simple-squeezing,[10] dry piece of formality, with his physical cant, and his nonsense!——Why don't you go, you booby, when I bid you?

SIMON. Yes, Sir; I am gone, Sir.

Exit.

WINGATE. This son of mine will be the death of me. I can't sleep in my bed for thinking of him. He'll be undone; he'll be ruin'd; ——well! it's his own fault; what care I? My advice is all lost. A scatter-brain puppy! To stand in his own light——death and fire! that we can't get children without having a regard for them! I have been turmoiling for him all my days, and now the villain is run away.——Suppose I advertise the dog, and promise a reward to anyone that can give an account of him. There, more expence! Why should I throw away money upon such a profligate? Why, as I don't say what reward, I may give what I please when they come. But then if the young rakehell should deceive me and happen to be dead? Why then he tricks me out of three shillings [11]

---

[8] Murphy alludes to La Calprenède, *Cassandre* (1642-5), a romance, rather than to Cassander in Nathaniel Lee's tragedy *The Rival Queens* or *The Death of Alexander the Great* (1677), which was influenced by the romance.

[9] Costly stone shoe buckles were in vogue before the triumph of the shoestring.

[10] Squeezing medicinal plants. Added in 1786 edition.

[11] "Two shillings" in earlier editions.

for the advertisement; there's my money thrown into the fire. I'll think no more about him; let him follow his nose; it's nothing at all to me: what care I?——What do you come back for, friend?

Enter SIMON.

WINGATE. Why don't you speak?

SIMON. As I was going out, Sir, the post came to the door, and brought this letter.

WINGATE. Let me see it——the gypsies have got hold of him! (*Looks at him and laughs*) Ha! ha! What a conjurer you are? ——Ha! ha!——Why don't you go where I ordered you?

SIMON. Yes, Sir.

Exit.

WINGATE. Well, well; I'm resolved, and it shall be so; I'll advertise him tomorrow morning, and promise, if he comes home, that all shall be forgiven: if he bites at the hook, then when I have him fast, I may do as I please. Ay, it shall be so; (*Laughs*) I may then do as I please. Ha! ha! Right! Very good! Let me see, how must I describe him? He had on, a silver-looped hat; I never liked those damn'd silver-loops;——a silver-looped hat, and——and——confusion! What signifies what he had on? I'll read my letter, and think no more about him. Hey! What in the name of wonder have we here? (*Reads*) "Bristol!"——How! What is all this?

"Esteemed Friend,

Last was 20th ultimo, since none of thine, which will occasion brevity. The reason of my writing to thee at present, is to inform thee, that thy son came to our place with a company of strolling players, who were taken up by the magistrate, and committed as vagabonds to jail." That's good news; I am glad of it; let the villain lie there; let him beat hemp. (*Laughs*) What a fine figure he'll cut in the jail!——Ha! ha! Alexander the Great at hard labour! I rejoice at this. Ha! ha! Let me see, what more does he say? (*Reads*) "I am sorry thy lad should follow such profane courses; but out of the esteem I bear unto thee, I have taken thy boy out of confinement, and sent him off for your city in the waggon, which left this four days ago. He is consigned to thy address; being the needful from thy friend and servant,

Ebeeneezer Broadbrim."

My esteemed friend, Ebeeneezer Broadbrim, you are as great a fool as the rest of them: what did you take the puppy out of jail for? Could not you let him lie there?——Ha! ha! The spirit moved him, I suppose.——Turned stage-player! I'll never see the villain's face. Who comes there?

Enter SIMON.

SIMON. Our cares are over.

WINGATE. You lie, you blockhead: our cares are but just begun.

SIMON. All's safe and well; make us thankful for it. I met Mr. Gargle on the way, and he has got such news for you, and he is coming as fast as he can, and here he is.

WINGATE. Let him come in, and do you go and recover your breath, you gaping, staring, open-mouthed, fly-catching son of a——

SIMON. We're all alive and merry.

Exit.

Enter GARGLE.

WINGATE. So, friend Gargle, here's a fine piece of work. Dick's turn'd vagabond.

GARGLE. He must be put under a proper regimen directly. He arrived at my house within these ten minutes, but in such a trim! I brought him with me; he is now belowstairs. I judged it proper to leave him there, till I have felt your pulse, and in due course prepared you for his reception.

WINGATE. Death and fire! What could put it into his head to turn buffoon?

GARGLE. Nothing so easily accounted for: when he ought to

be reading the dispensatory, there was he constantly poring over plays, and farces, and Shakespeare.

WINGATE. Ay, that damn'd Shakespeare! I hear the fellow was nothing but a deer-stealer in Warwickshire. If he had sold the venison, there would have been some sense in that; he would have made money by it; a better trade than writing plays. Zookers! If they had hanged the fellow out of the way, he would not now be the ruin of honest men's children. What right has my son to read Shakespeare? I never read Shakespeare. Wounds! I caught the rascal, myself, reading that Bartholomew Fair play of *Hamlet*,[12] *Prince of*——I don't know what, not I——*Sweden* I believe——and there was the Prince keeping company with strollers and vagabonds. A fine example, Master Gargle!

GARGLE. His disorder is of the malignant kind, and my daughter has taken the infection from him. Bless my heart! She was as innocent as water-gruel till he spoiled her. I caught her the other night in the very fact.

WINGATE. Zookers! You don't say so! Caught her in the fact? [13]

GARGLE. As sure as you are there, he has debauched the poor girl.

WINGATE. Debauched your daughter?

GARGLE. Even so.

WINGATE. I don't much wonder at that, friend Gargle. (*Looks at him and laughs*) The boy has good blood in his veins.

GARGLE. Poor Charlotte! I caught her in the very fact, reading a play-book in bed.

WINGATE. Is that the fact?

GARGLE. Yes, and bad enough of all conscience.

WINGATE. Why, you metaphorical blockhead, why could not you say so at first?

GARGLE. That was my meaning; but I have done for my young madam; I have locked up all her books, and confined her to her room.

---

[12] The allusion is to a puppet show at Bartholomew Fair, Smithfield, London.

[13] Murphy added the next four speeches in 1786.

WINGATE. You have served her right. Look you here, friend Gargle; I'll never see the villain's face; let him follow his own courses; let him bite the bridle.

GARGLE. Lenitives, Mr. Wingate, lenitives are properest at present. His habit requires gentle alteratives. Leave him to my management: twenty ounces of blood, a cephalic tincture, and a cool regimen, will bring him to himself, and then he may do very well.

WINGATE. Po! Truce with your jargon. Where is the scoundrel?

GARGLE. Dear Sir, moderate your anger. Harsh language may——

WINGATE. Harsh language! If he behaves like a profligate shan't I tell him of it?

GARGLE. Violence may inflame: gentle means may work a reformation: the boy has good sentiments.

WINGATE. Sentiments! Don't tell me of sentiment; what have I [to] do with sentiment?——Let the booby mind his business, learn how to get money, and never miss an opportunity. I never missed an opportunity; got up at five in the morning; struck a light; made my own fire; worked my fingers' ends; and this vagabond is now going to destruction. Let him have his full swing. Let him go on: a ridiculous——

GARGLE. Ay; ridiculous indeed! For a long time past he could not converse in the language of common sense. Ask him a trivial question, he gave you a cramp answer out of some of his plays, that are always running in his head. No understanding a word that he says!

WINGATE. Death and fury! This comes of his keeping company with wits, and be damn'd to 'em for wits.——Ha! ha! Wit is a fine thing indeed. I never knew one of your men of genius worth sixpence. There's my friend Bookworm; he has parts and talents; everybody says so; we went to school together; he studied well. (*Laughs*) Ha! ha! Yes, he studied well! He made verses, and I learned vulgar fractions. Where is he now? Looking through iron bars at the King's Bench prison.[14]——Ha! ha! Wit is the most rascally, contemptible, beggarly thing on the face of the earth.

---

[14] A prison for debtors in Southwark.

GARGLE. Would you believe it, Mr. Wingate? I have found out that your son went three times a week to a spouting club.

WINGATE. A spouting club, friend Gargle! What's a spouting club?

GARGLE. A meeting of prentices, and clerks, and giddy young men, all intoxicated with plays! And so they meet at public houses, and there they repeat speeches, and alarm the neighbourhood with their noise, and neglect their business, and despise the advice of their friends, and think of nothing but of becoming actors.

WINGATE. You don't tell me so! A spouting club! Zookers! they are all mad.

GARGLE. Ay, mad, indeed, Sir: madness is occasioned in a very extraordinary manner; the spirits flowing in particular channels——

WINGATE. 'Sdeath! You are as mad yourself as any of them.

GARGLE. And continuing to run in the same ducts——

WINGATE. Ducks!——What ducks? Roast ducks for supper?

GARGLE. No, sir, no; but the finer juices running in the same capillary ducts or vessels, the texture of the brain becomes disordered.

WINGATE. Friend Gargle, don't plague me. (*Walks away*) Who's below there?

GARGLE. (*Following him*) And by the pressure on the nervous system, the head is disturbed: obstructions are formed, and thus your son's malady is contracted.

WINGATE. (*Walking away*) Will nobody answer? Who is below?

GARGLE. (*Following him*) But I shall alter the morbid state of the juices, correct his blood, sweeten the humours, and produce laudable chyle.

WINGATE. Produce a laudable fortune; that's the true use of guile. Who's below there? Tell that fellow to come up.

GARGLE. Nay, be a little cool: inflammatories may be dangerous. He may reform; there is now some prospect of it.

WINGATE. Po! None of your prospects; give me a prospect of gain. Prithee, don't tease me, man; here the rascal comes.

Enter DICK.

DICK. (*Walking slow and sullen, with his arms folded: he looks at his father, then fixes his eyes on the ground*) There's an attitude! If I had chains on, Bajazet [15] could not do it better. (*Aside*)

WINGATE. Did you ever see such a fellow? So, friend!

DICK. "Now, my good father, what's the matter?" [16]

WINGATE. You have been upon your travels, have you?——You have had your frolic?——Look you, young man, I'll not put myself in a passion; but death and fire! you scoundrel, what right have you to plague me in this manner? Do you think I am to fall in love with your face? Must I bear with you because I am your father?

DICK. "A little more than kin, and less than kind." [17]

WINGATE. What a pretty figure you cut now? (*Stands laughing at him*) Such a poverty-struck rascal I never saw! Why don't you speak, you blockhead? Have you nothing to say for yourself?

DICK. (*Aside*) Nothing to say for yourself? What an old prig it is!

WINGATE. Mind me, friend; I have found you out. How often must I tell you that you will never come to good? Turn stage-player! Wounds! You'll not have an eye in your head in a month. (*Looks at him and laughs*) Ha! ha! You'll have 'em knocked out of the sockets with withered apples. Remember I tell you so, friend.

DICK. A critic too! (*Whistles*) Well said, old square-toes. [18]

WINGATE. Look you, young man; my advice is all thrown away upon you. But once for all, mind what I say. I made my own fortune, and I could do the same again. Wounds! If I were placed

---

[15] Bajazet is a ruler of the Ottomans in Nicholas Rowe's *Tamerlane* (1701) rather than in Christopher Marlowe's *Tamburlaine* (1587). Murphy added passage in 1786.

[16] Altered from *Hamlet* III.iv.8.

[17] *Hamlet* I.ii.65.

[18] An old-fashioned person with narrow ideas.

at the bottom of Chancery Lane [19] with a brush and blackball,[20] I know the world, and could make my own fortune again. You read Shakespeare! Get *Cocker's Arithmetick;* [21] you may buy it for a shilling upon a stall; the best book that ever was wrote.

DICK. (*Aside*) Pretty well that! Ingenious, truly! Egad, the old buck has a pretty notion of letters.

WINGATE. Can you tell me how much is five-eighths of three-sixteenths of a pound?——I see you are a blockhead. Five-eighths of three-sixteenths of a pound! You can't tell me; I would not give a farthing for all you know. If you have a mind to thrive in this world, study figures, and make yourself useful.

DICK. "How weary, stale, flat and unprofitable seem to me all the uses of this world!" [22]

WINGATE. Mind the scoundrel now!

GARGLE. Do, Mr. Wingate, let me speak to him. Softly, softly; I'll touch him with a gentle hand. Come, young man, lay aside this sulky humour, and speak as becomes a son.

DICK. "O Jephthah, judge of Israel, what a treasure hadst thou!" [23]

WINGATE. What does the fellow say?

GARGLE. He relents, Sir; come, come, young man, make peace with your father.

DICK. "They fool me to the top of my bent." [24] Egad, I'll bamboozle 'em, and so get out of the scrape.——"A truant disposition, good my lord." [25]——No, no, stay, stay, that's not right: my friend Ranger can supply a better speech.——"It is as you say, when we are sober, and reflect but ever so little on our follies, we are ashamed and sorry; and yet, the very next minute, we rush again into the very same absurdities." [26]

------

[19] In the heart of the legal district of London north of Fleet Street.

[20] The tools of a bootblack.

[21] Edward Cocker (1631-1675) published his arithmetic in 1664, and it had more than a hundred editions.

[22] *Hamlet* I.ii.133-134.

[23] *Ibid*. II.ii.422-423.

[24] *Ibid*. III.ii.401.

[25] *Ibid* I.ii.169.

[26] Benjamin Hoadly, *The Suspicious Husband* (1747) IV.iv.223-227.

WINGATE. Well said, lad, well said; that's very good sense; I like you when you talk sense. Listen to me, friend: commanding our own passions, and artfully taking advantage of other people's,[27] is the sure road to wealth. And without wealth, what is life?—— Die a beggar rather than live a beggar. A man should always have a thousand pounds at his banker's. Wounds! It's ridiculous not to have a thousand pounds at your banker's.

DICK. Without doubt, Sir. (*Stifling a laugh*)

WINGATE. I'll tell you what, friend; I have a great regard for you in the main. What do I mind my business for, and get up at five in the morning? Is not it all for you? I never lost an opportunity in my life. There was my friend Barlow, I knew he could not live; he drank brandy in a morning; I saw it; fixed my eye upon him; sold him an annuity: he did not live to receive the first quarter. Ha! ha!——My poor friend Barlow!——I knew what I was about: and is not all that for you? Mind me friend: if I abuse you, it is because I wish you well. Death and fire! Do you think I'd call you a scoundrel if I had not a regard for you?

DICK. To be sure, Sir.

WINGATE. You don't hear me call a stranger a scoundrel.

DICK. No bad mark of prudence.

WINGATE. Prudence!——What do I care for a stranger? Mind me, and I'll make a man of you. If you want anything, you shall be provided: have you any money in your pocket? Not a sixpence, I warrant. (*Looks at him and laughs*) There is nothing I hate like poverty. Let me see if I have any money in my purse. How is this? A ten-pound note! Now if I was to give you a bank-note——no; I'll keep it for you; that will do better; and so mind what I say, and go and make yourself useful.

DICK. "Else, wherefore breathe I in a Christian land?" [28]

WINGATE. Very well; I like that: you had better stick to your business than turn mountebank, and get truncheons broke upon your arm, and tumble about upon carpets.

---

[27] Correct case form in earlier editions.
[28] Colley Cibber, *Richard III* (1700) III.i.352.

DICK. "I shall in all my best obey you, Sir." [29]

WINGATE. Very well; very well said. You may do very well: I'll say no more to you now: go change your dress; make yourself fit to be seen, and go home to your business. And let me see no more play-books: let me never hear that you wear a laced waistcoat: what right have you to wear a laced waistcoat? I never wore a laced waistcoat; never wore one till I was forty. But I'll not put myself in a passion; go, and remember what I have said to you.

DICK. I shall, Sir.

"I must be cruel only to be kind;
   Thus bad begins, and worse remains behind." [30]

Cocker's Arithmetick, Sir?

WINGATE. Ay, *Cocker's Arithmetick:* study figures; figures and the true Italian method of bookkeeping will carry you through the world.

DICK. Yes, Sir. (*Stifling a laugh*) *Cocker's Arithmetick!*

Exit.

WINGATE. Let him mind me, friend Gargle, and I'll make a man of him.

GARGLE. Ay, Sir, you know the world. Your son will do very well: I wish he were out of his time; he shall then have my daughter.

WINGATE. Yes, but not a stiver of her fortune; I must touch the cash myself; he shan't finger it during my life. I must keep a tight hand over him. (*Goes to the door*) Do you hear, friend? Mind what I say, and go home to your business immediately.——Friend Gargle, let him follow my directions, and I'll make a man of him.

Enter DICK.

DICK. "Who call'd on Achmet? Did not Barbarossa require me here?" [31]

---

[29] Altered from *Hamlet* I.ii.120.
[30] *Hamlet* III.iv.178-179.
[31] John Brown, *Barbarossa* (1754) IV.i.208-209.

WINGATE. What's the matter now? Barossa! Wounds! What's Barossa? Does the fellow call me names? What makes the booby stand in such confusion?

DICK. "That Barbarossa should suspect my truth." [32]

WINGATE. Mad, stark-staring mad!——Get out of the room, you villain; get out of the room.

DICK. I thought you called me back, to give me the bank-note, Sir.

WINGATE. Give you a bank-note!——Death and confusion! You oaf; you scrub; you ridiculous coxcomb; give you a bank-note! The more you expect it, the less I'll give it. What right have you to expect it?

DICK. If you had not mentioned it yourself, Sir——

WINGATE. I mention it!

DICK. I thought so, Sir; and as your word is as good as your bond——

WINGATE. There now I see you're a blockhead: my word as good as my bond! You fool, you numskull, you'll never succeed in the world. Death and fire! How is my word as good as my bond? My word is one thing, and my bond is another; all the world knows that. Let me hear such another word out of your mouth and I'll turn you out of my house immediately. My word as good as my bond. Wounds! I have a mind never to see your face. I hate poverty and nonsense: never say that to me again.

GARGLE. Come, young man; everything was quietly settled: do as your father bids you, and don't spoil all again. Be advised by me: go, make yourself clean, and then come home to your business. (*He pushes Dick out*)

DICK. "Oh! I am Fortune's fool." [33]

Exit.

WINGATE. I can be very peremptory, friend Gargle: if he vexes me once more, I'll have nothing to say to him. But I still have hopes; he can do very well: and now I think of it, I have *Cocker's Arith-*

---

[32] *Ibid.* IV.i.124.
[33] *Romeo and Juliet* III.i.141.

metick belowstairs in the counting-house. I'll step and get it for him, and he shall take it home with him.

GARGLE. Mr. Wingate, I wish you a good evening. I have a slow fever in the neighbourhood, that I must pay a visit to. You'll send him home to his business.

Exit.

WINGATE. He shall follow you directly. Five-eighths of the three-sixteenths of a pound!——Multiply the numerator by the dominator; five times sixteen is ten times eight; ten times eight is eighty; and then——a——five and carry one.

Exit.

SCENE [II]

Another Apartment

Enter DICK *and* SIMON.

DICK. Simon, did you ever such a queer old putt [34] as my father?

SIMON. Good enough when he is pleased; but main choleric; merciful! how he storms and raves! Blows up like gunpowder.

DICK. His character will do for the stage, and I'll act it myself.

SIMON. Lord love you, Master, I am so glad you are come home; but methinks we had better get away from this house; all fishing in troubled waters here; much quieter at Mr. Gargle's.

DICK. No, no, Simon; stay a moment. This is but a scurvy sort of a coat I have on: I know old square-toes has always something smart locked up in his closet; I know his ways; he takes them in pawn; never parts with a guinea without a good pledge in hand.

SIMON. Odds my life, take care; as sure as a gun he'll hear you. Hush! I believe he's coming upstairs.

DICK. (*Goes to the door and listens*) No——no——no——he is going downstairs, growling and grumbling——"scoundrel, rascal——bite

---

[34] Blockhead. Added in 1786.

the bridle——make yourself useful——six times twelve is seventy-two."——All is safe, Simon; he is gone down; we have nothing to fear. Stand you there, and I'll dispatch this business in two minutes "by Shrewsbury clock." [35]

SIMON. Blessings on him, what is he about?——Why, the closet door is locked, Master.

DICK. I know it, Simon, but I can unlock it.——You shall see me do it with as much dexterity as any Sir John Brute [36] of 'em all.—— This right leg here is the best locksmith in England. Come, sur-render up your trust—— (*Kicks the door open and goes in*)

SIMON. He is at his plays again: odds my heart, he is wondrous comical; pure diverting; he will go through with it, I warrant him. Old Drybeard [37] must not smoke that I have any concern. I must be main cautious. What's he about? Bless his heart, he is to teach me to act Scrub. He began with me long ago, and I got as far as the Jesuit before he went out of town. "Scrub!——Coming Sir—— Why Scrub!——Ma'am——Lord Ma'am, I have a whole packet full of news; some say one thing, and some another, but for my part, Ma'am, I believe he is a Jesuit." [38]——That's main pleasant—— "I believe he is a Jesuit."

Enter DICK.

DICK. "I have done the deed; didst thou not hear a noise?" [39]

SIMON. No, Master; don't look so frightened; not a mouse stir-ring; all snug.

DICK. This coat will do charmingly. I have outwitted the old gentleman nicely. "In a dark corner of" his cabinet "I found this paper; what it is this light will show." [40] (*Reads*) *I promise to pay*

---

[35] Hoadly, *The Suspicious Husband* IV.i.127. Added in 1786.

[36] In John Vanbrugh, *The Provok'd Wife* (1697).

[37] Old man with a withered beard. Added in 1786.

[38] George Farquhar, *The Beaux' Stratagem* (1707) II.i.98-99; III.i.53-55, 70-71.

[39] *Macbeth* II.ii.15.

[40] William Congreve, *The Mourning Bride* (1697) III.i.6-7.

——ha!——*I promise to pay to Mr. Moneytrap or order on de-mand*——" 'tis his hand"; a note of his; "——yet more" [41]——*the sum of seven pounds fourteen shillings and seven pence, value received by me, London, this 15th June 1775.*[42] " 'Tis wanting what should follow"; his name "should follow, but 'tis torn off," [43] because the note is paid.

SIMON. Oh! Lud! Dear heart, I'm frighted out of my senses. You'll spoil all; I wish we were well out of the house. Our best way, Master, is to make off directly.

DICK. I'll do it; we'll sound a retreat in a moment; but first help me on with this coat. (*Puts it on*) Simon, you shall be my dresser when I am a great actor; you'll be pure happy behind the scenes.

SIMON. As happy as the day is long, Master. I shall like of it hugeously. I have been behind the scenes in the country, when I lived with the man that showed wild beastices.

DICK. Hark ye, Simon; when I am playing some deep tragedy, and "cleave the general ear with horrid speech," [44] you must stand at the side of the scenes, and cry bitterly. (*Teaches him*) Oh!——It's so moving, I can't stand it.

SIMON. Yes, I'll do it; I am rare one to cry.

DICK. And when I am playing a gay, sprightly, genteel part in comedy, you must be ready to crack your sides with laughing. (*Teaches him*) I shall be damn'd pleasant.

SIMON. Never doubt me, Master. (*Both laugh*)

DICK. Very well; now go and open the street door; I'll steal down, and we'll leave old Multiplication Table to himself.

SIMON. Ay, so best: we are dancing upon thorns here: I am gone to serve you, Master.

DICK. "To serve thyself; for look, when I am manager, claim thou of me the care o' th' wardrobe, with all those moveables whereof the property-man now stands possest." [45]

---

[41] *Ibid.* III.i.13.
[42] In earlier editions, "1755."
[43] Congreve, *The Mourning Bride* III.i.18-19.
[44] *Hamlet* II.ii.589.
[45] Based on Cibber, *Richard III* III.i.144-147.

SIMON. I does not understand it, but I likes to hear you talk. Hush! I am gone.

DICK. Hold, hold; Simon, come hither. "What money have you about you, Master Matthew?" [46]

SIMON. But a tester.[47]

DICK. A tester!——Something of the least, Master Matthew. Let me see it.

SIMON. You have had fifteen sixpences now.

DICK. Never mind; I'll pay you all at my benefit.

SIMON. I does not fear you. Hush!——I'll go and open the door.

Exit.

DICK. (*Solus*) "Thus far we run before the wind." [48]——An apothecary! Make an apothecary of me! What, cramp my genius over a pestle and mortar, or mew me up in a shop with an "alligator stufft, and a beggarly account of empty boxes!" [49] To be culling simples, and constantly adding to the bills of mortality. No, no, I'll add to the play-bills rather: it will be much better to be pasted up in capitals, *The part of Romeo by a young gentleman who never appeared upon any stage before!*——My ambition fires at the thought. But hold, hold; mayn't I run some chance of failing in my attempt? Hissed, pelted, laughed at, not admitted into the greenroom! That will never do; "down busy devil, down, down." [50]——Take it t'other way——loved by the women, envied by the men, applauded by the pit, clapped by the gallery, admired by the boxes; "Colonel, is not he a charming creature?——My Lord, don't you like him of all things? Makes love like an angel.——What an eye he has? The sweetest figure!——I'll certainly go to his benefit." Celestial sounds! ——And then I'll get in with all the painters, and have myself put up in every shop;——in the character of Macbeth, "This is a sorry sight." [51] (*Stands in an attitude*) In the character of Richard, "Give

---

[46] Jonson, *Every Man in His Humour* (1598) I.iv.165-166.
[47] A sixpence.
[48] Cibber, *Richard III* II.iii.130.
[49] *Romeo and Juliet* V.i.43,45.
[50] Thomas Otway, *Venice Preserv'd* (1682) IV.ii.282.
[51] *Macbeth* II.ii.21.

me another horse, bind up my wounds; have mercy." [52]——Oh! it will do rarely; and then the chance of some great fortune falling in love with me——"O glorious thought! By Heav'n, I will enjoy it, though but in fancy; imagination shall make room to." [53]——I wonder what o'clock it is: (*Looks at his watch*) 'sdeath! almost ten.[54] I'll away at once; this is club-night; the spouters will be all met. I'll make one among 'em. Little do they think I am in town; they will be surprised to see me; I'll beat up their quarters, and then for my assignation with my master Gargle's daughter. Poor Charlotte! By her letter I find she is locked up, but I shall contrive means to favour her escape. I'll carry her off. A pretty theatrical genius. If she flies to my arms "like a hawk to its perch," [55] it will be so rare an adventure, and so dramatic an incident! As my friend Polydore says,

"Limbs do your office, and support me well;
    Bear me but to her, then fail if you can." [56]

End of the FIRST ACT.

---

[52] Shakespeare, *Richard III* V.iii.177-178. Murphy added "have mercy" in 1786.

[53] Rowe, *Tamerlane* II.ii.134-136. Murphy added the last five words in 1786.

[54] In earlier editions, "it must be almost nine."

[55] Farquhar, *The Constant Couple: or, A Trip to the Jubilee* (1699) IV.i. 136.

[56] Otway, *The Orphan* (1680) III.i.483-484.

ACT the SECOND
SCENE [I]

The Spouting Club: the Members seated, and roaring out "Bravo," while one stands at a distance, acting Pierre.

FIRST MEMBER.

"Curs'd be your senate; curs'd your constitution;
  The curse of growing factions and divisions
  Still vex your councils"—— [57]

SECOND MEMBER. Don't you think his action rather confined?

FIRST MEMBER. Confin'd!——Don't you know that I am in chains? You know nothing of the stage. A blockhead!

SECOND MEMBER. (*Advancing to him*) Blockhead, say you?—— I know more of the stage than such upstarts as you can pretend to. Blockhead!——Was not I the first that took compassion on you, when you lay, like a sneaking fellow, under the counter, and swept your master's shop in a morning? When you read nothing but *The Young Man's Pocket Companion, or The True Clerk's Vade Mecum*,[58] did not I show you the way to the upper gallery, teach you the use of a catcall, and put *Chrononhotonthologos* [59] into your hand?

ALL. Well argued; bravo! bravo!

PRESIDENT. Come, gentlemen; no disputes; no quarrelling. Consider where you are: this is the Honourable Society of Spouters; and so to put an end to all animosities, read the seventh rule of this society.

---

[57] Otway, *Venice Preserv'd* IV.ii.156-158.

[58] Probably not a real title. There were *The Young Clerk's Companion* (1672); William Mather, *The Young Man's Companion* (1681); *The Young Clerk's Assistant* (1733); and Samuel Richardson, *The Apprentice's Vade Mecum: or Young Man's Pocket-Companion* (1733).

[59] Henry Carey, *The Tragedy of Chrononhotonthologos* (1734), a burlesque opera.

THIRD MEMBER. (*Reads*) "That business, or want of money, shall not be received as an excuse for non-attendance; nor the anger of parents, masters, guardians, or relations be a restraint to genius; to the end that this society may boast its own mimic heroes, and be a seminary of young actors, to grace the sock and buskin, in spite of the low mechanic notions of people fit only for the drudgery of trade and business."

PRESIDENT. That is not the rule I meant to read. But come——"Fill a measure the table round." [60] ——"Now good digestion wait on appetite, and health on both."—— [61]

ALL. Huzza! huzza! huzza!

SCOTCHMAN. What say you, lads?——Now I'll gee you a touch of *Macbeeth.*

FIRST MEMBER. Well done, highlander; let us have it.

SCOTCHMAN. What do'st leer at, mon? I have had muckle applause at Edinburgh, when I enacted in the *Reegiceede.*[62] I now intend to do *Macbeeth.* I seed the degger yesterneet, and I thought I should ha' killed everyone that came athwart my gate.

IRISHMAN. Arrah, stand out of the way, my boys, and you shall see me give a touch of *Othollo,* my dear. Now for the truth of it. (*Burns a cork, and blacks his face*) The devil burn the cork, it would not do it fast enough.

FIRST MEMBER. Here, here; I'll lend you a helping hand.

A rap at the door.

SECOND MEMBER. "Open locks, whoever knocks." [63]

Enter DICK.

DICK.

"How now, ye secret, black, and midnight *wags!* [64]
    What is't you do?" [65]

---

[60] *Macbeth* III.iv.11-12.

[61] *Ibid.* III.iv.38-39.

[62] T. G. Smollett, *The Regicide* (1749). Since *The Regicide* was never produced, the braggadocio is obvious!

[63] *Macbeth* IV.i.46-47.

[64] "Hags" in earlier editions.

[65] *Macbeth* IV.i.48-49.

ALL. Ha! The genius! The genius come to town!——The genius! ——Huzza!

DICK. "How fare the honest partners of my heart?" [66] Natt Pigtail, give us your hand; Jack Oakstick, yours; Bob Nankeen, how goes it my boy? Billy Saplin, I rejoice to see you.——Gentlemen, I rejoice to see you all. But come, the news; the news of the town, for I am but just arrived. Has anything been damned? Any new performer this winter? How often has *Romeo and Juliet* been acted? What new plays on the stocks? Come, my bucks, inform me; for I want news.

FIRST MEMBER. Bravo, Sir Harry! [67] You shall know all in good time. But prithee, my dear boy, how was it? You played at Bristol: the first dash is over with you: come, let us hear.

SECOND MEMBER. Ay, the particulars, my dear Dick.

DICK. Look you there now; as Ranger says, "Let us have it, dear boy, and dear Dick." [68]

FIRST MEMBER. Nay, nay, let us hear; how was you received?

DICK. Romeo was my part: I touch'd 'em to the quick. Every pale face from the Wells [69] was there. Not in the least frightened; on I went. Easy at first; came to the Garden Scene: Juliet thought to have it hollow: she tuned her silver pipe: are you at that work says I? Three strides to the stage door, turned short, and here goes. I gave 'em a volley. I tickled 'em, as you will see in the papers. But come, "What bloody scene has Roscius now to act?" [70]

FIRST MEMBER. All well studied; ready in several characters. But Genius, why come among us so late? Why was not you here in the beginning of the night?

DICK. Why, "*stap* my vitals," [71] I longed to see you all; but whom should I meet in my way but my friend Catcall! A devilish good critic. He has been in at the death of many a piece. He and I went

---

[66] Altered slightly from Otway, *Venice Preserv'd* I.i.121.

[67] Sir Harry Wildair, a character in Farquhar, *The Constant Couple* (1699) and *Sir Harry Wildair* (1701). Added in 1786.

[68] Based on Hoadly, *The Suspicious Husband* IV.i.185,188.

[69] The medicinal warm springs at Clifton, near Bristol, were popular.

[70] Cibber, *Richard III* I.ii.17.

[71] Vanbrugh, *The Relapse* (1696) I.iii.19-20. Added in 1786.

together and had our pipe, "to close the orifice of the stomach" [72] you know, and what do you think I learned of him?

FIRST MEMBER. Something deep.

DICK. "Not as deep as a well, but it will do." [73] Can you tell whether the *emphasis* should be laid upon the *epitaph* [74] or the *substantive?*

FIRST MEMBER. The *epitaph*, or the *substantive?*

DICK. Ever while you live, lay your *emphasis* upon the *epitaph*.

IRISHMAN. Arrah, my dear, what is that same *epitaph* now?

DICK. Arrah, "my dear Cousin Macshane, won't you put a remembrance upon me?" [75]

IRISHMAN. But is it mocking me you are?——I believe it's a knock you have a mind to take. Hark you, my jewel; if you'd be taking me off——don't you call it taking off?——By my shoul, I would be making you take yourself off.——What?——Don't you like it?——If you are for a carte over the arm, I would not matter you three skips of a flay.[76]

DICK. Nay, prithee, no offence: I hope we shall be brother players.

IRISHMAN. Ow! then we'd be very good friends; for you know two of a trade can never agree, my dear.

SCOTCHMAN. Locke is certainly reet in his chapter aboot innate ideas; for this mon was born without any at all. A sheet of blank paper: *tabula rasa:* and t'other mon yonder——I ken not his name; they call him the Genius; I doot he has no great heedpiece.

DICK. What character do you intend to appear in?

IRISHMAN. Othollo, my dear. Let me alone: you'll see how I'll bodder 'em. Though, by my shoul, myself does not know but I would be frightened, when everything is in a hubbub, and nothing to be heard but "Throw him over"——"Over with him"——"Off, off, off the stage"——"Music"——"Won't y' ha' some orange chips" ——"Ha! some nonpareils"——"Prologue"——"Hornpipe"——"Roast

---

[72] Jonson, *Every Man in His Humour* I.iv.170.
[73] *Romeo and Juliet* III.i.99-100. Added in 1786.
[74] A slip for "epithet," as Murphy's note in earlier editions explains.
[75] Farquhar, *The Beaux' Stratagem* IV.ii.80,91-92.
[76] If you are for a fight, I would not value you three skips of a flea.

beef"——My dear, it is not like going to the sod.[77] A body could do that, fresh and fasting in a morning, without fee or reward; becaze, why? You are as terrible yourself as your enemy.——But the critics have the advantage—— Ow! never mind that; who knows but the dear craturs in the boxes will be lucking at my legs? To be sure! The Devil burn the luck they'll give 'em.

SCOTCHMAN. By St. Andrew, the cheeld of North Britain has taken that trade out of your hands.

IRISHMAN. That trade out of our hands, is it?——Why sure, my dear, the legs are the manufacture of Ireland. Ow! never fear it. Let me alone, my jewel; maybe I would see a little round face from Dublin in the pit; maybe I would.[78]

SCOTCHMAN. For the elocution you will see that we have the preference: I'll gee you a specimen.

DICK. What, with that impediment?

SCOTCHMAN. Impeediment! What impeediment? I do not leesp, do I? I do not squeent. I am well leem'd, am I not?

IRISHMAN. Why then, if you go to that, I am as well timber'd myself as any of them; and by and by you will see what a figure I will make in genteel and top comedy.

SCOTCHMAN. Out a waw! Stand clear, mon, and I'll gee you a touch of *Macbeeth*. (*Repeats*)

"Is this a dagger that I see before me?
    The haundle tow'rds my haund!" [79]

IRISHMAN. (*Collaring him*) "Villain, be sure you prove my love a whore." [80] (*Repeats the rest of the speech*)

THIRD MEMBER. (*With his face powder'd, and a pipe in his hand*)

"I am thy father's spirit;
    Doom'd for a certain time to walk the night——" [81]

---

[77] Meeting a dueling antagonist. Added in 1786.

[78] In earlier editions there followed an autobiographical passage in which the Irishman alluded to the objections of Murphy's own relatives to the author's acting career.

[79] *Macbeth* II.i.33-34.

[80] *Othello* III.iii.359.

[81] *Hamlet* I.v.9-10.

DICK. Po! Prithee, man; you are not fat enough for a ghost.

ALL. No, no; it stands to reason that a ghost should be the fattest actor on the stage.

THIRD MEMBER. I intend to make my first appearance in the Ghost: but I am a little puzzled about one thing. The audience, you know, always applaud a man at his first appearance: now I want to know, when I come on, and they all fall a clapping, whether I should make a bow to the pit and boxes?

IRISHMAN. To be sure you would; and then if you are damned, being a ghost, you are at home you know, my dear.

SECOND MEMBER. Now, gentlemen, for the true way of dying—— (*Spreads a blanket*) you must suppose me wounded—— (*Falls*)

> "Oh! Altamont, thy genius is the stronger;
> Thou hast prevail'd——" [82]

WATCHMAN. (*Within*) Past five o'clock, and a cloudy morning.

DICK. How! Past five o'clock!——'Sdeath! I shall miss my appointment with Charlotte—— "I have staid too long, and I shall lose my proselyte." [83]——Come, my boys; let us sally out.

ALL. Ay! let us adjourn; let us beat the rounds.

IRISHMAN. Ow! never fear me; I am ready for anything, my dear; though if they had stayed, I should have boddered 'em finely in *Othollo*.

SCOTCHMAN. I should have sheened in *Macbeeth*. But never mind it now. I'll go to my friend the bookseller, and translate *Cornelius Tacitus*, or *Grotius de Jure Belli*.

ALL. Huzza! huzza! huzza!

DICK. We'll scour the watch——"confusion to morality! I wish the constable was married" [84]——Huzza!

IRISHMAN. Why then, myself did not care if I was well married too; a wife with a good fortune would be hindering me from going on the stage. Ow! no matter; I may meet with a willing cratur somewhere.

Exit singing.

---

[82] Rowe, *The Fair Penitent* (1703) IV.i.109-110. Added in 1786.

[83] Otway, *Venice Preserv'd* II.ii.11-12.

[84] Vanbrugh, *The Provok'd Wife* III.ii.47-48.

DICK. Now for the Montagues and the Capulets, and if they bite their thumbs at me—— [85]

Exit.

ALL. Huzza! huzza! huzza!

Exeunt omnes.

SCENE [II]

A Street

Enter WATCHMAN.

WATCHMAN. Past five o'clock, and a cloudy morning.——All mad I believe in this house. This is their trade three nights in the week, I think.——Past five o'clock, and a cloudy morning.

ALL. (*Within*) Huzza! "Down with the watch: I wish the constable was married."

WATCHMAN. What in the name of wonder are they about now?

Enter the SPOUTERS.

DICK. "Angels and ministers of grace defend us." [86]

FIRST MEMBER.

"By Heav'n, I'll tear thee joint by joint,
 And strew this hungry churchyard with your limbs." [87]

DICK.

"Avaunt, and quit my sight: thy bones are marrowless;
 There's no speculation in those eyes, that thou dost glare
  withal." [88]

---

[85] *Romeo and Juliet* I.i.48 ff. Added in 1786.
[86] *Hamlet* I.iv.39.
[87] *Romeo and Juliet* V.iii.35-36.
[88] *Macbeth* III.iv.93-96.

WATCHMAN. You are disposed to be merry, Master.

SECOND MEMBER. "Be sure you write him down an ass." [89]

DICK.

"Be alive again
And dare me to the desert with thy pole." [90]

FIRST MEMBER. "Approach thou like the rugged Russian bear." [91]

SECOND MEMBER. "The arm'd rhinoceros, or Hyrcanian tiger"——[92]

DICK.

"Take any shape but that, and my firm nerves
Shall never tremble."——[93]

WATCHMAN. Soho! soho!

Enter WATCHMEN *from all parts, some drunk, some coughing, and many standing at a distance.*

SECOND WATCHMAN. What's the matter here?

FIRST WATCHMAN. I charge 'em all in the King's name; they have broke the peace; they have committed burglary.

WATCHMEN. Down with 'em; bring 'em along.

DICK.

"Unmanner'd slave!
Advance your *lanthorn* higher than my breast,
Or by St. Paul, I'll strike thee to my foot,
And spurn the beggar for this insolence." [94]

WATCHMEN. Upon 'em; fall on; to the roundhouse. (*They fight; Dick falls; several run away; Watchmen follow*)

---

[89] *Much Ado about Nothing* IV.ii.79.
[90] *Macbeth* III.iv.103-104.
[91] *Ibid.* III.iv.100.
[92] *Ibid.* III.iv.101.
[93] *Ibid.* III.iv.102-103.
[94] Altered from Cibber, *Richard III* II.ii.40-43.

DICK.

"I am not valiant neither.
  Man but a rush against Othello's breast,
  And he retires. Where should Othello go?" [95]

Go! Where should I go?——To my little Charlotte to be sure.
Egad, I'll make my escape. "Now Love direct me, like the surest
arrow from your quiver." [96]

Exit.

Enter WATCHMAN *and several* SPOUTERS.

FIRST WATCHMAN. Bring 'em along.

SECOND WATCHMAN. Ay, ay; bring 'em along; they shall answer
this.

FIRST MEMBER. "Good ruffians, hold a while." [97]

FIRST WATCHMAN. Hold 'em fast.

SECOND MEMBER. "I am unfortunate, but not asham'd of being
so." [98]

SECOND WATCHMAN. No, asham'd of nothing, I'll warrant.

FIRST MEMBER. Rascals! Here is the most prevailing, powerful
rhetoric. (*Throws money down*)

FIRST WATCHMAN. Stay, stay; the money need not be lost.

SECOND WATCHMAN. We came honestly by it, whatever they
did. (*Watchmen pick up the money, and the Spouters run away* [99])

FIRST WATCHMAN. Come, neighbour; no bad booty.

Exeunt WATCHMEN.

---

[95] *Othello* V.ii.243,270-271. Added in 1786.
[96] Altered from Hoadly, *The Suspicious Husband* II.i.159-161.
[97] Altered from Edward Young, *The Revenge* (1721) V.ii.377.
[98] Thomas Southerne, *Oroonoko* (1695) I.ii.256-257.
[99] In earlier editions the Watchmen led away the Spouters.

SCENE [III]

Another Street

Enter DICK, *with a Lanthorn and Ladder.*

DICK. All's quiet here; the coast clear. Now for my adventure with Charlotte. This ladder will do the business, though it would be more theatrical if it was a ladder of ropes. That does not signify much: I have seen it done this way in one of the pantomimes.—— This is my master Gargle's. "I remember an apothecary, and here-about he dwells." [100]——Not being yet broad day, "the beggar's shop is shut.——What ho! apothecary!" [101]——"Soft; what light breaks from yonder window?——

It is the east, and Juliet is the Sun.
Arise, fair Sun, and kill the envious Moon"—— [102]

CHARLOTTE. (*At the window*) Who's there? My Romeo?
DICK. "The same, my love, if it not thee displease." [103]
CHARLOTTE. Not so loud; be a little natural now; you'll wake my father.
DICK.

"Alas! there's more peril in thy eye,
Than twenty of" [104] his gallypots.

CHARLOTTE. Pshaw! How can you? Don't be in heroics now; never mind poetry and plays. How could you stay so long?

---

[100] *Romeo and Juliet* V.i.37-38.
[101] *Ibid.* V.i.56-57.
[102] *Ibid.* II.ii.2-4.
[103] Altered from *ibid.* II.ii.61. As in the First Quarto, the line in Pope's edition ends with "displease," a reading that Garrick retained.
[104] *Romeo and Juliet* II.ii.71-72. Murphy added the second line in 1786.

DICK.

"Chide not, my fair, but let the god of love
  Laugh in thy eyes, and revel in thy heart." [105]

CHARLOTTE. As I live and breathe, you'll ruin everything. I shall be discovered. Be silent; make no noise, and I'll come down to you.

DICK. No, no; not so fast; let us act the Garden Scene first.

CHARLOTTE. And my next scene will be a prison scene. My father will lock me up, where I shall have no possibility of escaping. Have patience, and I'll be with you in a moment.

DICK. Nay, then, I'll act Ranger: "Up I go, neck or nothing." [106]

CHARLOTTE. Was there ever such a man? You are enough to fright a body out of one's wits. I have settled everything with Simon: he is going to open shop, and has promised to let me out that way. Can't you stay where you are? Don't come up. I tell you there is no occasion for the ladder.

DICK. But I tell you, I would not give a farthing for it without the ladder. "Up I go: if it was as high as the garret, I should mount." [107]

Enter SIMON, *at the Door.*

SIMON. Sir, Sir; Master, Madam——

DICK. (*Going up the ladder*) Prithee be quiet, Simon. I am ascending "the high top-gallant of my joy." [108]

SIMON. Always some new comical notion in his head. An't please you, Master, my young mistress may come through the shop: I am going to sweep it out, and she may pass that way safe and fast enow.

CHARLOTTE. That will be the best way: do you go down again; stay at the door, and be ready to receive me. (*She goes in*)

---

[105] Rowe, *The Fair Penitent* IV.i.20-21
[106] Expanded from Hoadly, *The Suspicious Husband* III.i.170.
[107] *The Suspicious Husband* V.ii.396-397.
[108] *Romeo and Juliet* II.iv.201.

DICK. But I tell you that will not do: you shan't hinder me from going through my part. (*Goes up and looks in at the window*) "A woman by all that's lucky; neither old nor crooked; in I go." [109] (*Gets in*) "And for fear of" my master Gargle, "and the pursuit of the family, I'll make sure of the ladder." [110] (*Pulling up the ladder*)

SIMON. Hist! Hist! Master; leave the ladder; it may save me from being suspected. I can say that young mistress got out of the house that way.

DICK. Very true, Simon: take care of a single rogue: I'll leave the ladder, and be with you in a moment. (*He goes in*)

SIMON. Lord love him, how pleasant he is!——It will be fine diversion for me, when we are all playing the fool together in the stage-play, to call him Brother Martin—— "Brother Martin; Brother Martin." [111]

Enter CHARLOTTE.

CHARLOTTE. Dear me! I am frighted out of my senses: where is he?

SIMON. He is a coming, Ma'am—— "Brother Martin."

Enter DICK.

DICK. "Cuckold him, Ma'am, by all means: I'm your man." [112]

CHARLOTTE. Well, I protest and vow, I wonder how you can serve a body so. Feel how my heart goes, thump, thump: it flutters like a bird in a cage.

DICK. " 'Tis an alarm to love." [113]——But stay; I have not done my part right: here has been no rapture at our meeting—— "Quick let me snatch thee to thy Romeo's arms." [114]

CHARLOTTE. Hush! Don't you consider the danger?

---

[109] *The Suspicious Husband* III.i.176-178.
[110] *Ibid.* III.i.179-182.
[111] Farquhar, *The Beaux' Stratagem* III.iii.44,227-228; IV.i.395,446.
[112] *The Suspicious Husband* III.ii.30-31.
[113] Congreve, *The Old Bachelor* (1693) IV.vi.6.
[114] David Garrick, *Romeo and Juliet* (1748) V.v.70.

DICK. But I tell you, in spite of all danger we should indulge our rapture. It is not dramatic otherwise. (*Embraces her*) "Curls like a vine, and touches like a god." [115]

WATCHMAN. (*Within*) Past six o'clock, and a cloudy morning.

CHARLOTTE. As I live and breathe, we shall be discovered and taken. We have not a moment to lose: if you love me, let us make our escape without more foolery.

WATCHMAN. (*Within*) Past six o'clock, and a cloudy morning.

CHARLOTTE. It comes nearer and nearer: let us get away.

DICK. Give me your hand, my fair adventurer; I attend you. "He must fight damn'd hard that takes you from me now." [116]

> "Yes, my dear Charlotte, we will go together;
> Together to the theatre we'll go;
> There to their ravish'd eyes our skill we'll show,
> And point new beauties——to the pit below." [117]

Exit with CHARLOTTE.

SIMON. Heaven bless the couple of 'em!——Lud! somebody coming!——Hush; I must get out of the way. (*Goes in and shuts the door*)

Enter CATCHPOLE *and his* FOLLOWER.

CATCHPOLE. That's he yonder, as sure as you're alive. Yes, yes; 'tis he. And by that token there (*Pointing to the ladder*) he has been about some mischief.

FOLLOWER. Yes, it is; no, no: that an't he. That one has a laced coat on him: thof I can't say——yes, it is——as sure as a gun it is he.

---

[115] Lee, *The Rival Queens* I.i.371. Added in 1786.
[116] Hoadly, *The Suspicious Husband* III.iii.195-196. Added in 1786.
[117] A rewriting of Ambrose Philips, *The Distrest Mother* (1712) I.v.6-9:

ANDROMACHE
"Yes, my Astyanax, we'll go together!
Together, to the realms of night, we'll go!
There to thy ravish'd eyes thy sire I'll show!
And point him out among the shades below."

CATCHPOLE. Ay, I smoked him at once.——Do you run that way, and stop at the bottom of Catherine Street; I'll turn into Drury Lane, and between us both, it's odds but we nab him.

Exeunt.

Enter WATCHMAN.

WATCHMAN. Past six o'clock——a troublesome riotous night I have had of it——hey! what's here? A ladder at Master Gargle's window! I must alarm the family. Ho! ho! Master Gargle! (*Raps at the door*)

GARGLE. (*At the window*) What's the matter? How comes this window to be open? Ha!——a ladder: who's below there?

WATCHMAN. Good morning, Master Gargle: you an't robbed, I hope: going my rounds I found a ladder here, and saw that window open.

GARGLE. My mind misgives; some misfortune has happened; that young Graceless has been at work, I fear. Take away the ladder: where is Charlotte? my daughter, Charlotte——(*He goes in*)

Enter SIMON *imitating* SCRUB.

SIMON. "Thieves! murder! thieves! robbery! popery!" [118]

WATCHMAN. What's the matter with the man? Are you crazy?

SIMON. (*With his coat half off*) "Spare all I have, and take my life." [119]

WATCHMAN. Any mischief within?

SIMON. "They broke in with fire and sword. They'll be here in a moment—— Five and forty!" [120] (*Aside*)——This will do——young master taught me this: I should not know what to say but for he: this will deceive 'em all. [*To Watchman*] "Five and forty, Sir; with sword and pistol!" [121]

---

[118] Farquhar, *The Beaux' Stratagem* V.ii.96.
[119] *Ibid.* V.ii.99-100.
[120] *Ibid.* V.ii.119-121,174.
[121] *Ibid.* V.ii.174,138.

WATCHMAN. Robbers in the house?

SIMON. "With sword and pistol——five and forty, I saw 'em all." [122]

WATCHMAN. Nay, an that be the case, it's time for me to march off: I may happen to have the worst on't, and so I'll go and sleep in whole bones.——Half an hour past six o'clock.

Exit.

SIMON. If it was not for my friend Scrub I don't know what I should do.

Enter GARGLE.

GARGLE. She's gone; the villain has robbed me; my daughter is run away; he has carried her off; Simon, I say, Simon; where is the fellow?

SIMON. "Down o' your knees; down o' your marrowbones; five and forty! robbers, villains, thieves, murderers, with sword and pistol; down o' your marrowbones." [123]

GARGLE. What a fright the poor fellow is in!——Get up, Simon. My daughter is lost; I am ruined.

SIMON. (*Aside*) He does not suspect me: young master has taught me rarely, blessings on him for it. (*To Gargle*) "Spare all I have, Sir, and take my life." [119]

Enter WINGATE, *with a Newspaper.*

WINGATE. (*Reading*) "Wanted on good security, FIVE HUNDRED POUNDS, for which lawful interest will be given, and a GOOD PREMIUM. Whoever this may suit, enquire for S. T. at the CROWN AND ROLLS in Chancery Lane. *Nota bene:* the utmost secrecy may be depended upon."——This may be worth looking after. If the fellow's a fool, I'll fix my eye upon him. Other people's [124] follies are an estate to the man who knows how to make himself useful. Hey!

---

[122] *Ibid.* V.ii.138,174,120.

[123] *Ibid.* V.ii.103-104,174,96,138.

[124] Correct case form in earlier editions.

whom have we here?——Friend Gargle!——Up early I see; nothing like it; nothing to be got by lounging in bed, like a great lubberly fellow. What's the matter with you? You look as if you had been taking your own physic.

GARGLE. No wonder; no wonder; my daughter Charlotte!

WINGATE. Your daughter! What signifies a foolish girl?

GARGLE. Poor girl! Out at that window there!

WINGATE. Fallen out of the window! If she is dead, she is provided for. Here, I have brought the book; I could not find it last night. Here it is; more sense in it than in all their *Macbeths* and their trumpery: (*Reads the title-page*) *Cocker's Arithmetick;* let that booby son of mine study this, and he will know how to fight his way in the world. Look you here now: suppose you have a sixteenth part of a ship, and I buy one-fifth of you; what share of the ship do I buy?

GARGLE. Dear heart! dear heart! Mine is a melancholy case.

WINGATE. So it is, if you can't answer the question. Why should not a man know everything? How can you settle partnership accounts? One-fifth of one-sixteenth, what share of the whole do I buy? Let me see; I'll do it a short way.

GARGLE. To lose my daughter in this manner! Seduced out of my house! She is gone, beyond redemption.

WINGATE. Zookers! be quiet man; you put me out. Can't you hold your tongue? Five times sixteen is equal to ten times eight; ten times eight is eighty. Wounds! I'll give the book to that ignorant scoundrel, though, for aught I see, you are as ignorant yourself.

GARGLE. Deliver me! I don't know which way to turn myself. Your son is returned to his old tricks.

WINGATE. His old tricks! What, on the stage again?

GARGLE. I suppose so; and he has carried off poor Charlotte.

WINGATE. Carried off your daughter! How did the rascal contrive that?

GARGLE. Oh! I am distracted. The watch alarmed us a little while ago, and I found a ladder at the window. I wish I had never taken him into my house. He may debauch the poor girl.

WINGATE. Suppose he does; what then? She's a woman, is not she?

The fellow will have sense enough for that, I warrant him.——Ha! ha! And that's what she wants I suppose.

GARGLE. I never suspected her: their intrigue was all a secret to me.

SIMON. (*Aside*) Now I may venture to speak—— "Secrets! Secrets!" [125]

WINGATE. What does the fellow say?——Are you in the secret, rascal?

SIMON. "There be secrets in all families, but for my part I'll not speak a word pro or con till there's a peace." [126]

WINGATE. You won't speak, sirrah? Speak out this moment, you villain; do you know anything of this plot?

SIMON. Who, I, Sir? Not I, Sir, I know no secret, Sir; he came home last night from your house, and went out again directly.

WINGATE. You saw him then?

SIMON. Yes, Sir; I saw him to be sure, Sir. He made me open the shop-door for him: he stopt on the threshold, and looked as if he saw something, and pointed at one of the clouds, and asked if it was like an ouzel.[127]

WINGATE. Like an ouzel! Wounds! what's an ouzel?

GARGLE. And then he came back in the dead of the night, and stole away my daughter.

WINGATE. Po! what signifies your daughter? All women are ruined some time or other. Wounds! I'll not put myself in a passion: what right has the scoundrel to put me in a passion? I'll think no more about him. Let him bite the bridle. I'll go and mind my business, and not lose an opportunity for such a worthless numskull.

GARGLE. What shall I do? Mr. Wingate, do not leave me in this affliction. Consider, Sir, Sir, when the animal spirits are properly employed, the whole system is exhilarated; a proper circulation in the smaller ducts or capillary vessels.

---

[125] *The Beaux' Stratagem* III.iii.31,38.
[126] *Ibid.* III.iii.29-30; IV.i.433-435.
[127] *Hamlet* III.ii.396. "Ouzle" is the reading of Pope and Theobald.

WINGATE. Look you there now; the fellow is at his ducks again. Ha! ha! What a mountebank of a doctor you are!

GARGLE. But when the spirits are under undue influence——

WINGATE. Po! you are as mad with your physical jargon as my son is with his Shakespeare, and his ridiculous beggarly poets.

GARGLE. Dear Sir, let us go in quest of him. He shall be well phlebotomized, and for the future I will keep his solids and fluids in a proper balance.

WINGATE. Don't tell me of solids. The blockhead will never be solid. I'll mind my own affairs. What care I for him? Let me see; my chap [128] is at——(*Reads the newspaper*) ay, at the Crown and Rolls. Friend Gargle, make your mind easy: go and study vulgar fractions. Arithmetical proportion is when the antecedent and the consequent——

Enter a PORTER.

WINGATE. Who are you, friend? What do you want?

PORTER. Is one Mr. Gargle here?

GARGLE. My name is Gargle: anybody taken sick?

PORTER. Here's a letter for you.

GARGLE. Let me see it. What can this be? "To Mr. Gargle at the Pestle and Mortar"—— A letter from your son, Mr. Wingate; this is his hand.

WINGATE. Let me see it. (*Snatches it*) This will unravel all, I suppose——his writing sure enough: what can the villain say for himself? (*Reads*)

"To Mr. Gargle.

Most potent, grave, and reverend doctor, my very noble and approved good master" [129]—— The fellow is mad: what a reverend doctor you are! (*Looks at Gargle and laughs*) Ha! ha! You look like a mummy—— (*Reads*) "That I have ta'en away your daughter it is most true; true I will marry her.[130] 'Tis true 'tis pity, and pity

---

[128] A contemptuous name for a customer. Above, Wingate calls the same man "a fool."

[129] Altered from *Othello* I.iii.76-77.

[130] *Ibid.* I.iii.78-79.

'tis 'tis true." [131] I never read such nonsense in my life. His friend Shakespeare has taught him this. (*Reads*) "I have done your shop some service, and you know it; no more of that.[132] Yet I could wish, that at this time, I had not been this thing." [133] What does the scoundrel mean? (*Reads*) "For time may have yet one fated hour to come, which wing'd with liberty, may overtake occasion past." [134] ——His poets have taught him that too, and it's all flat nonsense: time and tide wait for no man. (*Reads*) "Here is a ruffian making villainous jests at my undoing. Even the lewd rabble, when they beheld him seizing me, grumbled pity. I could have hugged the greasy rogues; they pleased me. I expect redress from thy noble sorrows.[135] Farewell, remember me.[136]   Richard Wingate."
I don't understand a word of it. Mad as a March hare; stark-staring mad.

PORTER. An't please ye, I fancy's the gentleman is a little beside himself. He took me hold by the collar, and called me villain, and bid me prove his wife a whore.[137] Lord help him! I never seed the gentleman's spouse in my born days before.

GARGLE. Is she with him now?

PORTER. There's a likely young woman with him, all in tears.

GARGLE. My daughter to be sure.

WINGATE. Let him stay there. Wounds! I would not go the length of my arm to save the villain from the gallows. Where was he, friend, when he gave you this letter?

PORTER. I fancy the gentleman's in troubles: I brought it from a spunging-house.

WINGATE. A spunging-house!

PORTER. Yes, Sir——Mr. Catchpole's in Gray's Inn Lane.

WINGATE. Let him lie there; I am glad of it.

---

[131] *Hamlet* II.ii.97-98.
[132] Altered from *Othello* V.ii.339-340.
[133] Congreve, *The Mourning Bride* III.i.175,176.
[134] *Ibid.* III.i.182-184.
[135] Otway, *Venice Preserv'd* I.i.238,241-242,264-267; V.iii.59.
[136] *Hamlet* I.v.88,91.
[137] *Othello* III.iii.359.

GARGLE. Let us go to him, Mr. Wingate, I entreat you; we may save him from ruin.

WINGATE. No; let him suffer for it. This it is to have a genius ——ha! ha! Genius is a fine thing indeed!

GARGLE. We may still do some good. We may retrieve him. Step into my house. I'll slip on my coat. This honest porter will show us the way.

WINGATE. Come in, and I'll talk to you: but I will have nothing to do with the scoundrel——

Exit.

GARGLE. Honest friend, come with us; I shall be ready in a moment. Simon, do you stay and take care of the house.

Exeunt.

SIMON. Oh! I understand it now: my poor young master shut up in a jail. I have three shillings, and a tester, and I should like to give it to him all, an it would do him any good.

GARGLE. (*Within*) Simon, Simon.

SIMON. Anan; I'm a coming.

Exit.

SCENE [IV]

A Spunging-House

Dick and Catchpole at a table; Charlotte sitting in a disconsolate manner.

CATCHPOLE. Here's my service to you, young gentleman. Don't let your spirits sink. The debt is no such great matter. Why so sad?

DICK. "Because captivity has robbed me of a just and dear re-venge." [138]

CATCHPOLE. Never look out of humour at me. I never uses anybody ill. No complaints of my house. Come, this has been many a

---

[138] Congreve, *The Mourning Bride* I.ii.145-146.

good man's lot. Don't be dejected. I have taken a liking to you. Your look bespeaks something. My heart warms to you, methinks. Here's my service to you. Hey! the liquor out. Come, we'll have t'other bowl.

DICK. "I've now not fifty ducats in the world; yet still I am in love, and pleas'd with ruin." [139]

CATCHPOLE. What do you say? You have fifty shillings I hope.

DICK. "Now thank Heav'n, I'm not worth a groat." [140]

CATCHPOLE. Not worth a groat!——Then there's no credit here, I can tell you that. You must get bail or go to Newgate. The county jail is the place for the like of you. Who do you think is to pay house-rent for you? I saw something sneaking in you at the first cast of my eye. I knew you was nobody. My heart turned against you at once. Such poverty-struck devils as you have no business in my house.

DICK.

"The insolence of office, and the spurns
    That patient merit from th' unworthy takes!" [141]

CATCHPOLE. Merits! The plaintiff will show you that he has merits, I warrant him. And you see your friends won't come near you. They have all answered in the old cant, "I've promised my wife never to be bail for anybody"——"I have sworn not to be security"——"I would lend you the money if I had it, but I desire to be excused from justifying bail"——And the porter you sent but just now will bring the same answer. Don't think to stay snivelling here. You shall go to quod,[142] I can tell you that. (*Knocking at the door*) Coming, coming; I'm a coming. I shall lodge you in Newgate before night. Not worth a groat!——I'll keep no such low-lived company in my house. (*Knocking at the door*) Knock the house down, do, will you? A parcel of actor-folks coming I

---

[139] Otway, *Venice Preserv'd* I.i.116-117.
[140] *Ibid.* I.i.250,251.
[141] *Hamlet* III.i.73-74. Added in 1786.
[142] Slang for prison.

suppose. None but players will come after you. I'll take none of 'em for bail. They shan't jibe me, I promise you.

Exit.

DICK. "Has this fellow no feeling in his business, that he laughs in making prisoners?" [143] Come, clear up, Charlotte; never mind this; let us act the Prison Scene in *The Mourning Bride.*

CHARLOTTE. How can you think of acting plays now, when we are in such distress?

DICK. Why that's the time to imitate great examples. "Unbend that brow and look more kindly on me." [144] Come, we'll practice an attitude. How many of 'em have you?

CHARLOTTE. Oh! attitudes enough, if that would pay the debt. Let me see; one, two, three, and then in the fourth act, and then ——as I live and breathe, I believe, I have ten at least.

DICK. That will do swimmingly. I believe I have a round dozen myself.

Enter WINGATE *and* GARGLE.

GARGLE. Hush! Let us listen to him. I dare say he repents.

WINGATE. Wounds! What cloaths are those he has on? The villain has robbed me.

DICK. Ay, we will show 'em attitudes enough. Let us try, Charlotte. Come; you fancy me dead, and I think the same of you. (*They stand in attitudes*)

WINGATE. The fellow ought to be in a strait waistcoat——there, there; mind him now.

DICK. "Oh! thou soft fleeting form of Lindamira!"

CHARLOTTE. "Illusive shade of my beloved lord!" [145]

DICK. "She lives, she speaks, and we shall still be happy." [146]

WINGATE. You lie, you villain, you shan't be happy. (*Knocks him down*)

---

[143] Altered from *Hamlet* V.i.73-74. Added in 1786.

[144] Otway, *The Orphan* II.i.213,216. Added in 1786.

[145] Murphy borrows the name Lindamira from William Whitehead's burlesque outline tragedy *Fatal Constancy or Love in Tears* (1754).

[146] Altered from Garrick, *Romeo and Juliet* V.v.66.

DICK. (*On the ground*) "Perdition catch thy arm, the chance is thine." [147]

GARGLE. So, young madam, I have found you again. (*Seizes Charlotte*)

DICK.

> "Capulet, forbear; Paris, let loose your hold;
> She is my wife; our hearts are twin'd together." [148]

WINGATE. Sirrah! villain! I'll teach you what it is to torment your father. (*Striking him*)

DICK. "Parents have flinty hearts; no tears can move 'em; children must be wretched." [149]

WINGATE. Get off the ground; rise up this moment, or——

DICK. (*Rising*) A pity there are no scene-drawers to carry me off.

WINGATE. What a vile profligate! Where did you get that coat? Rascal, I have a mind to break your head.

Enter CATCHPOLE, *listening at a distance.*

DICK. "What, like this?" [150] (*Pulls off his wig, and shows two patches on his head*) [151]

WINGATE. Have not I told you what your follies would bring you to? Can nothing sting you to reflection? A thousand circumstances might before now have touched you to the quick. Your own sufferings; a sense of filial duty; the ingratitude that marks your conduct, and the certain ruin that must be the consequence of irregular and wild pursuits.

CATCHPOLE. (*Aside*) Vastly well! He speaks more naturally than any of them.

DICK. Sir, with your permission, "Rude am I in my speech, and

---

[147] Cibber, *Richard III* V.iii.224.
[148] Altered from Garrick, *Romeo and Juliet* V.v.121-122.
[149] Altered from *ibid.* V.v.118-119.
[150] John Brown, *Barbarossa* II.i.351.
[151] In 1786 Murphy added the next eight speeches.

little shall I grace my cause in speaking for myself, yet by your gracious favour"——[152]

CATCHPOLE. (*Aside*) No; that won't do; sad stuff and ill-spoken.

WINGATE. What do you deserve for this behaviour? Where do you think it will end? Without experience and knowledge of the world, must you presume to judge for yourself? Is there nothing due to your superiors? No deference to authority? By persisting in a wild career of error and dissipation, you may plant thorns upon a father's pillow, but the uneasiness you give him will only serve to embitter your own reflections, when you are left in ruin and distress to think of what you have done.

CATCHPOLE. Very good! (*Goes up to Wingate and claps him on the shoulder*) I like to hear you: you are the best actor among them. (*Embraces him*)

WINGATE. What does the fellow mean?

CATCHPOLE. You do it admirably: give us another speech. You have a good salary, I warrant you.

WINGATE. Zookers! Do you take me for a mountebank? Mighty well, young man; you see what disgrace you bring upon your father. Wounds! Friend Gargle, I have done with him. I made my own fortune, and sooner than he shall spend a shilling of my money, I'll take a boy out of the Bluecoat Hospital,[153] and give him all I have. The scoundrel has robbed me, and so, Mr. Catchpole, you may take him to Newgate.

CATCHPOLE. Well, I thought I never heard a better actor in my life. I'll take him if you be so minded, and are in good earnest.

GARGLE. If you go to that extremity, Mr. Wingate, then you know the fortune I intended to give my daughter must go into another channel.

WINGATE. How is that?——[*Aside*] I must not lose the handling of his money.——Why, you know, friend Gargle, I am not hard-hearted in the main.

GARGLE. Very true, Sir, and if you'll make the young gentleman

---

[152] *Othello* I.iii.81,88-89. Added in 1786.
[153] Christ's Hospital, a famous charity school.

serve out the last year of his apprenticeship, I shall be giving over business; he may then set up for himself, and have all my practice into the bargain.

WINGATE. Right, you are right——I don't like to lose an opportunity: if the blockhead would get as many crabbed physical phrases from your *Hippocrates and Allen* [154] as he has from his plays and farces, I don't know, between you and me, but he may pass for a good physician.

DICK. "And must I leave thee, Juliet?" [155]

CHARLOTTE. Have done with speeches now: you see we are in the last distress: you had better make it up. (*Aside to Dick*)

DICK. Why, for your sake, I could almost find it in my heart—— (*Aside*)

WINGATE. You'll settle your money on your daughter?

GARGLE. You know it was always my intention.

WINGATE. I must not let the cash slip through my hands. (*Aside*) Look ye here, young man: I am the best-natured man in the world.——Mr. Catchpole, how much is the debt?

CATCHPOLE. The gentleman gave his note at Bristol, I understands, where he boarded. 'Tis but twenty pounds, debt and costs. I have treated him kindly, as I always do to everybody, and so what you please for civility money.——The gentleman knows I have been very civil.

WINGATE. Twenty pounds! What right have you to owe twenty pounds? Why don't you send for your friend Shakespeare to bail you?——Ha! ha! I should like to see Shakespeare attempt to justify bail.——Mr. Catchpole, will you take bail of Ben Thomson, and Shakespeare, and Odyssey Popes?

CATCHPOLE. No such people have been here. Are they housekeepers?

DICK. "You do not come to mock my miseries?" [156]

---

[154] John Allen, a physician and inventor, wrote the Latin *Synopsis Medicinae* (London, 1719), which included the opinions of Hippocrates and other ancient authorities.

[155] Garrick, *Romeo and Juliet* V.v.115.

[156] Congreve, *The Mourning Bride* III.ii.37.

GARGLE. Hush! you'll spoil all. (*Takes him by the hand*) Bless me! You are in a high fever. When you come home, I'll administer a gentle febrifuge.

DICK. "Throw physic to the dogs, I'll none of it." [157]

WINGATE. What does he say, Gargle?

GARGLE. He repents; he promises to reform.

WINGATE. That's right, lad; now you are right. Serve out your time, and my friend Gargle will make a man of you. Wounds! You'll have his daughter and all his money; and if I hear no more of your trumpery, and you mind your business, and stick to my little Charlotte, and make me a grandfather in my old days, why, then, you will have all my money too, that is, when I am dead.

DICK. And then, Charlotte, we may go to the play as often as we please. (*Aside*)

CHARLOTTE. That will be the purest thing in the world, and we may see *Romeo and Juliet* every time it's acted. (*Aside*)

DICK. So we may: I'll buy a renter's share.[158] And besides, it will look like a play now, if I reform in the end.——(*Aside*)——Sir (*To Wingate*), "free me so far in your most generous thoughts that I have shot my arrow o'er the house, and hurt my brother." [159]

WINGATE. What do you say? Speak out, friend.

CHARLOTTE. Tell him in plain English. (*Aside to Dick*)

DICK. I will: he knows nothing of metaphors. Sir, you shall find for the future that we will both endeavour to give you all the satisfaction in our power.

WINGATE. Very well; that's right. You may still do very well. Friend Gargle, I am overjoy'd.

GARGLE. Cheerfulness is the principal ingredient in the composition of health.

WINGATE. Wounds! No more of your physic. Here young man, put this book in your pocket, and let me see how soon you'll be master of vulgar fractions. Mr. Catchpole, step home with me, and I'll pay you the money. You seem a notable sort of a fellow, Mr.

---

[157] *Macbeth* V.iii.47.
[158] A share of a stockholder of a theater. Added in 1786.
[159] *Hamlet* V.ii.253-255.

Catchpole, and I dare say mind your opportunities. Could you nab a man for me?

CATCHPOLE. Ay, fast enow, when I have the writ.

WINGATE. Very well, step with me. I lent a young gentleman a hundred pounds. A cool hundred he called it——ha! ha!——it did not stay to cool with him. I touched a premium there; but I shan't wait a moment. Come, young man; do you know anybody that will give you twenty pounds? I never was obliged to my family for twenty pounds. But I'll say no more. If you have a mind to thrive in the world, make yourself useful; that's the only rule I know, and it's the golden rule.

DICK. Charlotte, as you are to be my reward, I intend now to be a new man.

CHARLOTTE. And now I shall see how much you love me.

DICK. It shall be my study to deserve you. And since we don't go on the stage it is some comfort that "the world's a stage, and all the men and women merely players." [160]

> Some act the upper, some the under parts,
> And most assume what's foreign to their hearts.
> Thus life is but a tragi-comic jest,
> And all is FARCE and MUMMERY at best.

---

[160] *As You Like It* II.vii.139-140.

EPILOGUE,

Written by a Friend.[161]

Spoken by Mrs. Clive.

Enters reading the Play-Bill.

A very pretty bill——as I'm alive!
The part of——Nobody——by Mrs. Clive!
A paltry, scribbling fool——to leave me out——
He'll say, perhaps——he thought I could not spout.
Malice and envy to the last degree!
And why?——I wrote a farce as well as he.[162]
And fairly ventur'd it, without the aid
Of prologue dress'd in black, and face in masquerade;
O pit——have pity——see how I'm dismay'd!
Poor soul!——this canting stuff will never do,
Unless, like Bayes, he brings his hangman too.[163]
But granting that from these same obsequies,
Some pickings to our bard in black arise;
Should your applause to joy convert his fear,
As Pallas turns to feast——Lardella's bier;[164]

---

[161] Christopher Smart.
[162] Catharine Clive's farce *The Rehearsal: or, Bays in Petticoats* was acted at Drury Lane in 1750.
[163] See Second Duke of Buckingham, *The Rehearsal* (1671) I.ii.144-150.
[164] See *ibid.* IV.i.201-210.

Yet 'twould have been a better scheme by half
T'have thrown his weeds aside, and learnt with me to laugh.
I could have shown him, had he been inclin'd,
A spouting junto of the female kind.
There dwells a milliner in yonder row,
Well-dress'd, full-voic'd, and nobly built for show,
Who, when in rage, she scolds at Sue and Sarah,
Damn'd, damn'd dissembler!——thinks she's more than Zara.[165]
She has a daughter too that deals in lace,
And sings——"O ponder well" [166]——and "Chevy Chase," [167]
And fain would fill the fair Ophelia's place.
And in her cockt up hat, and gown of camblet,
Presumes on "something——touching the Lord Hamlet." [168]
A cousin too she has, with squinting eyes,
With waddling gait, and voice like London cries;
Who, for the stage too short by half a story,
Acts Lady Townly [169]——thus——in all her glory.
And, while she's traversing the scanty room,
Cries——"Lord, my Lord, what can I do at home!" [170]
In short, there's girls enough for all the fellows,
The ranting, whining, starting, and the jealous,
The Hotspurs, Romeos, Hamlets, and Othellos.
Oh! little do those silly people know,
What dreadful trials——actors undergo.
Myself——who most in harmony delight,
Am scolding here from morning until night.
Then take advice from me, ye giddy things,
Ye royal milliners, ye apron'd kings;
Young men beware, and shun our slipp'ry ways,

---

[165] A Moorish queen in Congreve's *The Mourning Bride*.
[166] The old ballad *The Children in the Wood*.
[167] A famous historical ballad.
[168] *Hamlet* I.iii.89.
[169] In Cibber, *The Provok'd Husband* (1728).
[170] *Ibid.* I.i.28-29.

Study arithmetic, and burn your plays;
And you, ye girls, let not our tinsel train
Enchant your eyes, and turn your madd'ning brain;
Be timely wise, for oh! be sure of this!——
A shop with virtue is the height of bliss.

THE UPHOLSTERER (1758)

INTRODUCTION

IN 1757 Murphy composed *The Upholsterer or What News?*, a two-act laughing farce. The play opened at Drury Lane Theatre on March 30, 1758, with a brilliant cast, which included David Garrick as Pamphlet, Richard Yates as Quidnunc, Henry Woodward as Razor, Kitty Clive as Termagant, and Mary Ann Yates as Harriet. The farce became a stock piece in the repertoires of the London and provincial theaters. It was produced, for instance, at Covent Garden Theatre every year from 1763 to 1782. The role of Termagant attracted such comediennes as Ann Elliott and Isabella Mattocks.

The Upholsterer satirizes the neglect of private business and of domestic life for an unwarrantable interest in petty political news. With a political upholsterer, a crackbrained political barber, a political writer and trimmer, and a long-winded lawyer, the play depicts the life of the time. But newsmongers, talkative barbers, two-sided writers, pedants, and gullible readers of news are also perennial. Murphy never restricts his satire to any one political party. This satire actually influenced some members of the audience to give more attention to their families and less time to trifling news. The love affair of the upholsterer's daughter and the wanderings of his son provide the play with a simple plot structure appropriate as a frame for the satiric characterization. The genial satire never diminishes the laughter of the audience. The lively comic servant Termagant, who is one of the sources of Sheridan's Mrs. Malaprop, is an excellent characterization. Unbiased criticism prefers Termagant to Mrs. Malaprop as a comic creation. For her

and other characters, the dramatist writes equally well fragmentary
dialogue and long, natural soliloquies.

For *The Upholsterer*, Murphy received forty guineas from the
bookseller Paul Vaillant, and the first edition appeared in 1758.
Compared with the 1757 acting manuscript in the Larpent Collection of the Huntington Library, which was submitted for the
approval of the Lord Chamberlain, the printed version is improved
by a number of additions, cuts, alterations, and transpositions. The
most pronounced changes are the excision of four tradesmen from
the end of Act I, Scene ii—with the adaption of most of their
dialogue for Razor and Quidnunc in the following scene—and of
three watchmen from the final scene. The rare 1760 edition shows
no sign of the hand of the author.

For the opening of *The Upholsterer* at Covent Garden on
October 26, 1763, Murphy wrote what the title page of the 1763
edition designates as alterations and additions. The new material
follows Act II, Scene iii. First, there is added a scene in which
Quidnunc calls on Razor. This scene ends with the famous passage
that concerns the supplying of Jamaica with Florida peat. Then,
the final scene of the farce is rewritten with transpositions, cuts,
and insertions. For instance, Brisk's mistake in delivering a letter
for Bellmour is omitted, Quidnunc now does not immediately discover the presence of the lover Bellmour, Rovewell enters to rescue
Bellmour rather than to hunt female game, and Razor appears in
this scene and delivers a miniature epilogue. The added situation
in which Termagant cries after she has inadvertently revealed to
Quidnunc the presence of Bellmour utilizes material taken from
Muslin's similar situation near the conclusion of the three-act
version of Murphy's *The Way to Keep Him* (1760)—material not
retained in the five-act version of the comedy (1761). The most
interesting acting variations in the 1763 Larpent manuscript, which
corresponds to this 1763 edition, are the deletion of the characters
Brisk and Codicil * and the transposition of Act II, Scene iv, to
Act II, Scene iii. The two printings of 1765 and the printing of

---

* The role of Codicil had been dropped from the acting version in 1758.

1769 have no author's alterations, though the punctuation is progressively better. The title page of the second printing of 1765 reads "The Second Edition"; and that of 1769, "The Third Edition."

For the 1786 edition of his *Works*, Murphy revised *The Upholsterer*. The only untouched parts are those of Feeble and his maid. Murphy clarified the exposition, added figures of speech, and provided better transitions, exit lines, and stage directions. And the dramatist had become more chastened in his diction. Most markedly, he rewrote and expanded the final scene of the farce. Here, Harriet and Bellmour no longer quarrel before she consents to flee with him; she long hesitates because of her duty to Quidnunc and Feeble. Also, Rovewell does not enter to rescue Bellmour but is forced in after he has pursued the "game" Harriet.†

In January, 1791, for performance at Covent Garden, Murphy again revised *The Upholsterer*, chiefly by introducing up-to-date political references. This material survives in a 1791 Larpent manuscript, which ostensibly consists of so-called "additions" only. However, it submits certain 1786 changes, which had not been previously licensed for acting by the Lord Chamberlain, and unnecessarily includes some lines approved in 1757 and others in 1763.

In this present edition, the editor prints the text of 1786, with the dedication and dramatis personae of 1758. The footnotes indicate the most interesting differences between the versions of 1769 and 1786, and two outstanding alterations of 1791.

Texts Collated

MS., LA, 131, Mar. 16, 1757. Larpent Collection, Huntington Library.

By the Author of *The Apprentice, The Upholsterer, or, What News?*. London: P. Vaillant, 1758. [Temple University; Library Company, Philadelphia]

---

† In the 1758 edition Rovewell entered voluntarily in pursuit of Harriet.

By the Author of *The Apprentice, The Upholsterer; or, What News?*. London: P. Vaillant, 1760. [British Museum]

MS., LA, 227, [1763]. Larpent Collection, Huntington Library.

Murphy, [Arthur], *The Upholsterer, or, What News?*. With Alterations and Additions. London: P. Vaillant, 1763. [Yale University]

——, *The Upholsterer, or, What News?*. With Alterations and Additions. London: P. Vaillant, 1765. [Yale University]

——, *The Upholsterer, or, What News?*. With Alterations and Additions. The Second Edition. London: P. Vaillant, 1765. [University of Wisconsin; Columbia University]

——, *The Upholsterer, or, What News?*. With Alterations and Additions. The Third Edition. London: P. Vaillant, 1769. [Copy of Editor]

The Works of Arthur Murphy, II, 75-154. London: T. Cadell, 1786. [University of Pennsylvania; Copy of Editor]

MS., LA, 890, Jan. 21, 1791. Larpent Collection, Huntington Library.

THE UPHOLSTERER;

OR

WHAT NEWS?

A

COMEDY,

In TWO ACTS.

Performed at the

THEATRE ROYAL

IN

DRURY-LANE.

. . . O Bone (nam te
Scire, Deos quoniam propius contingis, oportet)
Num quid de Dacis audisti?

Hor.[1]

¹ Horace, *Satirae* II.6,51-53. "Oh, good sir, have you heard anything of the Dacians? (for it must be that you know, because you readily associate with the great)."

To Mr. Garrick

Sir,

The Upholsterer would be a bankrupt even in thanks could he think of going abroad into the world without making his compliments to Mr. Garrick for the civilities he has shown him. Whatever figure the poor, broken politician might make before the Commissioners of Bankruptcy at Guildhall, you have taken care of his appearance before the self-chosen Commissioners of Criticism at the Theatre Royal in Drury Lane.

I am not willing to flatter myself that you were drawn forth on this occasion by any extraordinary touches in the capital figure or in the *accompagnements du tableau*. I rather suppose that you approved the justness of the design than that you were an admirer of the colouring.

The design, Sir, was conceived and executed long since, because the author judged that something in this way might have a seasonable tendency to allay the intemperance of too violent a political spirit, or at least to laugh it into good humour. With the same view it was lately retouched and given to Mr. Mossop to be presented to the public at his benefit. And however men of a serious cast may depreciate amusements of this nature, I shall never blush for having dedicated a few hours to them, as I am of opinion that such-like avocations will more profitably unbend the mind from graver studies than the solitary pleasures of the recluse or any of the more open dissipations of life.

I am aware that you will, very probably, recollect a passage in a celebrated writer which may seem to render the scope of this little piece somewhat questionable. "Dans une nation libre," saith he, "il est très-souvent indifférent que les particuliers raisonnent bien ou mal; il suffit qu'ils raisonnent: de-là sort la liberté, qui garantit des effets de ces mêmes raisonnemens." [2] But you know that the question here is not concerning the indisputable right of the people to canvass their national concerns, but the vicious excess of a propensity to politics when it gives a wrong bias to the mind and is attended with circumstances which create the ridiculous absurd. In this light it was considered by Mr. Addison, who tells us in the *Tatler* that he designed his paper "for the benefit of those citizens who live more in a coffee-house than in their shops, and whose thoughts are so taken up with the affairs of the Allies that they forget their customers." [3] For the very same species of people, the Upholsterer was brought on the stage, being perhaps as proper an object of ridicule as modern ideas and manners will afford.

With regard to the execution, I shall not detain you any longer on that head than to remark that to preserve the gravity which is a specific quality in Mr. Addison's fine vein of humour has been my endeavour throughout the whole, though I am not insensible that grave humour is sometimes dangerous on the stage. In the principal character I considered myself rather describing a passion than a man; and this you remember is mentioned by an excellent critic [4] to belong to the province of farce. For this reason the Upholsterer's scenes are strongly tinctured with his predominant foible; and as this foible is generally fed and inflamed by a swarm of political writers, I judged it coincident with my plan to expose the duplicity of their conduct by introducing the character of Pamphlet.

This character I have had the pleasure of seeing set off with all the exquisite strokes of so fine a comic genius as Mr. Garrick's, without being indebted for success to the aid of personal satire, having entirely levelled it against those who are the ready mer-

---

[2] Montesquieu, *L'Esprit des Lois* (1748), Livre XIX, Chapitre 27.

[3] Conclusion of Addison's *Tatler*, No. 155, Apr. 6, 1710.

[4] Richard Hurd, "Of the Province of Farce," *A Dissertation on the Provinces of the Drama*, Chap. IV, Par. 2.

cenaries of all parties; and with all such I have the happiness not to be acquainted.

I could here enlarge in the just praise of Mr. Woodward, Mr. Yates, and Mrs. Clive, *&c.*, but I have already deviated too far from the purpose I set out with; which was not to inscribe a farce to you, for neither of us thinks so highly of these matters; nor to become your panegyrist, for your extended reputation does not stand in need of it. My intention was to embrace a public opportunity of subscribing myself,

Sir,
Your most obedient,
Very humble servant,
The Author.

Lincoln's Inn,
7th April, 1758.

PROLOGUE,

Spoken by Mr. Mossop.

The love of news, now grown the ruling passion,
In ev'ry age has been the gen'ral fashion.
'Twas so at Athens:——when in evil hour
Ambition aim'd at universal pow'r;
When the fierce man of Macedon began
Of a new monarchy to form the plan;
Each Greek (as fam'd Demosthenes relates [5])
Politically mad! wou'd rave of states!
And help'd to form, where'er the mob could meet,
A band of Senators in ev'ry street.
What news, what news? was their eternal cry:⎤
Is Philip sick! then soar'd their spirits high; ⎟
Philip is well!——dejection in each eye. ⎦
Athenian coblers join'd in deep debate,
While gold in secret undermin'd the state;
Till Wisdom's bird the vulture's prey was made;
And the sword gleam'd in Academus' shade.

Now modern Philips threaten this our land, [6]
What say Britannia's sons?——along the Strand
What news? ye cry——with the same passion smit;

---

[5] *First Philippic,* 10-11.

[6] The Seven Years' War, with England and Prussia versus France, Austria, and others, had begun in 1756.

74

And there at least you rival Attic wit.
A Parliament of porters here shall muse
On state affairs, "swall'wing a tailor's news"; [7]
For ways and means no starv'd projector sleeps;
And ev'ry shop some mighty statesman keeps;
He Britain's foes, like Bobadil,[8] can kill;
Supply th' Exchequer, and neglect his till.
In ev'ry alehouse legislators meet;
And patriots settle kingdoms in the Fleet.

To show this phrensy in its genuine light,
A modern newsmonger appears to-night!
Trick'd out from Addison's accomplish'd page,
Behold th' Upholsterer ascends the stage.

No minister such trials e'er hath stood;
He turns a bankrupt for the public good!
Undone himself, yet full of England's glory!
A politician!——neither Whig nor Tory!
Nor can ye high or low the Quixote call;
"He's Knight o' th' Shire,[9] and represents ye all."

As for the Bard, to you he yields his plan;
For well he knows, you're candid where you can.
One only praise he claims; no party stroke
Here turns a public character to joke.
His panacea is for all degrees,
For all have more or less of this disease.
Whatever his success, of this he's sure,
There's merit even to attempt the cure.

---

[7] *King John* IV.ii.195.

[8] Captain Bobadill, a braggart and coward in Ben Jonson, *Every Man in His Humour* (1598).

[9] A county representative in Parliament. The quotation is line 16 of John Dryden's epilogue to Sir George Etherege's *The Man of Mode; Or, Sir Fopling Flutter* (1676).

DRAMATIS PERSONAE

Men

Quidnunc, the upholsterer,	Mr. Yates.
Pamphlet,	Mr. Garrick.
Razor, a barber,	Mr. Woodward.
Feeble,	Mr. Blakes.
Bellmour,	Mr. Usher.
Rovewell,	Mr. Palmer.
Codicil, a lawyer,	Mr. Taswell.
Brisk,	Mr. Vernon.
Watchman,	Mr. Clough.

Women

Harriet,	Mrs. Yates.
Termagant,	Mrs. Clive.
Maid to Feeble,	Mrs. Simpson.

THE

UPHOLSTERER;

OR

WHAT NEWS?

ACT the FIRST
SCENE [I]

Bellmour's Lodging

Enter BELLMOUR *beating* BRISK.

BRISK. Mr. Bellmour,——let me die, Sir,——As I hope for mercy,[10] Sir——

BELLMOUR. Sirrah! rogue! villain!——I'll teach you, I will, you rascal, to speak irreverently of her I love.

BRISK. As I am a sinner, Sir, I only meant——

BELLMOUR. Only meant! You could not mean it, varlet; you had no meaning, booby.——

BRISK. Why no, Sir, that's the very thing, Sir, I had no meaning.

BELLMOUR. Then, sirrah, I'll make you know your meaning before you give a loose to your tongue for the future.

BRISK. Yes, Sir, to be sure, Sir, and yet upon my word if you

---

[10] 1769: "to be saved"; 1786: "for mercy."

would be but a little cool, Sir, you would find I am not much to blame. Besides, Master, you can't conceive the good it would do your health if you would but keep your temper a little.

BELLMOUR. Mighty well, Sir, give your advice.

BRISK. Why, really now, this same love hath metamorphosed us both very strangely, Master; for to be free, here have we been at this work these six weeks, stark-staring mad [11] in love with a couple of baggages not worth a groat: and yet, Heav'n help us! they have as much pride as comes to the share of a lady of quality before she has been caught in the fact with a handsome young fellow; or indeed after she has been caught, for that matter.

BELLMOUR. You won't have done, rascal?

BRISK. In short, my young mistress and her maid have as much pride and poverty as——as——no matter what, they have the devil and all, when at the same time everybody knows the old broken Upholsterer, Miss Harriet's father, might give us all he has in the world and not eat the worse pudding on a Sunday.

BELLMOUR. Insolent, scurrilous wretch! Detract from that heaven of beauty! I'll reform your notions, I will, thou profligate, abandoned, vile blasphemer! [12] (*Striking him*)

BRISK. Hold, hold, Sir; for mercy-sake, a little patience; not so hard, Sir.

Enter ROVEWELL.

ROVEWELL. Bellmour, your servant. What, at loggerheads with my old friend Brisk!

BELLMOUR. Confusion! Mr. Rovewell, your servant. This is your doing, hang-dog.——Jack Rovewell, I am glad to see thee.

ROVEWELL. Brisk used to be a good servant: he has not been destroying the game, instead of springing it for his master, has he?

BELLMOUR. Do you know, Rovewell, that he had the impudence to talk detractingly and profanely of the idol of my heart?

---

[11] Utterly mad.

[12] The 1769 version of this speech is: "Impious execrable Atheist! What, detract from Heaven! I'll reform your Notions, I will, you saucy —— ——."

BRISK. For which, Sir, I have suffered in a most inhuman and unchristian-like manner, I assure you, Sir.

BELLMOUR. Will you leave prating, booby?

ROVEWELL. Well, but Bellmour, where does she live?——I'm but just arrived you know: don't grudge your friend a little intelligence: I may have occasion to beat up her quarters.

BELLMOUR. Beat up her quarters!——(*Looks at him, then half aside*)

"Favours to none; to all she smiles extends,
  Oft she rejects, but never once offends." [13] (*Stands musing*)

ROVEWELL. Hey, what, fallen into a reverie!——Prithee, Brisk, what does all this mean?

BRISK. Why, Sir, you must know, I am over head and ears in love.

ROVEWELL. But I mean your master; what ails him?

BRISK. That's the very thing I am going to tell you: as I said, Sir, I am over head and ears in love with a whimsical, queer kind of an odd piece of affectation here in the neighbourhood, and so nothing can serve my master, but he must fall in love with the mistress. Look at him now, Sir. (*Bellmour continues musing and talking to himself*)

ROVEWELL. Ha, ha, ha,——poor Bellmour, I pity thee with all my heart——(*Strikes him on the shoulder*)

"Ye Gods, annihilate both space and time,——
  And make two lovers happy." [14]

BELLMOUR. My dear Rovewell, such a girl!——Ten thousand Cupids play about her mouth, you rogue.

ROVEWELL. Ten thousand pounds had better play about her pocket. What fortune has she?

BRISK. Heaven help us, not much to crack of.——

BELLMOUR. Not much to crack of, Mr. Brazen! Prithee, Rovewell, how can you be so ungenerous as to ask such a question? You know I don't mind fortune, though by the way she has an

---

[13] Alexander Pope, *The Rape of the Lock* II.11-12.
[14] Pope (?), *The Art of Sinking in Poetry* (1727), Chap. XI.

uncle who is determined to settle very handsomely upon her; and on the strength of that expectancy, does she give herself as many airs as the most finished coquette that ever fluttered in a side box.

ROVEWELL. Fortune not to be minded!——I'll tell you what, Bellmour, though you have a good one already, there's no kind of inconvenience in a little more. I'm sure if I had not minded fortune, I might have been in Jamaica still, not worth a sugar-cane; but the Widow Molosses took a fancy to me; heaven or a worse destiny has taken a fancy to her: and so, after ten years' exile, and being turn'd adrift by my father, here I am again a warm planter, and a widower, most woefully tired of matrimony. But, my dear Bellmour, we were both so overjoyed to meet one another yesterday evening, just as I arrived in town, that I did not hear a syllable from you of your love fit: how, when, and where did this happen?

BELLMOUR. Oh! by the most fortunate accident that ever was. I'll tell thee, Rovewell: I was going one night from the tavern, about six weeks ago; I had been with a parcel of blades, whose only joy is centered in their bottle, and, faith, till this accident I was a mere town-rake myself. But from that time I am grown a new man.

ROVEWELL. Ay, a new man indeed!——Who in the name of wonder would take thee, sunk as thou art into a musing, moping, melancholy lover, for the gay Charles Bellmour, whom I knew in the West Indies?

BELLMOUR. Po, the West Indies! The object there was to kill time, you know. What could I do? My father took me against my will from the university, and consigned me over to the academic discipline of a man-of-war; so that to prevent a dejection of spirits, I was obliged to run into the opposite extreme, as you yourself were wont to do.

ROVEWELL. Why, yes, I had my moments of reflection; thoughts were uneasy, and I was glad to dissipate them. You know I always told you there was something extraordinary in my story; and so there is still; I suppose it must be cleared up in a few days. I'm in no hurry about it; I must see the town a little this evening, and have my frolic first. But to the point, Bellmour; you was going from the tavern you say.

BELLMOUR. Yes, Sir, about two in the morning, and I perceived an unusual blaze in the air: I was in a rambling humour, and so resolved to know what it was.

BRISK. I and my master went together.

BELLMOUR. Oh! Rovewell! My better stars ordain'd it to light me on to happiness; by sure attraction led, I came to the very street where a house was on fire: water-engines playing, flames ascending, all hurry, confusion, and distress; when on a sudden the voice of despair, silver sweet, came thrilling down to my heart. "Poor dear, lovely angel, what can she do!" cried the neighbours. Again she scream'd, the fire gathering force, and gaining upon her every instant. "Here, ma'am," said I, "leap into my arms; I'll be sure to receive you." And wou'd you think it? Down she came——my dear Rovewell, such a girl! I caught her in my arms, you rogue, safe, without harm. The dear naked Venus, just risen from her bed, my boy! Her slender waist, Rovewell, the downy smoothness of her whole person, and her limbs "harmonious, swell'd by Nature's softest hand." [15]

ROVEWELL. Raptures and paradise!——What seraglio in Covent Garden did you carry her to?

BELLMOUR. There again now! Do, prithee, correct your way of thinking: take a *quantum sufficit* [16] of virtuous love, and purify your ideas. Her lovely bashfulness, her delicate fears, her beauty heightened and endeared by distress, dispersed my wildest thoughts, and melted me in tenderness and respect.

ROVEWELL. But, Bellmour, surely she has not the impudence to be modest after you have had possession of her person?

BELLMOUR. My views are honourable I assure you, Sir; but her father is absurdly positive. The man's distracted about the balance of power, and will give his daughter to none but a politician. When there was an execution in his house, he thought of nothing but the camp at Pyrna; [17] and now he's a bankrupt, his head runs upon

---

[15] Altered from James Thomson, *Summer* (1727), line 1316.

[16] As much as suffices.

[17] Augustus, Elector of Saxony and King of Poland, established a camp in Pirna, Saxony, in 1756, at the beginning of the Seven Years' War, before he was surrounded by Frederick the Great of Prussia.

ways and means, and schemes for paying off the national debt: the affairs of Europe engross all his attention, while the distresses of his lovely daughter pass unnoticed.

ROVEWELL. Ridiculous enough! But why do you mind him? Why don't you go to bed to the wench at once? Take her into keeping, man.

BELLMOUR. How can you talk so affrontingly? Have not I told you, though her father is ruin'd, that she has great expectancies from a rich relation?

ROVEWELL. Then what do you stand watering at the mouth for? If she is to have money enough to pay for her china, her gaming debts, her dogs, and her monkeys, marry her at once, if you needs must be ensnar'd; amuse yourself in a fool's paradise for a honeymoon; then come to yourself, wonder at what you've done, and mix with honest fellows again. Carry her off I say, and never stand whining for the father's consent.

BELLMOUR. Carry her off! I like the scheme: will you assist me?

ROVEWELL. No, no; there I beg to be excused. I'll have no hand in that business. My friend may marry if he will, but he shall never say that I helped to fasten the noose. Don't you remember what the satirist says——"Never marry while there's a halter to be had for money, or a bridge to afford a convenient leap." [18]

BELLMOUR. Prithee leave fooling.

ROVEWELL. I am in serious earnest I assure you; I'll drink with you, game with you, go into any scheme or frolic with you, but war [19] matrimony. Nay, if you'll come to the tavern this evening, I'll drink your mistress' health in a bumper; but as to your conjugal scheme, I have no relish for that business. It is not my talent. I will serve my friend with all my heart, but will do no mischief.

BELLMOUR. Well, well, I'll take you at your word, and meet you at ten exactly, at the same place where we spent last night; then and there I'll let you know what further measures I have concerted.

ROVEWELL. Till then, farewell; apropos——do you know that I've seen none of my relations yet?

---

[18] Based on Juvenal, *Satire VI*, lines 30, 32.
[19] Beware.

BELLMOUR. Time enough tomorrow.

ROVEWELL. Ay, tomorrow will do.——Well, your servant. If you must marry, *bon voyage!*

Exit.

BELLMOUR. Rovewell, yours.——Brisk, do you come to me in my study, that I may give you a letter to Harriet; and hark you Sir,—— be sure you see Harriet yourself, and let me have no messages from that officious go-between, her maid,——Mrs. Termagant, I think you call her.

BRISK. Yes, Sir, Mrs. Termagant. You know by experience that love spies certain perfections in the object of its esteem, which nobody else can discover, and I may possibly be in the same case with the maid as you are with Miss Harriet.

BELLMOUR. Again taking liberties!——Rascal! Your Mrs. Termagant is the veriest blunderer that ever perverted the use of language. Another Mrs. Slipslop! [20] With an eternal fund of unintelligible jargon, and a medley of words, of which she neither knows the meaning nor the pronunciation. Go, and order a coach.

BRISK. Yes, Sir.——

Exit.

BELLMOUR. I'll write to Harriet this moment; acquaint her with the soft tumult of my desires, and, if possible, make her mine this very night.

"Love first taught letters for some wretch's aid,
    Some banish'd lover, or some captive maid." [21]

Exit.

---

[20] In Henry Fielding, *Joseph Andrews* (1742).
[21] Pope, *Eloisa to Abelard*, 51-52. Murphy substitutes "Love" for "Heav'n."

SCENE [II]

The Upholsterer's House

Enter HARRIET *and* TERMAGANT.

TERMAGANT. Well, but Ma'am, he has made love to you six weeks *successfully;* he has been as constant in his *'moors,* poor gentleman, as if you had the *subversion* of *'state* to settle upon him ——and if he slips thro' your fingers now, Ma'am, you have nobody to *depute* it to but yourself.

HARRIET. My gracious! [22] How you run on!——I tell you, Termagant, my pride was touched, because he seemed to presume on his opulence, and my father's distresses.

TERMAGANT. La, Miss Harriet, how can you be so *paradropsical* in your *'pinions?*

HARRIET. Well, but you know, though my father's affairs are ruin'd, I am not in so desperate a way; consider, my uncle's fortune is no trifle, and I think that prospect entitles me to give myself a few airs before I resign my person.

TERMAGANT. I grant ye, Ma'am, you have very good pretensions; but then it's waiting for dead men's shoes: I'll venture to be perjur'd Mr. Bellmour ne'er *disclaim'd* an *idear* of your father's distress.

HARRIET. Supposing that.

TERMAGANT. Suppose, Ma'am——I know it *disputably* to be so.

HARRIET. Indisputably I guess you mean;——but I'm tired of wrangling with you about words.

TERMAGANT. By my troth you're in the right on't;——there's ne'er a she in all Old England (as your father calls it) is mistress of such *physiology* as I am. Incertain I am, as how you does not know nobody that puts their words together with such a *curacy* as myself. I once lived with a *mistus,* Ma'am,——*mistus!*——she was a lady; a great tallow-chandler's wife! And she wore as fine cloaths as any

---

[22] 1769: "Lard."

person of quality, let her get up as early as she will; and she used to call me——"Tarmagant," says she, "what's the signification of such a word?" And I always told her; I told her the *importation* of all my words, though I could not help laughing, Miss Harriet, to see so fine a lady such a downright *ignoranimus*.

HARRIET. Well——but pray now, Tarmagant, would you have me directly upon being asked the question, throw myself into the arms of a man?

TERMAGANT. O' my conscience, you did throw yourself into his arms with scarce a shift on, that's what you did.

HARRIET. Yes, but that was a leap in the dark, when there was no time to think of it.

TERMAGANT. Well, it does not signify *argifying*. I wish we were both warm in bed, you with Mr. Bellmour, and I with his coxcomb of a man; instead of being *minured* [23] here with an old crazy fool—— *axing* your pardon, Ma'am, for calling your father so——but he is a fool, and the worst of fools, with his policies, and his news, and his pamphlets, and his one side of the question, and then t'other side, when all the time his house is full of *statues of bankressy*.[24]

HARRIET. It is too true, Termagant; but he is my father still, and I must always think of him with respect, with gratitude and love.

TERMAGANT. Love! I should not have thought of that. He is an *anecdote* against love.

HARRIET. Hush! Here he comes.

TERMAGANT. No, it's your Uncle Feeble. Poor gentleman, I pity's him, eaten up with *infirmaries*, and yet always taking pains about a crack-brained politician, asking your pardon, Madam.

Enter FEEBLE.

HARRIET. Well, Uncle, have you been able to console him?

FEEBLE. He wants no consolation, child. Lackaday! I am so infirm I can hardly move. I found him tracing in the map, Prince Charles

---

[23] 1769: "*manured*."
[24] 1769: "*Bangcressy*."

of Lorraine's passage over the Rhine,[25] and comparing it with Julius Caesar's.

TERMAGANT. An old blockhead! I've no patience with him, with his fellows coming after him every hour in the day with news. Well now, I wishes there was no such thing as a newspaper in the world, with such a pack of lies, and such a deal of good authority today, and such flat contradiction tomorrow, that there is no such a thing as believing a word they say.

FEEBLE. Ay, there were three or four shabby fellows with him when I went into his room. I can't get him to think of appearing before the Commissioners tomorrow, to disclose his effects; but I'll send my neighbour Counsellor Codicil to him. Don't be dejected, Harriet; my poor sister, your mother, was a good woman; I love you for her sake, child, and all I am worth shall be yours. But I must be going; I find myself very ill; good night, Harriet, good night.

Exit FEEBLE.

HARRIET. You'll give me leave to see you to the door, Sir.

Exit HARRIET.

TERMAGANT. O' my conscience, this master of mine within here, might have pick'd up his crumbs as well as Mr. Feeble, if he had any *idear* of his business. I'm sure if I have not hopes from Mr. Feeble, I should not tarry in this house. By my troth, if all who have nothing to say to [26] the *'fairs* of the nation, would mind their own business; and those who should take care of our *'fairs*, would mind their business too, I fancy poor Old England (as they call it) would fare the better among 'em. This old crazy pate within here! Playing the fool, when the man is past his grand *clytemnester*.

Exit TERMAGANT.

---

[25] In 1744, in the War of the Austrian Succession, Prince Charles of Lorraine, on the side of Maria Theresa, abandoned Alsace to the French by an extremely skillful retreat over the Rhine towards Bohemia.

[26] 1786 omits "to," found in 1758.

SCENE [III]

Quidnunc at a Table, with Newspapers, Pamphlets, *&c.* all around
him.

QUIDNUNC. Six and three is nine; seven and four is eleven, and
carry one. Let me see, one hundred and twenty-six million, one
hundred and ninety-nine thousand, three hundred and twenty-
eight: and all this with about——where, where's the amount of the
specie? Here, here; with about fifteen million in specie, all this
great circulation! Good, good; why, then, how are we ruined?——
How are we ruined? What says the land tax [27] at four shillings in
the pound? Two million! Now where's my new assessment?——
Here, here, the 5th part of twenty, five in two I can't, but five in
twenty (*Pauses*) right, four times: why, then, upon my new assessment there's four million. How are we ruined?——What says malt,
cider, and mum? Eleven and carry one, nought and go two——
good, good, malt, hops, cider, and mum; then there's the wine
licence, and the gin act. The gin act is no bad article. If the people
will shoot fire down their throats, why in a Christian country they
should pay as dear as possible for suicide. Salt! good; sugar! very
good; window lights! good again! stamp duty! that's not so well;
it will have a bad effect upon newspapers, and we shan't have
enough of politics. But there's the lottery: where's my new scheme
for a lottery?——Here it is.——Now for the amount of the whole:
how are we ruined? Seven and carry nought; nought and carry one.

Enter TERMAGANT.

TERMAGANT. Sir, Sir,——
QUIDNUNC. Hold your tongue, you baggage, you'll put me out.
Nought and carry one.

---

[27] The land tax had been instituted in 1692.

TERMAGANT. Counsellor Codicil will be with you presently.

QUIDNUNC. Prithee be quiet, woman. How are we ruined?

TERMAGANT. Ay, I'm *confidous* as how you may thank yourself for your own ruination.

QUIDNUNC. Ruin the nation!——Hold your tongue, you jade; I am raising the supplies within the year. How many did I carry?

TERMAGANT. Yes, you've carried your pigs to a fine market.

QUIDNUNC. Get out of the room, hussy; you trollop, you jade, you baggage, get out of the room.

(*Turns her out*)

Enter RAZOR, *with a Shaving Bason in his Hand.*

QUIDNUNC. Friend Razor, I am glad to see thee. Well, hast got any news?

RAZOR. A budget! I left a gentleman half shaved in my shop over the way; it came into my head of a sudden, so I could not be at ease till I told you.

QUIDNUNC. That's kind, that's kind, friend Razor: never mind the gentleman, he can wait.

RAZOR. Yes, so he can, he can wait.

QUIDNUNC. Come, now let's hear, what is it?

RAZOR. I shav'd a great man's butler today.

QUIDNUNC. Did ye?

RAZOR. I did.

QUIDNUNC. Ay!

RAZOR. Very true. (*Both shake their heads*)

QUIDNUNC. What did he say?

RAZOR. Nothing.

QUIDNUNC. Hum——how did he look?

RAZOR. Full of thought.

QUIDNUNC. Ay! full of thought! What can that mean?

RAZOR. It must mean something. (*Staring at each other*)

QUIDNUNC. Mayhap somebody may be going out of place.

RAZOR. Like enow: there is always something at the bottom when a great man's butler looks grave. Things can't hold out in this manner, Master Quidnunc!——Luxury will be the ruin of us all, it will indeed.——Kingdoms rise and fall! (*Stares at him*)

QUIDNUNC. (*Staring at Razor*) So they do.——They rise and fall like the stocks.——Here today, gone tomorrow. Pity! Great pity!

RAZOR. Yes, yes; the more the pity. (*Both stand musing*)

QUIDNUNC. Pray, friend Razor, do you find business as current now as before the war?

RAZOR. No, no: I have not made a wig the Lord knows when. I can't mind it for thinking of my poor country.

QUIDNUNC. That's generous, friend Razor.

RAZOR. Yes, I can't gi' my mind to anything for thinking of my country. When I was in Bedlam,[28] it was the same; I cou'd think of nothing else in Bedlam, but poor Old England, and so they said as how I was incurable for it.

QUIDNUNC. Ay! And so they laugh at all virtue, and true patriotism. They might as well say the same of me.

RAZOR. So they might. Well, your servant, Mr. Quidnunc. I'll go now and shave the rest of the gentleman's face.——Poor Old England! (*Sighs and shakes his head going*)

QUIDNUNC. But hark ye, friend Razor, ask the gentleman if he has got any news.

RAZOR. I will——I will.

QUIDNUNC. And d'ye hear, come and tell me if he has.

RAZOR. I will, I will——poor Old England! (*Going, returns*) Oh, Mr. Quidnunc, I want to ask you——pray now——

Enter TERMAGANT.

TERMAGANT. My stars! O gemini! Are you mad? How can a man have so little *difference* for his customers?

QUIDNUNC. I tell you, Mrs. Malapert——

TERMAGANT. And I tell you, the gentleman keeps such a bawling yonder; for shame, Mr. Razor; you'll be a *bankrupper* like my mas-

---

[28] St. Mary of Bethlehem, a London hospital for lunatics. This entire sentence in 1786 becomes in the 1791 MS: "and so the Neighbours all call me a Blockhead for it."

ter, with such a house full of children as you have, pretty little things——that's what you will.

RAZOR. I'm a coming, I'm a coming, Mrs. Termagant.——I say, Mr. Quidnunc, I can't sleep in my bed for thinking what will become of the Protestants if the Papists should get the better in the present war.[29]

QUIDNUNC. I'll tell you.——The geographer of our coffeehouse was saying the other day, that there is an huge tract of land about the Pole, where the Protestants may retire, and that the Papists will never be able to beat 'em thence, if the Northern Powers[30] hold together, and the Grand Turk made a diversion in their favour.

RAZOR. That makes me easy——I'm glad the Protestants will know where to go, if the Papists shou'd get the better. (*Going, returns*) Oh! Mr. Quidnunc——harkye——India Bonds[31] are risen.

QUIDNUNC. Are they?——How much?

RAZOR. A Jew pedlar said in my shop as how they are risen three-sixteenths.

QUIDNUNC. Why then that makes some amends for the price of corn.[32]

RAZOR. So it does, so it does; if they but hold up, and the Protestants know where to go, I shall then have a night's rest mayhap. Poor Old England!

Exit RAZOR.

QUIDNUNC. I shall never be rightly easy till those careening wharfs at Gibraltar are repaired.[33]

TERMAGANT. A fiddle for you *dwarfs; impair* your ruin'd fortune, do that.

QUIDNUNC. If only one ship can heave down at a time, there will

---

[29] In the Seven Years' War, Frederick the Great of Prussia and William Pitt, the elder, of England were Protestant leaders against Catholic Austria and France.

[30] England and Prussia.

[31] East India Bonds.

[32] In 1757 the price of wheat reached its highest level since 1710.

[33] This is the only evidence that Gibraltar had careening wharves as early as 1757.

be no end of it——and then, why should watering be so tedious there?

TERMAGANT. Look where your daughter comes, and yet you'll be *ruinating* about *Give-a-halter*, while that poor thing is breaking her heart.

Enter HARRIET.

QUIDNUNC. It's one comfort, however, they can always have fresh provisions in the Mediterranean.

HARRIET. Dear papa, what's the Mediterranean to people in our situation?

QUIDNUNC. The Mediterranean, child? Why if we should lose the Mediterranean, we're all undone.

HARRIET. Dear Sir, that's our misfortune; we are undone already.

QUIDNUNC. No, no,——here, child; I have raised the supplies within the year.

TERMAGANT. I tell you, you're a *lunadic* man.

QUIDNUNC. Yes, yes, I'm a lunatic to be sure.——I tell you, Harriet, I have saved a great deal out of my affairs for you.

HARRIET. For Heav'n sake, Sir, don't do that: you must give up everything; my Uncle Feeble's lawyer will be here to talk with you upon that subject.

QUIDNUNC. Po, po, I tell you, I know what I am about. You shall have my books and pamphlets, and all the manifestoes of the powers at war.

HARRIET. And so make me a politician, Sir?

QUIDNUNC. It would be the pride of my heart to find I had got a politician in petticoats. A female Machiavel! 'Sbodikins, you might then know as much as most people that talk in coffeehouses; and who knows but in time you might be a Maid of Honour, or Sweeper of the Mall,[34] or——

HARRIET. Dear Sir, don't I see what you have got by politics?

---

[34] The Mall was a fashionable promenade or walk in St. James's Park, London. For patriotic reasons, even noblewomen were sometimes sweepers of malls. See the London *Examiner*, Oct. 18, 1812, no. 251, p. 671.

QUIDNUNC. Pshaw! My country's of more consequence to me; and let me tell you, you can't think too much of your country in these worst of times; for Mr. *Monitor* [35] has told us, that affairs in the North, and the Protestant interest, begin to grow ticklish.

TERMAGANT. And your daughter's affairs are very ticklish. Poor thing to be in such jeopardy.

HARRIET. Prithee, Termagant——

TERMAGANT. Nay, I must speak to him——I know you are in a ticklish situation, Ma'am.

QUIDNUNC. I tell you, trull——

TERMAGANT. But I am *convicted* it is so——and the posture of my affairs is very ticklish too; and so for my part I *imprecate* that Mr. Bellmour may come, and——

QUIDNUNC. Mr. Bellmour come! I tell you, Mrs. Impudence, that my daughter shall never be married to a man that has not better notions of the balance of power.

TERMAGANT. But what *purvision* will you make for her now, with your balances?

QUIDNUNC. There again now!——Why, do you think I don't know what I'm about? I'll look in the papers for a match for you, child; there's often good matches advertised in the papers. Evil betide it, evil betide it!——I once thought to have struck a great stroke, that would have astonished all Europe.——I thought to have married my daughter to Theodore, King of Corsica.

HARRIET. What, and have me perish in a jail,[36] Sir!

QUIDNUNC. 'Sbodikins, my daughter would have had her Coronation Day; I should have been allied to a crowned head, and been First Lord of the Treasury of Corsica!——But come,——now I'll go and talk over the *London Evening*,[37] till the *Gazette* [38] comes in. I shan't sleep to-night unless I see the *Gazette*.

---

[35] The *Monitor*, a Whig political periodical.

[36] Baron Theodor von Neuhof (1690-1756), German adventurer, became Theodor I, King of Corsica, in 1736. After the opposition of the Genoese, he finally settled in London, where his creditors had him imprisoned for debt for seven years until a short time before his death.

[37] The *London Evening Post* was a triweekly newspaper.

[38] The official *London Gazette* was a semiweekly newspaper.

Enter SERJEANT CODICIL.

CODICIL. Mr. Quidnunc, your servant. Your street door was open, and I entered upon the premises. I am just come from the great Hall of Pleas.[39]

QUIDNUNC. This man is come to keep me at home. What, from the Hall at this late hour in the evening?

CODICIL. Yes; afternoon sittings have detained me. Upon my word, Miss Harriet is as pretty a young lady as a man would desire to have and to hold. Ma'am, your most obedient; I have drawn my friend Feeble's will, in which you have all his goods and chattels, lands, tenements and hereditaments.

HARRIET. I thank you, Sir, for the information.

CODICIL. And I hope soon to draw your marriage settlement for my friend Mr. Bellmour.

HARRIET. Hush, dear Sir; not a word of that before my father. I wish you'd try, Sir, to get him to think of his affairs.

CODICIL. Why yes, I have instructions for that purpose. Mr. Quidnunc, I am instructed to expound the law to you.

QUIDNUNC. What, the law of nations? [40] Termagant, get out of the room; Harriet, leave me with this gentleman——I say, Termagant, begone and leave me. Leave me this moment. (*Puts them both out*)

CODICIL. I am instructed, Sir, that you're a bankrupt; *quasi bancus ruptus; banque route faire.*[41] And my instructions say further, that you are summoned to appear before the Commissioners tomorrow.

QUIDNUNC. That may be, Sir, but I can't go tomorrow, and so I shall send 'em word. I am to be tomorrow at Slaughter's Coffee-house with a private committee, about business of great consequence to the affairs of Europe.

---

[39] Westminster Hall, main seat of justice.

[40] International law.

[41] Codicil suggests alternate Latin and French etymologies: as it were the counter (or table of a tradesman) broken; counter trace (bankrupt has removed his counter and left only a trace or track behind) to make (persons who make bankrupt is a French idiom).

CODICIL. Then, Sir, if you don't go, I must instruct you, that you'll be guilty of a felony: it will be deem'd to be done *malo animo;* [42] it is held so in the books; and what says the statute? By the 5th George 2d, *Cap.* 30.[43] Not surrendering or imbezzling is felony without benefit of clergy.

QUIDNUNC. Ay——you tell me news.

CODICIL. Give me leave, Sir.——I am instructed to expound the law to you; felony is thus described in the books; "*Felonia,*" saith Hotoman,[44] *De Verbis Feudalibus,*[45] "*significat capitale facinus,*" [46] a capital offence.

QUIDNUNC. You tell me news, you do indeed.

CODICIL. It was so apprehended by the Goths and the Longo-bards,[46] and what saith Sir Edward Coke? [47] *Fieri debeat felleo animo.* [48]

QUIDNUNC. You've told me news: I did not know it was felony; but if the Flanders mail should come in while I am there, I shall know nothing at all of it.

CODICIL. But why should you be uneasy? *Cui bono,* Mr. Quid-nunc, *cui bono?* [49]

QUIDNUNC. Not uneasy! If the Papists should beat the Protestants in the present war.

CODICIL. But I tell you, they can get no advantage of us. The laws against the further growth of Popery will secure us. There are provisoes in favour of Protestant purchasers under Papists——10th Geo. I, *Cap.* 4., and 6th Geo. II, *Cap.* 5.

QUIDNUNC. Ay!

---

[42] With evil intent.

[43] An act to prevent the committing of frauds by bankrupts.

[44] François Hotman or Francisci Hotomanni (1524-1590), a French jurist.

[45] A Latin alphabetical commentary concerning feudal words.

[46] "*Felonia*" entry.

[47] Sir Edward Coke (1552-1634), lord chief justice of England, famous for *Commentary upon Littleton.*

[48] Let him find it necessary to be made with malignant mind—that is, he ought to be arraigned for felony (felony is from Latin fel, gall). Based on *Commentary upon Littleton,* Bk. 3, Chap. 13, Sect. 745.

[49] Who benefits by it? Cicero, *Oratio pro Milone* XII.xxxii.

CODICIL. And besides, Popish recusants can't carry arms, so can have no right of conquest, *vi & armis*.[50]

QUIDNUNC. That's true; that's true; I'm easier in my mind.

CODICIL. To be sure: what are you uneasy about? The Papists can have no claim to Silesia.[51]

QUIDNUNC. Can't they?

CODICIL. No, they can set up no claim. If the Queen on her marriage had put all her lands into hotchpot,[52] then indeed——and it seemeth, saith *Littleton*,[53] that this word *hotchpot* is in English a pudding.[54]

QUIDNUNC. You reason very clearly, Mr. Codicil, upon the rights of the powers at war, and so now if you will, I am ready to talk a little of my affairs.

CODICIL. Nor does the matter rest here; for how can she set up a claim, when she [55] has made a conveyance to the House of Brandenburgh? [56] The law, Mr. Quidnunc, is very severe against fraudulent conveyances.——

QUIDNUNC. 'Sbodikins, you have satisfied me.

CODICIL. Why therefore then, if he will levy fines and suffer a common recovery,[57] he can bequeath it as he likes in *feodum simplex*,[58] provided he takes care to put in *ses heres*.[59]

QUIDNUNC. I'm heartily glad of it; so that with regard to my effects——

CODICIL. Why, then, suppose she was to bring it to a trial at bar——

---

[50] With force and arms.

[51] Maria Theresa, ruler of Austria, had lost Silesia to Frederick the Great of Prussia in 1748.

[52] A throwing of property into a common stock for equality of division.

[53] Coke, *Commentary upon Littleton*, Bk. 3, Chap. 2, Sec. 267.

[54] A dish of many ingredients.

[55] Maria Theresa.

[56] Brandenburgh is an older designation for Prussia.

[57] A mode of conveying land through an action and judgment at law.

[58] In fee simple.

[59] His heirs.

QUIDNUNC. I say with regard to the full disclosure of my effects——

CODICIL. What wou'd she get by that? At common law she would have no chance, and as to equity——

QUIDNUNC. Pray, must I now surrender my books and my pamphlets?

CODICIL. What wou'd equity do for her? Equity can't relieve her; she might be kept at least twenty years before a master to settle the account.

QUIDNUNC. You have made me easy about the Protestants in this war, you have indeed; so that with regard to my appearing before the Commissioners——

CODICIL. And as to the Ban of the Empire,[60] he may demur to that. For all tenures by Knight's Service [61] are abolished, and the Statute 12 Char. II [62] has declared all lands to be held in common socage.[63]

QUIDNUNC. To the point, Mr. Serjeant. Why will you ramble thus? I want to hear about my own affairs. To the point. Is there no way of compelling the creditors to grant my certificate? [64]

CODICIL. Why, therefore, then, if they're held in common socage, I submit it to the court, whether the empire can have any claim to Knight's Service? They can't call upon him for a single man for the war.

QUIDNUNC. But I say as to my certificate.

CODICIL. They can't demand *unum hominem ad guerram;* [65]—— for what is common socage?——*Socagium idem est quod servitium socae,*[66] the service of the plough.

QUIDNUNC. I tell you I am willing to attend the Commissioners.

---

[60] An imperial interdict that took away political rights and privileges.

[61] Tenure of lands in return for military service.

[62] *Anno 12° Caroli, II.A.D. 1660* [*sic*], Chap. xxiv.

[63] Free tenure not military.

[64] A paper by which the majority of an insolvent's creditors agree to his discharge.

[65] One man for war.

[66] Socage is the same as service of the plough. Coke, *Commentary upon Littleton,* Bk. 2, Chap. 5, Sec. 119. Socage is tenure by any certain or determinate service.

But pray now.——It is of great consequence to me to know this point. I say, Mr. Serjeant——

CODICIL. A number of cases may be cited——

QUIDNUNC. Truce with your cases. I say, when my certificate is signed, may not I then——hey! (*Starting up*) Hey!——What do I hear?

CODICIL. I apprehend, I humbly conceive, when your certificate is signed——

QUIDNUNC. Hold your tongue, man——did not I hear the *Gazette?*

NEWSMAN. (*Within*) Great news in the *London Gazette.*

QUIDNUNC. Yes, yes it is——it is the *Gazette*——Termagant, Termagant; I say, Termagant; where is the jade? Stop the newsman; he is going by now; Termagant, I say. (*Stands bawling at the side of the scene*)

CODICIL. The law in that case, Mr. Quidnunc, prima facie——

QUIDNUNC. I can't hear you now; I have not time. Termagant, run, fly, make haste; get me the *Gazette;* bring it directly. (*Stamping violently*)

CODICIL. I say it is held in the books——

QUIDNUNC. I care for no books; I want the papers—— (*Stamping*)

CODICIL. It is held throughout the books that your certificate, if not obtained by fraud——

QUIDNUNC. You shan't defraud me of my newspaper. Where is it? Bring it this moment.

Enter TERMAGANT.

TERMAGANT. What do you keep such a bawling for?

CODICIL. *Non compos,* that's his case. Mr. Quidnunc, your politics——

QUIDNUNC. Mr. Serjeant, your cases, and your statutes, and your musty old books——

CODICIL. Bo! as mad as any man in Bedlam. Have you no such thing as a strait waistcoat in the house?

QUIDNUNC. Give me the news, I say.

CODICIL. There again! His friends, instead of a commission of bankrupts, should take out a commission of lunacy.

Exit.

TERMAGANT. He is an old *Don Quickset* sure enough. The newsman says as how the Emperor of *Molocco* is dead.

QUIDNUNC. The Emperor of Morocco! [67]

TERMAGANT. Yes, him.

QUIDNUNC. The Emperor of Morocco had a regard for the Balance of Europe. (*Sighs*) Well, well, come, come, give me the paper.

TERMAGANT. The newsman would not trust, because you're a *bankrupper,* and so I paid twopence, halfpenny for it.

QUIDNUNC. Let me see; let me see.

TERMAGANT. Give me the money first. (*Running from him*)

QUIDNUNC. Give it me this instant, you jade. (*After her*)

TERMAGANT. Give me the money, I say. (*From him*)

QUIDNUNC. I'll teach you, I will, you baggage. (*After her*)

TERMAGANT. I won't part with it till I have the money. (*From him*)

QUIDNUNC. I'll give you no money, hussy. (*After her*)

TERMAGANT. Your daughter shall marry Mr. Bellmour. (*From him*)

QUIDNUNC. I'll never accede to the treaty. (*After her*)

TERMAGANT. Go, you old fool. (*From him*)

QUIDNUNC. You vile minx, worse than the Whore of Babylon.[68] (*After her*)

TERMAGANT. There, you old crack'd-brain politic! There's your paper for you.

(*Throws it down and exit*)

QUIDNUNC. (*Sitting down*) Oh! Heavens!——I am quite out of breath. A jade, a vile baggage, to keep my news from me. What does it say? (*Reads very fast*) "Whereas a commission of bankrupt is awarded and issued forth against Abraham Quidnunc, of the parish of St. Martin in the Fields, upholsterer, dealer, and chapman,

---

[67] Moulay Abdallah died in 1757.
[68] The Roman Catholic Church.

the said bankrupt is hereby required to surrender himself." Po, what signifies this stuff? I don't mind myself when the balance of power is concerned. However, I shall be read of in the same paper, in the *London Gazette*, by the powers abroad; together with the Pope, and the French King, and the Mogul,[69] and all of 'em. Good, good, very good! Here's a pow'r of news——let me see. (*Reads*) "Letters from the Vice-Admiral, dated *Tiger*, off Calcutta." [70]——(*Mutters to himself very eagerly*) Odsheart, those baggages will interrupt me, I hear their tongues agoing, clack, clack, clack; I'll run into my closet and lock myself up. A vixen! a trollop! to want money from me, when I may have occasion to buy *The State of the Sinking Fund*,[71] or *Faction Detected*, or *The Barrier Treaty*,[72]——or——and besides, how could the jade tell but tomorrow we may have a *Gazette Extraordinary?*

Exit.

End of the FIRST ACT.

ACT the SECOND
SCENE [I]

The Upholsterer's House

Enter QUIDNUNC.

QUIDNUNC. Where, where, where is he?——Where's Mr. Pamphlet?——Mr. Pamphlet!——Termagant, Mr. a——a——Termagant, Harriet, Termagant, you vile minx, you saucy——

---

[69] Alamgir II, mogul in 1757-1758, had little power in India.

[70] On Jan. 2, 1757, Vice-Admiral Charles Watson, in command of the *Tiger* and other ships, captured Calcutta, then controlled by Surajah Dowlah.

[71] In 1716 the British government had established a sinking fund to reduce the national debt.

[72] In 1709 England had agreed that the Netherlands could garrison certain forts near the French border.

Enter TERMAGANT.

TERMAGANT. Here's a racket indeed!

QUIDNUNC. Where's Mr. Pamphlet? You baggage, if he's gone——

TERMAGANT. Did not I *intimidate* that he's in the next room? Why, sure, the man's out of his wits.

QUIDNUNC. Show him in here then. I would not miss seeing him for the discovery of the Northeast passage.

TERMAGANT. Go, you old Gemini Gomini!

Exit TERMAGANT.

QUIDNUNC. Show him in I say. I had rather see him than the whole state of the Peace at Utrecht,[73] or the *Paris A-la-main*,[74] or the *Votes*,[75] or the *Minutes*,[76] or——here he comes, the best political writer of the age.

Enter PAMPHLET, *with a surtout Coat, a Muff, a long campaign Wig*[77] *out of Curl, and a Pair of black Garters, buckled under the Knees.*

QUIDNUNC. Mr. Pamphlet, I am heartily glad to see you; as glad as if you were an express from the Groyn,[78] or from Berlin, or Zell,[79] or from Calcutta overland, or from——

PAMPHLET. Mr. Quidnunc, your servant. I am come from a place of great importance.

QUIDNUNC. Look ye there now! Well, where, where?

PAMPHLET. Are we alone?

QUIDNUNC. Stay, stay, till I shut the door. Now, now, where do you come from?

---

[73] The Peace of Utrecht ended the War of the Spanish Succession in 1713.
[74] This unrecorded work seems to be a Parisian guidebook.
[75] Printed records of the proceedings of the House of Commons.
[76] Printed records of committees of the House of Commons.
[77] A wig worn for traveling, with a twisted lock on each side and curls about the forehead.
[78] Seaport in northwestern Spain.
[79] In Hanover, Prussia.

PAMPHLET. From the Court of Requests.[80] (*Laying aside his surtout coat*)

QUIDNUNC. The Court of Requests! (*Whispers*) Are they up?

PAMPHLET. Hot work.

QUIDNUNC. Debates arising may be?

PAMPHLET. Yes, and like to sit late.

QUIDNUNC. What are they upon?

PAMPHLET. Can't say.

QUIDNUNC. What carried you thither?

PAMPHLET. I went in hopes of being taken up.[81]

QUIDNUNC. Lookye there now. (*Shaking his head*)

PAMPHLET. I have been aiming at it these three years.

QUIDNUNC. Indeed! (*Staring at him*)

PAMPHLET. Indeed: sedition is the only thing an author can live by now. Time has been I could turn a penny by an earthquake; or live upon a jail-distemper; or dine upon a bloody murder; but now that's all over; nothing will do now but roasting a minister; or telling the people that they are ruined (*Whispers*); the people of England are never so happy as when you tell 'em they are ruined.

QUIDNUNC. Yes, but they an't ruined: I have a scheme for paying off the national debt.

PAMPHLET. Let me see it; let me see. (*Puts on his spectacles*) Well enough! Well imagined.——A new thought this; I must make this my own. (*Aside*) Silly, futile, absurd, abominable, this will never do——I'll put it in my pocket, and read it over in the morning for you. Now look you here; I'll show you a scheme. (*Rummaging his pockets*) No, that's my *Conduct of the Ministry*, by a Country Gentleman——I proved the nation undone here; this sold hugely——and here now, here's my answer to it, by a Noble Lord;——this did not move among the trade.

QUIDNUNC. What, do you write on both sides?

PAMPHLET. Yes, both sides. I have two hands, Mr. Quidnunc, always impartial, *ambo dexter*.——Now here, here's my *Dedica-*

---

[80] In the eighteenth century, the London Court of Requests was merely a court for small debts!

[81] Taken into custody.

tion to a Great Man——touched twenty for this! And here——here's my libel upon him.

QUIDNUNC. What, after being obliged to him.

PAMPHLET. Yes, for that reason: it excites curiosity. Whitewash and blackball,[82] Mr. Quidnunc! *In utrumque paratus* [83]——no thriving without it.

QUIDNUNC. What have you here in this pocket? (*Prying eagerly*)

PAMPHLET. That's my account with Jacob Zorobabel, the broker, for writing paragraphs to raise or tumble the stocks, or the price of lottery tickets, according to his purposes.

QUIDNUNC. Ay, how do you do that?

PAMPHLET. As thus.——Today the Protestant interest declines, Madras is taken,[84] and England's undone; then all the long faces in the Alley look as dismal as a blank, and so Jacob buys away and thrives upon our ruin.——Then tomorrow, we're all alive and merry again, Ponticherry's taken;[85] a certain Northern Potentate will shortly strike a blow, to astonish all Europe, and then every true-born Englishman is willing to buy a lottery ticket for twenty or thirty shillings more than it is worth; so Jacob sells away, and reaps the fruit of our success.

QUIDNUNC. What, will the people believe that now?

PAMPHLET. Believe it!——Believe anything; no swallow like a true-born Englishman's: a man in a quart bottle, or a victory, it's all one to them.——They give a gulp, and down it goes——glib, glib, they swallow all.

QUIDNUNC. Yes, but they an't at the bottom of things.

PAMPHLET. No, not they; they dabble a little, but can't dive.

QUIDNUNC. Pray now, Mr. Pamphlet, what do you think of our situation?

---

[82] 1769: "Blacking-ball."

[83] Prepared for either.

[84] In 1746 the French had seized temporary control of Madras, British India.

[85] Ponticherry, in French India, was first besieged in 1748 and finally captured in 1761.

PAMPHLET. Bad, Sir, bad, and how can it be better?——The people in power never send to me, never consult me; it must be bad. Now here, here (*Goes to his loose coat*), here's a manuscript! ——This will do the business, a masterpiece! I shall be taken up for this.

QUIDNUNC. Shall ye?

PAMPHLET. As sure as a gun I shall. I know the bookseller's a rogue, and will give up his author.

QUIDNUNC. But pray now what shall you get by being taken up?

PAMPHLET. I'll tell you——(*Whispers*) in order to make me hold my tongue.

QUIDNUNC. Ay, but you won't hold your tongue for all that.

PAMPHLET. No, no, not a jot the more for that: abuse them the next day.

QUIDNUNC. Well, I wish you success. But do you hear no news? Have you seen the *Gazette?*

PAMPHLET. Yes, I've seen it. Great news, Mr. Quidnunc: but harkye!——(*Whispers*) and kiss hands next week.

(*Each in deep thought without looking at the other*)

QUIDNUNC. Ay!

PAMPHLET. Certain.

QUIDNUNC. Nothing permanent in this world.

PAMPHLET. All is vanity.

QUIDNUNC. Ups and downs.

PAMPHLET. Ins and outs.

QUIDNUNC. Wheels within wheels.

PAMPHLET. No smoke without fire.

QUIDNUNC. All's well that ends well.

PAMPHLET. It will last our time.

QUIDNUNC. Whoever lives to see it, will know more of the matter.

PAMPHLET. Time will tell all.

QUIDNUNC. Ay, we must leave all to the determination of time. Mr. Pamphlet, I'm heartily obliged to you for this visit: I love you better than any man in England. To think the same of the commonwealth is the truest and best foundation of friendship.

PAMPHLET. And for my part, Mr. Quidnunc, I love you better than I do England itself.

QUIDNUNC. That's kind, that's kind: there is nothing I would not do, Mr. Pamphlet, to serve you.

PAMPHLET. Mr. Quidnunc, I know you are a man of integrity and honour; I know you are; and now since we have opened our hearts, there is a thing, Mr. Quidnunc, in which you can serve me. You know, Sir, this is in the fullness of our hearts——you know you have my note for a trifle. Hard dealing with assignees.—— Now, could not you, to serve a friend, could not you throw that note into the fire?

QUIDNUNC. How! But would that be honest?

PAMPHLET. Leave that to me: a refin'd stroke of policy: papers have been destroyed in all governments.

QUIDNUNC. So they have; it shall be done; it will be political; it will indeed. It will balance accounts between us. But now that I have mentioned a balance of accounts, pray, Mr. Pamphlet, what do you take to be the true political balance of power?

PAMPHLET. What do I take to be the balance of power?

QUIDNUNC. Ay; what do you take to be the balance of power?

PAMPHLET. The balance of power: what do I take to be the balance of power? The balance of power——(*Shuts his eyes*) what do I take to be the balance of power?

QUIDNUNC. The balance of power, I take to be, when the Court of Aldermen sits.

PAMPHLET. No, no, no such thing: wide of the mark.

QUIDNUNC. Yes, yes, I am right: the bird in the eye.[86]

PAMPHLET. No, no: the balance of power is, when the foundations of government and the superstructures are natural.

QUIDNUNC. How do you mean natural?

PAMPHLET. Prithee be quiet man; this is the language. The balance of power is, when the superstructures are reduced to proper balances, or when the balances are not reduced to unnatural superstructures.

---

[86] The arrow in the center of the target.

QUIDNUNC. That won't do: I differ; with submission I differ: I take the balance of power to be, when the fortifications of Dunkerque are demolish'd.

(*Both in a passion and walking about*)

PAMPHLET. But I tell you, Mr. Quidnunc——

QUIDNUNC. I say, Mr. Pamphlet——

PAMPHLET. Hear me, Mr. Quidnunc.

QUIDNUNC. Give me leave, Mr. Pamphlet.

PAMPHLET. I must observe, Sir,——

QUIDNUNC. I am convinc'd, Sir, that——

PAMPHLET. That the balance of power——

QUIDNUNC. That the fortifications of Dunkerque——

PAMPHLET. (*Making towards the door, and Quidnunc following him*) Depends upon the balances and the superstructures——

QUIDNUNC. Constitute the true political equilibrium.

PAMPHLET. Nor will I converse with a man——

QUIDNUNC. And, Sir, I never desire to see your face——

PAMPHLET. Of such anti-constitutional principles——

QUIDNUNC. Nor the face of any man who is such a Frenchman in his heart, and has such notions of the balance of power.

Exeunt.

QUIDNUNC. (*Re-entering*) Ay, I have found him out: such abominable principles! I never desire to converse with any man of his notions; no, never while I live. He does not think of the constitution as I do: I will have no connection with a man of his character.

Re-enter PAMPHLET.

PAMPHLET. Mr. Quidnunc, one word, Sir, if you please.

QUIDNUNC. Sir, I never desire to see your face.

PAMPHLET. My property, Mr. Quidnunc: I shan't leave my property in the house of a bankrupt. (*Twisting his handkerchief round his arm*) A silly, empty, incomprehensible blockhead!

QUIDNUNC. Blockhead, Mr. Pamphlet?

PAMPHLET. A blockhead to use me thus, when I have you so much in my power.

QUIDNUNC. In your power!

PAMPHLET. In my power, Sir: it's in my power to hang you.

QUIDNUNC. To hang me!

PAMPHLET. Yes, Sir; to hang you. (*Drawing on his coat*) Did not you propose, but this moment, did not you desire me to combine and confederate to burn a note, and defraud your creditors?

QUIDNUNC. I desire it!

PAMPHLET. Yes, Mr. Quidnunc, but I shall detect you to the world. I'll give your character.——You shall have a sixpenny touch next week.

    Flebit et insignis tota cantabitur urbe.[87]

Exit PAMPHLET.

QUIDNUNC. Mercy on me! There's the effect of his anti-constitutional principles! The spirit of his whole party; I never desire to exchange another word with him.

Enter TERMAGANT.

TERMAGANT. Here's a pother indeed!——Did you call me?

QUIDNUNC. No, you trollop, no.

TERMAGANT. Will you go to bed?

QUIDNUNC. No, no, no, no——I tell you, no.

TERMAGANT. Better go to rest, Sir; I heard a doctor of physic say as how, when a man is past his grand *crime*——what the deuce makes me forget my word?——his grand *crime-hysteric*, no, no, that's not it——*clytemmester*, ay, that's it: when a man is past his grand *clytemmester*, nothing is so good to assist nature as rest, and the *nonnaturals*.

QUIDNUNC. Hold your prating: I'll not go to bed; I'll step to my

---

[87] Horace, *Satirae* II.i.46. "He shall lament and be proclaimed infamous through all the city."

brother Feeble; I want to have some talk with him, and I'll go to him directly.

Exit QUIDNUNC.

TERMAGANT. Go thy ways for an old hocus-pocus of a news-monger.——You'll have good luck if you find your daughter here when you come back: Mr. Bellmour will be here in the *intrim,* and if he does not carry her off, why, then I shall think him a mere shilly-shally *feller;* and by my troth I shall think him as bad a *politishing* as yourself.——Well, as I live and breathe I wonders what the dickens the man sees in these newspapers, to be forever *toxicated* with them. Let me see one of them, to try if I can *westigate* anything——(*Takes the newspaper and reads*)

"Yesterday at noon arrived at his lodgings in Pall Mall, John Stukely, Esq.; for the remainder of the winter season."

Where the devil has the man been?——Who knows him, or cares a minikin pin about him? He may go to Jericho for what I cares.

"The same day Mr. William Tabby, an eminent man-milliner, was married to Miss Minikin, daughter of Mr. Minikin, a consid-erable haberdasher in Bearbinder Lane."

What the dickens is this to me? Can't Miss Minikin and her man-milliner go to bed, and hold their tongues? Why must they kiss and tell?

"By advices from *Violenna*"——this is *policies* now——(*Reads to herself*)——"and promises a general peace."——Why can't that make the old curmudgeon happy?

"By letters from Paris"——this is more *policies*——(*Reads to her-self*) "and all seems tending to a general rupture."——What the devil does the *feller* mean?——Did not he tell me this moment there was to be a peace? And now it's bloody news again! To go to tell me such an impudent lie to my face!

"At the Academy in Essex Street, Grown People are taught to dance."

Grown people are taught to dance! I likes that well enough; I should like to be *betterer* in my dancing. I likes the *figerre* of a *minute* as well as a *figerre* in speech (*Dances and sings*); but such *trumpry* as the news is, with kings, and cheesemongers, and bishops, and *highwarman*, and ladies' prayer-books, and lap-dogs, and the *domodary* and *camomile*, and ambassadors, and hair-cutters, all higgledy-piggledy together. As I hope for *marcy*, I'll never read another paper. And I wishes old Quidnunc would do the same. If the man would do as I do, there would be some sense in it. If, instead of his *policies*, he would *manure* his mind like me, and read good *altars*, and improve himself in fine *langidge*, and *bombast*, and *polite accollishments*——

Exit singing and dancing.

SCENE [II]

The Street

Enter BELLMOUR, ROVEWELL, *and* BRISK.

BELLMOUR. Women ever were, and ever will be fantastic beings, vain, capricious, and fond of mischief.

BRISK. Well argued, Master.

ROVEWELL. (*Sings*)

> Deceit is in every woman,
> But none in a bumper can be, my brave boys,
> But none in a bumper can be.[88]

BELLMOUR. To be insulted thus, with such a contemptuous answer to a message of such tender import! She might methinks at least have treated me with good manners, if not with a more grateful return.

ROVEWELL. Confusion to her manners! Let us go and drink t'other bumper to drown sorrow.

---

[88] Based on the proverb "there is no Deceit in a Bumper," found in Robert Heath, "Description of Cornwall," *A Natural and Historical Account of the Islands of Scilly* (London: R. Manby and H. S. Cox, 1750), p. 443.

BELLMOUR. I'll shake off her fetters: I will, Brisk, this very night
I will.

BRISK. That's right, Master, and let her know we have found her
out, and as the poet says,

"She that will not when she may,
    When she will, she shall have nay," [89] Master.

BELLMOUR. Very true, Brisk, very true; the ingratitude of it
touches to the quick. My dear Rovewell, only come and see me
take a final leave.

ROVEWELL. No, truly, not I: none of your virtuous minxes for
me. I'll set you down there, if you've a mind to play the fool. I
know she'll melt you with a tear, and make a puppy of you with
a smile, and so I'll not be witness to it.

BELLMOUR. You're quite mistaken, I assure you: you shall see
me most manfully upbraid her with her ingratitude, and with more
joy than a fugitive galley slave, escape from the oar to which I have
been chain'd.

BRISK. Master, Master, now's our time, for look by the glimmering of yonder lamp, who comes along by the side of the wall.

BELLMOUR. Her father, by all that's lucky; my dear Rovewell,
let us drive off.

ROVEWELL. No, I'll speak a good word to him for you.

BELLMOUR. Not for the world; prithee come along.

Exeunt.

Enter QUIDNUNC, *with a dark Lanthorn.*

QUIDNUNC. If the Grand Turk should actually commence open
hostility, and the House-bug [90] Tartars make a diversion upon the
frontiers, why then it's my opinion, time will discover to us a great
deal more of the matter.

---

[89] A variant of the proverb:

"He that will not when he may,
    When he would he shall have nay."

[90] Bed-bug.

WATCH. (*Within*) Past eleven o'clock, a cloudy night.

QUIDNUNC. Hey! Past eleven o'clock! 'Sbodikins, my brother Feeble will be gone to bed: but he shan't sleep till I have some chat with him. Harkye, watchman, watchman.

Enter WATCHMAN.

WATCH. Call, Master!

QUIDNUNC. Ay, step hither, step hither: have you heard any news?

WATCH. News, Master!

QUIDNUNC. Ay, about the Prussians or the Russians? [91]

WATCH. Russians, Master!

QUIDNUNC. Yes; or the movements in Pomerania? [92]

WATCH. La, Master, I know nothing——poor gentleman——(*Pointing to his head*) Good night to you, Master.——Past eleven o'clock.

Exit WATCHMAN.

QUIDNUNC. That man now has a place under the government, and you see how guarded he is. The discretion of office! His mouth is padlockt. Not a word: he won't speak. But I am losing time. (*Knocks at the door*) Hazy weather (*Looking up*); the wind's fix'd in that quarter, and we shan't have any mails this week to come. Come about, good wind, do, come about.

Enter BETTY.

BETTY. La, Sir, is it you?

QUIDNUNC. Is your master at home, Mrs. Betty?

BETTY. Gone to bed, Sir.

QUIDNUNC. Well, well, I'll step up to him.

BETTY. Must not disturb him for the world, Sir.

QUIDNUNC. Business of the utmost importance.

BETTY. Pray consider, Sir, my master an't well.

QUIDNUNC. Prithee be quiet, woman; I must see him.

Exeunt.

---

[91] In 1758 the Prussians were winning over the Russians.
[92] In 1757 the Swedes had entered Pomerania to oppose the Prussians.

SCENE [III]

A Room in Feeble's House

Enter FEEBLE *in his Nightgown.*

FEEBLE. I was just stepping into bed; bless my heart, what can this man want?——I know his voice: I hope no new misfortune brings him at this hour.

QUIDNUNC. (*Within*) Hold your tongue you foolish hussy—— he'll be glad to see me.——Brother Feeble——Brother Feeble!

FEEBLE. What can be the matter?

Enter QUIDNUNC.

QUIDNUNC. Brother Feeble, I give you joy. The Nabob's demolish'd. (*Sings*) "Britons strike home, revenge," *&c.*[93]

FEEBLE. Lackaday, Mr. Quidnunc, how can you serve me thus?

QUIDNUNC. Surajah Dowlah is no more.[94]

FEEBLE. Poor man! He's stark-staring mad.

QUIDNUNC. Our men diverted themselves with killing their bullocks and their camels, till they dislodged the enemy from the octagon, and the counterscarp, and the bunglo.[95]

FEEBLE. I'll hear the rest tomorrow morning. Oh! I'm ready to die.

QUIDNUNC. Odsheart, man, be of good cheer. The new Nabob

---

[93] From a song of Henry Purcell for Act III, Scene II, of George Powell's edition of the opera *Bonduca* (1695), altered from John Fletcher.

[94] Surajah Dowlah, Nawab of Bengal, who had sided with the French against Clive, was defeated by Clive and killed by the son of his general Mir Jafar in 1757.

[95] A spelling of "bungalow," here a house for officers near a military post.

Jaffier Ali Khan has acceded to a treaty;[96] and the English Company have got all their rights in the Phirmaund and the Hushbulhoorums.[97]

FEEBLE. But dear heart, Mr. Quidnunc, why am I to be disturb'd for this?

QUIDNUNC. We had but two sepoys[98] killed, three Chokeys,[99] four Gaulwalls,[100] and two Zemidars.[101] (*Sings*) "Britons never shall be slaves!"[102]

FEEBLE. Would not tomorrow morning do as well for this?

QUIDNUNC. Light up your windows, man, light up your windows. Chandernagore is taken.[103]

FEEBLE. Well, well, I'm glad of it. Good night. (*Going*)

QUIDNUNC. Here, here's the *Gazette*.

FEEBLE. Oh, I shall certainly faint. (*Sits down*)

QUIDNUNC. Ay, ay, sit down: I'll read it to you. (*Reads*) Nay, don't run away——I've more news to tell you, there's an account from Williamsburg in America. The Superintendent of Indian Affairs——

FEEBLE. Dear Sir, dear Sir,——(*Avoiding him*)

QUIDNUNC. Has settled matters with the Cherokees——[104] (*Following him*)

FEEBLE. Enough, enough,——(*Avoiding him*)

---

[96] Jaffier Ali Khan or Mir Jafar had signed a treaty with the English against Surajah Dowlah, and after the latter's death, the former became Nawab of Bengal in 1757.

[97] Here, both the Phirmaund and the Hushbulhoorums are official documents of rights for the East India Company agreed to by the Nawab of Bengal.

[98] Sepoys were natives of India employed as soldiers by England.

[99] Indian tollmen.

[100] Gorawallahs are grooms or horsekeepers.

[101] Landholders who pay revenue to the government directly.

[102] James Thomson, "Rule, Britannia!" line 6, from the masque *Alfred* (1740) II.v.

[103] Robert Clive captured the French settlement Chandernagore, near Calcutta, in March, 1757.

[104] The British and the Cherokees had signed a treaty in 1730, and in 1757 the British built for the Cherokees Fort Loudoun on the Tennessee River.

QUIDNUNC. In the same manner he did before with the Cataw-bas.[105] (*After him*)

FEEBLE. Well, well, your servant.——(*From him*)

QUIDNUNC. So that the back inhabitants——(*After him*)

FEEBLE. I wish you would let me be a quiet inhabitant in my own house.

QUIDNUNC. So that the back inhabitants will now be secured by the Cherokees and the Catawbas.

FEEBLE. You'd better go home, and think of appearing before the Commissioners.

QUIDNUNC. Go home! No, no, I'll go and talk the matter over at our coffeehouse.

FEEBLE. Do so, do so.

QUIDNUNC. (*Returning*) Mr. Feeble——I had a dispute about the balance of power.——Pray now can you tell——

FEEBLE. I know nothing of the matter.

QUIDNUNC. Well, another time will do for that——I have a great deal to say about that. (*Going, returns*) Right, I had like to have forgot, there's an erratum in the last *Gazette*.

FEEBLE. With all my heart.

QUIDNUNC. Page 3, line I, col. I, and 3, for *bombs* read *booms*.

FEEBLE. Read what you will.

QUIDNUNC. Nay, but that alters the sense, you know. Well, now your servant. If I hear any more news I'll come and tell you.

FEEBLE. For Heaven's sake no more.

QUIDNUNC. I'll be with you before you're out of your first sleep.

FEEBLE. Good night, good night.

(*Runs off*)

QUIDNUNC. I forgot to tell you: the Emperor of Morocco is dead. Brother Feeble, do you hear? (*Bawls through the keyhole*) The Emperor of Morocco is dead. So, now I have made him happy, I'll go to our coffeehouse, and make them all happy there. (*Sings*) "Rule, Britannia, Britannia, rule the waves"——[106]

Exit.

---

[105] The Catawbas were friends of the British of South Carolina.

[106] Thomson, "Rule, Britannia!" line 5, from *Alfred* II.v.

SCENE [IV]

A Street: A shabby house in front, with a barber's pole, and the
windows lighted up.

Enter QUIDNUNC.

QUIDNUNC. Ha! friend Razor! He is a good subject, a true English heart. He makes a right use of a rejoicing night. Our victories
are not thrown away upon him. Who knows but he may have heard
more intelligence? (*Knocks at the door*)

RAZOR. (*Looking out of the window*) Anan!

QUIDNUNC. Friend Razor.

RAZOR. My Master Quidnunc! I'm rejoicing for the news. Will
you partake of a pipe? I'll open the door.

QUIDNUNC. Not now, friend Razor.

RAZOR. I've something to tell you; I'll come down.

QUIDNUNC. This may be worth staying for: what can he have
heard!

Enter RAZOR,
in a Cap, a Pipe in his Mouth, and a Tankard in his Hand.

RAZOR. Say, here's to you, Master Quidnunc.

QUIDNUNC. What have you heard? What have you heard?

RAZOR. The Consumers of Oats [107] are to meet next week.

QUIDNUNC. Those Consumers of Oats have been meeting any
time these ten years to my knowledge, and I never could find what
they are about.

RAZOR. Things an't right, I fear: it's enough to pull down a
body's spirits——(*Drinks*)

---

[107] This may actually be an unrecorded Scottish club in London to promote the use of oats at a time when the price of corn or wheat was high!

QUIDNUNC. No, nothing to fear. I can tell you some good news. A certain great potentate has not heard high mass the Lord knows when.

RAZOR. That puts a body in spirits again. (*Drinks*) Here, drink no wooden shoes.[108]

QUIDNUNC. With all my heart.——(*Drinks*) Good liquor this, Master Razor, of a cold night.

RAZOR. Yes, I put a quartern of British brandy in my beer. Whu! ——Do you know what a rebel my wife is?

QUIDNUNC. A rebel!

RAZOR. Ay, a rebel——I earned nineteen pence, halfpenny today, and she wanted to lay out all that great sum upon the children. Whu——but I bought those candles for the good of my country, to rejoice with as a body may say, a little *Virginy* [109] for my pipe, and this sup of hot. Whu. Bitter cold.

QUIDNUNC. Ay, you're an honest man, and if everybody were like you and me, what a nation we should be!

RAZOR. Very true! (*Shakes his head*)

QUIDNUNC. I can give you the *Gazette* to read.

RAZOR. Can you! A thousand thanks. I'll take it home to you when I have done.——(*Drinks and staggers*)

QUIDNUNC. Friend Razor, you begin to be a little in for't.

RAZOR. Yes, I have a whirligig of a head. But a body shou'd take a cheering glass [110] sometimes for the good of one's country.

QUIDNUNC. Well, I shall be at home in half an hour!——Harkye.

RAZOR. Anan!

QUIDNUNC. I have made a rare discovery. Florida will be able to supply Jamaica with peat for their winters' firings. I had it from a deep politician.[111]

---

[108] A toast against France, where many peasants wore wooden shoes.

[109] Virginia tobacco.

[110] 1769: "get drunk"; 1786: "take a cheering glass."

[111] Murphy added the Florida passage in 1763. Spain temporarily ceded Florida to England on Feb. 10 of that year. Murphy himself had been imposed upon concerning peat for the West Indies in his political periodical *The Auditor*, Dec. 18, 1762.

RAZOR. Ay! I am glad the poor people of Jamaica will have Florida peat to burn.[112] They may now have a little firing in the winter. I don't know what the news is, but I have been rejoicing for the good of my country. I'll go and read the *Gazette*, to see a little what it's about. After all is said and done, O rare Old England! (*Goes into his house*)

QUIDNUNC. Ay! Rare Old England! Strong enough still for all our enemies; we shan't be a bankrupt nation yet, and that's some comfort.——I will now go and see who is up at our coffeehouse, and discuss points with our political club.

Exit.

SCENE [V]

The Upholsterer's House

Enter HARRIET *and* BELLMOUR.

HARRIET. I don't know what to say, Mr. Bellmour. It is difficult to refuse you. A heart touched as mine has been cannot easily resolve to give you a moment's uneasiness. And yet your proposal——

BELLMOUR. It is a fair and honourable proposal. It springs from esteem and true affection. You cannot doubt my honour.

HARRIET. No, Mr. Bellmour: to form an ill opinion of you is impossible: but you may judge otherwise of me. What will be your sentiment hereafter, should I now be wanting in that duty which I owe my father?

BELLMOUR. You have promised me your hand. Your father unreasonably withholds it. To all his just commands you owe obedience: but when the whims and oddities of a wild, disordered imagination have no other tendency than to involve you in the ruin which has unhappily befallen himself, why must you be a sacrifice to his humours? And why must I be rendered miserable, Harriet?

---

[112] 1769: scene ends at this point.

HARRIET. But then, to comply with your solicitations, and leave my father in a scene of trouble and misfortune——

BELLMOUR. It will be the means of making his misfortunes lighter. In his moments of reflection he will feel with pleasure that his conduct has not prevented your happiness. You will then have the means of behaving to him with gratitude and generosity.

HARRIET. But my Uncle Feeble, what will he say?

BELLMOUR. You may depend upon his approbation. I will be answerable for it: a coach is now waiting at the end of the street to receive you. Harriet, will you refuse me your hand?

HARRIET. Must I give it? I don't know what to say. Why don't you take it?

Enter TERMAGANT.

TERMAGANT. Undone, undone! Oh! my stars, I am all over in such a tribulation. The old newsmonger is coming.

BELLMOUR. Distraction!——What brings him here so soon?

HARRIET. Oh! Mr. Bellmour, this overpowers me quite. What can I say to him?

TERMAGANT. The devil is in it: this is such a cross accident. I am at my wit's end. No; that's not true neither. I have it: I'll tell you what to do. Don't *frustrate* yourself, Ma'am. Away, Mr. Bellmour, into that room. He never will find you out. Away, fly Mr. Bellmour. Do you stay, Miss Harriet, and talk to the old gentleman. When you have seen him, and wished him a good night, you may slip downstairs, and so make the best of your way to the coach at the end of the street.——I shall find some nonsense news for the old politician, and when I get him to bed, Mr. Bellmour may follow you, Madam. Why don't you go, Mr. Bellmour? You are enough to ruin a body.

BELLMOUR. I am gone, I'll be govern'd by you.

Exit.

HARRIET. Oh! Termagant, I shall never be able to go through this business: my strength fails me.

TERMAGANT. Have courage, Madam. I hear him coming. Let me see: have I nothing in my pocket to amuse him? Yes, yes; this will do; never fear, Miss Harriet. Now let the old walking *Gazette* come as soon as he will. I am ready for him, I warrant me.

Enter QUIDNUNC.

QUIDNUNC. Fie upon it, fie upon it! All the coffeehouses shut up. Harriet, what makes you out of bed at this late hour?

TERMAGANT. A rejoicing night, Sir: but this love of her country does not agree much with her. She is quite sick for the good of Old England.——Speak to him, Madam.

HARRIET. I am frightened out of my wits, Termagant. I shall faint.

QUIDNUNC. It is well we have not a female Parliament. Late debates would be too much for her spirits. Get to rest, Harriet; get to bed.

HARRIET. I wish you a good night, Sir.

Exit.

TERMAGANT. (*Going with her*) This will do purely, Ma'am.

QUIDNUNC. Where is my *Salmon's Gazetteer*,[113] and my maps of the world? I must see all these places before I sleep. They are in that room, I believe. (*Going towards the door*)

TERMAGANT. (*Returning*) What is he about now?——Sir, Sir, Sir——here has been Mr.——I forget his name——he that writes letters in the newspapers about paying off the national debt——Mr. Ruin, Sir——he has been here, and he desires you'll read his new project, and give him your thoughts about it.

QUIDNUNC. Give me the paper; let me see it.

TERMAGANT. The deuce fetch it. Here is something that so catches and hitches in my pocket. There, there it is. (*Gives him the paper, and drops a letter*) Had not you better go and read it in bed, Sir? Bed is a pure place for thinking.

---

[113] Thomas Salmon, *The Modern Gazetteer or A Short View of the Several Nations of the World* (London, 1746; 3rd ed. 1756).

QUIDNUNC. So it is, Termagant. Go and lock the street door, and then——

TERMAGANT. Yes, Sir. I'll be with you in an instant. And so now I shall get Miss Harriet clear off——

Exit.

QUIDNUNC. Po! the foolish jade! This is an old paper. Hey; what have we here? (*Takes up a letter*) How, how is this? "To Miss Harriet Quidnunc." Let me see; let me see. (*Reads eagerly*) "My dearest Harriet——no longer in suspense——given you every proof ——constancy and love——your happiness——father's obstinacy"—— Here's a villain for you——"convey you to a family"——Will you so? ——"and there you may remain in perfect security, till you resign your person to the arms of your eternal admirer——Bellmour."—— So, so! This is as good as a state paper: here is Machiavel at work. Why daughter Harriet, where is she? Harriet I say. (*Bawls violently*) A plot! A conspiracy! Gunpowder treason! Robbery! Murder!

Enter TERMAGANT.

TERMAGANT. Law, Sir, what is the matter now?

QUIDNUNC. I have found you out, traitress. Here is Mr. Bellmour's letter. Rob me of my daughter! Where is Harriet? Search the house; call the watch; alarm the neighbours; I'll go and rouse the whole world.

Exit.

TERMAGANT. I am all over in such a quandary. Dear me! What shall I do?

BELLMOUR. (*Peeping in*) Blundering busybody! You have marr'd all. This is your doing. What possessed you to give him that letter?

TERMAGANT. I did not do it on purpose; as I hope for mercy, I did not. Don't be angry with me, Sir. (*Cries*)

BELLMOUR. Why do you scream so? Is the woman crazy?

TERMAGANT. I did not go for to give it him; (*Cries*) I would have seen him gibbeted first. I found the letter in my mistress's bed-chamber, and my Curiosity did make me peep into it. Says my

Curiosity, "Now, Termagant, you may gratify yourself by finding out the contents of that letter, which you have had such a plaguy itching for." My Curiosity did say so; and then I own my respect for my mistress did say to me, "Hussy, how dare you to meddle with what does not belong to you? Keep your distance, and let your mistress's secrets alone." And then upon that in comes my unlucky Curiosity again, "Read it, I tell you, Termagant; a woman of spirit should know everything."—"Let it alone, you jade," says my Respect; "it's as much as your place is worth."—"What *significations* a place with an old *bankrupper?*" says my Curiosity; "there's more places than one; and so read it, I tell you, Termagant." —And I did so. (*Cries bitterly*) I did read it; what could I do, Heaven help me? I did read it; I don't go to deny it, I don't, I don't. —(*Cries very bitterly*)

BELLMOUR. Hush; have you a mind to ruin me?

TERMAGANT. And after I had read it, thinks me I, I'll give it safe into Miss Harriet's own hand, and her crazy old father shan't see it; and so as my ill stars would have it, as I was giving him a news-paper, I run my hand full into the lion's mouth. (*Cries*)

A loud rap at the door.

BELLMOUR. There, there; you have roused the neighbourhood, and I shall be detected.

QUIDNUNC. (*Within*) Bring him along; bring the villain in.

BELLMOUR. Death and distraction! Our whole scheme is ruin'd.

Enter QUIDNUNC, *leading* HARRIET.

QUIDNUNC. Walk in, Jezebel; I have caught you. Lead that traitor this way.

TERMAGANT. Oh! my dear, young mistress. (*Taking her by the hand*)

QUIDNUNC. Let me see the plunderer, that would rob me of my daughter.

WATCHMAN. (*Within*) Ay, ay; this way, Sir.

RAZOR. (*Within*) Rob my Master Quidnunc! Secure him; knock him down.

Enter RAZOR *and* WATCHMAN, *leading in* ROVEWELL.

WATCHMAN. We have him fast: now who are you?

RAZOR. Ay, who are you? Whence come you?

QUIDNUNC. Away with him to the roundhouse.[114] I'll go with him: I may meet a Parliament-man in the roundhouse to tell me some news. What business have you with my daughter?

ROVEWELL. Wounds! If your daughter will walk the streets at this late hour, a gentleman has a right to consider her as fair game.

BELLMOUR. Rovewell, was this well done? What unlucky planet sent you this way?

QUIDNUNC. How! Bellmour here! The enemy in my very camp.

BELLMOUR. I am no enemy, Sir. My designs are honourable. You see I scorn to conceal myself.

QUIDNUNC. I see you do: a bold-faced ruffian! Here, seize 'em both. I charge them both. Away with them.

RAZOR. Put 'em both in irons; handcuff 'em; secure 'em this moment.

BELLMOUR. Don't frighten the lady: here is my sword: I surrender.

RAZOR. (*Strips off his coat*) Lay hold of that traitor. (*Attacking Rovewell*) Seize him; bind him fast.

ROVEWELL. Dastards! Villains! Stand off.

RAZOR. Fall on him, neighbours; that's right; now we have him. (*Rovewell is seized*)

ROVEWELL. Rascals, you have overpower'd me.

RAZOR. Victory!——I have conquered. (*Puts on his coat*) Here, Master Quidnunc, I have brought you back the *Gazette*.

TERMAGANT. I believes as sure as anything that he is a *highwareman*, and as how it was he that robbed the mail.

QUIDNUNC. Rob the mail, and stop all the news! Search him: he may have the letters belonging to the mail in his pocket. Here, here; here's a letter. What is it? (*Reads*) "To Mr. Abraham Quidnunc."

---

[114] Jail.

How! How is this? (*Opens and reads*)——"Your dutiful son, John Quidnunc." Quidnunc! Is that your name?

ROVEWELL. Quidnunc is my name, Sir, and Rovewell was but assumed; a travelling title.

QUIDNUNC. And are you my son?

RAZOR. (*Looking at him*) Oh! my dear Sir; it is he. (*Embraces him and powders him all over*) It is he sure enough——I remember the mole on his cheek. I shaved his first beard.

QUIDNUNC. What, just returned from the West Indies?

ROVEWELL. Even so, and the owner of a rich plantation.

QUIDNUNC. By being a great politician, I suppose.

ROVEWELL. By marrying a planter's widow. I have now fortune sufficient to afford you, Sir, the comforts and enjoyments of life.

RAZOR. This is true joy. You'll let Razor shave you, I hope, Master.

ROVEWELL. Honest Razor, I shan't forget you. This is a lucky discovery. I have both ability and inclination, Sir, to convince you that I know and feel the duty I owe to a father. I shall now atone for the irregularities of my youth.[115] Bellmour, give me your hand. He is an honest fellow, Sir, and if you will bestow my sister upon him, you will add to the joy of this unexpected meeting.

QUIDNUNC. Why, I think it will make a good paragraph in the papers.

TERMAGANT. There, Madam, *calcine* your person to him.

ROVEWELL. What, do you hesitate, Bellmour? Here, take her, man; take her at once. I hope to know her better, and to find that she is worthy of so honest a fellow.

QUIDNUNC. Pray now, what are the Spaniards doing in the Bay of Honduras? [116]

ROVEWELL. Truce with politics for the present, if you please, Sir. We will think of our own affairs before we concern ourselves about the balance of power.

---

[115] The preceding three sentences first appear in 1786. In 1791 Murphy rewrote them: "And since chance has brought me to my father's house, I hope, Sir, that I shall be able to extricate you out of all your misfortunes."

[116] The bay is east of British Honduras. The Spanish were harassing English woodcutters.

RAZOR. With all my heart: I am pure happy now.

Come, Master Quidnunc, now with news have done,
Bless'd in your wealth, your daughter and your son.
May discord cease; faction no more be seen;
Be *high* and *low* [117] for COUNTRY, KING, and QUEEN.

___

[117] High Church and Low Church.

THE WAY TO KEEP HIM (1761)

INTRODUCTION

N 1758 and 1759 Murphy composed the three-act form of *The Way to Keep Him*, a comedy of manners. David Garrick produced it at Drury Lane Theatre, with the successful opening on January 24, 1760. In accordance with his original design of composition, Murphy soon expanded the play to five acts. Garrick had paid Murphy £100 for the additions before the dramatist had written them. At Drury Lane on January 10, 1761, this version began a continual stage history that was to last until late in the nineteenth century. *The Way to Keep Him* attracted many great actors. David Garrick, Charles Holland, William Smith, and Richard Wroughton played Lovemore; Mary Ann Yates, George Anne Bellamy, Elizabeth Farren, and Sarah Siddons, Mrs. Lovemore; Susannah Maria Cibber, Jane Pope, Frances Abington, Maria Macklin, Elizabeth Farren, Dorothea Jordan, and Julia Glover, Widow Bellmour; Henry Woodward and Charles Kemble, Sir Brilliant Fashion; Richard Yates, John Quick, John Bannister, and Joseph Munden, Sir Bashful Constant; Elizabeth Inchbald and Harriet Mellon, Lady Constant; and Kitty Clive, Jane Hippisley Green, and Isabella Mattocks, Muslin.

Allardyce Nicoll justly ranks *The Way to Keep Him* above Sheridan's *The Rivals*.* Suspense is strong. The characters become distinctive immediately. The same character is realistically different in different circumstances. No audience could resist the varied incitements to laughter—the connubial eccentricity of the incomparable Sir Bashful Constant; the predicaments of the embarrassed, philandering husband Lovemore; the dramatic irony when Sir Bash-

---

* *The Way to Keep Him* (London, 1926), p. viii.

ful Constant believes that Lovemore is attempting to aid him in his relations with Lady Constant and when Lovemore calls on the vivacious and noble Widow Bellmour, who still thinks that he is single.

The first edition of the three-act form of *The Way to Keep Him,* for which the bookseller Paul Vaillant paid Murphy fifty guineas, appeared shortly after the opening performance early in 1760. The Fourth Edition of 1761 is the first edition of the five-act form. Vaillant had paid Murphy fifty more guineas for the enlarged play, but a new comedy of as many as five acts was so unusual at that time that the dramatist only with difficulty prevented the bookseller from severely cutting the text for publication.

The main difference between the three-act and the five-act forms is that the longer play has as additional characters Sir Bashful Constant, Lady Constant, and their servants, Sideboard and Furnish. Sir Bashful Constant appears in every act except the third and Lady Constant in every act except the first and third, and their introduction into the play makes the second act and the second and last scene of the fourth act almost entirely new. Thus, Murphy expertly interweaves with the original situation of Mrs. Lovemore, who for some time does not know how to keep her straying husband, the situation of the delightful Sir Bashful Constant, who feels so bound by modish society that he is ashamed to admit loving his own wife; in the expanded comedy, the versatile Lovemore hunts Lady Constant as well as Widow Bellmour. Other noteworthy alterations are the added realistic domestic scene of the Lovemores at the opening of the third act; the new farewell scene for William, a servant of Lovemore, and Mignionet, a servant of Widow Bellmour, at the opening of the fourth act; and the excision of Muslin, the maid of Mrs. Lovemore, from the last part of the final scene of the play.

The Fifth Edition of *The Way to Keep Him* appeared in 1765; The Sixth Edition, in 1770. Neither reveals the hand of the author.

For the 1786 edition of his *Works,* Murphy revised *The Way to Keep Him.* Thomas Cadell, the publisher and bookseller for the

Works, issued the revised text of the comedy separately in both 1785 and 1787. However, after the publication of the 1785 octavo, Murphy continued to revise the text of this play for his *Works*, particularly Act III, in which there are more cuts, additions, transpositions, and alterations. Some of the omitted material concerns moralization. The text of 1787 is that of 1785, though the former follows 1786 in sixty-six typographical details. The editor reproduces the text of 1786 with a little assistance from those of 1770, 1785, and 1787, as explained in the footnotes.

The rewriting of the 1770 text for the 1786 edition evinces the dramatist's artistry. Murphy deletes the farewell scene of William and Mignionet at the opening of Act IV; and the domestic scene of the Lovemores that opens Act III becomes the new opening of Act IV. The placing of this domestic scene after Lovemore's call on Widow Bellmour increases suspense and, with added dialogue, promotes the dramatic irony, for the audience and Mrs. Lovemore are aware of Lovemore's defection. In every scene of the 1786 version, Murphy rewrites speeches for every character; in fact, he rewrites most speeches except in Act V. He expands, adds, transposes, combines, divides, cuts, and expunges speeches, with the total effect a lengthening of the play. The manifold improvements include clearer exposition, an added illustrative instance, the interruption of a long speech, the elimination of repetition, a more effective exit, more stage directions, the excision of a topical allusion, the removing of moralizing, an increase in humour, and more fluent, subtler, and more sophisticated dialogue. It is also interesting to note that the servant William uses better grammar and that at the opening of Act I, Scene ii, Murphy deletes an unnamed maid of Mrs. Lovemore.

Texts Collated

[Murphy, Arthur], *The Way to Keep Him*. A Comedy In Three Acts. London: P. Valliant [Vaillant], 1760. [Princeton University]

Murphy, [Arthur], *The Way to Keep Him.* A Comedy In Five Acts. The Fourth Edition. London: P. Vaillant, 1761. [Haverford College]

——, *The Way to Keep Him.* A Comedy In Five Acts. The Fifth Edition. London: P. Vaillant, 1765. [Columbia University]

——, *The Way to Keep Him.* A Comedy In Five Acts. The Sixth Edition. London: P. Vaillant, 1770. [University of Pennsylvania]

——, *The Way to Keep Him.* London: T. Cadell, 1785. [Library of Congress]

The Works of Arthur Murphy, III, v-viii, 1-197. London: T. Cadell, 1786. [University of Pennsylvania; Copy of Editor]

[Murphy, Arthur], *The Way to Keep Him.* London: T. Cadell, 1787. [Harvard University]

THE
WAY TO KEEP HIM:

A
COMEDY,

Performed at the

THEATRE ROYAL
IN
DRURY-LANE.

. . . Ut ameris, amabilis esto:
Quod tibi non facies solvave forma dabit.
Ovid.[1]

Nam facit ipsa suis interdum faemina factis,
Morigerisque modis, et mundo corpore cultu,
Ut facile insuescat secum vir degere vitam.
Lucret. *Lib*. 4.[2]

¹ Ovid, *Ars Amatoria* II.107-108. "That you may be loved, be lovable: and this nor face nor figure alone will bring you." [Loeb translation]

² Lucretius, *De Rerum Natura* IV.1280-1282. "For a woman sometimes so manages herself by her own conduct, by obliging manners and bodily neatness and cleanliness, that she easily accustoms a man to live with her." [Modified Loeb translation]

To Mrs. Abington [3]

Madam,

You will be surprised, at this distance of time, and in this public manner, to receive an answer to a very polite letter, which you addressed to me in the course of the last summer at Yarmouth. In a strain of vivacity, which always belongs to you, you invite me to write again for the stage. You tell me that having gone through the comedies of *The Way to Keep Him*,[4] *All in the Wrong*,[5] and *Three Weeks after Marriage*,[6] you now want more from the same hand. I am not bound, you say, by my resolution, signified in a prologue about ten years ago,[7] to take my leave of the Dramatic Muse. At the perjuries of poets, as well as lovers, Jove laughs; and the public, you think, will be ready to give me a general release from the promise. All this is very flattering. If the following scenes, at the end of five and twenty years, still continue to be a part of the public amusement, I know to what cause I am to ascribe it. Those graces of action with which you adorn whatever you undertake have given to the piece a degree of brilliancy, and even novelty, as often as you have repeated it. I am not unmindful of the performers who first obtained for the author the favour of the town: a Garrick, a Yates, a Cibber, united their abilities; and who can forget Mrs. Clive? They have all passed away, and the comedy might have

---

[3] Frances Abington (1737-1815).

[4] Her role of Widow Bellmour "established her fame in London." (*Roach's Authentic Memoirs of the Green Room*, 1796, p. 5.)

[5] Belinda was her "favourite character." (The London *Chronicle*, Oct. 11, 1785, LVIII, 351.)

[6] As Lady Rackett, she ended her acting career Apr. 12, 1799.

[7] The prologue of *Know Your Own Mind*.

passed with them if you had not so frequently placed it in a conspicuous light.

The truth is, without such talents as yours, all that the poet writes is a dead letter. He designs for representation, but it is the performer that gives to the draught, however justly traced, a form, a spirit, a countenance, and a mind. All this you have done for the Widow Bellmour; and that excellence in your art, which you are known to possess, can, no doubt, lend the same animation to any new character. But alas! I have none to offer. That tinder in the poet's mind, which, as Doctor Young says, takes fire from every spark,[8] I have not found, even though you have endeavoured to kindle the flame. Could I write as you can act, I should be proud to obey your commands: but after a long disuse, how shall I recover the train of thinking necessary for plot, humour, incident, and character?

In the place of novelty, permit me to request that *The Way to Keep Him* may be inscribed to you. You are entitled to it, Madam; for your talents have made the play your own. A dedication, I grant, at this period of time, comes rather late; but being called upon for a new edition, I have retouched the dialogue and perhaps so reformed the whole, that, in its present state, it may be deemed less unworthy of your acceptance. It is, therefore, my wish, that this address may in future attend the comedy, to remain (as long as such a thing can remain) a tribute due to the GENIUS OF MRS. ABINGTON, and a mark of that esteem with which I subscribe myself,

Madam,
        Your real admirer,
                And most obedient servant,
                        Arthur Murphy.
Lincoln's-Inn,
  25th Nov. 1785.

_____
[8] Edward Young, *A Discourse on Lyric Poetry* (1728), par. 4.

PROLOGUE,

Spoken by Mr. Holland.

When first the haughty critic's dreadful rage,
With Gothic fury, overran the stage,
Then prologues rose, and strove with varied art
To gain the soft accesses to the heart.
Thro' all the tuneful tribe th' infection flew,
And each great genius——his petition drew;
In *forma pauperis* [9] address'd the pit,
With all the gay antithesis of wit.
Their sacred art poor poets own'd a crime;
They sigh'd in simile; they bow'd in rhyme.
For charity they all were forc'd to beg;
And ev'ry prologue was "a wooden leg."
   Next these a hardy, manly race appear'd,
Who knew no dullness, and no critics fear'd. [10]
From Nature's store each curious tint they drew,
Then boldly held the piece to public view:
"Lo! here, exact proportion! just design!
The bold relief! and the unerring line!
Mark in soft union how the colours strike!
This, Sirs, you will, or this you ought to like."
They bid defiance to the foes of wit,

---

[9] To sue in the form of a pauper is to sue without liability for costs.
[10] 1770: "no audience fear'd."

135

"Scatter'd like ratsbane up and down the pit." [11]

　　Such prologues were of yore;——our bard to-night
Disdains a false compassion to excite:
Nor too secure your judgment would oppose;
He packs no jury, and he dreads no foes.
To govern here no party can expect;
An audience will preserve its own respect.
　　To catch the foibles, that misguide the fair,
From trifles spring, and end in lasting care,
Our author aims; nor this alone he tries, ⎤
But as fresh objects, and new manners rise, ⎬
He bids his canvas glow with various dyes; ⎦
Where sense and folly mix in dubious strife,
Alternate rise, and struggle into life.
Judge if with art the mimic strokes he [12] blend;
If amicably light and shade contend;
The mental features if he trace with skill;
See the piece first, then damn it if you will.

———

[11] William Congreve, *The Mourning Bride* (1697), "Epilogue," line 8.
[12] 1770: "he"; 1786: "be."

DRAMATIS PERSONAE

Men

Lovemore,	Mr. Garrick.
Sir Bashful Constant,	Mr. Yates.
Sir Brilliant Fashion,	Mr. Palmer.
William, serv. to Lovemore,	Mr. King.
Sideboard, serv. to Sir Bash.,	Mr. Ackman.
Pompey, black boy,	Mr. Hurst.[13]

Women

The Widow Bellmour,	Mrs. Cibber.
Mrs. Lovemore,	Mrs. Yates.
Lady Constant,	Mrs. Davies.
Muslin, maid to Mrs. Lovemore,	Mrs. Clive.
Mignionet, maid to the Widow,	Miss Bradshaw.
Furnish, maid to Lady Constant,	Miss Hippisley.

SCENE: LONDON [14]

---

[13] 1785: "Mr. Hurst." Lacking in 1786.
[14] From 1785. Lacking in 1786.

THE

WAY TO KEEP HIM

ACT the FIRST
SCENE [I]

An Apartment in Lovemore's House
William and Sideboard discovered at a game of cards.

WILLIAM. A plague go with it! I have turned out my game. Is forty-seven good? [15]

SIDEBOARD. Equal.[16]

WILLIAM. Confound the cards! Tierce to a queen?

SIDEBOARD. Equal.[17]

WILLIAM. There again! Ruined, stock and block:[18] nothing can save me. I don't believe there is a footman in England plays with worse luck than myself. Four aces are fourteen.[19]

---

[15] In piquet, after the discarding and the passing of *carte blanche*, the first stage of the scoring, William, the nondealer, announces that he has completed his count in point, the second stage of the scoring. In his suit of greatest strength, an ace counts eleven; a court card, ten; and each of the other cards from ten to seven, the number of its pips. He asks if his count of forty-seven is better than Sideboard's count in his suit of greatest strength.

[16] Since Sideboard's count is equal or forty-seven also, neither player scores for point.

[17] In sequences, the third stage of the scoring, each has a sequence of three cards in a suit with the queen the highest, so that again neither player scores.

[18] Everything, all one's possessions.

[19] In quatorzes, part of the fourth stage of the scoring, four aces count fourteen.

SIDEBOARD. That's hard, cruel, by Jupiter! Aces against me every time.

WILLIAM. Four aces are fourteen: fifteen.[20] (*Plays*)

SIDEBOARD. There's your equality.

WILLIAM. Very well: I turned out my point.[21] Sixteen, (*Plays*) seventeen. (*Plays*)

Enter MUSLIN.

MUSLIN. There's a couple of you, indeed! You are so fond of the vices of your betters that you are scarce out of your beds but you must imitate them and their profligate ways. Set you up,[22] forsooth!

WILLIAM. Prithee, be quiet, woman, do. Eighteen. (*Plays*)

MUSLIN. Upon my word!——With your usual ease, Mr. Coxcomb.

WILLIAM. Manners, Mrs. Muslin: you see Mr. Sideboard here; he is just come on a message from Sir Bashful Constant. Have some respect for a stranger. Nineteen, clubs.——(*Plays*)

MUSLIN. It would become Mr. Sideboard to go back with his answer, and it would become you to send my lady word——

WILLIAM. Command your tongue, Mrs. Muslin: you'll put me out. What shall I play?——He will go back with his answer in good time. Let his master wait till it suits our conveniency. Nineteen, clubs: where shall I go now?

MUSLIN. Have done with your folly, Mr. Impertinent. My lady desires to know——

WILLIAM. I tell you, woman, my master and I desire to have nothing to do with you and your lady. Twenty, diamonds. (*Plays*)

MUSLIN. But I tell you, Mr. Brazen, that my lady desires to know at what hour your master came home last night, and how he does this morning?

WILLIAM. Ridiculous! Don't disturb us with that nonsense now: you see I am not at leisure. I and my master are resolved to be

---

[20] In points made in play, the fifth stage of the scoring, William adds one point for each card that he leads above a nine.

[21] He announces that he has begun to play his suit with the greatest number of pips.

[22] Muslin ironically suggests that they put themselves on a pedestal.

teased no more by you; and so Mrs. Go-between, you may return as you came. What the devil shall I play? We will have nothing to do with you, I tell you.

MUSLIN. You'll have nothing to do with us! But you shall have to do with us, or I'll know the reason why. (*She snatches the cards from him and throws them about*)

WILLIAM. Death and fury! This meddling woman has destroyed my whole game. A man might as well be married as be treated in this fashion.

SIDEBOARD. I shall score you for this, Mr. William: I was sure of the cards,[23] and that would have made me up.

WILLIAM. No, you'll score nothing for this. You win too much of me. I am a very pretty annuity to you.

SIDEBOARD. Annuity say you? I lose a fortune to you in the course of the year. How could you, Mrs. Muslin, behave in this sort to persons of our dignity?

MUSLIN. Decamp with your dignity; take your answer to your master; turn upon your rogue's heel, and rid the house.

SIDEBOARD. I shan't dispute with you. I hate wrangling: I leave that to lawyers and married people; they have nothing else to do. Mr. William, I shall let Sir Bashful know that Mr. Lovemore will be at home for him. When you come to our house, I'll give you your revenge. We can have a snug party there, and I promise you a glass of choice Champagne: it happens to be a good batch; Sir Bashful gets none of it: I keep it for my own friends. Au revoir.

Exit.

WILLIAM. (*To Muslin*) You see what mischief you have made.

MUSLIN. Truce with your foolery, and now, Sir, be so obliging as to send my lady an answer to her questions. How and when your rakehelly master came home last night.

WILLIAM. I'll tell you one thing, Mrs. Muslin; you and my master will be the death of me at last. In the name of charity, what do you both take me for? Whatever appearances may be, I am but of mortal mould; nothing supernatural about me.

---

[23] The sixth stage of the scoring. Sideboard might have scored twenty-three points in cards.

MUSLIN. Upon my word, Mr. Powder-Puff!

WILLIAM. I have not, indeed; and flesh and blood, let me tell you, can't hold it always at this rate. I can't be for ever a slave to Mr. Lovemore's eternal frolics, and to your second-hand airs.

MUSLIN. Second-hand airs!

WILLIAM. Yes, second-hand airs! You take them at your ladies' toilets with their cast gowns, and so you descend to us with them. ——And then on the other hand, there's my master!——Because he chooses to live upon the principal of his health, and so run out his whole stock as fast as he can, he must have my company with him in his devil's dance to the other world! Never at home till three, four, five, six in the morning.

MUSLIN. Ay, a vile ungrateful man! Always ranging abroad, and no regard for a wife that doats upon him. And your love for me is all of a piece. I have no patience with you both; a couple of false, perfidious, abandoned profligates.

WILLIAM. Hey! Where is your tongue running? My master, as the world goes, is a good sort of a civil kind of a husband; and I, heaven help me! a poor simpleton of a constant, amorous puppy, who bear with all the whims of my little tyrant here. Come and kiss me, you jade, come and kiss me.

MUSLIN. Paws off, Caesar. Don't think to make me your dupe. I know when you go with him to this new lady, this Bath acquaintance; and I know you are as false as my master, and give all my dues to your Mrs. Mignionet there.

WILLIAM. Hush! not a word of that. I am ruined, pressed, and sent on board a tender directly if you blab that I trusted you with that secret.——But to charge me with falsehood!——Injustice and ingratitude.——My master, to be sure, does drink an agreeable dish of tea with the Widow. He has been there every evening this month past. How long things are to be in this train, Heaven only knows. But he does visit there, and I attend him. I ask my master, "Sir," says I, "what time will you please to want me?" He fixes the hour, and I strut by Mrs. Mignionet, without so much as tipping her a single glance. She stands watering at the mouth, and "A pretty fellow that," says she. "Ay, gaze on," say I, "gaze on: I know what you would be at: you would be glad to have me." But sour grapes, my dear; and so home I come, to cherish my own lovely little wanton: you know I do, and after toying with thee, I fly back to my master, later indeed than he appoints, but always too soon for him. He is loth to part: he lingers and dangles, and I stand cooling my heels. Oh! to the devil I pitch such a life.

MUSLIN. Why don't you strive to reclaim the vile man?

WILLIAM. Softly; not so fast. I have my talent, to be sure; yes, I must acknowledge some talent. But can you suppose that I have power to turn the drift of his inclinations? Can I give him a new taste, and lead him as I please? And to whom? To his wife? Ridiculous! A wife has no attraction now; the spring of the passions flies back; it won't do.

MUSLIN. Fine talking! And you admire yourself for it, don't you? Can you proceed, Sir?

WILLIAM. I tell you a wife is out-of-date: the time was, but that's all over; a wife is a drug now; mere tar-water, with every virtue under heaven, but nobody takes it.

MUSLIN. Have done, or I'll print these ten nails upon your rogue's face.

WILLIAM. Come and kiss me, I say.

MUSLIN. A fiddlestick for your kisses, while you encourage your master to open rebellion against the best of wives.

WILLIAM. I tell you it's all her own fault. Why does not she study to please him as you do me? Come, and throw your arms about my neck.

MUSLIN. As I used to do, Mr. Impudence?

WILLIAM. Then I must force you to your own good. (*Kisses her*) Pregnant with delight! Egad, if my master was not in the next room ——(*Bell rings*)

MUSLIN. Hush! My lady's bell: how long has he been up?

WILLIAM. He has been up——(*Kisses her*) 'Sdeath! You have set me all on fire. (*Kisses her*)

MUSLIN. There, there; have done now; the bell rings again. What must I say? When did he come home?

WILLIAM. He came home——(*Kisses her*) he came home at five

this morning; damned himself for a blockhead. (*Kisses*) Went to bed in a surly humour; was tired of himself and everybody else. (*Bell rings, he kisses her*) And he is now in tiptop spirits with Sir Brilliant Fashion in that room yonder.

MUSLIN. Sir Brilliant Fashion? I wish my lady would mind what he says to her——you great bear! You have given me such a flush in my face! (*Takes a pocket looking glass*) I look pretty well, I think. There (*Kisses him*), have done, and let me be gone.

Exit.

WILLIAM. There goes high and low life contrasted in one person. She has not dived to the bottom of my master's secrets; that's one good thing. What she knows, she'll blab. We shall hear of this widow from Bath. But the plot lies deeper than they are aware of. Enquire they will; and let 'em, say I; their answer will do 'em no good. "Mr. Lovemore visit the Widow Bellmour! We know no such person." That's what they'll get for their pains. Their puzzle will be greater than ever, and they may sit down to chew the cud of disappointed malice.——Hush! My master and Sir Brilliant: I'll take care of a single rogue, and get me out of their way.

Exit.

Enter LOVEMORE *and* SIR BRILLIANT.

LOVEMORE. My dear Sir Brilliant, I must both pity and laugh at you. Thou art metamorphosed into the most whimsical being!

SIR BRILLIANT. If your raillery diverts you, go on with it. This is always the case: apply for sober advice, and your friend plays you off with a joke.

LOVEMORE. Sober advice! Very far gone indeed. There is no such thing as talking soberly to the tribe of lovers. That eternal absence of mind that possesses you all! There is no society with you. I was damnable company myself when I was one of the pining herd: but a dose of matrimony has cooled me pretty handsomely; and here comes *repetatur haustus*.[24]

---

[24] Let the draft [that cools me in regard to matrimony] be repeated.

Enter MUSLIN.

MUSLIN. My lady sends her compliments, and begs to know how you do this morning.

LOVEMORE. (*Aside to Sir Brilliant*) The novelty of the compliment is enlivening——it is the devil to be teased in this manner.—— What did you say, child?

MUSLIN. My lady hopes you find yourself well this morning.

LOVEMORE. Ay, your lady:——give her my compliments, and tell her——tell her I hope she is well, and——(*Yawns*)

MUSLIN. She begs you won't think of going out without seeing her.

LOVEMORE. To be sure, she has such variety every time one sees her——my head aches woefully——tell your lady——I shall be glad to see her; I'll wait on her——(*Yawns*) tell her what you will.

MUSLIN. [*Aside*] A brute!——I shall let my lady know, Sir.

Exit.

LOVEMORE. My dear Sir Brilliant, you see me an example before your eyes. Put the Widow Bellmour out of your head, and let my Lord Etheridge be the victim for you.

SIR BRILLIANT. Positively no; my pride is piqued. My Lord Etheridge shall find me a more formidable rival than he imagines. By the way, how long has the noble peer been in England?

LOVEMORE. His motions are unknown to me.——(*Aside*) I don't like that question.——His Lordship is in France, is not he?

SIR BRILLIANT. No; he is certainly returned. The match is to be concluded privately.——He visits her *incog*.

LOVEMORE. (*Forcing a laugh*) Oh! no; that can't be; my Lord Etheridge loves parade. I cannot help laughing. The jealousy of you lovers is forever conjuring up phantoms to torment yourselves. My dear Sir Brilliant, wait for realities; there are enough in life, and you may teach your fancy to be at rest and give you no further trouble.

SIR BRILLIANT. Nay, don't let your fancy run away with you. What I tell you, is the real truth.

LOVEMORE. Well, if it be true, and if Lord Etheridge is come to England to marry, do you go to France not to marry, and you will have the best of the bargain.

Enter WILLIAM.

WILLIAM. Sir Bashful Constant is in his chariot at the upper end of the street, and if your Honour is at leisure, he will wait upon you.

LOVEMORE. Have not I sent him word I should be at home? Let him come as soon as he will. (*Exit William*) Another instance, Sir Brilliant, to deter you from all thoughts of matrimony.

SIR BRILLIANT. Po! Hang him; he is no precedent for me. A younger brother, who lived in middling life, comes to a title and an estate on the death of a consumptive baronet; marries a woman of quality, and now carries the primitive ideas of his narrow education into high life. Don't you remember when he had chambers in Fig Tree Court,[25] and used to saunter and lounge away his time in Temple coffeehouses? [26] The fellow is as dull as a bill in chancery.

LOVEMORE. But he is improved since that time.

SIR BRILLIANT. Impossible; don't you see how he goes on? He knows nothing of the world; if his eyes meet yours, he blushes up to his ears, and looks suspicious, as if he imagined you have a design upon him.

LOVEMORE. I can explain that part of his character. He has a mortal aversion to wit and raillery, and dreads nothing so much as being laughed at for being particular.

SIR BRILLIANT. And so, fearing to be ridiculous, he becomes substantially so every moment.

LOVEMORE. Even so, and if you look at him, he shrinks back from your observation, casting a sly, slow, jealous eye all round him, like Miss Bumpkin in a country village, awkwardly endeav-

---

[25] One of the courts of The Temple district of London.
[26] No section of London had more coffeehouses than that of the Inns of Court.

ouring to conceal what the increase of her shape discovers to the whole parish.

SIR BRILLIANT. And then his behaviour to his lady!

LOVEMORE. Why, as to that point, I don't think he hates her. His fear of ridicule may be at the bottom. He has strange notions about the dignity of a husband. There is a secret which he would fain tell me, and yet he is shy, and he hints, and he hesitates, and then he retreats back into himself, and ends just where he began. But with all his faults, he has fits of good nature. There;——his chariot's at the door.

SIR BRILLIANT. Lady Constant, you mean, has fits of good nature. Have you made any progress there?

LOVEMORE. That's well from you, who are the formidable man in that quarter.

SIR BRILLIANT. Oh! no; positively, no pretence, no colour for it.

LOVEMORE. Don't I know that you have made advances?

SIR BRILLIANT. Advances! I pity my Lady Constant, and——

LOVEMORE. Well, that's generous——hush! I hear him coming. Sir Brilliant, I admire your amorous charity of all things.

Enter SIR BASHFUL CONSTANT.

SIR BASHFUL. Mr. Lovemore, I have taken the liberty——but you seem to be busy, and I intrude perhaps.

LOVEMORE. Oh, by no means: walk in, Sir Bashful.

SIR BASHFUL. Sir Brilliant, I am glad to see you. (*Bows awkwardly*)

SIR BRILLIANT. You do me honour, Sir. I hope you left my Lady well.

SIR BASHFUL. I can't say, Sir; I am not her physician.

SIR BRILLIANT. (*Aside*) An absurd brute!——Lovemore, I'll just step and pay a short visit to our friend over the way.

LOVEMORE. Why in such a hurry?

SIR BRILLIANT. I shall return immediately. I'll be with you before you are dressed. Sir Bashful, I kiss your hand.

Exit.

SIR BASHFUL. I am glad he is gone. I have something, Mr. Lovemore, that I want to advise with you about.

LOVEMORE. Have you!

SIR BASHFUL. I have had another brush with my wife.

LOVEMORE. I am sorry for it, Sir Bashful.——(*Aside*) I am perfectly glad of it.

SIR BASHFUL. Pretty warm the quarrel was. She took it in a high tone. "Sir Bashful," says she, "I wonder you will disgrace yourself at this rate. You know my pin money is not sufficient. The mercer and everybody dunning me! I can't go on after this fashion," says she, and then something about her quality.——You know, Mr. Lovemore, (*Smiling*) she is a woman of high quality.

LOVEMORE. Yes, and a very fine woman.

SIR BASHFUL. No, no, no; not much of that——and yet——(*Looks at him and smiles*) Do you think her a fine woman?

LOVEMORE. Undoubtedly; where do you see anybody that outshines her?

SIR BASHFUL. Why, to be sure——(*Smiling*) one does not often see her eclipsed. I think she is what you may call a fine woman. She keeps good company.

LOVEMORE. The very best.

SIR BASHFUL. Yes, yes; your tiptop, none else. And yet to encourage her too far were dangerous. Too complying a husband makes but a sorry figure in the eyes of the world.

LOVEMORE. The world will talk, Sir Bashful.

SIR BASHFUL. Too fast, Mr. Lovemore. Their tongues will run on, and one does not like to give them a subject. I answered her stoutly: "Madam," says I, "a fig for your quality: I am master in my own house, and who do you think"——(*Winks at Lovemore*) putting myself in a passion, you know——"who do you think is to pay for your cats and your dogs, and your monkeys, and your squirrels, and your gaming debts?"

LOVEMORE. How could you? That was sharply said.

SIR BASHFUL. Yes; I gave it her. But for all that I am main good-natured at the bottom.

LOVEMORE. You was not in earnest then?

SIR BASHFUL. No, no; that's the point: a man must keep up his own dignity. I'll tell you what I did.

LOVEMORE. Well;——you did what's proper I dare say.

SIR BASHFUL. I hope you'll think so——don't laugh at me.—— Come, I will tell you. I went to her mercer slyly and paid him the money. (*Smiling*)

LOVEMORE. Did you?

SIR BASHFUL. (*Looking alarmed*) Was not it right?

LOVEMORE. It was elegant.

SIR BASHFUL. I am glad you approve. I took care to save appearances. One would not have the world know it.

LOVEMORE. By no means.

SIR BASHFUL. It would make them think me too uxorious.

LOVEMORE. So it would——(*Aside*) I must encourage that notion. While you live, guard against being too uxorious. Though our wives deserve "our fondness," [27] the world will laugh at us;——and hark ye, if our wives don't deserve it, they'll laugh at us the more.

SIR BASHFUL. I know it. And so says I, "Mr. Lutestring, there's your money; but tell nobody that I paid it slyly."

LOVEMORE. Why, that's doing a genteel thing by stratagem.—— Admirably contrived!

SIR BASHFUL. I think it was. But I have a deeper secret for you.

LOVEMORE. Have you?

SIR BASHFUL. I have.——May I trust you?

LOVEMORE. Now there you hurt me. I feel that, Sir Bashful.

SIR BASHFUL. I beg your pardon. I know you are my friend. I have great confidence in you. You must know——look ye, Mr. Lovemore,——you must know——

Enter MUSLIN.

MUSLIN. My lady desires to know if you choose a dish of tea this morning.

---

[27] Edward Young, *The Brothers* (1753) V.i.192. Added in 1785.

LOVEMORE. Po! Ridiculous!——Tell your mistress——go about your business. (*Turns her out*)

SIR BASHFUL. I see how it is. He does not care a cherry-stone for his wife. [*Aside*]

LOVEMORE. Such impertinence!——Well, Sir Bashful.

SIR BASHFUL. He does not value her a pinch of snuff. (*Aside*)

LOVEMORE. Well, I am all attention.

SIR BASHFUL. It does not signify. A foolish affair; I won't trouble you.

LOVEMORE. Nay, that's unkind. It will be no trouble.

SIR BASHFUL. Well, well, I——I——do you think Muslin did not overhear us?

LOVEMORE. Not a syllable. Come, we are safe.

SIR BASHFUL. I don't know but——let me ask you a question, first. ——Have you any regard for your lady?

LOVEMORE. The highest value for her. But then you know appearances——

SIR BASHFUL. Right!——I repose it with you.——You must know, Mr. Lovemore, as I told you, I am at the bottom very good-natured, and though it may be thought——we are interrupted again.

Enter SIR BRILLIANT.

SIR BRILLIANT. Lovemore, I have paid my visit.

LOVEMORE. Pshaw!——This is unlucky.——You are as good as your word, Sir Brilliant.

SIR BRILLIANT. Perhaps you have business?

SIR BASHFUL. No, no business——(*Turns to Lovemore*) there's no proceeding now——I was going, Sir Brilliant. Mr. Lovemore, I wish you a good day.

LOVEMORE. Po! Prithee, you shan't leave me yet.

SIR BASHFUL. I must; I can't stay. (*Aside to Lovemore*) Another time. Suppose you call at my house at one o'clock.

LOVEMORE. With all my heart.

SIR BASHFUL. Do so; nobody shall interrupt us. Mr. Lovemore, I take my leave. Sir Brilliant, I kiss your hand. You won't forget, Mr. Lovemore.

LOVEMORE. Oh! no; depend upon me

SIR BASHFUL. A good morning. He is the only friend I have.

Exit.

LOVEMORE. Ha! ha! You broke in in the most critical moment. He was just going to be delivered of his secret.

SIR BRILLIANT. I beg your pardon. How could you let me?

LOVEMORE. Nay, no matter. I shall worm it out of him.

Enter MUSLIN.

MUSLIN. My lady, Sir, is quite impatient.

LOVEMORE. Po! For ever teasing! I'll wait upon her presently.

Exit MUSLIN.

SIR BRILLIANT. I'll step and chat with her while you dress. May I take the liberty?

LOVEMORE. You know you may: no ceremony. How could you ask me such a question?——Apropos, Sir Brilliant; I want a word with you. Step with me into the study for a moment.

SIR BRILLIANT. I attend you.

LOVEMORE. Poor Sir Bashful!——Ha! ha!——A ridiculous, unac-countable——what does he mean?

Exeunt.

SCENE [II]

Another Apartment

Mrs. Lovemore at her tea-table.

MRS. LOVEMORE. This trash of tea! I don't know why I drink so much of it. Heigh-ho——What keeps Muslin? Surely never was an unhappy woman treated with such cruel indifference; nay, with such open, such undisguised insolence of gallantry.

Enter MUSLIN.

MRS. LOVEMORE. Well, Muslin? Have you seen his prime minister?

MUSLIN. Yes, Ma'am, I have seen Mr. William. He says his master is going out, according to the old trade, and he does not expect to see him again till tomorrow morning. Mr. Lovemore is now in the study. Sir Brilliant Fashion is with him: I heard them, as I passed by the door, laughing as loud as two actors in a comedy.

MRS. LOVEMORE. About some precious mischief, I'll be sworn, and all at my cost. Heigh-ho!

MUSLIN. Dear Ma'am, why chagrin yourself about a vile man, that is not worth——no, as I hope for mercy, not worth a single sigh?

MRS. LOVEMORE. What can I do, Muslin?

MUSLIN. Do, Ma'am——if I was as you, I'd do for him. If I could not cure my grief, I'd find some comfort, that's what I would.

MRS. LOVEMORE. Comfort? Alas; there is none for me.

MUSLIN. And whose fault then?——Would anybody but you—— it provokes me to think of it——would any but you——young, handsome, with wit, graces, talents, would anybody with so many accomplishments sit at home here, as melancholy as a poor servant out of place?——And all for what? For a husband? And such a husband! What do you think the world will say of you, Ma'am?

MRS. LOVEMORE. I care not what they say. I am tired of the world, and the world may be tired of me if it will. My troubles are to myself only, and I must endeavour to bear them. Who knows what patience may do? If Mr. Lovemore has any feeling left, my conduct and his own heart may one day incline him to do me justice.

MUSLIN. But, dear Ma'am, that's waiting for dead men's shoes.[28] Incline him to do you justice!——What signifies expecting and expecting? Give me a bird in the hand. If all the women in London

---

[28] Waiting for another's death in order to inherit his wealth.

who happen to be in your case were to sit down and die of the spleen, what would become of the public places? They might turn Vauxhall [29] to a hop-garden; make a brewhouse of Ranelagh,[30] and let both the playhouses to a Methodist preacher. We should not have the racketting [31] we have now. "John, let the horses be put to." ——"John, go to my Lady Trump-abouts, and invite her to a small party of twenty or thirty card tables."——"John, run to my Lady Catgut, and let her know I'll wait upon her Ladyship to the opera." ——"John, run as fast as ever you can, with my compliments to Mr. Varney,[32] and tell him it will be the death of me if I have not a box for the new play."——Lord bless you, Ma'am, they rantipole it about this town, with as unconcerned looks, and as florid outsides, as if they were treated at home like so many goddesses; though everybody knows possession has ungoddessed them all long ago, and their husbands care no more for them, no, by jingo, no more than they do for their husbands.

MRS. LOVEMORE. At what a rate you run on!

MUSLIN. It is enough to make a body run on. If everybody thought like you, Ma'am——

MRS. LOVEMORE. If everybody loved like me!

MUSLIN. A brass thimble for love if it is not returned by love. What the deuce is here to do? Love for love is something: but to love alone, where's the good of that? Shall I go and fix my heart upon a man, who shall despise me for that very reason? And, "Ay," says he, "poor fool! I see she adores me. The woman's well enough, only she has one inconvenient circumstance about her; I am married to her, and marriage is the devil."

MRS. LOVEMORE. Will you have done?

MUSLIN. I have not half done, Ma'am. And when the vile man goes a roguing, he smiles impudently in your face, "And I am going

---

[29] Vauxhall pleasure gardens were south of the Thames.

[30] The somewhat more fashionable Ranelagh gardens were north of the Thames near Chelsea.

[31] The whirl of social life.

[32] Varney, the housekeeper, was in charge of the advance sale of tickets at Drury Lane Theatre.

to the chocolate house, my dear; amuse yourself in the meantime, my love." Fie upon 'em; I know 'em all. Give me a husband that will enlarge the circle of my innocent pleasures; but a husband nowadays is no such a thing. A husband now is nothing but a scarecrow, to show you the fruit, but touch it if you dare. The devil's in 'em, the Lord forgive me for swearing. A husband is a mere bugbear, a snap-dragon,[33] a monster; that is to say, if one makes him so, then he is a monster indeed; and if one does not make him so, then he behaves like a monster; and of the two evils, by my troth——but here, Ma'am, here comes one who can tell you all about it. Here comes Sir Brilliant: ask his advice, Ma'am.

MRS. LOVEMORE. His advice?——Ask advice of the man who has estranged Mr. Lovemore's affections from me?

MUSLIN. Well I protest and vow, I think Sir Brilliant a very pretty gentleman. He is the very pink of the fashion. He dresses fashionably, lives fashionably, wins your money fashionably, loses his own fashionably, and does everything fashionably; and then he looks so lively, and so much to say, and so never at a loss!—— But here he comes.

Enter SIR BRILLIANT.

SIR BRILLIANT. Mrs. Lovemore, my dear Ma'am, always in a *vis-à-vis* party with your *suivante?* [34]——Afford me your pardon if I say this does a little wear the appearance of being out of humour with the world.

MRS. LOVEMORE. Far from it, Sir Brilliant. We were engaged in your panegyric.

SIR BRILLIANT. My panegyric? Then am I come most apropos to give the portrait a few finishing touches. Mr. Lovemore, as soon as he is dressed, will wait upon you: in the meantime, I can help you to some anecdotes, which will enable you to colour your canvas a little higher.

[33] A pageant dragon that snapped its jaws—that is, a bugbear.
[34] Waiting maid.

MRS. LOVEMORE. Among those anecdotes, I hope you will not omit the bright exploit of seducing Mr. Lovemore from all domestic happiness. (*She makes a sign to Muslin to go*)

SIR BRILLIANT. I, Madam?——Let me perish if ever——

MRS. LOVEMORE. Oh! Sir, I can make my observations.

SIR BRILLIANT. May fortune eternally forsake me, and beauty frown on me, if I am conscious of any plot upon earth.

MRS. LOVEMORE. Don't assert too strongly, Sir Brilliant.

SIR BRILLIANT. May I never throw a winning cast——

MRS. LOVEMORE. It is in vain to deny it, Sir.

SIR BRILLIANT. May I lose the next sweepstakes if I have ever, in thought, word or deed, been accessary to his infidelity. I alienate the affections of Mr. Lovemore! Consider, Madam, how would this tell in Westminster Hall? [35] Sir Brilliant Fashion, what say you, guilty of this indictment or not guilty? Not guilty, *poss.*[36] Thus issue is joined. You enter the court: but, my dear Madam, veil those graces that adorn your person: abate the fire of those charms: so much beauty will corrupt the judges: give me a fair trial.

MRS. LOVEMORE. And thus you think to laugh it away.

SIR BRILLIANT. Nay, hear me out. You appear in court: you charge the whole upon me, without a syllable as to the how, when, and where? No proof positive; the prosecution ends, and I begin my defence.

MRS. LOVEMORE. And by playing these false colours you think I am to be amused?

SIR BRILLIANT. Nay, Mrs. Lovemore, I am now upon my defence. Only hear.——You will please to consider, Gentlemen of the Jury, that Mr. Lovemore is not a minor, nor I his guardian. He loves gaiety, pleasure, and enjoyment: is it my fault? He is possessed of talents and a taste for pleasure, which he knows how to gratify: can I restrain him? He knows the world, makes the most of life, and plucks the fruit that grows around him: am I to blame? This is the whole affair.——How say you, Gentlemen of the Jury?——Not Guilty. There, you see how it is. I have cleared myself.

---

[35] Still the main seat of justice in the eighteenth century.

[36] Latin possessor, the defendant in a suit.

MRS. LOVEMORE. Brisk, lively, and like yourself, Sir Brilliant! But if you can imagine this bantering way——

SIR BRILLIANT. Acquitted by my country, Ma'am; fairly acquitted.

MRS. LOVEMORE. After the very edifying counsel which you give to Mr. Lovemore, this loose strain is not in the least surprising. And, Sir, your late project——

SIR BRILLIANT. My late project!

MRS. LOVEMORE. Your late project, Sir. Not content with leading Mr. Lovemore into a thousand scenes of dissipation, you have introduced him lately to your mistress Bellmour. You understand me, Sir.

SIR BRILLIANT. Ma'am, he does not so much as know the Widow Bellmour.

MRS. LOVEMORE. Nay, Sir Brilliant, have a care: justify it if you can, or give it a turn of wit. There is no occasion to hazard yourself too far.

SIR BRILLIANT. Falsehood I disdain, Madam, and I, Sir Brilliant Fashion, declare that Mr. Lovemore is not acquainted with the Widow Bellmour. And if he was, what then? Do you know the lady?

MRS. LOVEMORE. I know her, Sir? A person of that character?

SIR BRILLIANT. Oh!——I see you don't know her: but I will let you into her whole history.——Pray be seated——you shall know her whole history, and then judge for yourself. The Widow Bellmour, Madam——

LOVEMORE. (*Within*) William, are the horses put to?

SIR BRILLIANT. We are interrupted.

Enter LOVEMORE.

LOVEMORE. Very well: let the carriage be brought round directly. ——How do you do, my dear?——Sir Brilliant, I beg your pardon. ——My love, you don't answer me: how do you do this morning? (*With an air of cold civility*)

MRS. LOVEMORE. A little indisposed in mind: but indisposition of the mind is of no consequence: nobody pities it.

LOVEMORE. I beg your pardon, Mrs. Lovemore. Indisposition of the mind—— Sir Brilliant, that's a mighty pretty ring on your finger.

SIR BRILLIANT. A bauble: will you look at it? (*Gives the ring*)

MRS. LOVEMORE. Though I have but few obligations to Sir Brilliant, I suppose I am to ascribe to him the favour of this visit, Mr. Lovemore.

LOVEMORE. (*Looking at the ring, and laughing*) Now there you wrong me.——Your enquiries about my health have been very obliging this morning, and I came to return the compliment before I go out.——It is set very neatly. (*Gives back the ring*)

MRS. LOVEMORE. Are you going out, Sir?

LOVEMORE. A matter of business.——How I do hate business!—— But business (*Examining his ruffles*)——business must be done.—— Pray is there any news?——Any news, my dear?

MRS. LOVEMORE. It would be news to me, Sir, if you would be kind enough to let me know whether I may expect the favour of your company at dinner today.

LOVEMORE. It would be impertinent in me to answer such a question, for I can give no direct answer to it.——I am the slave of events; just as things happen; perhaps I may; perhaps not. But don't let me be of any inconvenience to you. Is it material where a body eats?——Have you heard what happened to me? (*Aside to Sir Brilliant*)

SIR BRILLIANT. When and where?

LOVEMORE. A word in your ear——with your permission, Ma'am?

MRS. LOVEMORE. That cold contemptuous civility, Mr. Lovemore——

LOVEMORE. Po! prithee now, how can you?——That is very peevish and very ill-natured.——(*Turning to Sir Brilliant*) I lost everything I played for after you went. The foreigner and he understand one another.——I beg your pardon, Mrs. Lovemore; it was only about an affair at the opera.

MRS. LOVEMORE. The opera or anything is more agreeable than my company.

LOVEMORE. Now there again you wrong me. (*To Sir Brilliant*) We dine at the St. Alban's.[37]——How can you, Mrs. Lovemore? I make it a point not to incommode you. You possibly may have some private party; and it would be unpolite in me to obstruct your schemes of pleasure. Would not it, Sir Brilliant?

SIR BRILLIANT. Oh!——Gothic to the last degree!

LOVEMORE. Very true; vulgar and mechanic! (*Both stand laughing*)

MRS. LOVEMORE. Go on; make sport for yourselves, gentlemen.

LOVEMORE. Ho! ho! ho! I am sore with laughing.——If you, Madam, have arranged an agreeable party, for me to be present, it would look as if we lived together like Sir Bashful Constant and his lady, who are always, like two gamecocks, ready armed to goad and spur one another. Hey! Sir Brilliant?

SIR BRILLIANT. Oh! the very thing: or like Sir Theodore Traffic at Tunbridge taking his wife under the arm in the public rooms, and "Come along home, I tell you."

LOVEMORE. Exactly so. (*Both continue laughing*) Odds my life! I shall be beyond my time. (*Looks at his watch*) Any commands into the City, my dear?

MRS. LOVEMORE. Commands!——No, Sir, I have no commands.

LOVEMORE. I have an appointment at my banker's. Sir Brilliant, you know old Discount?

SIR BRILLIANT. He that was in Parliament, and had the large contract?

LOVEMORE. The same: Entire Butt,[38] I think, was the name of his borough. Can I set you down?

SIR BRILLIANT. No, my carriage waits. I shall rattle half the town over presently.

LOVEMORE. As you will. Sir Brilliant will entertain you, Ma'am. Au revoir, my love.——Sir Brilliant, yours.——Who waits there?

Exit singing.

---

[37] The fashionable St. Alban's Tavern was near Pall Mall.

[38] A secluded small piece of ground!

SIR BRILLIANT. *Bon voyage.*——You see, Madam, that I don't deprive you of his company.

MRS. LOVEMORE. Your influence is now unnecessary. It is grown habitual to him: he will drive to your Mrs. Bellmour, I suppose.

SIR BRILLIANT. Apropos; that brings us back to the little history I was going to give you of that lady. What is your charge against her? That she is amiable? Granted. Young, gay, rich, handsome, with enchanting talents, it is no wonder all the pretty fellows are on their knees to her. Her manner so entertaining! That quickness of transition from one thing to another! That round of variety! And every new attitude does so become her; and she has such a feeling heart, and with an air of giddiness so nice a conduct!

MRS. LOVEMORE. Mighty well, Sir: she is a very vestal. Finish your portrait. A vestal from your school of painting must be a curiosity.——But how comes it, Sir, if she is this wonder, that your honourable proposals are at an end there?

SIR BRILLIANT. Compulsion, Ma'am: it is not voluntary. My Lord Etheridge is the happy man. I thought he was out of the kingdom; but his Lordship is with her ev'ry evening. I can scarce gain admittance; and so all that remains for me, is to do justice to the lady, and console myself in the best way I can for the insufficiency of my pretensions.

MRS. LOVEMORE. And am I to believe all this?

SIR BRILLIANT. May the first woman I pay my addresses to, strike me to the centre with a supercilious eyebrow, if every syllable is not minutely true.——So that you see, I am not the cause of your inquietude.——There is not in the world a person who more earnestly aspires to prove the tender esteem he bears you.——I have long panted for an opportunity——by all that's soft she listens to me (*Aside*)——I have long panted, Ma'am, for a tender moment like this——

MRS. LOVEMORE. (*Looking gravely at him*) Sir!

SIR BRILLIANT. I have panted with all the ardour which charms like yours must kindle in every heart——

MRS. LOVEMORE. (*Walks away*) This liberty, Sir——

SIR BRILLIANT. Consider, Madam: we have both cause of discontent; both disappointed; both crossed in love; and the least we can do is both to join, and sweeten each other's cares.

MRS. LOVEMORE. And your friend, Sir, who has just left you——

SIR BRILLIANT. He, Madam, for a long time——I have seen it, with vexation seen it——yes, he has long been false to honour, love, and you.

MRS. LOVEMORE. Sir Brilliant, I have done. You take my wrongs too much to heart, Sir——(*Rings a bell*)

SIR BRILLIANT.

> "Those eyes that tell us what the sun is made of;
> Those hills of driven snow!"——[39]

MRS. LOVEMORE. Will nobody answer there?

Enter MUSLIN.

SIR BRILLIANT. Madam, I desist: when you are in better humour, recollect what I have said. Your adorer takes his leave.——(*Aside*) Sir Brilliant, mind your hits, and her strait-laced virtue will surrender at last.——Madam—— (*Bows respectfully; exit.*)

MUSLIN. As I live and breathe, Ma'am, if I was as you, I would not fluster myself about it.

MRS. LOVEMORE. About what?

MUSLIN. What signifies mincing the matter? I heard it all.

MRS. LOVEMORE. You did? did you? (*Looks angrily*)

MUSLIN. Ma'am!

MRS. LOVEMORE. Impertinence! (*Walks about*) Oh! Mr. Lovemore!——To make his character public, and render him the topic of every tea table throughout this town: I must avoid that.

MUSLIN. What the deuce is here to do?——An unmannerly thing, for to go for to huff me in this manner! (*Aside*)

MRS. LOVEMORE. That would only widen the breach, and instead of neglect, might call forth resentment, and settle at last into a fixed aversion: lawyers, parting, and separate maintenance!—— What must be done?

---

[39] Edward Young, *The Revenge* (1721) I.i.142,144. Added in 1785.

MUSLIN. [*Aside*] What is she thinking of now?——A sulky thing, not to be more familiar with such a friend as I am.——Did you speak to me, Ma'am?

MRS. LOVEMORE. It may succeed: suppose I try it.——Muslin.

MUSLIN. Ma'am. (*Running to her*)

MRS. LOVEMORE. You heard Sir Brilliant say that Mr. Lovemore is not acquainted with the Widow?

MUSLIN. Lard, Ma'am, he is as full of tricks as a French milliner. I know he does visit there: I know it from William. I'll be hanged in my own garters if he does not.

MRS. LOVEMORE. I know not what to do. Let my chair be got ready.

MUSLIN. Your chair, Ma'am!——Are you going out?

MRS. LOVEMORE. Let me hear no more questions: do as I order you.

Exit.

MUSLIN. Which way is the wind now? No matter; she does not know what she'd be at. If she would but take my advice——go abroad, visit everywhere, see the world, throw open her doors, give balls, assemblies, concerts; sing, dance, dress, spend all her money, run in debt, ruin her husband; there would be some sense in that: the man would stay at home then to quarrel with her. She would have enough of his company. But no; mope, mope for ever; heigh-ho! tease, tease. "Muslin, step to William; where's his master? When did he come home? How long has he been up?" A fine life truly!——I love to be in the fashion, for my part. Bless me, I had like to have forgot. Mrs. Marmalet comes to my rout tonight. She might as well stay away: she is nothing but meer lumber. The formal thing won't play higher than shilling whist. How the devil does she think I can make a shilling party for her? There is no such a thing nowadays; nobody plays shilling whist now, unless I was to invite the tradespeople: but I shan't let myself down for Madam Marmalet, that I promise her.

End of the FIRST ACT

ACT the SECOND
SCENE [I]

An Apartment at Sir Bashful Constant's

Enter SIR BASHFUL.

SIR BASHFUL. Did not I hear a rap at the door? Yes, yes, I did; I am right. The carriage is just now driving away. Who answers there? Sideboard; step hither, Sideboard. I must know who it is: my wife keeps the best company in England. Hold, I must be wary. Servants love to pry into their masters' secrets.

Enter SIDEBOARD.

SIR BASHFUL. Whose carriage was that at the door?
SIDEBOARD. The Dutchess of Hurricane, your Honour.
SIR BASHFUL. The Dutchess of Hurricane? (*Walks aside and smiles*) A woman of great rank!——What did she want?
SIDEBOARD. She has left this card for my Lady.
SIR BASHFUL. A card? Let me see it. (*Reads*) "The Dutchess of Hurricane presents compliments to Lady Constant. She has left the hounds and the foxes, and the brutes that gallop after them, to their own dear society for the rest of the winter. Her Grace keeps Wednesdays at Hurricane House [40] for the rest of the winter."——Make me thankful, here's a card from a dutchess!——What have you there?
SIDEBOARD. A parcel of cards, that have been left here this morning.
SIR BASHFUL. All these in one morning? (*Looks at them*) Why I may as well keep an inn; may as well keep the coach and horses in Piccadilly. (*Reads fast*) "Lady Riot"——"Mrs. Allnight"——

---

[40] A hurricane is a large private reception.

"The Dutchess of Carmine"——look ye there, another dutchess! "Lady Basset" [41]——"Lord Pleurisie"——"The Countess of Ratifie" [42]——"Sir Richard Lungs"——"Lord Laudanum"——"Sir Charles Valerian" [43]——"Lady Hectick"——"Lady Mary Gabble" ——I can't bear all this, Sideboard——(*Aside and smiling*) I can't bear the pleasure of it: all people of tiptop condition to visit my wife!

Enter FURNISH.

SIR BASHFUL. What's the matter, Furnish?

FURNISH. The matter, Sir?——Nothing's the matter.

SIR BASHFUL. What are you about? Where are you going? What have you to do now?

FURNISH. Only to tell the chairmen they must take Black George with his flambeau with them this evening, and carry the chair to pay visits for my Lady.

SIR BASHFUL. An empty chair to pay visits!——What polite ways people of fashion have got of being intimate with each other!—— (*Aside*) Absurd as it is, I am glad to see my wife keep pace with the best of them. I laugh at it, and yet I like it.——Wounds! I shall be found out by my servants.——I tell you, Sideboard, and you Mrs. Busy Body, that your mistress leads a life of noise and hurry, and cards and dice, and vanity, and nonsense, and I am resolved to bear it no longer.——Don't I hear her coming?

FURNISH. My Lady is coming, Sir.

SIR BASHFUL. (*Aside and smiling*) She looks charmingly.——Now I'll tell her roundly a piece of my mind. You shall see who commands in this house.

Enter LADY CONSTANT.

---

[41] Basset was a popular eighteenth-century card game resembling the later faro.

[42] Ratafia is a liqueur with almond flavor.

[43] Valerian is a drug used as a carminative and sedative.

SIR BASHFUL. (*Steals a look*) I could almost give up the point when I look at her.——So, Madam, I have had my house full of duns again today.

LADY CONSTANT. Obliging creatures, to call so often. What did they want?

SIR BASHFUL. Want!——What should they want but money?

LADY CONSTANT. And you paid them, I suppose.

SIR BASHFUL. You suppose!——'sdeath, Madam, what do you take me for?

LADY CONSTANT. I took you for a husband: my brother prescribed you. But his prescription has done me no good.

SIR BASHFUL. Nor me either: I have had a bitter pill of it.

LADY CONSTANT. But the pill was gilded for you. My fortune, I take it, has paid off the old family mortgage on your estate.

SIR BASHFUL. And at the rate you go on, a new mortgage will swallow up my estate.——I see you are an ungrateful woman.

LADY CONSTANT. That is, as you keep the account.

SIR BASHFUL. And my accounts will show it. Day after day nothing but extravagance to gratify your vanity. Did not I go into Parliament to please you? Did not I go down to the Borough of Smoke and Sot, and get drunk there for a whole month together? Did not I get mobbed at the George and Vulture? And pelted and horsewhipped the day before the election? And was not I obliged to steal out of the town in a rabbit-cart? [44] And all this to be somebody as you call it? Did not I stand up in the house to make a speech to show what an orator you had married? And did not I expose myself? Did I know whether I stood upon my head or my heels for half an hour together? And did not a great man from the Treasury-bench tell me never to speak again?

LADY CONSTANT. And why not take his advice?

SIR BASHFUL. What in the name of common sense had I to do in Parliament? My country! What's my country to me? The debts of the nation, and your gaming debts are nothing to me. I must help to pay both, must I? I can vote against taxes, and I can advertize in the

[44] A small, inelegant cart.

Gazette [45] to secure me from your extravagance. I have not lived in the Temple [46] for nothing.

FURNISH. He slept there, and calls it studying the law.

SIR BASHFUL. Hold you your tongue, Mrs. Pert: leave the room. Go both about your business.

Exeunt FURNISH *and* SIDEBOARD.

SIR BASHFUL. (*Aside*) I have kept it up before my servants. (*Looks at Lady Constant*) She is a fine woman after all.

LADY CONSTANT. Is there never to be an end of this usage, Sir? Am I to be for ever made unhappy by your humours.

SIR BASHFUL. Humours! Good sense and sound judgment, in the fine lady's dictionary, are to be called humours.

LADY CONSTANT. And your humours are now grown insupportable.

SIR BASHFUL. Your profusion is insupportable. At the rate you go on, how am I to find money for my next election?——If you would but talk this matter over coolly——(*Aside*) she talks like an angel, and I wish I could say the same of myself.——What will the world think?——Only command your temper——what will they think, if I am seen to encourage your way of life?

LADY CONSTANT. Amuse yourself that way, Sir.——Avoid one error and run into the opposite extreme.

SIR BASHFUL. (*Aside*) There; a translation from Horace——*Dum vitant stulti vitia.*[47]——She is a notable woman.

LADY CONSTANT. Let me tell you, there is not in life a more ridiculous sight than the person who guards, with imaginary wisdom, against one giant-vice and leaves himself open to a million of absurdities.

SIR BASHFUL. (*Aside*) I am nothing to her in an argument——she has a tongue that can reason me out of my senses.——I could almost find it in my heart to tell her the whole truth.——You know, my Lady Constant, that when you want anything in reason——

LADY CONSTANT. Is it unreasonable to live with decency? Is it un-

---

[45] The *London Gazette* was a semiweekly newspaper.
[46] An Inn of Court, a set of buildings for law students and lawyers.
[47] *Satirae* I.2.24. While fools shun vices.

reasonable to keep the company my rank and education have entitled me to? Is it unreasonable to conform to the modes of life when your fortune can so well afford it?

SIR BASHFUL. (*Aside*) She is a very reasonable woman, and I wish I had but half her sense.——You know I am good-natured in the main, and if a sum of money within a moderate compass——if a brace of hundreds—— (*Aside*) why should not I make it three?——I know that you have contracted habits of life, and (*In a softened tone*) habit I know is not easily conquered: and if three (*Smiling*) hundred pounds will prevent disputes, why, why (*Smiling*), as to the matter of three hundred pounds——

Enter FURNISH, *with a Bandbox.*

FURNISH. Your Ladyship's things from the milliner's.

SIR BASHFUL. Death and fury! This woman has overheard me. Three hundred pounds, Madam! (*In a violent passion*) Let me tell you that three hundred pounds——what right have you to shovel away three hundred pounds?

LADY CONSTANT. Why does the man fly out into such a passion?

SIR BASHFUL. I will allow no such doings in my house. Don't I often come when my hall is besieged with a parcel of powder-monkey servants? And did not I the other day, before I could get into my own doors, entangle myself among the chairmen's poles, and was not I confined there, like a man in the stocks?

LADY CONSTANT. Why would you be so awkward?

SIR BASHFUL. An eternal scene of routs [48] and drums. [49] Have not I seen you put the fee simple of a score of my best acres upon a single card? And have not I muttered to myself, if that woman was as much in love with me as she is with pam, what an excellent wife she would make?

LADY CONSTANT. Pam is very obliging: why won't you strive to be as agreeable?

---

[48] Large evening parties.
[49] Noisy private assemblies in the world of fashion.

SIR BASHFUL. 'Sdeath, Madam, you are so fond of play that I should not wonder to see my next child marked on the forehead with a pair royal [50] of aces.

FURNISH. I am sure you deserve to be marked on the forehead with a pair of——[51]

SIR BASHFUL. Malapert hussy! Do you meddle? Begone this moment.

Exit FURNISH.

LADY CONSTANT. Fie upon it, Sir Bashful! I am tired of blushing for you.

SIR BASHFUL. I am afraid I have gone too far: she is ashamed of me. (*Aside*)

LADY CONSTANT. You agreed to a separation the other day, and there remains nothing but to execute articles, and make an end of all this disquiet.

SIR BASHFUL. A separate maintenance will go but a little way to answer the bawling of milliners, mercers, jewellers, and gaming debts.

LADY CONSTANT. It will purchase content, and nothing can obtain that under your roof.

SIR BASHFUL. (*Aside*) I have shot my bolt too far.——I fancy, my Lady Constant, that you don't know me. We might explain matters, and——'sdeath! (*Aside*) I am going to blab.——I say, Madam, if you understood me rightly——as to the authority of a husband, I might perhaps be brought to give it up, in part at least; and if nobody was the wiser, I might connive——po! confusion! Interrupted again by that——

Enter FURNISH.

FURNISH. A servant from Mrs. Lovemore, Madam, to know——

SIR BASHFUL. The authority of a husband I never will give up——

LADY CONSTANT. A storm, a whirlwind is fitter to converse with.

---

[50] Three cards of the same value.
[51] An allusion to the horns of the cuckold.

SIR BASHFUL. I will storm like a whirlwind in my own house. I have done, Madam; you are an ungovernable woman——(*Aside and smiling*) she is a charming woman, and if nobody saw it, I would let her govern me with all my heart.

Exit.

LADY CONSTANT. Did anybody ever see such behaviour?

FURNISH. Never, and how your Ladyship bears it, I can't tell.

LADY CONSTANT. That it should be my fate to be married to such a quicksand! What does Mrs. Lovemore say?

FURNISH. If your Ladyship will be at home, she intends to do herself the pleasure of waiting upon you, Madam.

LADY CONSTANT. Very well; I shall be at home. Upon recollection, I want to see her. Let the servant wait: I'll write an answer.

Exeunt.

SCENE [II]

Another Apartment

Enter SIR BASHFUL *and* LOVEMORE.

SIR BASHFUL. Walk in, Mr. Lovemore, walk in. I am heartily glad to see you. This is kind.

LOVEMORE. I am ready, you see, to attend the call of friendship.

SIR BASHFUL. Mr. Lovemore, you are a friend indeed.

LOVEMORE. You do me honour, Sir Bashful. And your Lady, how does she do?

SIR BASHFUL. Perfectly well: in great spirits. (*Smiling at Lovemore*) I never saw her look better: but we have had t'other skirmish since I saw you.

LOVEMORE. Another!

SIR BASHFUL. Ay, another; and I did not bate her an ace. She is a rare one to argue. She is fit to discuss a point with any man.—— Nobody like her. Wit at will; I thought I managed the dispute, and that I should soon have had her at what [52] you call a *non-plus*. But no, no; no such thing. She can give you a sharp turn in a moment.

LOVEMORE. Ay!

SIR BASHFUL. Give her her due, I am nothing to her. I thought I had her fast, but she went round me, quick as lightning; and would you believe it? (*Looks highly pleased*) She did not leave me a word to say.

LOVEMORE. Well! That was hard upon you.

SIR BASHFUL. No, not hard at all. Those little victories I don't mind. You know I told you I have something for your private ear. Have you observed nothing odd and singular in me?

LOVEMORE. Not in the least. In the whole circle of my acquaintance I know nobody so little tinged with oddity.

SIR BASHFUL. What, have you seen nothing? (*Laughs*) Have you remarked nothing particular in regard to my wife?

LOVEMORE. Why, you don't live happy with her: but that is not a singular case.

SIR BASHFUL. But I tell you——this must be in confidence——I am at the bottom a very odd fellow.

LOVEMORE. You do yourself injustice, Sir Bashful.

SIR BASHFUL. No, not in the least. It is too true——I am in the main a very odd fellow; I am indeed; as odd a fish as lives; and you must have seen it before now.

LOVEMORE. I see it?——I am not apt to spy defects in my friends. What can this be? You are not jealous, I hope.

SIR BASHFUL. You have not hit the right nail on the head. No, not jealous. Do her justice, I am safe as to that point. My Lady has high notions of honour. No, it is not that.

LOVEMORE. Not a ray of light to guide me: explain, Sir Bashful.

SIR BASHFUL. (*Smiling at him*) You could never have imagined it. But first let me shut this door.

LOVEMORE. (*Aside*) What whim has got possession of him now?

SIR BASHFUL. Mr. Lovemore, I have great dependence upon you. I am going to make a discovery——I blush at the very thought of it. (*Turns away*)

---

[52] 1785, 1787: "what"; 1786: "a what."

LOVEMORE. Be a man, Sir Bashful; out with it at once; let me advise you.

SIR BASHFUL. The very thing I want. The affair is——[*Aside*] but then if he should betray me!——Mr. Lovemore, I doubt you, and yet esteem you. Some men there are who, when a confidence is reposed in them, take occasion from thence to hold a hank over their friend, and tyrannize him all the rest of his days.

LOVEMORE. O fie! This is ungenerous. True friendship is of another quality: it feels from sympathy; honour is the active principle; and the strictest secrecy is an inviolable rule.

SIR BASHFUL. Mr. Lovemore, I have no further doubt——stay; did not you hear a noise?——Don't I see a shadow moving under the bottom of that door? (*Goes to the door*)

LOVEMORE. What has got into his head?

SIR BASHFUL. (*Looking out*) Servants have a way of listening.

LOVEMORE. Rank jealousy! He has it through the very brain!

SIR BASHFUL. No, no; all's safe. Mr. Lovemore, I will make you the depositary——the faithful depositary of a secret: let it pass from the bottom of my heart to the inmost recess of yours: there let it rest concealed from every prying eye.——My inclination——there ——I see a laugh already forming in every feature of your face.

LOVEMORE. Then my face is no true index of the mind. Were you to know the agitations in which you keep me by this suspense——

SIR BASHFUL. I believe it. To make an end at once, my inclinations are totally changed——no; not changed; but they are not what they seemed to be. Love is the passion that possesses me.——I am in love, and——(*Turns from him*) and I am ashamed of myself.

LOVEMORE. Ashamed! Love is a noble passion: but don't let me hear any more about it. Lady Constant will discover all, and then the blame will fall on me. If your heart revolts from her, don't let me be thought in league with you. You need not involve me in a quarrel with her Ladyship.

SIR BASHFUL. You don't take me right. You are wide, quite wide of the mark. Hear me out.

LOVEMORE. No, no more. You must excuse me.

SIR BASHFUL. You shall hear me. The object of my passion, this charming woman, whom I dote on to distraction——

LOVEMORE. Your pardon; I won't hear it.——(*Walks away from him*) When her Ladyship hears of his gallantry, the devil is in the dice if the spirit of revenge does not mould her to my purposes.

SIR BASHFUL. (*Following Lovemore*) I say, Mr. Lovemore, this adorable creature——

LOVEMORE. Keep your secret, Sir Bashful. (*Avoiding him*)

SIR BASHFUL. (*Following him*) Who looks so lovely in my eyes——

LOVEMORE. Well; I don't desire to know her.

SIR BASHFUL. You do know her. (*Following him*) This idol of my heart——is my own wife.

LOVEMORE. (*Stares at him*) Your own wife?

SIR BASHFUL. Yes, my own wife. (*Looks silly, and turns away*) It's all over with me: I am undone.

LOVEMORE. This is the most unexpected discovery.

SIR BASHFUL. Look ye there now; he laughs at me already.

LOVEMORE. (*Aside*) His wife must not know this. The grass is cut under my feet if she ever hears a word of it.

SIR BASHFUL. (*Aside*) He is struck with amazement, and does not say a word to me.

LOVEMORE. (*Aside*) I must not encourage him.——And can this be possible, Sir Bashful?——In love with your own wife!

SIR BASHFUL. Spare my confusion. I have made myself very ridiculous. (*Looks at him, and turns away*) I know I have.

LOVEMORE. Ridiculous? Far from it. Can it be wrong to love a valuable woman? Not to feel the impressions of beauty and of merit were downright insensibility; but then we should always admire with discretion. The folly of us married men consists in letting our wives perceive the vehemence with which we love; and the consequence is, we are enslaved for the rest of our lives.——I could trust you with a secret, which, perhaps, would keep you in countenance. Could you imagine it? I love my wife.

SIR BASHFUL. How?

LOVEMORE. I am in love with my wife.

SIR BASHFUL. Oh! no, no;——hey! (*Looking highly pleased*) You make me laugh. You don't love her, do you?

LOVEMORE. Passionately; tenderly; with all the ardour of affection.

SIR BASHFUL. Give me your hand. Ha! ha!——I did not expect this. This is some relief. Ha! ha!——you have made me happy. And have you led the life you have done all this time, on purpose to conceal your regard from her?

LOVEMORE. For that very purpose. I esteem her; I love her; but I would not have her know it.

SIR BASHFUL. No?

LOVEMORE. Upon no consideration, nor would I have the world know it.

SIR BASHFUL. Perfectly right.

LOVEMORE. To be sure. Tell your wife that you esteem her good qualities, and admire her person, she cries VICTORIA, falls to plundering, and then you must either break her chain, or wear it in the face of the world, a laughing stock for all your acquaintance.

SIR BASHFUL. That is what I have always been afraid of.

LOVEMORE. Not without reason. The world delights in ridicule. Do you know, if our secrets were to transpire, that we should have nothing but wit, raillery, and fleers, and taunts, flying about our ears?

SIR BASHFUL. But I have taken good care. I have quarrelled with my Lady ten times a day on purpose to cloak the affair, and prevent all suspicion.

LOVEMORE. Admirable! I commend your prudence. Besides——my Lady Constant, you know, has some youthful vigour about her; a graceful person, and an eye that inflames desire; and desire at your time of life, you know——

SIR BASHFUL. Po! It is not for that; that is nothing. I wear admirably well, Mr. Lovemore.

LOVEMORE. Do you?

SIR BASHFUL. As young as ever: but I don't let her know it.

LOVEMORE. Well! If you are discreet in that point, you are a very Machiavel!

SIR BASHFUL. Yes, yes; I fight cunning. (*Laughs*)

LOVEMORE. Let nothing betray you. Be upon your guard: that is my own plan exactly. You want no advice from me.

SIR BASHFUL. Pardon me: you can assist me.——My dear brother sufferer, give me your hand. We can in a sly way be of great use to each other.

LOVEMORE. As how?

SIR BASHFUL. I'll tell you. There are some things which you know our wives expect to be done.

LOVEMORE. So there are.——(*Aside*) What the devil is he at now?

SIR BASHFUL. Now if you will assist me——

LOVEMORE. You may depend upon my assistance.

SIR BASHFUL. Thus it is: my wife, you know, keeps a power of company, and makes a great figure there. I could show her in any company in England: I wish she could say the same of me.

LOVEMORE. Why truly I wish she could.

SIR BASHFUL. But that's out of the question. Now if you will come into my scheme——it must be a deep secret.——How? Is that Sir Brilliant's voice?

Enter SIR BRILLIANT.

SIR BRILLIANT. Sir Bashful, you see what attraction you have. Lovemore, I did not expect to see you here.

LOVEMORE. Nor did I expect you, Sir Brilliant. (*Aside*)

SIR BASHFUL. Confusion!——This unseasonable visit——(*Aside*)

SIR BRILLIANT. And your Lady, is she at home, Sir Bashful?

SIR BASHFUL. Her own people keep that account, Sir: I know nothing of her.

SIR BRILLIANT. Nay, never talk slightingly of a lady who possesses so many elegant accomplishments. She has spirit, sense, wit, and beauty.

SIR BASHFUL. (*Aside*) Spirit, sense, wit, and beauty! She has them all, sure enough.——Sir, I am no sworn appraiser to take an inventory of her effects.——(*Aside*) Hey, Lovemore? (*Looks at him and laughs*)

LOVEMORE. (*To Sir Bashful*) Vastly well!

SIR BRILLIANT. Is her Ladyship visible this morning?

SIR BASHFUL. Whether she is visible or not, is no business of mine, but I know she is unintelligible this morning, and incomprehensible this morning. She has the vapours; but your conversation I suppose will brighten her up for the rest of the day.

SIR BRILLIANT. Why, as it happens, I have the rarest piece of news to communicate to her. Lovemore, you know Sir Amorous La Fool?

LOVEMORE. He that was sheriff the other day? Came up with an address, and got himself knighted?

SIR BRILLIANT. The same. He declared he would live with his friends upon the same familiar footing as before, and his new dignities should make no alteration.

SIR BASHFUL. I have seen the knight. What of him?

SIR BRILLIANT. Poor devil. He is in such a scrape!

SIR BASHFUL. What's the matter? Bubbled at play,[53] I suppose.

SIR BRILLIANT. Worse, much worse.

LOVEMORE. He has been blackballed at one of the clubs?

SIR BASHFUL. Or run through the body in a duel?

SIR BRILLIANT. Why that's a scrape indeed: but it is not that.

SIR BASHFUL. What then?

SIR BRILLIANT. So unfortunate a discovery! He is fallen in love—— I cannot help laughing at him.

LOVEMORE. Po! Fallen in love with some coquette, who plays off her airs, and makes a jest of him.

SIR BASHFUL. A young actress maybe, or an opera singer?

SIR BRILLIANT. No, you will never guess. Sir Bashful——like a silly devil, he is fallen in love with his own wife.

SIR BASHFUL. Fallen in love with his own wife! (*Stares at him*)

SIR BRILLIANT. Yes; he has made up all quarrels; his jealousy is at an end,[54] and he is to be upon his good behaviour for the rest of his life.——Could you expect this, Lovemore?

---

[53] Cheated at gambling.

[54] 1785, 1787: "at an end"; 1786: "at end."

LOVEMORE. No, Sir; neither I nor my friend Sir Bashful expected this.

SIR BASHFUL. It is a stroke of surprise to me. (*Looking uneasy*)

SIR BRILLIANT. I heard it at my Lady Betty Scandal's, and we had such a laugh: the whole company were in astonishment: whist stood still; quadrille laid down the cards, and brag was in suspense. Poor Sir Amorous! It is very ridiculous, is not it, Sir Bashful?

SIR BASHFUL. Very ridiculous indeed.——(*Aside*) My own case exactly, and my friend Lovemore's too.

SIR BRILLIANT. The man is lost, undone, ruined, dead and buried.

LOVEMORE. (*Laughing*) He will never be able to show his face after this discovery.

SIR BRILLIANT. Oh, never; it's all over with him. Sir Bashful, this does not divert you; you don't enjoy it.

SIR BASHFUL. Who I?——I——I——nothing can be more pleasant, and——I——I laugh as heartily as I possibly can. (*Forcing a laugh*)

SIR BRILLIANT. Lovemore, you remember Sir Amorous used to strut, and talk big, and truly he did not care a pinch of snuff for his wife, not he; pretended to be as much at ease as Sir Bashful about his Lady, and as much his own master as you yourself, or any man of pleasure about town.

LOVEMORE. I remember him: but as to Sir Bashful and myself, we know the world; we understand life.

SIR BASHFUL. So we do; the world will never have such a story of us. Will they Lovemore?

LOVEMORE. Oh! we are free: we are out of the scrape.

SIR BRILLIANT. Sir Amorous La Fool will be a proverb. Adieu for him the side-box whisper, the soft assignation, and all the joys of freedom. He is retired with his Penelope, to love one another in the country; and next winter they will come to town, to hate one another.

SIR BASHFUL. Do you think it will end so?

SIR BRILLIANT. No doubt of it. That is always the denouement of modern matrimony. But I have not told you the worst of his case. Our friend Sir Charles Wildfire, you know, was writing a comedy, and what do you think he has done? He has drawn the

character of Sir Amorous, and made him the hero of the play.

SIR BASHFUL. What, put him into a comedy?

SIR BRILLIANT. Even so: it is called *The Amorous Husband; or, The Man in Love with His Own Wife.* Oh! ho! ho! ho!

LOVEMORE. We must send in time for places. (*Laughs with Sir Brilliant*)

SIR BASHFUL. Lovemore carries it with an air. (*Aside*)

SIR BRILLIANT. Yes, we must secure places. Sir Bashful, you shall be of the party.

SIR BASHFUL. The party will be very agreeable. I shall enjoy the joke prodigiously. Ha! ha! (*Forces a laugh*)

LOVEMORE. Yes, Sir Bashful, we shall relish the humour. (*Looks at him and laughs*)

SIR BRILLIANT. The play will have a run: the people of fashion will crowd after such a character.——I must drive to a million of places and put it about; but first, with your leave, Sir Bashful, I will take the liberty to give a hint of the affair to your Lady. It will appear so ridiculous to her!

SIR BASHFUL. Do you think it will?

SIR BRILLIANT. Without doubt: she has never met with anything like it: has she, Lovemore?

LOVEMORE. I fancy not: Sir Bashful, you take care of that.

SIR BASHFUL. Yes, yes; I shall never be the town-talk.——Hey, Lovemore?

SIR BRILLIANT. Well, I'll step and pay my respects to my Lady Constant. Poor Sir Amorous! He will have his horns added to his coat of arms in a little time. Ha! ha!

Exit.

SIR BASHFUL. There, you see how it is. I shall get lampooned, berhymed, and niched into a comedy.

LOVEMORE. Po! Never be frightened at this. Nobody knows of your weakness but myself, and I can't betray your secret for my own sake.

SIR BASHFUL. Very true.

LOVEMORE. This discovery shows the necessity of concealing our loves. We must act with caution. Give my Lady no reason to suspect that you have the least regard for her.

SIR BASHFUL. Not for the world.

LOVEMORE. Keep to that.

SIR BASHFUL. I have done her a thousand kindnesses, but all by stealth; all in a sly way.

LOVEMORE. Have you?

SIR BASHFUL. Oh! a multitude. I'll tell you.——She has been plaguing me a long time for an addition to her jewels. She wants a diamond cross, and a better pair of diamond buckles. "Madam," says I, "I will have no such trumpery"; but then goes I and bespeaks them of the first jeweller in town.——All under the rose. The buckles are finished: worth five hundred! She will have them this very day, without knowing from what quarter they come.——I can't but laugh at the contrivance——the man that brings them will run away directly, without saying a word. (*Laughs heartily*)

LOVEMORE. Sly, sly.——You know what you are about.

SIR BASHFUL. Ay, let me alone——(*Laughs with Lovemore*) And then, to cover the design still more, when I see her wear her baubles, I can take occasion to be as jealous as bedlam.

LOVEMORE. So you can: ha! ha!——(*Aside*) I wish he may never be jealous of me in good earnest.

SIR BASHFUL. Give me your hand. (*Looks at him and laughs*) I am safe I think.

LOVEMORE. (*Laughing with him*) Perfectly safe——(*Aside*) if it was not for his own folly.

SIR BASHFUL. But I was telling you, Mr. Lovemore:——we can be of essential use to each other.

LOVEMORE. As how pray?

SIR BASHFUL. Why, my Lady is often in want of money. It would be ridiculous in me to supply her. Now if you will take the money from me, and pretend to lend it to her, out of friendship, you know——

LOVEMORE. Nothing can be better.——(*Aside*) Here is a fellow pimping for his own horns.——I shall be glad to serve you.

SIR BASHFUL. I am for ever obliged to you——here, here; take it now——here it is in bank notes——one, two, three; there is three hundred——give her that, and tell her you have more at her service tomorrow or next day, if her occasions require it.

LOVEMORE. My good friend, to oblige you. (*Takes the money*) This is the rarest adventure!

SIR BASHFUL. I'll do anything for you in return.

LOVEMORE. I shall have occasion for your friendship——that is to forgive me if you find me out. (*Aside*)

SIR BASHFUL. Lose no time; step to her now——hold, hold; Sir Brilliant is with her.

LOVEMORE. I can dismiss him. Rely upon my friendship: I will make her Ladyship easy for you.

SIR BASHFUL. It will be kind of you.

LOVEMORE. It shall be her own fault if I don't.

SIR BASHFUL. A thousand thanks to you——well, is not this the rarest project?

LOVEMORE. It is the newest way——of satisfying a man's wife!

SIR BASHFUL. Ay! Let this head of mine alone.

LOVEMORE. (*Aside*) Not if I can help it!——Hush!——I hear Sir Brilliant; he is coming downstairs. I'll take this opportunity, and step to her Ladyship now.

SIR BASHFUL. Do so, do so.

LOVEMORE. I am gone. (*Aside*) Who can blame me now if I cuckold this fellow?

Exit.

SIR BASHFUL. Prosper you, prosper you, Mr. Lovemore. Make me thankful: he is a true friend. I don't know what I should do without him.

Enter SIR BRILLIANT.

SIR BRILLIANT. Sir Bashful, how have you managed this?

SIR BASHFUL. I have no art, no management. What's the matter?

SIR BRILLIANT. I don't know what you have done, but your Lady laughs till she is ready to expire at what I have been telling her.

SIR BASHFUL. And she thinks Sir Amorous La Fool an object of ridicule?

SIR BRILLIANT. She does not give credit to a single syllable of the story. A man that loves his wife would be a phoenix indeed! Such a thing might exist formerly, but in this polished age is nowhere to be found. That's her opinion of the matter.

SIR BASHFUL. (*Laughs*) A whimsical notion of hers! And so she thinks you may go about with a lanthorn to find a man that sets any value upon his wife?

SIR BRILLIANT. You have managed to convince her of it. How the devil do you contrive to govern so fine a woman? I know several, without her pretensions, who have long ago thrown off all restraint. You keep up your own dignity.

SIR BASHFUL. Yes, I know what I am about.

SIR BRILLIANT. You!––you are quite in the fashion.––Apropos; I fancy I shall want you to afford me your assistance. You know my Lady Charlotte Modelove? She has a taste for the theatre: at Bellgrove Place she has an elegant stage, where her select friends amuse themselves now and then with a representation of certain comic pieces. We shall there act the new comedy, but we apprehend some difficulty in the arrangement of the several characters. Now you shall act Sir Amorous, and––

SIR BASHFUL. I act, Sir?––I know nothing of the character.

SIR BRILLIANT. Po! Say nothing of that. In time you may reach the ridiculous absurdity of it, and play it as well as another.

SIR BASHFUL. (*Aside*) Confusion! He does not suspect, I hope.–– Divert yourselves, Sir, as you may; but not at my expense I promise you.

SIR BRILLIANT. Never be so abrupt. Who knows but Lady Constant may be the happy wife, the *cara sposa* [55] of the piece! And then, you in love with her, and she laughing at you for it, will give a zest to the humour, which everybody will relish in the most exquisite degree.

SIR BASHFUL. Po! This is too much. You are very pleasant, but you won't easily get me to play the fool.

------

[55] Dear wife.

SIR BRILLIANT. Well, consider of it. I shall be delighted to see my friend Sir Bashful tied to his wife's apron-string, and with a languishing look melting away in admiration of her charms. Oh! ho! ho! ho!——Adieu; *à l'honneur;* good morning, Sir Bashful.

Exit.

SIR BASHFUL. I don't know what to make of all this. But there is no danger. As long as nobody knows it, I may venture to love my wife. There will be no harm, while the secret is kept as close as night, concealed in tenfold darkness, from the wits and scoffers of the age.

Enter LOVEMORE.

SIR BASHFUL. Well, well?——How have you managed?

LOVEMORE. As I could wish: she is infinitely obliged to me, and will never forget the civility.

SIR BASHFUL. A thousand thanks to you. I am not suspected?

LOVEMORE. She has not a distant idea of you in this business. She was rather delicate at first, and hesitated, and thought it an indecorum to accept of money even from a friend. But that objection soon vanished. I told her it is but too visible that she is unfortunately yoked with a husband whose humour will never be softened down to the least compliance with her inclinations.

SIR BASHFUL. That was well said, and had a good effect, I hope.

LOVEMORE. I hope so too.

SIR BASHFUL. It helps to carry on the plot, you know.

LOVEMORE. Admirably; it puts things in the train I wish.

SIR BASHFUL. And so, to cover the design, you gave me the worst of characters.

LOVEMORE. I painted you in terrible colours.

SIR BASHFUL. Do so always, and she will never suspect me of being privy to any civility you may show her.

LOVEMORE. I would not have you know anything of my being civil to her for the world. (*Aside*) [56] I have succeeded thus far. I talked a few musty sentences, such as, the person who receives a

---

[56] 1786 omits "(*aside*)"; it is in 1785, 1787.

civility confers the obligation, and so with some reluctance she complied at last, and things are now upon the footing I would have them.——Death and fury! There comes my wife.

SIR BASHFUL. Ay, and here comes my wife.

LOVEMORE. What the devil brings her hither?

SIR BASHFUL. (*Aside*) Now; now; now let me see how he will carry it before Mrs. Lovemore.——Walk in, Madam! Walk in, Mrs. Lovemore.

Enter MRS. LOVEMORE *and* LADY CONSTANT *at opposite doors.*

LADY CONSTANT. Mrs. Lovemore, to see you abroad is a novelty indeed.

MRS. LOVEMORE. As great perhaps as that of finding your Ladyship at home. Mr. Lovemore, I did not expect to have the pleasure of meeting you.

LOVEMORE. Then we are both agreeably surprised.

SIR BASHFUL. Now mind how he behaves. (*Aside*)

MRS. LOVEMORE. I thought you were gone to your city-banker.

LOVEMORE. And you find that you are mistaken. I have deferred it till the evening.——(*Aside*) 'Sdeath! To be teased in this manner.

SIR BASHFUL. (*Aside*) No, no; he won't drop the mask. (*Looks at Lady Constant*) She has touched the cash; I can see the bank notes sparkling in her eyes.

MRS. LOVEMORE. If you don't go into the City till the evening, may I hope for your company at dinner, Mr. Lovemore?

LOVEMORE. The question is entertaining, but as it was settled this morning, I think it has lost the graces of novelty.

SIR BASHFUL. He won't let her have the least suspicion of his regard. (*Aside*)

LADY CONSTANT. I dare say Mr. Lovemore will dine at home if it conduces to your happiness, Ma'am; and Sir Bashful, I take it, will dine at home for the contrary reason.

SIR BASHFUL. Madam, I will dine at home, or I will dine abroad, for what reason I please, and it is my pleasure to give no reason for either.——Lovemore! (*Looks at him and smiles*)

LOVEMORE. (*Aside to Sir Bashful*) Bravo! (*Aside*) What a block-head it is!

MRS. LOVEMORE. As you have your chariot at the door, Mr. Lovemore, if you have no objection, I will send away my chair, and you may do me the honour of a place in your carriage.

LOVEMORE. The honour will be very great to me, but——so many places to call at.——If I had known this sooner.——You had better keep your chair.

SIR BASHFUL. (*Aside*) Cunning! Cunning! He would not be seen in his chariot with her for the world. He has more discretion than I have.

LADY CONSTANT. Mrs. Lovemore, since you have at last ventured to come abroad, I hope you will think it a change for the better. You are too domestic. I shall expect now to see you often: and apropos, I am to have a rout tomorrow evening; if you will do me the honour of your company——

SIR BASHFUL. A rout tomorrow evening! You have a rout every evening, I think. Learn of Mrs. Lovemore; imitate her example, and don't let me have your hurricane months all the year round in my house.——Hip! (*Aside*) Lovemore, how do you like me?

LOVEMORE. (*Aside to Sir Bashful*) You improve upon it every time. But I am loitering here as if I had nothing to do.——My Lady Constant, I have the honour to wish your Ladyship a good morning. Sir Bashful, yours.——Madam——(*Bows gravely to Mrs. Lovemore, hums a tune, and exit*)

SIR BASHFUL. (*Aside*) He knows how to play the game. I'll try what I can do. Mrs. Lovemore, I have the honour to wish you a good morning. Madam——(*Bows gravely to Lady Constant, hums a tune, and exit*)

MRS. LOVEMORE. Two such husbands!

LADY CONSTANT. As to my swain, I grant you. Mr. Lovemore is at least well-bred; he has an understanding, and may in time reflect. Sir Bashful never qualifies himself with the smallest tincture of civility.

MRS. LOVEMORE. If civility can qualify the draught, I must allow Mr. Lovemore to have a skillful hand. But there is no end of his projects. Every day opens a new scene. Another of his intrigues is come to light. I came to consult with your Ladyship. I know you are acquainted with the Widow Bellmour.

LADY CONSTANT. The Widow Bellmour? I know her perfectly well.

MRS. LOVEMORE. Not so well, perhaps, as you may imagine. She has thrown out the lure for my wild gallant, and in order to deceive me——

LADY CONSTANT. My dear, you must be mistaken. Who tells you this?

MRS. LOVEMORE. Oh! I can trust to my intelligence. Sir Brilliant Fashion, by way of blind to me, has been this morning drawing so amiable a picture of the lady——

LADY CONSTANT. Sir Brilliant's authority is not always the best, but in this point, you may trust to him.

MRS. LOVEMORE. But when you have heard all the circumstances——

LADY CONSTANT. Depend upon it, you are wrong. I know the Widow Bellmour. Her turn of character, and way of thinking——

MRS. LOVEMORE. Excuse me, Madam. You decide without hearing me.

LADY CONSTANT. All scandal, take my word for it. However, let me hear your story. We'll adjourn to my dressing-room, if you will; and I promise to confute all you can say.——I would have you know the Widow Bellmour: you will be in love with her.——My dear Madam, have not you a tinge of jealousy?——Beware of that malady. If you see things through that medium, I shall give you up.

> That jaundice of the mind, whose colours strike
> On friend and foe, and paint them all alike.

End of the SECOND ACT.

ACT the THIRD
SCENE [I]

An Apartment at the Widow Bellmour's: several chairs, a toilette,[57] a bookcase, and a harpsichord disposed up and down.

MIGNIONET. (*Putting things in order*) I don't well know what to make of this same Lord Etheridge. He is coming here again today, I suppose: all this neatness, and all this care must be for him.—— Well, it does not signify: (*Arranging the chairs*) there is a pleasure in obeying Madam Bellmour. She is a sweet lady, that's the truth of it.——'Twere a pity any of these men, with their deceitful arts, should draw her into a snare.——But she knows them all. They must rise early who can outwit her. (*Settling the toilette*)

Enter MRS. BELLMOUR, *reading.*

"Oh! blest with temper, whose unclouded ray
    Can make tomorrow cheerful as today;
    She who can own a sister's charms, and hear
    Sighs for a daughter with unwounded ear;
    That never answers till a husband cools,
    And if she rules him, never shows she rules." [58]

Sensible, elegant Pope!

"Charms by accepting, by submitting sways,
    Yet has her humour most, when she obeys." [59]

                       (*Seems to read on*)

MIGNIONET. Lord love my mistress! Always so charming, so gay, and so happy!

---

[57] A dressing table.
[58] 1785, 1787: "*she rules*"; 1786: "*the rules*."
[59] *Moral Essays*, Epistle II, lines 257-264.

MRS. BELLMOUR. These exquisite characters of women! They are a sort of painter's gallery, where one sees the portraits of all one's acquaintance, and sometimes we see our own features too. Mignionet, put this book in its place.

MIGNIONET. Yes, Ma'am; and there's your toilet looks as elegant as hands can make it.

MRS. BELLMOUR. Does it? I think it does. You have some taste. Apropos, where is my new song?——Oh! here it is: I must make myself mistress of it. (*Plays upon the harpsichord and sings a little*) I believe I have conquered it. (*Rises and goes to her toilet*) This hair is always tormenting me, always in disorder: this lock must be forever gadding out of its place. I must and will subdue it. ——Do you know, Mignionet, that this is a very pretty song? It was written [60] by my Lord Etheridge. My Lord has a turn. (*Sings a little*) I must be perfect before he comes. (*Hums the tune*) Do you know that I think my Lord is one of those men who may be endured?

MIGNIONET. Yes, Ma'am, I know you think so.

MRS. BELLMOUR. Do you?

MIGNIONET. And if I have any skill, Ma'am, you are not without a little partiality for his Lordship.

MRS. BELLMOUR. Really? Then you think I like him perhaps. Do you think I like him? I don't well know how that is. Like him! No, not absolutely; it is not decided: and yet I don't know, if I had a mind to humour myself, and to give way a little to inclination, there is something here in my heart that would be busy, I believe. ——The man has a softness of manner, a turn of wit, and does not want sentiment. Can I call it sentiment? Yes, I think I may. He has sentiment; and then he knows the manners, the usage of the world, and he points out the ridicule of things with so much humour!

MIGNIONET. You'll be caught, Ma'am; I see that.——To be sure, my Lord has a quality-air, and can make himself agreeable. But what of that? You know but very little of him. Is a man's character known in three or four weeks' time? (*Mrs. Bellmour hums a tune*)

---

[60] 1770: "written"; 1786: "writ."

Do, my dear Madam, mind what I say: I am at times very considerate. I make my remarks, and I see very plainly——Lord, Ma'am, what am I doing? I am talking to you for your own good, and you are all in the air, and no more mind me, no, no more than if I was nothing at all.

MRS. BELLMOUR. (*Continues humming a tune*) You talk wonderfully well upon the subject; but as I know how the cards lie, and can play the best of the game; and as I have a song to amuse me, one is inclined to give musical nonsense the preference.

MIGNIONET. I assure you, Ma'am, I am not one of those servants that bargain for their mistress's inclinations: but you are a going to take a leap in the dark. What does my Lord Etheridge mean, with his chair always brought into the hall, and the curtains close about his ears? Why does he not come like himself, and not care who sees him? There's some mystery at the bottom, I'll be sworn there is; and so you'll find at last.——Dear heart, Ma'am! If you are determined not to listen, what signifies my living with you? At this rate, I am of no service to you.

MRS. BELLMOUR. There;——I have conquered my song. (*Runs to her glass*) How do I look today? The eyes do well enough, I think.——And so, Mignionet, you imagine I shall play the fool, and marry my Lord Etheridge?

MIGNIONET. You have it through the very heart of you: I see that.

MRS. BELLMOUR. Do you?——I don't know what to say to it. Poor Sir Brilliant Fashion! If I prefer his rival, what will become of him? ——I won't think about it.

Enter POMPEY.

MRS. BELLMOUR. What's [61] the matter, Pompey?

POMPEY. A lady in a chair desires to know if your Ladyship is at home.

MRS. BELLMOUR. Has the lady no name?

POMPEY. Yes; I fancies she has, Ma'am; but she did not tell it.

---

[61] 1785, 1787: "What's"; 1786: "What."

MRS. BELLMOUR. How awkward!——Well, show the lady up-stairs.

Exit POMPEY.[62]

MIGNIONET. Had not you better receive her in the drawing-room, Ma'am? I have not half done my business here.

MRS. BELLMOUR. Oh! you have done very well. There will be less formality here. I dare say it is some intimate acquaintance, though that foolish boy does not recollect her name.——Here she comes. I don't know her.

Enter MRS. LOVEMORE.

MRS. LOVEMORE. (*Disconcerted*) I beg pardon for this intrusion.

MRS. BELLMOUR. Pray walk in, Ma'am. Mignionet, reach a chair. (*Mrs. Lovemore crosses the stage, and they salute each other with an air of distant civility*)

MRS. LOVEMORE. I am afraid this visit from one who has not the honour of knowing you——

MRS. BELLMOUR. Oh, make no apology, Ma'am.——Mignionet, you may withdraw.

Exit MIGNIONET.

MRS. LOVEMORE. It may appear extraordinary that a stranger thus intrudes upon you;——but a particular circumstance determined me to take this liberty. I hope you will excuse the freedom.

MRS. BELLMOUR. You do me honour, Ma'am; pray no excuses. A particular circumstance, you say?

MRS. LOVEMORE. I shall appear, perhaps, very ridiculous, and indeed I am afraid I have done the most absurd thing! But a lady of your acquaintance——you know my Lady Constant, Ma'am?

MRS. BELLMOUR. Extremely well.

MRS. LOVEMORE. She has given you such an amiable character for benevolence and a certain elegant way of thinking, entirely your own, that I flatter myself, if it is in your power, you will be generous enough to afford me your assistance.

---

[62] The exit for Pompey is last indicated in 1770.

MRS. BELLMOUR. Lady Constant is very obliging. Make a trial of me, Ma'am, and if I can be of any use——

MRS. LOVEMORE. I fear I shall ask you a strange question:——are you acquainted with a gentleman of the name of Lovemore?

MRS. BELLMOUR. Lovemore? No such name in my list.——Lovemore? No;——I recollect no such person. The circle of my acquaintance is small: I am almost a stranger in town.

MRS. LOVEMORE. That makes an end, Ma'am. I beg your pardon. I have given you an unnecessary trouble. (*Going*)

MRS. BELLMOUR. (*Aside*) Mighty odd this! Her manner is interesting.——You have given me no trouble, but my curiosity is excited. (*Takes her by the hand*) I beg you will keep your chair. Pray be seated.——What can this mean? (*Aside*) Will you be so good as to inform me who the gentleman is?

MRS. LOVEMORE. The story will be uninteresting to you, and to me it is painful. My grievances—— (*Puts her handkerchief to her eyes*)

MRS. BELLMOUR. (*Aside*) Her grief affects me. (*Looks at her till she has recovered herself*) I would not importune too much——

MRS. LOVEMORE. You have such an air of frankness and generosity, that I will open myself without reserve: I have the tenderest regard for Mr. Lovemore: I have been married to him these two years. I admired his understanding, his sensibility, and his spirit. My heart was his; I loved him with unbounded passion. I thought the flame was mutual, and, you may believe I was happy. But of late, there is such a revolution in his temper! I know not what to make of it. I am doomed to be unhappy.

MRS. BELLMOUR. Perhaps not: you may still have much in your power.

MRS. LOVEMORE. My power is at an end. Instead of the looks of affection, and the expressions of tenderness, with which he used to meet me, it is nothing now but cold, averted, superficial civility; while abroad he runs on in a wild career of pleasure, and to my deep affliction, has attached himself entirely to another object.

MRS. BELLMOUR. And if I had known Mr. Lovemore, do you imagine that my advice or persuasion would avail you anything?

MRS. LOVEMORE. I had such a fancy. (*Aside*) What can I think of her?

MRS. BELLMOUR. You are much mistaken. In these cases friends may interpose, but what can they do? They recommend a wife to the good will, the honour, and generosity of her husband. But when a woman, who should be esteemed and loved, is recommended as the object of compassion, she is humbled indeed: it is all over with her. A wife should recommend herself by the graces of her person, and the variety of her talents. Men will prove false, and if there is nothing in your complaint but mere gallantry on his side, I protest I do not see that your case is so very bad.

MRS. LOVEMORE. Can it be worse, Ma'am?

MRS. BELLMOUR. A great deal.——If his affections, instead of being alienated, had been extinguished, what would be the consequence?——A downright, sullen, habitual insensibility. From that lethargy of affection a man is not easily recalled. In all Love's bill of mortality there is not a more fatal disorder. But this is not the case with Mr. Lovemore: by your account, he still has sentiment; and where there is sentiment, there is room to hope for an alteration.——But where the heart has lost its feeling, you have the pain of finding yourself neglected; and for what? The man is grown stupid, and to the warm beams of wit and beauty, as impenetrable as an icehouse.

MRS. LOVEMORE. This is not my complaint. I have to do with one who is too susceptible of impressions from every beautiful object that comes in his way.

MRS. BELLMOUR. Why, so much the better. A new idea strikes his fancy. He is inconstant, but after wavering and fluttering, he may settle at last.

MRS. LOVEMORE. How light she makes of it! She apologizes for him! (*Aside*)

MRS. BELLMOUR. And perhaps, the fault is on the woman's side.——

MRS. LOVEMORE. The virtue of my conduct, Madam——

MRS. BELLMOUR. Oh! I would have laid my life you would be at that work. But virtue is not the question at present. I suppose virtue; that is always understood. The fault I mean, is the want of due attention to the art of pleasing. It is there that most women fail. In these times, virtue alone may be its own reward.

MRS. LOVEMORE. But after being married so long, and behaving all the time with such an equality——

MRS. BELLMOUR. Ay, that equality is the rock so many split upon. The men will change; they love variety. Excuse my freedom. Do you know your rival?

MRS. LOVEMORE. There I own I am somewhat puzzled.

MRS. BELLMOUR. Never throw up the cards for all that. Take my advice, Ma'am.——Employ but half the pains you now use perhaps in teasing yourself, to vie with the person who has struck your husband's fancy——to vie with her, I say, in the arts of pleasing; do this, and victory is yours. If I judge right, you have qualities that may dispute his heart with anybody.

MRS. LOVEMORE. You are pleased to compliment.

MRS. BELLMOUR. Oh! by no means; but you must exert yourself. It is the wife's business to bait the hook for her husband with variety. Virtue alone will not do it. Vice puts on allurements: why should not truth and innocence do the same? That is the whole affair, Ma'am: I would not make myself uneasy.

MRS. LOVEMORE. Not uneasy, when a wild, ungrateful libertine——

MRS. BELLMOUR. Give me leave. I have been married, and am a little in the secret.——To win a heart is easy; to keep it the difficulty. After the fatal words "for better, for worse," women in general relax into indolence, and while they are guilty of no infidelity, they think everything is right. But they are mistaken: a great deal is wanting; an address, vivacity, a desire to please.——A favourite poet——Prior——he expressed it with delicacy:

> "Above the fix'd and settled rules
> Of vice and virtue in the schools,
> The better part should set before 'em
> A grace, a manner, a decorum." [63]

---

[63] Matthew Prior, *Paulo Purganti and His Wife: An Honest but a Simple Pair*, lines 1-2, 5-6, altered slightly.

MRS. LOVEMORE. But when the natural temper——

MRS. BELLMOUR. Oh! the natural temper must be forced. Home must be made a place of pleasure to the husband. How is that to be done? Virtue of itself will not please the taste of this age; and that equality, which you talk of, is a sameness that palls and wearies. A wife should throw infinite variety into her manner. She should, as it were, multiply herself, and show a number of different women collected in her own person. The grave, the gay, the tender, affectionate, witty, silent, and talkative, all in their turns, all shifting the scene, and she succeeding to herself as quick as lightning. And this I take to be the whole mystery; the way to keep a man.——But I beg your pardon. I go on too fast: you will think me the giddiest creature.

MRS. LOVEMORE. Quite the reverse, Ma'am; you are so obliging—— (*Aside*) Sir Brilliant has told me the truth, I believe.

MRS. BELLMOUR. I have tired myself and you too.——But pray, may I now enquire, who was so kind as to intimate that I am acquainted with Mr. Lovemore?

MRS. LOVEMORE. It was a mere mistake. I have given you a great deal of trouble. You will excuse my frankness; I had heard that his visits were frequent here.

MRS. BELLMOUR. His visits frequent here! My Lady Constant could not tell you so?

MRS. LOVEMORE. She told me quite the contrary. She knows your amiable qualities, and does you justice.

MRS. BELLMOUR. The accident is lucky: it has procured me the honour of your acquaintance. And I suppose you imagined that I had robbed you of Mr. Lovemore's heart?——Scandal will be buzzing about. I can laugh at everything of that sort. (*A rap at the door*) Oh! Heavens! Some troublesome visit.——(*Rings a bell*)

Enter MIGNIONET.

MRS. BELLMOUR. I am not at home. Go, and give an answer.

MIGNIONET. It is Lord Etheridge, Ma'am: he is coming upstairs. The servants did not know you had changed your mind.

MRS. BELLMOUR. Was ever anything so cross? Tell his Lordship I have company; I am busy; I am not well; anything, don't let him come in. Make haste, dispatch: I won't see him.

MRS. LOVEMORE. I beg I may not hinder you: I shall take my leave.

MRS. BELLMOUR. By no means. Our conversation grows interesting. I positively will not see my Lord.

MRS. LOVEMORE. I can't agree to that. You must see his Lordship. I can step into another room.

MRS. BELLMOUR. Will you be so good?——You will find something to amuse you in that cabinet. (*Points to a door in the back scene*) We must talk further. My Lord shan't stay long.

MRS. LOVEMORE. Nay, but if you stand upon ceremony——

MRS. BELLMOUR. Very well: I'll contrive it. This is a lover of mine. A lover and a husband are the same thing. Perhaps it will divert you to hear how I manage him. I hear him on the stairs. Make haste: Mignionet show the way.

MRS. LOVEMORE *and* MIGNIONET *go out at the back scene.*

MRS. BELLMOUR. Let me see how I look to receive him. (*Runs to her glass*)

Enter LOVEMORE, *with a Star and Garter,*[64] *as* LORD ETHERIDGE.

LOVEMORE.

"A heav'nly image in the glass appears,
  To that she bends, to that her eyes she rears,
  Repairs her smiles——" [65]

MRS. BELLMOUR. Repairs her smiles, my Lord! You are satirical this morning. Pray, my Lord, are my features out of repair, like an old house in the country, that wants a tenant?

LOVEMORE. Nay, now you wrest the words from their visible intention. You can't suppose that I impute to such perfect beauty

---

[64] Two of the insignia of the Order of the Garter.
[65] Pope, *The Rape of the Lock* I.125-126, 141.

the least want of repair, whatever may be the case, Ma'am, with regard to the want of a tenant.

MRS. BELLMOUR. Oh! Then your opinion is, that I want a tenant. And perhaps you think I am going to put up a bill to signify to all passers-by, that here is a mansion to be let, enquire of the Widow Blackacre.[66] I like your notion; I don't think it would be a bad scheme. Shall I try it?

LOVEMORE. A palace needs no such invitation. Its natural beauty attracts admiring eyes. But who can bid up to the price? The person who is able to do it——

MRS. BELLMOUR. Will be happy; I know that is what you are going to say. But he must do homage for it; and then I will let it to none but a single gentleman. Do you know anybody whom those conditions will suit?

LOVEMORE. Those conditions, Ma'am—— (*Aside*) What the devil does she mean? I am not detected, I hope.——To be sure, Ma'am, those conditions——and——none but single gentlemen will presume to——

MRS. BELLMOUR. And then it must be a lease for life. But that will never do. Nobody will be troubled with it. I shall never get it off my hands: do you think I shall, my Lord?

LOVEMORE. There must be very little taste left if you have not a number of bidders. You know the ambition of my heart; you know I am devoted to you, upon any terms, even though it were to be bought with life.

MRS. BELLMOUR. Heavens! What a dying swain you are! And does your Lordship mean to be guilty of matrimony? Lord! what a question have I asked? To be sure I am the giddiest creature. My Lord, don't you think me a strange madcap?

LOVEMORE. A vein of wit, like yours, that springs at once from vivacity and sentiment, serves to exalt your beauty, and give animation to every charm.

MRS. BELLMOUR. Upon my word, you have said it finely!——But

---

[66] 1785, 1787: "Bellmour"; 1786: "Blackacre." The Widow Blackacre is in William Wycherley's *The Plain Dealer* (1676).

you are in the right, my Lord. Your pensive, melancholy beauty is the most insipid thing in nature. And yet we often see features without a mind; and the owner of them sits in the room with you, like a mere vegetable, for an hour together, till at last she is incited to the violent exertion of, "Yes, Sir"——"I fancy not, Ma'am," and then a matter of fact conversation! "Miss Beverly is going to be married to Captain Shoulder-Knot——My Lord Mortgage has had another tumble at hazard [67]——Sir Harry Wilding has lost his election——They say short-aprons are coming into fashion."

LOVEMORE. Oh! a matter of fact conversation is insupportable.

MRS. BELLMOUR. But you meet with nothing else. All in great spirits about nothing, and not an idea among them. Go to Ranelagh, or to what public place you will, it is just the same. A lady comes up to you; "How charmingly you look!——But my dear M'em, did you hear what happened to us the other night?——We were going home from the opera——you know my Aunt Roly-Poly; it was her coach.——There was she and Lady Betty Fidget——what a sweet blonde! How do you do, my dear? (*Curtsying as to another going by*) My Lady Betty is quite recovered; we were all frightened about her; but Doctor Snakeroot was called in; no, not Doctor Snakeroot, Doctor Bolus; and so he altered the course of the medicines, and so my Lady Betty is purely now.——Well, there was she, and my aunt, and Sir George Bragwell——a pretty man Sir George——finest teeth in the world——your Ladyship's most obedient——(*Curtsying*) We expected you last night, but you did not come.——He! he! he!——And so there was Sir George and the rest of us; and so turning the corner of Bond Street, the brute of a coachman——I humbly thank your Grace (*Curtsies*)——the brute of a coachman overturned us, and so my Aunt Roly-Poly was frighted out of her wits; and Lady Betty has had her nerves again. Only think! Such accidents!——I am glad to see you look so well; *à l'honneur;* he! he! he!"

LOVEMORE. Ho! ho! You paint to the life. I see her moving before me in all her airs.

---

[67] A dice game.

MRS. BELLMOUR. With this conversation their whole stock is exhausted, and away they run to cards. Quadrille has murdered wit!

LOVEMORE. Ay, and beauty too. Cards are the worst enemies to a complexion: the smallpox is not so bad. The passions throw themselves into every feature: I have seen the countenance of an angel changed, in a moment, to absolute deformity: the little loves and graces, that sparkled in the eye, bloomed in the cheek, and smiled about the mouth, all wing their flight, and leave the face, which they before adorned, a prey to grief, to anger, malice, and fury, and the whole train of fretful passions.

MRS. BELLMOUR. And the language of the passions is sometimes heard upon those occasions.

LOVEMORE. Very true, Ma'am; and if by chance they do bridle and hold in a little, the struggle they undergo is the most ridiculous sight in nature. I have seen a huge oath quivering on the pale lip of a reigning toast for half an hour together, and an uplifted eye accusing the gods for the loss of an odd trick. And then, at last, the whole room is a babel of sounds. "My Lord, you flung away the game."——"Sir George, why did not you rough the spade?" [68]—— "Captain Hazard, why did not you lead through the honour?" [69] ——"Ma'am, it was not the play."——"Pardon me, Sir."——"But Ma'am."——"But Sir——I would not play with you for straws; don't you know what Hoyle [70] says? [71]——If A and B are partners against C and D, and the game nine all,[72] A and B have won three tricks, and C and D four tricks; [73] C leads his suit, D puts up the King, then returns the suit; A passes,[74] C puts up the Queen, and B trumps it"; and so A and B and C and D are bandied about; they attack,

---

[68] In whist, trump the spade when unable to follow suit.

[69] To lead to one of the four highest trumps of the left-hand opponent.

[70] Edmond Hoyle (1672-1769), writer on card games. His rules for whist were in effect until 1864.

[71] *Mr. Hoyle's Games, The Fourteenth Edition*, p. 41.

[72] In whist, ten points constituted a game.

[73] Scoring depended upon honours as well as odd or seventh tricks.

[74] Declines to take a trick.

they defend, and all is jargon, and confusion, wrangling, noise, and nonsense; and high life, and polite conversation.——Ha! ha! ha!

MRS. BELLMOUR. Ho! ho! The pencil of Hogarth could not do it better. And yet one is dragged to these places. One must play sometimes. We must let our friends pick our pockets now and then, or they drop our acquaintance. Do you ever play, my Lord?

LOVEMORE. Play, Ma'am?——(*Aside*) What does she mean? I must play the hypocrite to the end of the chapter.——Play?——Now and then, as you say, one must; to oblige, and from necessity; but from taste, or inclination, no; I never touch a card.

MRS. BELLMOUR. Oh! very true; I forgot. You dedicate your time to the Muses; a downright rhyming peer. Do you know, my Lord, that I am charmed with your song?

LOVEMORE. Are you?

MRS. BELLMOUR. Absolutely; and I really think you would make an admirable Vauxhall poet.[75]

LOVEMORE. Nay, now you flatter me.

MRS. BELLMOUR. No, as I live; it is very pretty. And do you know that I can sing it already? Come, you shall hear how I murder it. I have no voice today, but you shall hear me. (*Sings*)

I.

Attend all ye fair, and I'll tell you the art
To bind ev'ry fancy with ease in your chains;
To hold in soft fetters the conjugal heart,
And banish from Hymen his doubts and his pains.

II.

When Juno was deck'd with the cestus of Love,
At first she was handsome; she charming became:
With skill the soft passions it taught her to move,
To kindle at once, and to keep up the flame.

---

[75] The vocalists at Vauxhall gardens specialized in love songs for young ladies.

III.

'Tis this gives the eyes all their magic and fire,
The voice melting accents; impassions the kiss;
Confers the sweet smile, that awakens desire,
And plants round the fair each incentive to bliss.

IV.

Thence flows the gay chat, more than reason that charms;
The eloquent blush, that can beauty improve;
The fond sigh, the fond vow; the soft touch that alarms;
The tender disdain, the renewal of love.

V.

Ye fair, take the cestus, and practice its pow'r:
The mind unaccomplish'd, mere features are vain;
With wit, with good humour enliven each hour,
And the Loves, and the Graces shall walk in your train.

LOVEMORE. My poetry is infinitely obliged to you. It grows into sense as you sing it. Your voice, like the cestus of Venus, bestows a grace upon everything.

MRS. BELLMOUR. Oh! fulsome! I sing horridly. (*Goes to the glass*) How do I look?——Don't tell me, my Lord; you are studying a compliment, but I am resolved to mortify you; I won't hear it.——Well! Have you thought of anything? Let it pass; it's too late now. Pray, my Lord, how came you to choose so grave a subject as connubial happiness?

LOVEMORE. Close and particular that question! (*Aside*)

MRS. BELLMOUR. Juno! Hymen! Doubts and pains! One would almost swear that you have a wife at home, who sat for the picture.

LOVEMORE. Ma'am, the——(*Embarrassed*) the compliment——you are only laughing at me——the subject, from everyday's experience——(*Aside*) does she suspect me?——the subject is common—— bachelors' wives, you know——ha! ha!——And when you inspire the thought; when you are the bright original, it is no wonder that the copy——

MRS. BELLMOUR. Horrid! Going to harp on the old string. Odious solicitations! I hate all proposals. I am not in the humour. You must release me now: your visit is rather long. I have indulged you a great while. And besides, were I to listen to your vows, what would become of poor Sir Brilliant Fashion?

LOVEMORE. Sir Brilliant Fashion?

MRS. BELLMOUR. Do you know him?

LOVEMORE. I know whom you mean. I have seen him; but that's all. He lives with a strange set, and does not move in my sphere. If he is a friend of yours, I have no more to say.

MRS. BELLMOUR. Is there anything to say against him?

LOVEMORE. Nay, I have no knowledge of the gentleman. They who know him best, don't rate him high. A sort of current coin that passes in this town. You will do well to beware of counterfeits.

MRS. BELLMOUR. But this is very alarming——

Enter MIGNIONET, *in a violent hurry.*

MIGNIONET. My dear Madam, I am frighted out of my senses. The poor lady——where are the hartshorn drops?

LOVEMORE. The lady! What lady?

MIGNIONET. Never stand asking what lady. She has fainted away all on a sudden: she is now in strong hysterics; give me the drops.

MRS. BELLMOUR. I must run to her assistance. Adieu, my Lord. I shall be at home in the evening. Mignionet, step this way. Your Lordship will excuse me: I shall expect to see you. Come, Mignionet; make haste, make haste.

Exit with MIGNIONET.

LOVEMORE. I hope the lady has not overheard me. What a villain am I to carry on this scheme against so much beauty, innocence, and merit! And to wear this badge of honour for the darkest purposes! And then my friend Sir Brilliant, will it be fair to supplant him?——Prithee, be quiet, my dear conscience! None of your meddling; don't interrupt a gentleman in his pleasures. Don't you know, my good friend, that love has no respect for persons, but soars above all laws of honour and of friendship? No reflection; have her I must, and that quickly too, or she will discover all. Besides, this is my wife's fault: why does not she make home agreeable? I am willing to be happy; I could be constant to her, but she is not formed for happiness. What the devil is Madam Fortune about now?——(*Sir Brilliant sings within*) Sir Brilliant, by all that's infamous. Confusion! No place to hide me? No escape? The door is locked. Mignionet, Mignionet, open the door.

MIGNIONET. (*Within*) You must not come in here.

LOVEMORE. What shall I do? This star and this ribbon will bring me to disgrace. Away with this telltale evidence. (*Takes off the ribbon*) Go, thou blushing devil, and hide thyself for ever. (*Puts it in his pocket*)

Enter SIR BRILLIANT, *singing.*

SIR BRILLIANT. Mrs. Bellmour, I have such a story for you.—— How!——Lovemore?

LOVEMORE. Your slave, Sir Brilliant, your slave. (*Hiding the star with his hat*)

SIR BRILLIANT. I did not think you had been acquainted here.

LOVEMORE. You are right. I came in quest of you. I saw the lady. I was drawn hither by mere curiosity. We have had some conversation; and I made it subservient to your purposes. I have been giving a great character of you.

SIR BRILLIANT. You are always at the service of your friends. But what's the matter? What are you fumbling about? (*Pulls the hat*)

LOVEMORE. 'Sdeath! Have care: don't touch me. (*Puts his handkerchief to his breast*)

SIR BRILLIANT. What the devil ails you?

LOVEMORE. Oh! keep off——(*Aside*) here's a business.——Taken in the old way: let me pass.——I have had a fling at Lord Etheridge: he will be out of favour with the Widow: I have done you that good.——Racks and torments, my old complaint! (*Wanting to pass him*)

SIR BRILLIANT. What complaint? You had better sit down.

LOVEMORE. No, no; air, the air. I must have a surgeon. A stroke of a tennis ball! My Lord Rackett's unlucky left hand. Let me pass. There is something forming here. (*Passes him*) To be caught is the devil. (*Aside*)——Don't mention my name. You will counter-act all I have said.——Oh! torture, torture!——I will explain to you another time. Sir Brilliant, yours. I have served your interest.—— Oh! there is certainly something forming.

Exit.

SIR BRILLIANT. What does all this mean?——So, so, Mrs. Love-more's suspicions are well-founded.——The Widow has her private visits, I see. Yes, yes, there is something forming here.

Enter MRS. BELLMOUR.

SIR BRILLIANT. So; here she comes. The whole shall be explained. I hope, Ma'am, that I don't interrupt you with any piquet-friend.

MRS. BELLMOUR. You are always a torment: what brings you hither?

SIR BRILLIANT. There are times, Ma'am, when a visit——

MRS. BELLMOUR. Is unseasonable, and yours is so now. How can you tease me?

SIR BRILLIANT. I thought as much.——There are some things that may require to be discussed between us.

MRS. BELLMOUR. Reserve them all for another time. I can't hear you now. You must leave me. There is a lady taken ill in the next room.

SIR BRILLIANT. And here has been a gentleman taken ill in this room.

MRS. BELLMOUR. How troublesome! You must be gone. Do you dispute my will and pleasure?——Fly this moment.

SIR BRILLIANT. But Ma'am——nay, if you insist upon it—— (*Goes*)

MRS. BELLMOUR. But, Sir!——I will be absolute: you must leave me. (*Puts him out*) There, and now I'll make sure of the door.

Enter MRS. LOVEMORE, *leaning on* MIGNIONET.

MIGNIONET. This way, Madam: here is more air in this room.

MRS. BELLMOUR. How do you find yourself? Pray sit down.

MRS. LOVEMORE. My spirits were too weak. I could not support it any longer. Such a scene of perfidy!

MRS. BELLMOUR. You astonish me: what perfidy?

MRS. LOVEMORE. Perfidy of the blackest dye! I told you that you were acquainted with my husband!

MRS. BELLMOUR. Acquainted with your husband! (*Angrily*)

MRS. LOVEMORE. A moment's patience.——Yes, Madam, you are acquainted with him.——The base man, who went hence but now——

MRS. BELLMOUR. Sir Brilliant Fashion?

MRS. LOVEMORE. No; your Lord Etheridge, as he calls himself——

MRS. BELLMOUR. Lord Etheridge? What of him, pray?

MRS. LOVEMORE. False, dissembling man! He is my husband, Ma'am: not Lord Etheridge, but plain Mr. Lovemore; my Mr. Lovemore.

MRS. BELLMOUR. And has he been base enough to assume a title to ensnare me to my undoing?

MIGNIONET. (*Going*) Well, for certain I believe the devil's in me: I always thought him a sly one.

Exit.

MRS. LOVEMORE. To see him carrying on this dark design——to see the man whom I have ever esteemed and loved——the man whom I must still love——esteem him, I fear, I never can——to see him before my face, with that artful treachery! It was too much for sensibility like mine; I felt the shock too severely, and I sunk under it.

MRS. BELLMOUR. I am ready to sink this moment with amazement. I saw him, for the first time, at old Mrs. Loveit's. She introduced him to me. The appointment was of her own making.

MRS. LOVEMORE. You know Mrs. Loveit's character, I suppose.

MRS. BELLMOUR. The practised veteran!——Could I suspect that a woman in her style of life would lend herself to a vile stratagem against my honour? That she would join in a conspiracy against her own sex?——Mr. Lovemore shall never enter these doors again. ——I am obliged to you, Ma'am, for this visit; to me a providential incident. I am sorry for your share in it. The discovery secures my peace and happiness; to you, it is a fatal conviction, a proof unanswerable against the person to whom you are joined for life.

MRS. LOVEMORE. After this discovery, it cannot be for life. I am resolved not to pass another day under his roof.

MRS. BELLMOUR. Hold, hold; no sudden resolutions. Consider a little: passion is a bad adviser. This may take a turn to your advantage.

MRS. LOVEMORE. That can never be: I am lost beyond redemption.

MRS. BELLMOUR. Don't decide too rashly. Come, come, the man, who has certain qualities, is worth thinking about before one throws the hideous thing away for ever. Mr. Lovemore is a traitor; but is not he still amiable? And besides, you have heard his sentiments. That song points at something. Perhaps you are a little to blame. He did not write upon such a subject without a cause to suggest it. We will talk over this matter coolly. You have saved me, and I must return the obligation. You shall stay dinner with me.

MRS. LOVEMORE. Excuse me. Mr. Lovemore may possibly go home. He shall hear of his guilt while the sense of it pierces here, and wounds me to the quick.

MRS. BELLMOUR. Now there you are wrong: take my advice first. I will lay such a plan as may ensure him yours for ever. Come, come, you must not leave me yet. (*Takes her hand*) Answer me one question: don't you still think he has qualities that do in some sort apologize for his vices?

MRS. LOVEMORE. I don't know what to think of it: I hope he has.

MRS. BELLMOUR. Very well then. I have lost a lover; you may gain one. Your conduct upon this occasion may reform him; and let me tell you that the man who has it in his power to atone for his faults should not be entirely despised.——Let the wife exert herself; let her try her powers of pleasing, and take my word for it,

The wild gallant [76] no more abroad will roam,
But find his lov'd variety at home.

End of the THIRD ACT.

ACT the FOURTH
SCENE [I]

An Apartment in Lovemore's House

Mr. and Mrs. Lovemore at table, after dinner; Servants taking
things out of the room.

LOVEMORE. (*Filling a glass*) I wonder you are not tired of the
same eternal topic. (*Sipping his wine*)

MRS. LOVEMORE. If I make it an eternal topic, it is for your own
good, Mr. Lovemore.

LOVEMORE. I know I have your good wishes, and you have mine.
All our absent friends, Mrs. Lovemore. (*Drinks*)

MRS. LOVEMORE. If you would but wish well to yourself, Sir, I
should be happy.——But in the way you go on, your health must be
ruined; day is night, and night day; your substance squandered;
your constitution destroyed; and your family quite neglected.

LOVEMORE. Family neglected! You see I dined at home, and this
is my reward for it.

MRS. LOVEMORE. You dined at home, Sir, because something
abroad has disconcerted you. You went, I suppose, after I saw you
at Lady Constant's, to your old haunt, your friend Mrs. Loveit——

LOVEMORE. Mrs. Loveit! Ha! ha! I dropt her acquaintance long
ago. No, my love, I drove into the City, and spent the rest of the
morning upon business. I had long accounts to settle with old Discount the banker.

---

[76] The allusion is to Loveby in John Dryden, *The Wild Gallant* (1663).

MRS. LOVEMORE. And that to be sure engrossed all your time. Business must be minded. Did you find him at home?

LOVEMORE. It was by his own appointment. I went to his house directly after I parted from you. I have been nowhere else. Matters of account always fatigue me.

MRS. LOVEMORE. I would not be too inquisitive, Sir.

LOVEMORE. Oh! no; you never are. I stayed at the banker's the rest of the time; and I came straight from his house to have the pleasure of dining with you. (*Fills a glass of wine*)

MRS. LOVEMORE. Were there any sincerity in that declaration, I should be happy. A tavern life has hitherto been your delight. I wonder what delight you can find in such an eternal round of gaming, riot and dissipation. Will you answer me one question?

LOVEMORE. With great pleasure——(*Aside*) if it is not inconvenient.

MRS. LOVEMORE. Lay your hand on your heart, and tell me—— have I deserved this usage?

LOVEMORE. My humble service to you, my love. (*Drinks*)

MRS. LOVEMORE. I am sure I have never been deficient in any one point of the duty I owe you. You won my heart, and I gave it freely.

LOVEMORE. (*Going to sleep*) It is very true.

MRS. LOVEMORE. Your interest has been mine. I have known no pleasure unconnected with your happiness. Diversions, show, and pomp have had no allurements for me.

LOVEMORE. (*Dropping asleep*) Yes——you are right——just as you please——

MRS. LOVEMORE. Had I been inclined to follow the example of other women, your fortune would have felt it before now. You might have been thousands out of pocket; but your interest has been the object of my attention; and your convenience——

LOVEMORE. (*Turns his chair from her*) You reason very—— you reason admir——ably——admi——rably——always——al——always ——gay——and——enter——entertaining—— (*Going to sleep*)

MRS. LOVEMORE. Marriage is generally considered as an introduction to the great scene of the world. I thought it a retreat to less noisy and serener pleasures. What is called polite company (*He falls fast asleep*) was not my taste. You was lavish in expense; I was therefore an economist. From the moment marriage made me yours, the pleasure arising from your company——there! fast asleep! Agreeable company indeed!——This is ever his way. (*She rises*) Unfeeling man!——It is too plain that I am grown his aversion. Mr. Lovemore! (*Looking at him*) You little think what a scene this day has brought to light. And yet he hopes with falsehood to varnish and disguise his treachery. How mean the subterfuge! Shall I rouse him now, and tax him with his guilt? My heart is too full, and reproach will only tend to exasperate, and perhaps make him irreconcilable. The pride that can stoop to low and wretched artifice, but ill can brook detection. Let him rest for the present. The Widow Bellmour's experiment may answer better.——I will try it at least.——Oh! Mr. Lovemore, you will break my heart.

Looks at him, and exit.

LOVEMORE. (*Talking in his sleep*) I do listen——I am not asleep. (*Sleeps and nods*) You are very right——always right——I am only thinking a little. No——no——no——(*Mutters indistinctly*) it was not two o'clock——in bed——in bed by twelve——Sir Bashful is an oaf.——The Widow Bellmour.——(*Sleeps, and his head rolls about*) What's the matter? (*Waking*) I beg your pardon; I was beginning to nod. What did you say, my dear? (*Leans on the table, without looking about*) One cannot always you know——(*Turns about*) 'sdeath! she is gone! Oh! fast asleep. This is ever the way when one dines at home. Let me shake it off. (*Rises*) What's o'clock?——No amusement in this house; what shall I do? The Widow?——I must not venture in that quarter. My evil genius Sir Brilliant will be busy there. Is anybody in the way? I must sally out. My dear Venus, favour your votary this afternoon:

"Your best arms employ,
All wing'd with pleasure, and all tipt with joy." [77]

Exit.

---

[77] Altered from Matthew Prior, *Henry and Emma*, lines 728-729.

SCENE [II]

Sir Bashful's

Enter LADY CONSTANT *and* FURNISH.

LADY CONSTANT. Who brought this letter?

FURNISH. A servant of Mrs. Lovemore's: he waits an answer.

LADY CONSTANT. My compliments to Mrs. Lovemore, and I shall wait upon her.

FURNISH. Yes, Ma'am. (*Going*)

LADY CONSTANT. And hark ye, Furnish;——have the things been carried to Sir Brilliant, as I ordered?

FURNISH. I have obeyed your Ladyship's commands. The steward went himself. Mr. Pounce, your Ladyship knows, is a trusty body. You may depend upon his care.

LADY CONSTANT. Go and send Mrs. Lovemore her answer. She may depend upon my being with her in time.

Exit FURNISH.

LADY CONSTANT. (*Alone*) What can Mrs. Lovemore want? (*Reads*) "Ladyship's company to a card-party: but cards are the least part of my object. I have something of higher moment in view, and the presence of my friends is absolutely necessary." There is some mystery in all this. What does she mean? I shall go, and then the scene will clear up. Those diamond buckles embarrass me more than Mrs. Lovemore's unintelligible letter. Diamond buckles to me! From what quarter? Who could send them? Nobody but Sir Brilliant. I am right in my conclusion: they came from him. Who could take the liberty but a person of his cast? A presuming man. But I have mortified his vanity. Before this time, he has found his diamonds thrown back upon his hands, with the disdain which such confidence deserves.——But if I have made a mistake!——Oh! no; no danger. Has not Sir Brilliant made overtures to me? Has not he declared himself? He sees Sir Bashful's behaviour, and his vanity plumes itself upon that circumstance. To give me my revenge against a crazy and insufferable husband, he would fain induce me to ruin myself with a coxcomb. Besides, he heard the whole of Sir Bashful's dispute about diamonds and trinkets: the thing is clear; it was Sir Brilliant sent them; and by that stratagem he hopes to bribe me into compliance.——That bait will never take; though here comes one who, I am sure, deserves to be treated without a grain of ceremony.

Enter SIR BASHFUL.

SIR BASHFUL. Here she is. Now let me see whether she will take any notice of the present I sent her. She has reason to be in good humour, I think.——Your servant, Madam.

LADY CONSTANT. Your address is polite, Sir.

SIR BASHFUL. (*Aside*) Still proud and obstinate!——Has anything happened to disturb the harmony of your temper?

LADY CONSTANT. Considering what little discord you make, it is a wonder that my temper is not always in tune.

SIR BASHFUL. If you never gave me cause, Madam——

LADY CONSTANT. Oh! for mercy sake, truce with altercation. I am tired out with the eternal violence of your temper. Those frequent starts of passion hurry me out of my senses: and those unaccountable whims, that hold such constant possession of you——

SIR BASHFUL. Whims, Madam?——Not to comply with you in everything is a whim, truly. Must I yield to the exorbitant demands of your extravagance? When you laid close siege to me for diamond baubles, and I know not what, was that a whim of mine? Did I take that fancy into my head, without cause, and without sufficient foundation?

LADY CONSTANT. Well, we have exhausted the subject. Have not you told me a thousand times that there is no living with me? I agree to it. And have not I returned the compliment? We have nothing new to say; and now, all that remains, is to let the lawyer reduce to writing our mutual opinions, and so we may part with the pleasure of giving each other a most woeful character.

SIR BASHFUL. (*Aside*) The buckles have had no effect. Stubborn! She has received them, and won't own it.

LADY CONSTANT. A dash of your pen, Sir, at the foot of certain articles now preparing, will make us both easy. (*Going*)

SIR BASHFUL. If we don't live happily, it is your own fault.

LADY CONSTANT. That is very old.

SIR BASHFUL. If you would control your passion for play——

LADY CONSTANT. Quite threadbare!

SIR BASHFUL. I have still a regard for you.

LADY CONSTANT. Worn-out to frippery!——I can't hear any more. The law will dress it up in new language for us, and that will end our differences.

Exit.

SIR BASHFUL. (*Alone*) I must unburthen my heart: there is no time to be lost. I love her; I admire her; she inflames my tenderest passions, and raises such a conflict here in my very heart, I cannot any longer conceal the secret from her. I'll go and tell her all this moment.——But then that meddling fiend, her maid, will be there. Po! I can turn her out of the room: but then the jade will suspect something.——Her Ladyship may be alone: I'll send to know where she is. Who is there? Sideboard——

Enter SIDEBOARD.

SIR BASHFUL. Go and tell your Lady that—— (*Pauses*)

SIDEBOARD. Did your Honour want me?

SIR BASHFUL. No matter; it does not signify.——(*Aside*) I shall never be able to tell her my mind: a glance of her eye, and my own confusion will undo all.

SIDEBOARD. I thought your Honour called.

SIR BASHFUL. (*Aside*) A thought comes across me: I'll write her a letter. Yes, yes, a letter will do the business. Sideboard, draw that table this way.——Reach me a chair.

SIDEBOARD. There, your Honour.

SIR BASHFUL. Do you stay while I write a letter. You shall carry it for me. (*Sits down to write*)

SIDEBOARD. Yes, Sir. (*Aside*) [78] I hope he has an intrigue upon his hands. A servant thrives under a master that has his private amusements. Love on, say I, if you are so given: it will bring grist to my mill.

SIR BASHFUL. (*Writing*) This will surprise her. Warm, passionate, and tender! And yet it does not come up to what I feel.

SIDEBOARD. What is he at?——I may as well read the newspaper. (*Takes it out of his pocket*) What in the name of wonder is all this?——Ha! ha! (*Bursts into a loud laugh*) I never heard the like of this before. Oh! ho! ho ho!

SIR BASHFUL. What does the scoundrel mean? (*Stares at him*)

SIDEBOARD. Ha! ha! ha! I can't help laughing.

SIR BASHFUL. Does the villain suspect me? (*Rises*) Hark ye, sirrah, if ever I find that you dare listen at any door in my house——

SIDEBOARD. Sir!

SIR BASHFUL. Confess the truth: have not you been listening to my conversation with Mr. Lovemore this morning?

SIDEBOARD. Who, I, Sir? I would not be guilty of such a thing: I never did the like in all my days.

SIR BASHFUL. What was you laughing at?

SIDEBOARD. A foolish thing in the newspaper, Sir, that's all. I'll read it to your Honour. (*Reads*) We hear that a new comedy is now in rehearsal, and will speedily be performed, entitled, *The Amorous Husband, or The Man in Love with His Own Wife*.

SIR BASHFUL. And what do you see to laugh at?

SIDEBOARD. See, Sir? I have lived in a great many families, and never heard of the like before.

SIR BASHFUL. (*Aside*) There, there, there!——I shall be the butt of my own servants.——Sirrah, leave the room. And let me never hear that you have the trick of listening in my house.

SIDEBOARD. No, Sir.——*The Man in Love with His Own Wife!*

Exit laughing.

---

[78] Aside is labeled in 1770, not in later editions.

SIR BASHFUL. What does the varlet mean?——No matter——I have finished my letter, and it shall be sent this moment.——But then, if I should get into a comedy? Po! no more scruples. I'll seal it directly.——Sideboard——

Enter SIDEBOARD.

SIR BASHFUL. (*Sealing the letter*) I have opened my heart to her. What do you bring your hat and stick for?

SIDEBOARD. To go out with your Honour's letter.

SIR BASHFUL. You have not far to go. Take this, and let nobody see you.

SIDEBOARD. I warrant me, your Honour.

Exit.

SIR BASHFUL. I feel much lighter now. A load is taken off my heart.

Enter SIDEBOARD.

SIR BASHFUL. What do you come back for?

SIDEBOARD. A word or two by way of direction, if you please.

SIR BASHFUL. Blockhead! Give it to me.——(*Aside*) If I direct it, he finds me out.——Go about your business: I have no occasion for you; leave the room.

SIDEBOARD. Very well, Sir.——Does he think to manage his own intrigues? If he takes my commission out of my hands, I shall give him warning. The vices of our masters are all the vails [79] a poor servant has left.

Exit.

SIR BASHFUL. What must be done?——Mr. Lovemore could conduct this business for me. He is a man of address, and knows all the approaches to a woman's heart. That fellow, Sideboard, coming again?——No, no; this is lucky. Mr. Lovemore, I am glad to see you.

---

[79] Tips.

Enter LOVEMORE.

LOVEMORE. A second visit you see, in one day; entirely on the score of friendship.

SIR BASHFUL. And I thank you for it; heartily thank you.

LOVEMORE. I broke away from company at the St. Alban's on purpose to attend you. Well, I have made your Lady easier in her mind, have not I?

SIR BASHFUL. We don't hit it at all, Mr. Lovemore.

LOVEMORE. No?

SIR BASHFUL. I think she has been rather worse, since you spoke to her.

LOVEMORE. A good symptom that. (*Aside*)

SIR BASHFUL. She has received the diamond buckles. They were delivered to her maid sealed up, and the man never stayed to be asked a question. I saw them in her own hand: but not a syllable escaped her. She was not in the least softened, obstinate as a mule!

LOVEMORE. The manner of conveying your present was not well judged. Why did not you make me the bearer?

SIR BASHFUL. I wish I had. She talks of parting; and so to avoid coming to extremities, I have even thought of telling her the whole truth at once.

LOVEMORE. How! Acquaint her with your passion?

SIR BASHFUL. Ay, and trust to her honour. I could not venture to speak; I should blush, and falter, and look silly; and so I have writ a letter to her. Here it is signed and sealed, but not directed. I got into a puzzle about that. Servants, you know, are always putting their own construction upon things.

LOVEMORE. No doubt: and then your secret flies all over the town.

SIR BASHFUL. That's what alarmed me. You shall write the superscription, and send it to her.

LOVEMORE. No, that won't do. Give her a letter under your hand? I'll speak to her for you: let me try how her pulse beats.

SIR BASHFUL. But a letter may draw an answer from her, and then, you know, (*Smiling at him*) I shall have it under her hand.

LOVEMORE. I don't like this hurry: we had better take time to consider of it.

SIR BASHFUL. No, I can't defer the business of my heart a single moment. It burns like a fever here. Sit down, and write the direction; I'll step and send the servant. He shall carry it, as if it were a letter from yourself.

Enter SIDEBOARD.

SIDEBOARD. Sir Brilliant Fashion is below, Sir.

LOVEMORE. What brings him? He will only interrupt us. Go and talk to him, Sir Bashful; hear what he has to say; amuse him; anything rather than let him come up.

SIR BASHFUL. I am gone: he shan't molest you.

Exit with SIDEBOARD.

LOVEMORE. Fly, make haste; and don't let him know that I am here.——A lucky accident this; I have gained time by it. All matters were in a right train, and he himself levelling the road for me, and now this letter blows me up into the air at once. Some unlucky planet rules today. First the Widow Bellmour; a hair-breadth scrape I had of it, and now almost ruined here! What in the name of wonder has he writ to her?——Friendship and wafer, by your leave.——But will that be delicate?——Po! Honour has always a great deal to preach upon these occasions; but then the business of my love!——Very true; the passions need but say a word, and their business is done. (*Opens the letter, and reads*) This must never reach her. I'll write a letter from myself. (*Sits down, writes, and starts up*) I hear him coming: no; all safe. (*Writes*) This will do: ——vastly well. Her husband's inhumanity! Ay, mention that.—— The diamonds may be a present from me: yes, I'll venture it.—— There, there; that will do.——Long adored——ay——sweetest revenge——ay——eternal admirer——Lovemore.[80]——Now, now, let me see it.——Admirable! This will do the business. (*Seals the letter*)

Enter SIR BASHFUL.

---

[80] The 1770 edition has the entire letter.

SIR BASHFUL. Well, have you sent it?

LOVEMORE. Not yet: I am writing the direction.

SIR BASHFUL. And where is that blockhead?——Sideboard!

Enter SIDEBOARD.

SIR BASHFUL. Numskull, why don't you wait?—— Mr. Lovemore wants you.

LOVEMORE. Step and deliver this to your Lady, and if she pleases I will wait upon her.

SIR BASHFUL. Charming!——Take it upstairs directly.

SIDEBOARD. Upstairs, Sir? My Lady is in the next room.

SIR BASHFUL. Take it to her; make haste; begone. (*Exit Sideboard*) I hope this will succeed: I shall be for ever obliged to you, and so will her Ladyship.

LOVEMORE. I hope she will, and I shall be proud to serve her.

SIR BASHFUL. You are very good. She won't prove ungrateful, I dare answer for her.——I should like to see how she receives the letter.——The door is conveniently open.——I will have a peep. Ay, there, there she sits.

LOVEMORE. Where, Sir Bashful?

SIR BASHFUL. Hush, no noise.——There, do you see her? She has the letter in her hand.——This is a critical moment: I am all over in a tremble.

LOVEMORE. Silence; not a word. She opens it.——(*Aside*) Now, my dear Cupid, befriend me now, and your altar shall smoke with incense.

SIR BASHFUL. She colours!

LOVEMORE. I like that rising blush: a soft and tender token.

SIR BASHFUL. She turns pale.

LOVEMORE. The natural working of the passions.

SIR BASHFUL. And now she reddens again!——What is she at now? ——There, she has tore the letter in two:——I am a lost, an undone man. (*Walks away*)

LOVEMORE. She has flung it away with indignation: I am undone too. (*Aside, and walks away from the door*)

SIR BASHFUL. Mr. Lovemore, you see what it is all come to.

LOVEMORE. I am sorry to see so haughty a spirit.

SIR BASHFUL. An arrogant, ungrateful woman! To make such a return to so kind a letter.

LOVEMORE. Ay, so kind a letter!

SIR BASHFUL. Did you ever see such an insolent scorn?

LOVEMORE. I never was so disappointed in all my life.

SIR BASHFUL. A letter full of the tenderest protestations!

LOVEMORE. Yes; an unreserved declaration of love!

SIR BASHFUL. Made with the greatest frankness; throwing myself at her very feet!

LOVEMORE. Did she once smile? Was there the faintest gleam of approbation in her countenance?

SIR BASHFUL. She repaid it all with scorn, with pride, contempt, and insolence. I cannot bear this; despised, spurned, and treated like a puppy.

LOVEMORE. There it stings——like a puppy indeed!

SIR BASHFUL. Is there a thing in nature so mortifying to the pride of man, as to find oneself rejected and despised by a fine woman, who is conscious of her power, and triumphs in her cruelty?

LOVEMORE. It is the most damnable circumstance!——

SIR BASHFUL. My dear Mr. Lovemore, I am obliged to you for taking this matter so much to heart.

LOVEMORE. I take it more to heart than you [are] aware of.

SIR BASHFUL. This is mortifying; enough to make one ashamed all the rest of one's life.

LOVEMORE. I did not expect this sullen ill humour.

SIR BASHFUL. Did you ever know so obstinate, so uncomplying a temper?

Enter SIR BRILLIANT.

SIR BRILLIANT. Sir Bashful, I forgot to tell you——

LOVEMORE. He again! He hunts me up and down, as the vice did the devil, with a dagger of lath, in the old comedy. (*Aside*)

SIR BRILLIANT. Hey!——what's the matter?——You seem both out of humour: what does this mean? Have you quarrelled?

SIR BASHFUL. No, Sir, no quarrel:——Why would my booby servants let him in again? (*Aside*)

SIR BRILLIANT. Strike me stupid, but you look very queer upon it.——Lovemore is borrowing money, I suppose: Sir Bashful is driving a hard bargain, and you can't agree about the premium. Sir Bashful, let my friend Lovemore have the money?

SIR BASHFUL. Money!——What does he mean?

SIR BRILLIANT. Both out of humour, I see: well, as you will. You have no reason to be in harmony with yourselves; my stars shine with a kinder aspect. Here, here, behold a treasury of love. I came back on purpose to show it to you. (*Takes a shagreen case out of his pocket*) See what a present I have received; a magnificent pair of diamond buckles, by all that's amiable.

LOVEMORE. How?

SIR BASHFUL. (*Walking up to him*) A pair of diamond buckles!

SIR BRILLIANT. How such a present should be sent to me is more than I can explain at present. Perhaps my friend Lovemore gained some intelligence in the quarter where I surprised him today, on a visit which I little suspected.

LOVEMORE. That was to serve you: I know nothing of this business.

SIR BRILLIANT. The pain in your side, I hope, is better.

LOVEMORE. Po! This is only to distract your attention, Sir Bashful.

SIR BASHFUL. So I suppose. And was this a present to you?

SIR BRILLIANT. A present, Sir. The consequence of having some tolerable phrase, a person, and a due degree of attention to the service of the ladies.——Do you envy me, Sir Bashful?

SIR BASHFUL. I can't but say I do.——(*Turns to Lovemore*) My buckles, by all that's false in woman!

LOVEMORE. Take no notice.——(*Walks aside*) Has he supplanted me here too, as well as with the Widow?

SIR BRILLIANT. What's the matter with you both?——Burning with envy!

SIR BASHFUL. And I suppose an elegant epistle, or a well-penned billet-doux, accompanied this token of the lady's affection.

SIR BRILLIANT. That would have been an agreeable addition, but it is still to come. Too many favours at once might overwhelm a body. A country-looking fellow, as my people tell me, left this, curiously sealed up, at my house: he would not say from whence he came: I should know that in time, was all they could get from him, and I am now panting to learn where this mighty success has attended me. Sir Bashful, I came, saw, and conquered; ha! ha! ha!

SIR BASHFUL. But may not this be from some lady who imagines that you sent it, and therefore chooses to reject your present?

SIR BRILLIANT. Oh! no; that cannot be the case. A little knowledge of the world would soon convince you that ladies do not usually reject presents from the man who has the good fortune to please by his manner, a taste for dress, and a certain *je ne sais quoi* in his person and conversation.

SIR BASHFUL. So I believe.——(*Walks aside*) What say you to this, Mr. Lovemore?

LOVEMORE. She would not have torn a letter from him.

SIR BRILLIANT. No, Sir Bashful; a present from me would not have been returned back upon my hands.

SIR BASHFUL. I dare say not.——(*To Lovemore*) I suppose she will give him my three hundred pounds into the bargain.

LOVEMORE. After this, I shall wonder at nothing.

SIR BRILLIANT. What mortified countenances they both put on! (*Looks at them, and laughs*)

SIR BASHFUL. (*Walking up to Sir Brilliant*) And I suppose you expect to have this lady?

SIR BRILLIANT. No doubt of it. This is the forerunner, I think. Hey, Lovemore!——Sir Bashful, this it is to be in luck. Ha! ha! (*Laughs at them both*)

LOVEMORE *and* SIR BASHFUL. (*Both forcing a laugh*) Ha! ha!

SIR BRILLIANT. You both seem strangely piqued.——Lovemore, what makes you so uneasy?

LOVEMORE. You flatter yourself, and you wrong me——I——I—— (*Walks away*)

SIR BASHFUL. He is a true friend: he is uneasy on my account. (*Aside, and looking at Lovemore*)

SIR BRILLIANT. And Sir Bashful, something has dashed your spirits. Do you repine at my success?

SIR BASHFUL. I can't but say I do, Sir.

SIR BRILLIANT. Oh! very well; you are not disposed to be good company. *A l'honneur*, gentlemen: finish your money matters. Lovemore, where do you spend the evening?

LOVEMORE. A good evening to you, Sir Brilliant: I am engaged. Business with Sir Bashful, you see——

SIR BRILLIANT. Well, don't let me be of inconvenience to you: fare ye well, gentlemen. Thou dear pledge of love (*Looking at the buckles*), thus let me clasp thee to my heart.——Sir Bashful, your servant.

Exit.

SIR BASHFUL. What think you now, Mr. Lovemore?

LOVEMORE. All unaccountable, Sir.

SIR BASHFUL. By all that's false, I am gulled, cheated, and imposed upon. I am deceived, and dubbed a rank cuckold. It is too clear; she has given him the buckles, and I suppose my bank notes have taken the same course.——Diamond buckles, and three hundred pounds for Sir Brilliant! A reward for his merit!

LOVEMORE. He is the favourite, and I have been working for him all this time.

SIR BASHFUL. I now see through all her artifices. My resolution is fixed. If I can but get ocular demonstration of her guilt, if I can but get the means of proving to the whole world that she is vile enough to cuckold me, I shall then be happy.

LOVEMORE. Why, that will be some consolation!

SIR BASHFUL. So it will: kind Heaven, grant me that at least; make it plain that she dishonours me, and I am amply revenged.—— Hark! I hear her coming. She shall know all I think, and all I feel. I have done with her for ever.

LOVEMORE. (*Aside*) Let me fly the impending storm. If I stay, detection and disgrace pursue me.——Sir Bashful, I am sorry to see matters take this turn. I have done all in my power, and since there is no room to hope for success, I take my leave, and wish you a good night.

SIR BASHFUL. No, no; you shall not leave me in this distress. You shall hear me tell her her own, and be a witness of our separation. (*Holding him*)

LOVEMORE. Excuse me: after what has passed, I shall never be able to endure the sight of her. Fare you well; I must be gone; good night, Sir Bashful. (*Struggling to go*)

SIR BASHFUL. You are my best friend: I cannot part with you. (*Stands between him and the door*) Stay and hear what she has to say for herself; you will see what a turn she will give to the business.

LOVEMORE. (*Aside*) What turn shall I give it?——Confusion! Here she comes: I must weather the storm.

Enter LADY CONSTANT.

LADY CONSTANT. After this behavior, Mr. Lovemore, I am surprised, Sir, that you can think of staying a moment longer in this house.

LOVEMORE. Madam, I——'sdeath! I have no invention to assist me at a pinch. (*Aside*)

SIR BASHFUL. Mr. Lovemore is my friend, Madam, and I desire he will stay in my house as long as he pleases.——Hey, Lovemore! (*Looks at him and smiles*)

LOVEMORE. (*Aside*) All must out, I fear.

LADY CONSTANT. Your friend, Sir Bashful!——And do you authorize him to take this unbecoming liberty? Have you given him permission to send me a letter so extravagant in the very terms of it?

LOVEMORE. (*Aside*) Ay, now it's coming, and impudence itself has not a word to say.

SIR BASHFUL. I desired him to send that letter, Madam.

LOVEMORE. Sir Bashful desired me, Ma'am. (*Bowing respect-fully*)

SIR BASHFUL. I desired him.

LOVEMORE. All at his request, Ma'am.

LADY CONSTANT. And am I to be made your sport?——I wonder, Mr. Lovemore, that you would condescend to make yourself a party in so poor a plot. Do you presume upon a trifling mark of civility, which you persuaded me to accept of this morning? Do you come disguised under a mask of friendship, to help this gentleman in his design against my honour and my happiness?

LOVEMORE. (*Aside*) Fairly caught, and nothing can bring me off——

SIR BASHFUL. A mask of friendship!——He is a true friend, Madam; he sees how ill I am treated, and let me tell you, there is not a word of truth in that letter.

LOVEMORE. Not a syllable of truth, Ma'am.——(*Aside*) This will do: his own nonsense will save me.

SIR BASHFUL. It was all done to try you, Madam.

LOVEMORE. Nothing more, Ma'am: merely to try you.

SIR BASHFUL. By way of experiment only; just to see how you would behave upon it.

LOVEMORE. Nothing else was intended; pure innocent mirth.

LADY CONSTANT. You have been both notably employed. The exploit is worthy of you. Your snare is spread for a woman, and if you had succeeded, the fame of so bright an action would add mightily to two such illustrious characters.

SIR BASHFUL. A snare spread for her! Mark that, Mr. Lovemore: she calls it ensnaring.

LOVEMORE. Ensnared to her own good. (*To Sir Bashful*)—— He has pleaded admirably for me. (*Aside*)

LADY CONSTANT. As to you, Sir Bashful, I have long ago ceased to wonder at your conduct: you have lost the power of surprising me; but when Mr. Lovemore becomes an accomplice in so mean a plot——

SIR BASHFUL. I am in no plot, Madam, and nobody wants to ensnare you: do we, Lovemore?

LOVEMORE. Sir Bashful knows that no harm was intended.

SIR BASHFUL. Yes, I am in the secret, and my friend Lovemore meant no harm.

LOVEMORE. If the letter had succeeded, Sir Bashful knows there would have been no harm in it.

SIR BASHFUL. No harm in nature; but I now see how things are; and since your Ladyship will listen to nothing for your own good, it is too plain from all that has passed between us, that our tempers are by no means fitted for each other, and I am ready to part whenever you please: nay, I will part.

LADY CONSTANT. And that is the only point in which we can agree, Sir.

SIR BASHFUL. Had the letter been sent from another quarter, it would have met with a better reception: we know where your smiles are bestowed.

LADY CONSTANT. Deal in calumny, Sir; give free scope to malice; I disdain your insinuations.

SIR BASHFUL. The fact is too clear, and reproaches are now too late. This is the last of our conversing together; and you may take this by the way, you are not to believe one syllable of that letter.

LOVEMORE. There is not a syllable of it deserves the least credit, Ma'am.

SIR BASHFUL. It was all a mere joke, Madam: was not it, Lovemore?——And as to your being a fine woman, and as to any passion that anybody has conceived for you, there was no such thing; you can witness for me, Lovemore: can't you?

LADY CONSTANT. Oh! you are witnesses for one another.

LOVEMORE. Sir Bashful knows the fairness of my intentions, and I know his.——(*Aside*) He has acquitted me better than I expected, thanks to his absurdity.

LADY CONSTANT. Go on, and aggravate your ill usage, gentlemen.

SIR BASHFUL. It was all a bam,[81] Madam, a scene we thought proper to act. Let us laugh at her. (*Goes up to Lovemore*)

LOVEMORE. With all my heart.——(*Aside*) A silly blockhead! I can't help laughing at him. (*Laughing heartily*)

---

[81] Hoax.

SIR BASHFUL. (*Laughing with him*) Ha! ha!——ha!——all a bam; nothing else; a contrivance to make sport for ourselves.——Hey, Lovemore?

LADY CONSTANT. This usage is insupportable. I shall not stay for an explanation. Two such worthy confederates!——Is my chair ready there? You may depend, Sir, that this is the last time you will see me in this house.

Exit.

SIR BASHFUL. Agreed; a bargain; with all my heart. Lovemore, I have managed this well.

LOVEMORE. Charmingly managed! I did not think you had so much spirit.

SIR BASHFUL. I have found her out. The intrigue is too plain. She and Sir Brilliant are both detected.

LOVEMORE. I never suspected that Sir Brilliant was the happy man. I wish I had succeeded, had it been only to mortify his vanity.

SIR BASHFUL. And so do I: I wish it too: but never own the letter: deny it to the last.

LOVEMORE. You may depend upon my secrecy.

SIR BASHFUL. I am for ever obliged to you. A foolish woman! How she stands in her own light!

LOVEMORE. Truly I think she does. But since I have no interest with her Ladyship, I shall now sound a retreat and leave matters to your own discretion. Success attend you. (*Going*)

SIR BASHFUL. You must not forsake me in this distress.

LOVEMORE. Had your lady proved tractable, I should not have cared how long I had stayed. But since things are come to this pass, I shall now go and see what kind of reception I am to meet with from Mrs. Lovemore.

SIR BASHFUL. Don't let her know that you have a regard for her.

LOVEMORE. Oh! no; I see the consequence.——(*Aside*) Well off this time; and, Madam Fortune, if I trust you again, you shall play me what prank you please. Sir Bashful, yours. (*Going*)

SIR BASHFUL. A thousand thanks to you. And harkye, if I can serve you with your lady——

LOVEMORE. I am much obliged to you: but I shall endeavour

to go on without giving you the trouble of assisting me. And do you hear? Assure my Lady Constant that I meant nothing but to serve your interest.

Exit.

SIR BASHFUL. Rely upon my management. I can acquit you.——My Lady Constant! Lady Constant!——Let me chase her from my thoughts: [82] can I do it? Rage, fury, love——no more of love! I am glad she tore the letter. Odso! yonder it lies. It is only torn in two, and she may still piece the fragments together. I'll pick up the letter this moment: it shall never appear in evidence against me. As to Sir Brilliant, his motions shall be watched: I know how to proceed with Madam, and if I can but prove the fact, everybody will say that I am ill-used by her.

End of the FOURTH ACT

ACT the FIFTH
SCENE [I]

An Apartment at Mr. Lovemore's

Enter MRS. LOVEMORE, *elegantly dress'd;* MUSLIN *following her.*

MUSLIN. Why, to be sure, Ma'am, it is so for certain, and you are very much in the right of it.

MRS. LOVEMORE. I fancy I am: I see the folly of my former conduct. I am determined never to let my spirits sink into a melancholy state again.

MUSLIN. Why, that's the very thing, Ma'am; the very thing I have been always preaching up to you. Did not I always say, see company, Ma'am, take your pleasure, and never break your heart for any man? This is what I always said.

---

[82] 1785, 1787: "from my thoughts"; 1786: "from thoughts."

MRS. LOVEMORE. And you have said enough: spare yourself the trouble now.

MUSLIN. I always said so! And what did the world say? Heavens bless her for a sweet woman! And a plague go with him for an in-human, barbarous, bloody——murdering brute.

MRS. LOVEMORE. Well, truce with your impertinence; your tongue runs on at such a rate.

MUSLIN. Nay, don't be angry: they did say so indeed. But dear heart, how everybody will be overjoy'd when they find you have pluck'd up a little! As for me, it gives me new life to have so much company in the house, and such a racketting at the door with coaches and chairs, enough to hurry a body out of one's wits. Lard, this is another thing, and you look quite like another thing, Ma'am, and that dress quite becomes you. I suppose, Ma'am, you will never wear your negligee again. It is not fit for you indeed, Ma'am. It might pass very well with some folks, Ma'am, but the like of you——

MRS. LOVEMORE. Will you never have done? Go and see who is coming upstairs.

Enter MRS. BELLMOUR.

MRS. LOVEMORE. Mrs. Bellmour, I revive at the sight of you. Muslin, do you step and do as I ordered you.

MUSLIN. What the deuce can she be at now?

Exit.

MRS. BELLMOUR. You see I am punctual to my time.——Well, I admire your dress of all things.——It's mighty pretty.

MRS. LOVEMORE. I am glad you like it. But under all this appearance of gaiety, I have at the bottom but an aching heart.

MRS. BELLMOUR. Be ruled by me, and I'll answer for the event. Why really, now you look just as you shou'd do.——Why neglect so fine a figure?

MRS. LOVEMORE. You are so obliging!

MRS. BELLMOUR. And so true!——What was beautiful before, is now heightened by the additional ornaments of dress; and if you will but animate and inspire the whole by those graces of the mind which I am sure you possess, the impression cannot fail of being effectual upon all beholders, and even upon the depraved mind of Mr. Lovemore.——You have not seen him since——have you?

MRS. LOVEMORE. He dined at home, but was soon upon the wing to his usual haunts.

MRS. BELLMOUR. If he does but come home time enough, depend upon it my plot will take. And have you got together a good deal of company?

MRS. LOVEMORE. Yes; a tolerable party.

MRS. BELLMOUR. That's right: show him that you will consult your own pleasure.

MRS. LOVEMORE. Apropos, as soon as I came home I received a letter from Sir Brilliant, in a style of warmth and tenderness that would astonish you. He begs to see me again, and has something particular to communicate. I left it in my dressing-room; you shall see it by-and-by: I took your advice, and sent him word he might come. That lure brought him hither immediately: he makes no doubt of his success with me.

MRS. BELLMOUR. Well! Two such friends as Sir Brilliant and Mr. Lovemore, I believe, never existed!

MRS. LOVEMORE. Their falsehood to each other is unparalleled. I left Sir Brilliant at the card-table: as soon as he can disengage himself, he will quit his company in pursuit of me. I forgot to tell you; my Lady Constant is here.

MRS. BELLMOUR. Is she?

MRS. LOVEMORE. She is, and has been making the strangest discovery: Mr. Lovemore has had a design there too!

MRS. BELLMOUR. Oh! I don't doubt him: but the more proof we have the better.

MRS. LOVEMORE. There is sufficient proof: you must know, Ma'am, (*A rap at the door*) as I live and breathe, I believe this is Mr. Lovemore.

MRS. BELLMOUR. If it is, everything goes on as I could wish.

MRS. LOVEMORE. I hear his voice, it is he. How my heart beats!

MRS. BELLMOUR. Courage, and the day's our own. He must not see me yet: where shall I run?

MRS. LOVEMORE. In there, Ma'am. Make haste; I hear his step on the stairs.

MRS. BELLMOUR. Success attend you. I am gone.

Exit.

MRS. LOVEMORE. I am frightened out of my senses. What the event may be I fear to think; but I must go through with it.

Enter LOVEMORE.

MRS. LOVEMORE. You are welcome home, Sir.

LOVEMORE. Mrs. Lovemore, your servant. (*Without looking at her*)

MRS. LOVEMORE. It is somewhat rare to see you at home so early.

LOVEMORE. I said I should come home, did not I? I always like to be as good as my word.——What could the Widow mean by this usage? To make an appointment, and break it thus abruptly (*Aside*)

MRS. LOVEMORE. He seems to muse upon it. (*Aside*)

LOVEMORE. (*Aside*) She does not mean to do so treacherous a thing as to jilt me? Oh Lord! I am wonderfully tired. (*Yawns, and sinks into an armed chair*)

MRS. LOVEMORE. Are you indisposed, my dear?

LOVEMORE. No, my love; I thank you, I am very well;——a little fatigued only, with jolting over the stones all the way into the City this morning. I have paid a few visits this afternoon.——Confoundedly tired.——Where's William?

MRS. LOVEMORE. Do you want anything?

LOVEMORE. Only my cap and slippers. I am not in spirits, I think. (*Yawns*)

MRS. LOVEMORE. You never are in spirits at home, Mr. Lovemore.

LOVEMORE. I beg your pardon: I never am anywhere more cheerful. (*Stretching his arms*) I wish I may die if I an't very happy at home——very (*yawns*), very happy!

MRS. LOVEMORE. I can hear otherwise. I am informed that Mr Lovemore is the promoter of mirth and good humour wherever he goes.

LOVEMORE. Oh! no, you overrate me; upon my soul, you do.

MRS. LOVEMORE. I can hear, Sir, that no person's company is so acceptable to the ladies; that your wit inspires everything; you have your compliment for one, your smile for another, a whisper for a third, and so on, Sir: you divide your favours, and are everywhere, but at home, all whim, vivacity, and spirit.

LOVEMORE. Ho! ho! (*Laughing*) How can you talk so? I swear I can't help laughing at the fancy. All whim, vivacity, and spirit! I shall burst my sides. How can you banter one so?——I divide my favours too!——Oh, heavens! I can't stand this raillery: such a description of me!——I that am rather saturnine, of a serious cast, and inclined to be pensive! I can't help laughing at the oddity of the conceit.——Oh Lord! Oh Lord! (*Laughs*)

MRS. LOVEMORE. Just as you please, Sir. I see that I am ever to be treated with indifference. (*Walks across the stage*)

LOVEMORE. (*Rises and walks the contrary way*) I can't put this Widow Bellmour out of my head. (*Aside*)

MRS. LOVEMORE. If I had done anything to provoke this usage, this cold, determined contempt——(*Walking*)

LOVEMORE. I wish I had done with that business entirely; but my desires are kindled, and must be satisfied. (*Aside*)

(*They walk for some time silently by each other*)

MRS. LOVEMORE. What part of my conduct gives you offence, Mr. Lovemore?

LOVEMORE. Still harping upon that ungrateful string!——But prithee don't set me a laughing again.——Offence!——Nothing gives me offence, child!——You know I am very fond——(*Yawns and walks*)——I like you of all things, and think you a most admirable wife;——prudent, managing,——careless of your own person, and very attentive to mine;——not much addicted to pleasure,——grave, retired, and domestic; you govern your house; pay the trademen's bills, (*Yawns*) scold the servants, and love your husband:——upon my soul, a very good wife!——As good a sort of a wife (*Yawns*) as a body might wish to have.——Where's William? I must go to bed.

MRS. LOVEMORE. To bed so early! Had not you better join the company?

LOVEMORE. I shan't go out tonight.

MRS. LOVEMORE. But I mean the company in the dining-room.

LOVEMORE. Company in the dining-room! (*Stares at her*)

MRS. LOVEMORE. Yes: I invited them to a rout.

LOVEMORE. A rout in my house!——And you dressed out too!—— What is all this?

MRS. LOVEMORE. You have no objection I hope.

LOVEMORE. Objection!——No, I like company, you know, of all things; I'll go and join them. Who are they all?

MRS. LOVEMORE. You know 'em all; and there's your friend Sir Brilliant.

LOVEMORE. Is he there? I shall be glad to see him. But pray, how comes all this about?

MRS. LOVEMORE. I intend to see company often.

LOVEMORE. Do you?

MRS. LOVEMORE. Ay, and not look tamely on, while you revel luxuriously in a course of pleasure. I shall pursue my own plan of diversion.

LOVEMORE. Do so, Ma'am: the change in your temper will not be disagreeable.

MRS. LOVEMORE. And so I shall, Sir, I assure ye. Adieu to melancholy, and welcome pleasure, wit, and gaiety. (*She walks about and sings*)

LOVEMORE. What the devil has come over her? And what in the name of wonder does all this mean?

MRS. LOVEMORE. Mean, Sir!——It means, it means——how can you ask me what it means?——Well, to be sure, the sobriety of that question!——Do you think a woman of spirit can have leisure to tell her meaning, when she is all air, alertness, rapture, and enjoyment?

LOVEMORE. She's mad!——Stark mad!

MRS. LOVEMORE. You're mistaken, Sir——not mad, but in spirits, that's all. Am I too flighty for you?——Perhaps I am: you are of a saturnine disposition, inclin'd to think a little, or so. Well, don't let me interrupt you; don't let me be of any inconvenience. That would be the unpolitest thing; a married couple to be interfering and encroaching on each other's pleasures! Oh hideous! It would be Gothic to the last degree. Ha! ha! ha!

LOVEMORE. (*Forcing a laugh*) Ha! ha!——Ma'am, you——ha! ha! You are perfectly right.

MRS. LOVEMORE. Nay, but I don't like that laugh now: I positively don't like it. Can't you laugh out as you were used to do? For my part, I'm determined to do nothing else all the rest of my life.

LOVEMORE. This is the most astonishing thing! Ma'am, I don't rightly comprehend——

MRS. LOVEMORE. Oh Lud! Oh Lud!——With that important face! Well, but come! What don't you comprehend?

LOVEMORE. There is something in this treatment that I don't so well——

MRS. LOVEMORE. Oh! are you there, Sir! How quickly they who have no sensibility for the peace and happiness of others can feel for themselves, Mr. Lovemore!——But that's a grave reflection, and I hate reflection.

LOVEMORE. What has she got into her head? This sudden change, Mrs. Lovemore, let me tell you——

MRS. LOVEMORE. Nay, don't be frighten'd: there is no harm in innocent mirth, I hope; never look so grave upon it. I assure you, Sir, that though, on your part, you seem determined to offer constant indignities to your wife, and though the laws of retaliation wou'd in some sort exculpate her if, when provok'd to the utmost, exasperated beyond all enduring, she should, in her turn, make him know what it is to receive an injury in the tenderest point——

LOVEMORE. Madam! (*Angrily*)

MRS. LOVEMORE. Well, well, don't be alarmed. I shan't retaliate: my own honour will secure you there; you may depend upon it. ——Will you come and play a game at cards? Well, do as you like; you won't come? No, no, I see you won't.——What say you to a bit of supper with us?——Nor that neither?——Follow your inclinations: it is not material where a body eats, you know; the company expects me; adieu, Mr. Lovemore, yours, yours.

Exit singing.

LOVEMORE. This is a frolic I never saw her in before!——Laugh all the rest of my life!——Laws of retaliation!——An injury in the tenderest point!——The company expects me!——Adieu! yours,

yours!——(*Mimicking her*) What the devil is all this? Some of her female friends have been tampering with her. So, so; I must begin to look a little sharp after madam. I'll go this moment into the card-room and watch whom she whispers with, whom she ogles with, and every circumstance that can lead to—— (*Going*)

Enter MUSLIN *in a hurry.*

MUSLIN. Madam, Madam——here's your letter; I wou'd not for all the world that my master——

LOVEMORE. What, is she mad too? What's the matter, woman?

MUSLIN. Nothing, Sir——nothing: I wanted a word with my lady, that's all, Sir.

LOVEMORE. You wou'd not for the world that your master—— what was you going to say?——What paper's that?

MUSLIN. Paper, Sir!

LOVEMORE. Paper, Sir! Let me see it.

MUSLIN. Lord, Sir! How can you ask a body for such a thing. It's a letter to me, Sir, a letter from the country; a letter from my sister, Sir. She bids me to buy her a *Shiver de Fize* [83] cap, and a six-teenth in the lottery; and tells me of a number she dreamt of; that's all, Sir; I'll put it up.

LOVEMORE. Let me look at it. Give it me this moment. (*Reads*) To Mrs. Lovemore!——Brilliant Fashion. This is a letter from the country, is it?

MUSLIN. That, Sir——that is——no, Sir——no;——that's not sister's letter.——If you will give me that back, Sir, I'll show you the right one.

LOVEMORE. Where did you get this?

MUSLIN. Sir?

LOVEMORE. Where did you get it?——Tell me truth.

MUSLIN. Dear heart, you fright a body so——in the parlour, Sir, ——I found it there.

LOVEMORE. Very well!——Leave the room.

---

[83] 1785, 1787: "*shiver de frize.*" Muslin means *chiveret de Frise*, a woollen fabric of Friesland.

MUSLIN. The devil fetch it, I was never so out in my politics, in all my days.

Exit.

LOVEMORE. A pretty epistle truly! (*Reads*) "When you command me, my dearest Mrs. Lovemore, never to touch again upon the subject of my love, you command an impossibility. You excite the flame, and forbid it to burn. Permit me once more to throw myself on my knees, and implore your compassion."——Compassion with a vengeance on him!——"Think you see me now with tender, melting, supplicating eyes, languishing at your feet."—— Very well, Sir!——"Can you find it in your heart to persist in cruelty?——Grant me but access to you once more, and in addition to what I already said this morning, I will urge such motives"—— Urge motives, will ye?——"as will convince you, that you should no longer hesitate in gratitude, to reward him who here makes a vow of eternal constancy and love.

Brilliant Fashion."

So! so! so! Your very humble servant, Sir Brilliant Fashion!——This is your friendship for me, is it?——You are mighty kind indeed, Sir, ——but I thank you as much as if you had really done me the favour: and, Mrs. Lovemore, I'm your humble servant too. She intends to laugh all the rest of her life! This letter will change her note. Yonder she comes along the gallery, and Sir Brilliant in full chase of her. They come this way. Could I but detect them both now! I'll step aside, and who knows but the devil may tempt them to their undoing. A polite husband I am: there's the coast clear for you, Madam.

Exit.

Enter MRS. LOVEMORE *and* SIR BRILLIANT.

MRS. LOVEMORE. I have already told you my mind, Sir Brilliant. Your civility is odious; your compliments fulsome; and your solicitations insulting.——I must make use of harsh language, Sir: you provoke it.

SIR BRILLIANT. Not retiring to solitude and discontent again, I hope, Madam! Have a care, my dear Mrs. Lovemore, of a relapse.

MRS. LOVEMORE. No danger, Sir: don't be too solicitous about me. Why leave the company? Let me entreat you to return, Sir.

SIR BRILLIANT. By Heaven, there is more rapture in being one moment *vis-à-vis* with you than in the company of a whole drawing room of beauties. Round you are melting pleasures, tender transports, youthful loves, and blooming graces, all unfelt, neglected, and despised by a tasteless, cold, unimpassioned husband, while they might be all so much better employed to the purposes of ecstasy and bliss.

MRS. LOVEMORE. I am amazed, Sir, at this liberty.——What action of my life has authorized this assurance?——I desire, Sir, you will desist. Were I not afraid of the ill consequences that might follow, I should not hesitate a moment to acquaint Mr. Lovemore with your whole behaviour.

SIR BRILLIANT. She won't tell her husband!——A charming creature, and blessings on her for so convenient a hint. She yields, by all my hopes!——What shall I say to overwhelm her senses in a flood of nonsense? (*Aside*)

"Go, my heart's envoys, tender sighs make haste,——
    Still drink delicious poison from thy eye,——
    Raptures and paradise
    Pant on thy lip, and to thy heart be press'd." [84]
                                    (*Forcing her all this time*)

Enter MR. LOVEMORE.

LOVEMORE. Hell and distraction! This is too much.

SIR BRILLIANT. What the devil's the matter now? (*Kneels down to buckle his shoe*) This confounded buckle is always plaguing me. Lovemore! I rejoice to see thee. (*Looking at each other*)

LOVEMORE. And have you the confidence to look me in the face?

---

[84] Line 1 is from Richard Steele, *The Tender Husband* (1705) I.i.221. Lines 2 and 4 are from Pope, *Eloisa to Abelard*, lines 122-123.

SIR BRILLIANT. I was telling your lady here, of the most whimsical adventure——

LOVEMORE. Don't add the meanness of falsehood to the black attempt of invading the happiness of your friend. I did imagine, Sir, from the long intercourse that has subsisted between us, that you might have had delicacy enough, feeling enough, honour enough, Sir, not to meditate an injury like this.

SIR BRILLIANT. Ay, it's all over, I am detected. (*Aside*) Mr. Lovemore, I feel that I have been wrong, and will not attempt a vindication of myself. We have been friends hitherto, and if begging your pardon for this rashness will anyways atone——

LOVEMORE. No, Sir, nothing can atone. The provocation you have given me, would justify my drawing upon you this instant, did not that lady and this roof protect you.

SIR BRILLIANT. Harsh language to a friend——

LOVEMORE. Friend, Sir Brilliant?

SIR BRILLIANT. If you will but hear me——

LOVEMORE. Sir, I insist; I won't hear a word.

SIR BRILLIANT. I declare upon my honour——

LOVEMORE. Honour! For shame, Sir Brilliant: honour and friendship are sacred words, and you profane them both.

SIR BRILLIANT. If imploring forgiveness of that lady——

LOVEMORE. That lady!——I desire you will never speak to that lady.

SIR BRILLIANT. Can you command a moment's patience?

LOVEMORE. Sir, I am out of all patience: this must be settled between us: I have done for the present.

Enter SIR BASHFUL.

SIR BASHFUL. Did not I hear loud words among you? I certainly did. What are you quarrelling about?

LOVEMORE. Read that, Sir Bashful. (*Gives him Sir Brilliant's letter*) Read that, and judge if I have not cause—— (*Sir Bashful reads to himself*)

SIR BRILLIANT. Hear but what I have to say——

LOVEMORE. No, Sir, no; we shall find a fitter time: as for you, Madam, I am satisfied with your conduct. I was indeed a little alarmed, but I have been a witness of your behaviour, and I am above harbouring low suspicions.

SIR BASHFUL. Upon my word, Mr. Lovemore, this is carrying the jest too far.

LOVEMORE. It is the basest action a gentleman can be guilty of; and to a person who never injured him, still more criminal.

SIR BASHFUL. Why so I think. Sir Brilliant, (*To him aside*) here, take this letter, and read it to him; his own letter to my wife.

SIR BRILLIANT. Let me see it—— (*Takes the letter*)

SIR BASHFUL. 'Tis indeed, as you say, the vilest action a gentleman can be guilty of.

LOVEMORE. An unparalleled breach of friendship.

SIR BRILLIANT. Not altogether so unparalleled: I believe it will not be found without a precedent—as for example—— (*Reads*)
                    "TO MY LADY CONSTANT——
Why should I conceal, my dear Madam, that your charms have awaken'd my tenderest passions?"

LOVEMORE. Confusion! My letter—— (*Aside*)

SIR BRILLIANT. (*Reading*) "I long have lov'd you, long adored. Could I but flatter myself"——(*Lovemore walks about uneasy; Sir Brilliant follows him*)

SIR BASHFUL. There, Mr. Lovemore, the basest treachery!

SIR BRILLIANT. (*Reads*) "Could I but flatter myself with the least kind return."

LOVEMORE. Confusion! Let me seize the letter out of his hand. (*Snatches it from him*)

SIR BASHFUL. An unparalleled breach of friendship, Mr. Lovemore.

LOVEMORE. All a forgery, Sir; all a forgery.

SIR BASHFUL. That I deny; it is the very identical letter my Lady threw away with such indignation. She tore it in two, and I have pieced it together.

LOVEMORE. A mere contrivance to varnish his guilt.

SIR BRILLIANT. Ha! ha! My dear Lovemore, we know one another. Have not you been at the same work with the Widow Bellmour?

LOVEMORE. The Widow Bellmour!——If I spoke to her, it was to serve you, Sir.

SIR BRILLIANT. Are you sure of that?

LOVEMORE. Po! I won't stay a moment longer among ye. I'll go into another room, to avoid ye all. I know little or nothing of the Widow Bellmour, Sir. (*Opens the door; enter Mrs. Bellmour*) Hell and destruction!——What fiend is conjured up here! Zoons! Let me make my escape out of the house. (*Runs to the opposite door*)

MRS. LOVEMORE. I'll secure this pass: you must not go, my dear.

LOVEMORE. 'Sdeath, Madam, give me way.

MRS. LOVEMORE. Nay, don't be in such a hurry: I want to introduce an acquaintance of mine to you.

LOVEMORE. I desire, Madam——

MRS. BELLMOUR. My Lord, my Lord Etheridge; I am heartily glad to see your Lordship. (*Taking hold of him*)

MRS. LOVEMORE. Do, my dear, let me introduce this lady to you. (*Turning him to her*)

LOVEMORE. Here's the devil and all to do! (*Aside*)

MRS. BELLMOUR. My Lord, this is the most fortunate encounter!

LOVEMORE. I wish I was fifty miles off. (*Aside*)

MRS. LOVEMORE. Mrs. Bellmour, give me leave to introduce Mr. Lovemore to you. (*Turning him to her*)

MRS. BELLMOUR. No, my dear Ma'am, let me introduce Lord Etheridge to you. (*Pulling him*) My Lord——

SIR BRILLIANT. In the name of wonder, what is all this?

SIR BASHFUL. This is another of his intrigues blown up.

MRS. LOVEMORE. My dear Ma'am, you are mistaken! This is my husband.

MRS. BELLMOUR. Pardon me, Ma'am, 'tis my Lord Etheridge.

MRS. LOVEMORE. My dear, how can you be so ill-bred in your own house?——Mrs. Bellmour,——this is Mr. Lovemore.

LOVEMORE. Are you going to toss me in a blanket, Madam?—— Call up the rest of your people, if you are.

MRS. BELLMOUR. Pshaw! Prithee now, my Lord, leave off your

humours. Mrs. Lovemore, this is my Lord Etheridge, a lover of mine, who has made proposals of marriage to me.

LOVEMORE. Confusion! Let me get rid of these two furies. (*Breaks away from them*)

SIR BASHFUL. He has been tampering with her too, has he?

MRS. BELLMOUR. (*Follows him*) My Lord, I say! My Lord Etheridge! Won't your Lordship know me?

LOVEMORE. This is the most damnable accident! (*Aside*)

MRS. BELLMOUR. I hope your Lordship has not forgot your appointment at my house this evening.

LOVEMORE. I deserve all this. (*Aside*)

MRS. BELLMOUR. Pray, my Lord, what have I done, that you treat me with this coldness? Come, come, you shall have a wife: I will take compassion on you.

LOVEMORE. Damnation! I can't stand it. (*Aside*)

SIR BASHFUL. Murder will out: murder will out.

MRS. BELLMOUR. Come, cheer up, my Lord: what the deuce, your dress is alter'd! What's become of the star and the riband? And so the gay, the florid, the *magnifique* Lord Etheridge, dwindles down into plain Mr. Lovemore, the married man! Mr. Lovemore, your most obedient, very humble servant, Sir.

LOVEMORE. I can't bear to feel myself in so ridiculous a circumstance. (*Aside*)

SIR BASHFUL. He has been passing himself for a lord, has he?

MRS. BELLMOUR. I beg my compliments to your friend Mrs. Loveit: I am much obliged to you both for your very honourable designs. (*Curtsying to him*)

LOVEMORE. I was never so ashamed in all my life!

SIR BRILLIANT. So, so, so, all his pains were to hide the star from me. This discovery is a perfect cordial to my dejected spirits.

MRS. BELLMOUR. Mrs. Lovemore, I cannot sufficiently acknowledge the providence that directed you to pay me a visit, though I was wholly unknown to you; and I shall henceforth consider you as my deliverer.

LOVEMORE. Ay, it was she that fainted away in the closet, and be damned to her jealousy. (*Aside*)

SIR BRILLIANT. By all that's whimsical, an odd sort of an adventure this. My Lord, (*Advances to him*) my Lord, my Lord Etheridge, as the man says in the play, "Your Lordship is right welcome back to Denmark." [85]

LOVEMORE. Now he comes upon me.——Oh! I'm in a fine situation. (*Aside*)

SIR BRILLIANT. My Lord, I hope that ugly pain in your Lordship's side is abated.

LOVEMORE. Absurd and ridiculous. (*Aside*)

SIR BRILLIANT. There is nothing forming there I hope, my Lord.

LOVEMORE. I shall come to an explanation with you, Sir.

SIR BRILLIANT. The tennis ball from Lord Rackett's unlucky left hand.

LOVEMORE. No more at present, Sir Brilliant. I leave you now to yourselves, and (*Goes to the door at the back scene*)——'sdeath, another fiend! I am beset by them.

Enter LADY CONSTANT.

LOVEMORE. No way to escape?——(*Attempts both stage doors and is prevented*)

LADY CONSTANT. Mr. Lovemore, it is the luckiest thing in the world that you are come home.

LOVEMORE. Ay, it's all over——all must come to light.

LADY CONSTANT. I have lost every rubber; quite broke; four by honours against me every time. Do, Mr. Lovemore, lend me another hundred.

LOVEMORE. I would give a hundred pound you were all in Lapland. (*Aside*)

LADY CONSTANT. Mrs. Lovemore, let me tell you, you are married to the falsest man; he has deceived me strangely.

MRS. LOVEMORE. I begin to feel for him, and to pity his uneasiness.

MRS. BELLMOUR. Never talk of pity; let him be probed to the quick.

---

[85] *Hamlet* V.ii.81-82.

SIR BASHFUL. The case is pretty plain, I think, now, Sir Brilliant.

SIR BRILLIANT. Pretty plain, upon my soul. Ha! ha!

LOVEMORE. I'll turn the tables upon Sir Bashful, for all this—— (*Takes Sir Bashful's letter out of his pocket*) where is the mighty harm now in this letter?

SIR BASHFUL. Where's the harm?

LOVEMORE. (*Reads*) "I cannot, my dearest life, any longer behold"——

SIR BASHFUL. Shame and confusion! I am undone. (*Aside*)

LOVEMORE. Hear this, Sir Bashful.——"the manifold vexations, of which, thro' a false prejudice, I am myself the occasion."

LADY CONSTANT. What is all this?

SIR BASHFUL. I am a lost man. (*Aside*)

LOVEMORE. Mind, Sir Bashful. "I am therefore resolved, after many conflicts with myself, to throw off the mask, and frankly own a passion, which the fear of falling into ridicule has in appearance suppressed."

SIR BASHFUL. 'Sdeath! I'll hear no more of it. (*Snatches at the letter*)

LOVEMORE. No, Sir; I resign it here, where it was directed.

LADY CONSTANT. It is his hand sure enough.

LOVEMORE. Yes, Madam, and those are his sentiments, which he explained to me more at large.

LADY CONSTANT. (*Reads*) "Accept the presents which I myself have sent you; money, attendance, equipage, and everything else you shall command; and in return, I shall only entreat you to conceal from the world that you have raised a flame in this heart which will ever show me,

Your admirer,

and your truly affectionate husband,

Bashful Constant."

ALL. Ha! ha!——

SIR BRILLIANT. So, so, so! He has been in love with his wife all this time, has he? Sir Bashful, will you go and see the new comedy with me?

SIR BASHFUL. I shall blush through the world all the rest of my life. (*Aside*)

SIR BRILLIANT. Lovemore, don't you think it a base thing to invade the happiness of a friend? Or to do him a clandestine wrong? Or to injure him with the woman he loves?

LOVEMORE. To cut the matter short with you, Sir, we have been traitors to each other; a couple of unprincipled, unreflecting profligates!

SIR BRILLIANT. Profligates!

LOVEMORE. Ay! both! We are pretty fellows indeed!

MRS. BELLMOUR. I am glad to find you are awakened to a sense of your error.

LOVEMORE. I am, Madam, and I am frank enough to own it. I am above attempting to disguise my feelings when I am conscious they are on the side of truth and honour. With the sincerest remorse, I ask your pardon.——I should ask pardon of my Lady Constant, too, but the fact is, Sir Bashful threw the whole affair in my way; and, when a husband will be ashamed of loving a valuable woman, he must not be surprised if other people take her case into consideration, and love her for him.

SIR BRILLIANT. Why, faith, that does in some sort make his apology.

SIR BASHFUL. Sir Bashful, Sir Bashful! Thou art ruined! (*Aside*)

MRS. BELLMOUR. Well, Sir, upon certain terms, I don't know but I may sign and seal your pardon.

LOVEMORE. Terms!——What terms!

MRS. BELLMOUR. That you make due expiation of your guilt to that lady. (*Pointing to Mrs. Lovemore*)

LOVEMORE. That lady, Ma'am!——That lady has no reason to complain.

MRS. LOVEMORE. No reason to complain, Mr. Lovemore!

LOVEMORE. No, Madam, none! For whatever may have been my imprudences, they have had their source in your conduct.

MRS. LOVEMORE. In my conduct, Sir!

LOVEMORE. In your conduct!——I here declare before this company, and I am above misrepresenting the matter; I here declare, that no man in England could be better inclined to domestic happiness if you, Madam, on your part, had been willing to make home agreeable.

MRS. LOVEMORE. There I confess he touches me. (*Aside*)

LOVEMORE. You could take pains enough before marriage; you would put forth all your charms; practice all your arts; and make your features please by rule; for ever changing; running an eternal round of variety: and all this to win my affections: but when you had won them, you did not think them worth your keeping; never dressed, pensive, silent, melancholy; and the only entertainment in my house, was the dear pleasure of a dull conjugal tête-à-tête; and all this insipidity, because you think the sole merit of a wife consists in her virtue: a fine way of amusing a husband, truly!

SIR BRILLIANT. Upon my soul, and so it is—— (*Laughing*)

MRS. LOVEMORE. Sir, I must own there is too much truth in what you say. This lady has opened my eyes, and convinced me there was a mistake in my former conduct.

LOVEMORE. Come, come, you need say no more. I forgive you; I forgive.

MRS. LOVEMORE. Forgive! I like that air of confidence, when you know that, on my side, it is at worst an error in judgment; whereas on yours——

MRS. BELLMOUR. Po! po! Never stand disputing: you know each other's faults and virtues: you have nothing to do but to mend the former, and enjoy the latter. There, there, there, kiss and be friends.[86] There, Mrs. Lovemore, take your reclaimed libertine to your arms.

LOVEMORE. 'Tis in your power, Madam, to make a reclaimed libertine of me indeed.

MRS. LOVEMORE. From this moment it shall be our mutual study to please each other.

LOVEMORE. A match with all my heart. I shall hereafter be ashamed only of my follies, but never ashamed of owning that I sincerely love you.

---

[86] 1770: "kiss and be friends"; 1785, 1786, 1787: "kiss and friends."

SIR BASHFUL. Shan't you be ashamed?

LOVEMORE. Never, Sir.

SIR BASHFUL. And will you keep me in countenance?

LOVEMORE. I will.

SIR BASHFUL. Give me your hand. I now forgive you all. My Lady Constant, I own the letter, I own the sentiments of it, (*Embraces her*) and from this moment I take you to my heart.—— Lovemore, zookers! You have made a man of me.

LADY CONSTANT. If you hold in this humour, Sir Bashful, our quarrels are at an end.

SIR BRILLIANT. And now I suppose I must make restitution here—— (*Gives Lady Constant the buckles*)

SIR BASHFUL. Ay, ay, make restitution. Lovemore! This is the consequence of his having some tolerable phrase, and a person, Mr. Lovemore! Ha! ha!——

SIR BRILLIANT. Why, I own the laugh is against me. With all my heart; I am glad to see my friends happy at last. Lovemore, may I presume to hope for pardon at that lady's hands? (*Points to Mrs. Lovemore*)

LOVEMORE. My dear confederate in vice, your pardon is granted. Two sad libertines we have been. But come, give us your hand: we have used each other scurvily: for the future we will endeavour to atone for the errors of our past misconduct.

SIR BRILLIANT. Agreed; we will henceforward behave like men who have not forgot the obligations of truth and honour.

LOVEMORE. And now I congratulate the whole company, that this business has had so happy a tendency to convince each of us of our folly.

MRS. BELLMOUR. Pray, Sir, don't draw me into a share of your folly.

LOVEMORE. Come, come, my dear Ma'am, you are not without your share of it. This will teach you for the future, to be content with one lover at a time, without listening to a fellow you know nothing of, because he assumes a title, and spreads a fair report of himself.

MRS. BELLMOUR. The reproof is just, I grant it.

LOVEMORE. Come, let us join the company cheerfully, keep our own secrets, and not make ourselves the town-talk.

SIR BASHFUL. Ay, ay; let us keep the secret.

LOVEMORE. What, returning to your fears again? You will put me out of countenance, Sir Bashful.

SIR BASHFUL. I have done.

LOVEMORE. When your conduct is fair and upright, never be afraid of ridicule. Real honour and generous affection may bid defiance to all the small wits in the kingdom. In my opinion, were the business of this day to go abroad into the world, it would prove a very useful lesson: the men would see how their passions may carry them into the danger of wounding the bosom of a friend: and the ladies would learn, that, after the marriage rites are performed, they ought not to suffer their powers of pleasing to languish away, but should still remember to sacrifice to the Graces.

> To win a man, when all your pains succeed,
> *The Way to Keep Him* is a task indeed.

Song for Mrs. Cibber in *The Way to Keep Him*.

Written, at the revival of the play,[87] by Mr. Garrick.

I.

Ye fair married dames, who so often deplore,
That a lover once blest, is a lover no more;
Attend to my counsel, nor blush to be taught,
That prudence must cherish, what beauty has caught.

II.

The bloom of your cheek, and the glance of your eye,
Your roses and lilies, may make the men sigh:
But roses, and lilies, and sighs pass away,
And passion will die, as your beauties decay.

---

[87] In 1761.

III.

Use the man that you wed, like your fav'rite guitar,
Tho' music in both, they are both apt to jar;
How tuneful and soft from a delicate touch,
Not handled too roughly, nor play'd on too much!

IV.

The sparrow and linnet will feed from your hand,
Grow tame by your kindness, and come at command:
Exert with your husband the same happy skill,
For hearts, like your birds, may be tam'd to your will.

V.

Be gay and good-humour'd, complying and kind,
Turn the chief of your care from your face to your mind:
'Tis there that a wife may her conquests improve,
And HYMEN shall rivet the fetters of LOVE.

THE OLD MAID (1761)

FOR the summer season of 1761, Murphy rented Drury Lane Theatre from David Garrick and James Lacy, and Murphy and Samuel Foote entered into a partnership as theatrical managers. On July 2 they first presented *The Old Maid*, a two-act farce of situation, which Murphy had composed the same year; and there were nine successful summer performances. During the following winter season, the farce opened at Drury Lane November 14 and was acted seventeen times. As a stock piece it held the stage until at least the middle of the nineteenth century, though it was perhaps not produced at Drury Lane or Covent Garden between 1778 and 1795. London casts included Ann Elliott and Jane Pope as Mrs. Harlow; Kitty Clive, Henry Woodward (in female attire), and Dorothea Jordan as Miss Harlow, the old maid; and Charles Kemble as Clerimont.

The farcical amusement of *The Old Maid* is well sustained. The central situation of the mistaken identity of two women who are sharp contrasts results in admirable dramatic irony. The farcical elements harmonize with the realistic dialogue, the development of the characters, and the exposure of Miss Harlow's comic foibles.

The bookseller Paul Vaillant paid Murphy forty guineas for *The Old Maid*, and the play was published late in 1761. There is no convincing evidence of any other separate genuine London edition. For his *Works* in 1786, Murphy extensively rewrote *The Old Maid*. He changed every part except the roles of the two insignificant servants. He shortened some speeches, as when he eliminated repetitious diction, and added a few new speeches; however, his main method was the expansion of existing speeches, particularly in Act I. It is indeed stimulating and rewarding to analyze this rewriting. The dramatist reveals exceptional sensitiveness to the opportunities for the improvement of clarity of exposition and of facility of style. His diction is better. His fluency of style is memorable. His dividing of sentences or his handling of pauses contributes to the smoothness of his dialogue. An aspiring playwright should study Murphy's artistry.

The editor reproduces the 1786 edition with five exceptions, where the text of 1761 is used. (See footnotes 2, 3, 10, 11, and 12.)

Texts Collated

Murphy, [Arthur], *The Old Maid*. London: P. Vaillant, 1761. [Library Company of Philadelphia]

The Works of Arthur Murphy, II, 155-214. London: T. Cadell, 1786. [University of Pennsylvania; Copy of Editor; British Museum (Copy of play removed from *Works* and given partially spurious title page)]

THE
OLD MAID:

A
COMEDY,
In TWO ACTS.

Performed at the

THEATRE ROYAL

IN

DRURY-LANE.

Tempus erit, quo tu, quae nunc excludis amantem,
Frigida deserta nocte jacebis anus.

Ovid.[1]

DRAMATIS PERSONAE

Men

Clerimont,	Mr. O'Brien.
Capt. Cape,	Mr. King.
Mr. Harlow,	Mr. Kennedy.
Mr. Heartwell,	Mr. Phillips.
Footman,	Mr. Castle.

Women

Mrs. Harlow,	Miss Haughton.
Miss Harlow,	Mrs. Kennedy.
Trifle,	Miss Hippisley.

THE
OLD MAID

ACT the FIRST
[SCENE I]

[A Room in the Harlow House]

Enter MRS. HARLOW *and* MISS HARLOW.

MRS. HARLOW. My dear sister, let me tell you——

MISS HARLOW. But, my dear sister, let me tell you it is in vain; you can say nothing that will have any effect.

MRS. HARLOW. Not if you won't hear me; only hear me.

MISS HARLOW. Oh! Ma'am, I know you love to hear yourself talk, and so please yourself; talk on at your usual rate, if your fancy so inclines you; but I have taken my resolution, and nothing shall alter it.

MRS. HARLOW. And yet, upon due reflection your mind may change.

MISS HARLOW. Never, Sister, never.

MRS. HARLOW. You can't be sure of that, Sister; when you have considered everything——

MISS HARLOW. Upon no consideration.

MRS. HARLOW. You don't know how that may be: recollect, Sister, that you are no chicken: you are not now in that sprightly season of life, when giddiness and folly are excusable, nay becoming. Your age, Sister——

MISS HARLOW. Age, Ma'am——

MRS. HARLOW. Do but hear me, Sister; do but hear me. A person of your years——

MISS HARLOW. My years, Sister!——Upon my word——

MRS. HARLOW. Nay, no offence, Sister——

MISS HARLOW. But there is offence, Ma'am: I don't understand what you mean by it. Always thwarting me with my years; my years, indeed! When perhaps, Ma'am, if I was to die of old age, some folks might have reason to look about them.

MRS. HARLOW. She feels it, I see——oh! how I delight in mortifying her.——(*Aside*)——Sister, if I did not love you, I am sure I should not talk to you in this manner. But how can you make so unkind a return as to alarm me about myself?——In some sixteen or eighteen years after you, to be sure, I own I shall begin to think of making my will. How could you be so severe?——

MISS HARLOW. Some sixteen or eighteen years, Ma'am!——If you would own [2] the truth, Ma'am,——I believe, Ma'am,——you would find,[3] Ma'am, that the disparity, Ma'am, is not so very great, Ma'am——

MRS. HARLOW. Well! I vow passion becomes you inordinately. It blends a few roses with the lillies of your cheek, and——

MISS HARLOW. And though you are married to my brother, Ma'am, I would have you to know, Ma'am, that you are not thereby any way authorized to take unbecoming liberties with his sister. I am independent of my brother, Ma'am: my fortune is in my own hands, Ma'am, and Ma'am——

MRS. HARLOW. Well! Do you know when your blood circulates a little, that I think you look mighty well? But you was in the wrong not to marry at my age. Sweet three and twenty! You can't conceive what a deal of good it would have done your temper and your spirits if you had married early.

---

[2] 1761: "If you would own"; 1786: "if you you would own."
[3] 1761: "you would find"; 1786: "you would not find."

MISS HARLOW. Insolent, provoking, female malice!

MRS. HARLOW. But to be waiting till it is almost too late in the day, and force one's self to say strange things; with the tongue and heart at variance all the time——"I don't mind the hideous men. I am very happy as I am.——I don't desire to change my condition." ——And while those words are at your tongue's end, the heart murmurs inwardly, and flutters upon the tenterhooks of expectation.

MISS HARLOW. I upon tenterhooks!

MRS. HARLOW. And to be at this work of sour grapes, till one is turned of three and forty!

MISS HARLOW. Three and forty, Ma'am!——I desire, Sister——I desire, Ma'am——three and forty, Ma'am!

MRS. HARLOW. Nay——nay——nay——don't be angry; don't blame me; blame my husband; he is your own brother, and he knows your age: he told me so.

MISS HARLOW. Oh! Ma'am, I see your drift: but you need not give yourself those airs, Ma'am——the men don't see with your eyes, Ma'am——years, indeed!——Three and forty, truly!——I'll assure you——upon my word——very fine!——But I see plainly, Ma'am, what you are at——Mr. Clerimont, Madam!——Mr. Clerimont, Sister! That's what frets you. A young husband, Ma'am; younger than your husband, Ma'am: Mr. Clerimont, let me tell you——

Enter TRIFLE.

TRIFLE. Oh! rare news, Ma'am, charming news: we have got another letter.

MISS HARLOW. From whom?——From Mr. Clerimont?——Where is it?

TRIFLE. Yes, Ma'am! From Mr. Clerimont, Ma'am.

MISS HARLOW. Let me see it; let me see it; quick; quick. (*Reads*)

"Madam,

The honour of a letter from you has so filled my mind with joy and gratitude, that I want words of force to reach but half my meaning; I can only say that you have revived a heart that was expiring for you, and now beats for you alone."

——There Sister, mind that! Years indeed! (*Reads to herself*)

MRS. HARLOW. I wish you joy, Sister: I wish I had not gone to Ranelagh [4] with her last week. Who could have thought that her faded beauties would have made such an impression? (*Aside*)

MISS HARLOW. Mind here again, Sister.——(*Reads*) "Ever since I had the good fortune of seeing you at Ranelagh, your idea has been ever present to me; and since you now give me leave, I shall, without delay, wait upon your brother. The terms he may think proper to demand, I shall readily subscribe to; for to be your slave is dearer to me than liberty. I have the honour to remain

The humblest of your admirers,
Clerimont."

There, Sister!

MRS. HARLOW. Well! I wish you joy again: but remember I tell you, take care what you do. He is young, and of course giddy and inconstant.

MISS HARLOW. He is warm, passionate, and tender.

MRS. HARLOW. But you don't know how long that may last; and here are you going to break off a very suitable match, which all your friends liked and approved, a match with Captain Cape, who to be sure——

MISS HARLOW. Don't name Captain Cape; I beseech you, don't name him.

MRS. HARLOW. Captain Cape, let me tell you, is not to be despised. He has acquired by his voyages to India a very pretty fortune: has a charming box of a house upon Hackney Marsh, [5] and is of an age every way suitable to you.

MISS HARLOW. There again now!——Age! age! age! for ever!—— Years——years——my years! But I tell you once for all, Mr. Clerimont does not see with your eyes. I am determined to hear no more

---

[4] Ranelagh pleasure gardens were north of the Thames near Chelsea.

[5] Hackney Marsh, east of Hackney, a village northeast of London in 1761.

of Captain Cape. Odious Hackney Marsh! Ah! Sister, you would be glad to see me married in a middling way.

MRS. HARLOW. I, Sister!——I am sure nobody will rejoice more at your preferment. I am resolved never to visit her if Mr. Clerimont marries her. (*Aside*)

MISS HARLOW. To cut the matter short, Sister, Mr. Clerimont has won my heart: young, handsome, rich, town house, country house, equipage! To him, and only him, will I surrender myself. Three and forty, indeed!——Ha! ha!——You see, my dear, dear sister, that these features are still regular and blooming; that the love-darting eye has not quite forsook me; and that I have made a conquest which your boasted youth might be vain of.

MRS. HARLOW. Oh! Ma'am, I beg your pardon if I have taken too much liberty; it has all arisen from affection and regard: your good is all I aim at, Sister.

MISS HARLOW. I humbly thank you for your advice, my sweet, dear, friendly sister; but don't envy me, I beg you won't; don't fret yourself; you can't conceive what a deal of good, serenity of mind will do your health. I'll go and write an answer directly to this charming, charming letter. Sister, yours. I shall be glad to see you, Sister, at my house in Hill Street,[6] when I am Mrs. Clerimont. And remember what I tell you: some faces retain their bloom and beauty longer than you imagine, my dear sister. Come, Trifle, let me fly this moment. Sister, your servant.

Exit with TRIFLE.

MRS. HARLOW. Your servant, my dear!——Well! I am determined to lead the gayest life in nature if she marries Clerimont.——I'll have a new equipage, that's one thing: and I'll have greater routs [7] than her, that's another: positively, I must outshine her there; and I'll keep up a polite enmity with her; go and see her, maybe once or twice in a winter; "Ma'am, I am really so hurried with such a number of acquaintances, that I can't possibly find time." And then to provoke her, "I wish you joy, Sister, I hear you are breeding." Ha! ha!——That will so mortify her.——"I wish it may be a boy,

---

[6] Hill Street, Berkeley Square, Mayfair.
[7] Fashionable evening parties.

Sister." Ha! ha!——And then when her husband begins to despise her: "Really, Sister, I pity you; had you taken my advice, and married the India captain——your case is a compassionate one."—— Compassion is so insolent when a body feels none at all. Ha! ha! It is the finest way of insulting.

Enter MR. HARLOW.

MR. HARLOW. So, my dear; how are my sister's affairs going on?

MRS. HARLOW. Why, my dear, she has had another letter from Mr. Clerimont. Did you ever hear of such a strange, unaccountable thing patched up in a hurry here?

MR. HARLOW. Why, it is sudden, to be sure.

MRS. HARLOW. Upon my word, I think you had better advise her not to break off with Captain Cape.

MR. HARLOW. No, not I——I wish she may be married to one or other of them. Her temper is really grown so very sour, and there is such eternal wrangling between you both, that I wish to see her in her own house, for the peace and quiet of mine.

MRS. HARLOW. Do you know this Mr. Clerimont?

MR. HARLOW. No; but I have heard of the family. There is [a] very fine fortune. I wish he may hold his intention.

MRS. HARLOW. I wish he may, but I doubt it.

MR. HARLOW. And truly so do I; for between ourselves, I see no charms in my sister.

MRS. HARLOW. For my part I can't comprehend it. How she could strike his fancy, is to me the most astonishing thing. After this, I shall be surprised at nothing.

MR. HARLOW. Well! strange things do happen. So she is but married out of the way, I am satisfied. An old maid in a house is the devil.

Enter a SERVANT.

SERVANT. Mr. Clerimont, Sir, to wait on you.

MR. HARLOW. Show him in. (*Exit* Servant) How comes this visit, pray?

MRS. HARLOW. My sister wrote to him to explain himself to you. The affair seems now to grow serious. The gentleman seems in earnest, and in a hurry too. Well, I suppose he wants to talk to you: I'll leave you to yourselves. (*Aside as she goes out*) The man must be mad to think of her. He must have a strange taste indeed.

Exit.

Enter CLERIMONT.

MR. HARLOW. Your most obedient, Sir: be pleased to walk in.

CLERIMONT. I presume, Sir, you are no stranger to the business that occasions this visit.

MR. HARLOW. Sir, the honour you do me and my family——

CLERIMONT. Oh! Sir, to be allied to your family by so tender a tie as a marriage with your sister, will at once reflect a credit upon me, and conduce to my happiness in the most essential point. I adore your sister, Sir: my sentiments are not to be expressed: she charmed me at the very first sight.

MR. HARLOW. (*Aside*) The devil she did!

CLERIMONT. The sensibility of her countenance, the elegance of her figure, the sweetness of her manner——

MR. HARLOW. Sir, you are pleased to——compliment!

CLERIMONT. Compliment! I speak the language of the heart. Where merit is so apparent, so transcending all praise, he must have great skill in flattery who can give an air of compliment to that justice which your sister claims from all.

MR. HARLOW. The sweetness of my sister's manner. (*Aside*) Ha! ha!

CLERIMONT. I saw her, for the first time, a few nights ago at Ranelagh: though there was a crowd of beauties in the room, thronging and pressing all around, yet she shone amongst them with superior lustre. She was walking arm in arm with another lady. No opportunity offered for me to form an acquaintance amidst the hurry and bustle of the place. I enquired their names as they were going into their chariot: I was told they were Mrs. and

Miss Harlow. From that moment she won my heart. At one glance I became the willing captive of her beauty.

MR. HARLOW. A very candid declaration, Sir!——How can this be? The bloom has been off the peach any time these fifteen years, to my knowledge. (*Aside*)——You see my sister with a favourable eye, Sir.

CLERIMONT. A favourable eye! He must greatly want discernment who has not a quick perception of her merit.

MR. HARLOW. You do her a great deal of honour. But this affair—— is it not somewhat sudden, Sir?

CLERIMONT. I grant it. You may indeed be surprised at it, Sir; nor should I have been hardy enough to make any overtures to you—— at least yet awhile——if she herself had not condescended to listen to my passion. She has authorized me under her own fair hand to apply to her brother for his consent.

MR. HARLOW. I shall be very ready, Sir, to give my approbation to my sister's happiness.

CLERIMONT. No doubt you will. But let me not cherish an unavailing flame, a flame that already lights up all my tenderest passions.

MR. HARLOW. To you, Sir, there can be no exception. I am not altogether a stranger to your family and fortune. His language is warm, considering my sister's age; but I won't hurt her preferment. (*Aside*)——You will pardon me, Sir, if I observe one thing: you are, as one may say, just coming into life. Have you left the university?

CLERIMONT. Left it, Sir?——Above a year. I am almost two and twenty.

MR. HARLOW. And yet, this is a delicate point: have you consulted your friends?

CLERIMONT. I have: my uncle, Mr. Heartwell, who proposes to leave me a very handsome addition to my fortune, which is considerable already, he, Sir——

MR. HARLOW. Well, Sir, if he has no objection, I can have none.

CLERIMONT. He has none, Sir; he has given his consent; he desires me to lose no time. I will bring him to pay you a visit. He approves my choice. You shall have it out of his own mouth. Name your hour, and he shall attend you.

MR. HARLOW. Any time today. I shall stay at home on purpose.

CLERIMONT. In the evening I will conduct him hither. In the meantime I feel an attachment here: the lady, Sir——

MR. HARLOW. Oh! you want to see my sister. I will send her to you, Sir, this instant. I beg your pardon for leaving you alone. Ha! ha! Who could have thought of her making a conquest at last?

Exit.

CLERIMONT. Your politeness, Sir, upon this occasion, will lay me under the most lasting obligation.——Now, Clerimont, now your heart may rest content: your doubts and fears may all subside, and joy and rapture take their place. Miss Harlow shall be mine: she receives my vows; she approves my passion. (*Sings and dances*) Soft! Here she comes.——Her very appearance controls my wildest hopes, and hushes my proud heart into respect and silent admiration.

Enter MRS. HARLOW.

MRS. HARLOW. I beg your pardon, Sir; I intrude, perhaps.

CLERIMONT. Madam, (*Bows respectfully*) you never can intrude, Madam. You——you must be ever welcome.

MRS. HARLOW. I thought Mr. Harlow was here, Sir.

CLERIMONT. Madam, he is but just gone. How a single glance of that deluding eye overawes and checks each wish that flutters in my heart. (*Aside*)

MRS. HARLOW. I wonder he would leave you alone, Sir. That is not so polite in his own house.

CLERIMONT. How her modesty throws a veil over her inclinations!——My tongue falters!——I can't speak to her. (*Aside*)

MRS. HARLOW. He seems in confusion. A pretty man too!——That this should be my sister's luck!——(*Aside*)

CLERIMONT. Madam!——(*Embarrassed*)

MRS. HARLOW. I imagine you have been talking to him on the subject of the letter you sent this morning.

CLERIMONT. Madam, I have presumed to——

MRS. HARLOW. You are the only person, Sir, that will call it presumption. Mr. Harlow has no objection, I hope.

CLERIMONT. She hopes! Heavens bless her for the word.—— (*Aside*)——Madam, he has frankly consented, if his sister will do me that honour.

MRS. HARLOW. You do his sister a great deal of honour, Sir,—— (*Aside*) a great deal more than she deserves, if he knew all.

CLERIMONT. How her modesty makes her turn aside that lovely countenance!——Mr. Harlow, Madam, encouraged me to entertain a gleam of hope.

MRS. HARLOW. I think you need not despair, Sir, if I may venture to hazard my sentiment.

CLERIMONT. No doubt you may.

MRS. HARLOW. Then, without doubt——(*Turns away*) her success is too provoking——(*Turns to him*) I believe, Sir,——I think you may entertain some degree of hope.

CLERIMONT. How coyly she pronounces it!——"Oh! sweet reluctant amorous delay." [8] [*Aside*]——Madam, you make me happy. If anything could add to the ardour of my affection, you have done it. (*Turns from her*) Generous Miss Harlow!

MRS. HARLOW. A proposal so honourable on your part, claims attention, and cannot easily be rejected; Mr. Harlow has too much regard for his sister; and the whole family hold themselves much obliged to you.

CLERIMONT. Madam, this extreme condescension has added rapture to the sentiments I felt before: it shall be the endeavour of my life to prove deserving of the amiable object I have dared to aspire to.

MRS. HARLOW. Sir, I make no doubt of your sincerity. I have already declared my sentiments. You know Mr. Harlow's; and if my

---

[8] Milton, *Paradise Lost* IV.311: "And sweet reluctant amorous delay." Added by Murphy in 1786.

sister gives her approbation, nothing will be wanting to conclude this business. If no difficulties arise from her——her temper is uncertain——as to my consent, Sir, your air, your manner have commanded it. Sir, your most obedient: I'll send my sister to you.

Exit.

CLERIMONT. Madam, (*Bowing*) I shall endeavour to repay this goodness with excess of gratitude. She is an angel!——And yet, stupid that I am, I could not give vent to the tenderness with which my heart is ready to dissolve. It is ever so with sincere and generous love; it fills the soul with rapture, and then denies the power of uttering what we so exquisitely feel. Generous Miss Harlow! Who could thus see thro' my confusion, interpret all appearances favourably, and with a dignity superior to her sex's little arts, forego the idle ceremonies of coquetting, teasing, and tormenting her admirer. I hear somebody. Oh! here comes Mistress Harlow: what a gloom sits upon her features!——She assumes authority here I find. But I'll endeavour by insinuation and respect to make her my friend, or at least to soften prejudices, and get the better of that sour, ill-natured temper.

Enter MISS HARLOW.

MISS HARLOW. My sister has told me, Sir——

CLERIMONT. Ma'am——(*Bowing cheerfully*)

MISS HARLOW. He is a sweet figure. (*Aside*)

CLERIMONT. She rather looks like Miss Harlow's mother than her sister-in-law——(*Aside*)

MISS HARLOW. He seems abash'd——his respect is the cause.—— (*Aside*)——My sister told me, Sir, that you was here. I beg pardon for making you wait so long.

CLERIMONT. Oh, Ma'am. (*Bows*) The gloom disappears from her face, but the lines of ill-nature remain. (*Aside*)

MISS HARLOW. In his confusion I see the ardour of his passion.—— He has not recovered himself!——I'll cheer him with affability.—— (*Aside*)——Sir, the letter you was pleased to send, my sister has seen, and——

CLERIMONT. And has assured me that she has no objection.

MISS HARLOW. I am glad of that, Sir.——I was afraid——

CLERIMONT. No objection. And Mr. Harlow——I have seen him too. He has honoured me with his consent. Now, Madam, the only doubt remains with you. May I be permitted to hope——

MISS HARLOW. Sir, you appear like a gentleman,——and——

CLERIMONT. Madam, believe me, never was love more sincere, more justly founded on esteem, or kindled into higher admiration.

MISS HARLOW. Sir, with the rest of the family I hold myself much obliged to you, and——

CLERIMONT. Obliged!——'Tis I that am obliged. There is no merit on my side: it is the consequence of impressions made upon my heart; and what heart can resist such beauty, such various graces!

MISS HARLOW. The warmth of your expression, Sir——I wish my sister heard him. (*Aside*) I am afraid you are lavish of your praise; and the short date of your love, Sir——

CLERIMONT. It will burn with unabating ardour. The same charms that first inspired it, will forever cherish, and add new fuel to the flame.——You cannot doubt me, Madam: no, you will not harbour an ungenerous suspicion. You use this style to put my sincerity to the proof. That, Madam, I perceive is your aim: but could you read the feelings of my heart, you would not thus cruelly keep me in suspense.

MISS HARLOW. Heavens! If my sister saw my power over him—— (*Aside*)——A little suspense cannot be deem'd unreasonable. Marriage is an important affair; an affair for life; and some caution you will allow to be necessary.

CLERIMONT. Madam!——(*Disconcerted*)——Oh! I dread the sourness of her look! (*Aside*)

MISS HARLOW. One thing, Sir, you will permit me to observe. You seem to dwell chiefly on articles of external and superficial merit; whereas the more valuable qualities of the mind, prudence, good sense, a well-regulated conduct——

CLERIMONT. Oh! Ma'am, I am not inattentive to those matters. She has a notable household understanding, I warrant her.——

(*Aside*)——But let me entreat you, Madam, to do justice to my principles, and believe that never yet a fond, fond heart declared itself with more sincerity.

MISS HARLOW. Sir, I will frankly own that I have been trying you all this time, and from henceforth all doubts are banished.

CLERIMONT. Your words recall me to new life. I shall for ever study to merit this goodness. But your fair sister, do you think I can depend upon her consent? May I flatter myself she will not change her mind?

MISS HARLOW. My sister cannot be insensible of your merit, and the honour you do her and the whole family. And, Sir, as far as I can act with propriety in the affair, I will endeavour to keep them all in a disposition to favour your pretensions.

CLERIMONT. Madam—— (*Bows*)

MISS HARLOW. You have an interest in my breast that will be busy for you.

CLERIMONT. I am eternally devoted to you, Madam—— (*Bows*)

MISS HARLOW. How modest, and yet how expressive he is! (*Aside*)

CLERIMONT. Madam, I shall be for ever sensible of this extreme condescension. I shall think no pains too great to prove the gratitude and esteem I bear you. I beg my compliments to Mr. Harlow. I shall be here with my uncle in the evening; as early as possible I shall come. My respects to your sister, Ma'am——and pray, Madam, keep her in my interest.——Madam, your most obedient. ——I have managed the motherly lady finely, I think. (*Aside*)

Bows, and exit.

MISS HARLOW. What will my sister say now? I shall hear no more of her taunts. A malicious thing! I fancy she now sees that your giddy flirts are not always the highest beauties. Set her up, indeed! Had she but heard him, the dear man! What sweet things he said! And what sweet things he looked. Well, I am enchanted with him. I shall love him to distraction.

Enter MRS. HARLOW.

MRS. HARLOW. Well, Sister!——How!——What does he say?

MISS HARLOW. Say, Sister!——Everything that is charming: he is the prettiest man! And so polite, so sensible, so elegant, so everything that is agreeable!

MRS. HARLOW. Well! I am glad of it. But all's well that ends well.

MISS HARLOW. Envy, Sister! Envy, and downright malice!—— Oh! had you heard all the tender things he uttered, and with that ecstasy too! That tenderness! That delight restrained by modesty!

MRS. HARLOW. All that is very true: but still I feel, methinks, as if everything was not right: I can't well explain myself; but there is to me something odd in the whole business.

MISS HARLOW. Oh! I don't doubt but you will say so. You will find, however, that I have beauty enough left to make some noise in the world. The men, Sister, are the best judges of female beauty. Don't concern yourself about the affair, Sister: the men are the best judges; leave it all to them.

MRS. HARLOW. But only think of a lover you never saw but once at Ranelagh.

MISS HARLOW. Very true! But even then I saw what work I made in his heart. Don't you remember how he followed us up and down the room? Oh! I am in raptures with him, and he is in raptures with me, and in a few days, Sister, Mrs. Clerimont will be glad to see you.

Enter MR. HARLOW.

MR. HARLOW. So, Sister! How stand matters now?

MISS HARLOW. As I could wish. I shall no more be a trouble to you. He has declared himself in the most warm and vehement manner; tho' my sister has her doubts; she is a good friend, she is afraid of my success.

MRS. HARLOW. Pray, Sister, don't think so meanly of me. I understand that sneer, Ma'am.

MISS HARLOW. And I understand you too, Ma'am.

MR. HARLOW. Come, come, I desire we may have no quarrelling. You two are always wrangling. But when you are separated, it is to be hoped you will then be more amicable. Things are now in a fair way. Tho', Sister, let me tell you I am afraid our India friend will think himself ill-treated.

MRS. HARLOW. That's what I fear too: that's my reason for speaking. Captain Cape, in my opinion, will have reason to think himself ill-used.

MISS HARLOW. Oh! never throw away a thought on him. Mr. Clerimont has my heart; and now I think I am settled for life, Sister.——I love to plague her. (*Aside*)——I say, Sister, whatever doubts you may have, you will see me settled for life, for life, for life, my dear sister.

Enter SERVANT.

SERVANT. Dinner is served, Sir.

MR. HARLOW. Very well! Come, Sister, I give you joy. Let us in to dinner.

MISS HARLOW. Oh! vulgar!——I can't eat.——I must go and dress my head over again, and do a thousand things;——for I am determined I'll look this afternoon as well as ever I can.

Exit.

MRS. HARLOW. Is not all this amazing, my dear? Her head is turned.

MR. HARLOW. Well, let it all pass: don't you mind it: don't you say anything. Let her get married if she can. I am sure I shall rejoice at it.

MRS. HARLOW. And upon my word, my dear, so shall I. If I interfere, it is purely out of friendship.

MR. HARLOW. Be advised by me: say no more to her. If the affair goes on, we shall fairly get rid of her. Her peevish humours, and her maiden temper, are become insupportable. Come, let us in to dinner. If Mr. Clerimont marries her, which indeed will be odd enough, we shall then enjoy a little peace and quiet in our own house.

Exit.

MRS. HARLOW. What in the world could the man see in her? He will repent of his bargain in a week or a fortnight; that I am sure he will. She is gone to dress now!——Ha! ha!——

"Oh! how she rolls her pretty eyes in spite,
    And looks delightfully with all her might!" [9]

Ha! ha! Delightfully she will look indeed!——

End of the FIRST ACT.

ACT the SECOND
[SCENE I]

[A Room in the Harlow House]

Enter a SERVANT, *and* CAPT. CAPE.

SERVANT. Yes, Sir, my master is at home: he has just done dinner, Sir.

CAPT. CAPE. Very well then; tell him I would speak a word with him.

SERVANT. I beg pardon, Sir; I am but a stranger in the family—— who shall I say?

CAPT. CAPE. Captain Cape, tell him.

SERVANT. Yes, sir.

Exit.

CAPT. CAPE. I can hardly believe my own eyes. 'Sdeath! I am almost inclined to think this letter, signed with Miss Harlow's name, a mere forgery by some enemy, to drive me into an excess of passion, and so injure us both: I don't know what to say to it.

---

[9] Edward Young, *Love of Fame, The Universal Passion* (1725-8), Satire V, lines 39-40. Murphy substitutes "pretty" for "charming."

Enter MR. HARLOW.

CAPT. CAPE. I have waited on you about an extraordinary affair; I can't comprehend it, Sir. Here is a letter with your sister's name.——Look at it, Sir: is that her handwriting?

MR. HARLOW. Yes, Sir; I take it to be her writing.

CAPT. CAPE. And do you know the contents?

MR. HARLOW. I can't say I have read it; but——

CAPT. CAPE. But you know the purport of it?

MR. HARLOW. Partly.

CAPT. CAPE. You do?——And is it not base treatment, Sir? Is it not unwarrantable? Can you justify her?

MR. HARLOW. For my part, I leave women to manage their own affairs. I am not fond of intermeddling.

CAPT. CAPE. But, Sir, let me ask you: Was not everything agreed upon? Are not the writings now in the lawyer's hands? Was not next week fixed for our wedding?

MR. HARLOW. I understood it so.

CAPT. CAPE. Very well then: you see how she treats me. She writes me here in a contemptuous style, that she recalls her promise; it was rashly given; she has thought better of it; she will listen to me no more; she is going to dispose of herself to a gentleman with whom she can be happy for life. There, that's free and easy, is not it? What do you say to that?

MR. HARLOW. Why really, Sir, it is not my affair. I have nothing to say to it.

CAPT. CAPE. Nothing to say to it!——Sir, I imagined I was dealing with people of honour.

MR. HARLOW. You have been dealing with a woman, and you know——

CAPT. CAPE. Yes, I know; I know the treachery of the sex. Who is this gentleman, pray?

MR. HARLOW. His name is Clerimont. They have fixed the affair among themselves, and amongst them be it for me.

CAPT. CAPE. Very fine! Mighty fine!——Is Miss Harlow at home, Sir?

MR. HARLOW. She is; and here she comes this way.

CAPT. CAPE. Very well!——Let me hear it from herself, that's all: I desire to hear her speak for herself.

MR. HARLOW. With all my heart. I'll leave you together: you know, Captain, I was never fond of being concerned in these affairs.

Exit.

Enter MISS HARLOW.

MISS HARLOW. Captain Cape, this is mighty odd: I thought my letter informed you——

CAPT. CAPE. Madam, I acknowledge the receipt of your letter, and, Madam, the usage is so extraordinary, that I hold myself excusable if I refuse to comply with the terms you impose upon me.

MISS HARLOW. Not comply? I don't understand you.

CAPT. CAPE. Mistake me not; I am not come to whimper or to whine, and to make a puppy of myself again. That, Madam, is all blown over.

MISS HARLOW. Well, there is no harm done, and you will survive this, I hope.

CAPT. CAPE. Survive it!

MISS HARLOW. Yes;——you won't grow desperate: suppose you were to order somebody to take care of you, because you know fits of despair are sudden, and you may rashly do yourself a mischief. Don't do any such thing, I beg you won't.

CAPT. CAPE. This insult, Madam!——Do myself a mischief! Don't flatter yourself that it is in your power to make me unhappy. It is not vexation brings me hither, that let me assure you.

MISS HARLOW. Then let vexation take you away. We were never designed for one another.

CAPT. CAPE. My amazement brings me hither; amazement that any woman can behave——but I don't want to upbraid——I only come to ask——for I can hardly as yet believe it——I only come to ask if I am to credit this pretty epistle?

MISS HARLOW. Every syllable: therefore take your answer, Sir, and truce with your importunity.

CAPT. CAPE. Very well, Ma'am, very well——your humble servant, Madam——I promise you, Ma'am, I can repay this scorn with scorn; with tenfold scorn, Madam, such as this treatment deserves; that's all: I say no more——your servant Ma'am.—— But let me ask you ——is this a just return for all the attendance I have paid you these three years past?

MISS HARLOW. Perfectly just, Sir; three years!——How could you be a dangler so long? I told you what it would come to: can you think that raising a woman's expectation, and tiring her out of all patience, is the way to make sure of her at last? You ought to have been a brisker lover, you ought indeed, Sir. I am now contracted to another, and so there is an end of everything between us.

CAPT. CAPE. Very well, Madam.——And yet I can't bear to be despised by her. [*Aside*]——And can you, Miss Harlow, can you find it in your heart to treat me with this disdain? Have you no compassion?

MISS HARLOW. No, positively none, Sir, none; none.

CAPT. CAPE. Your own Captain Cape, whom you——

MISS HARLOW. Whom I despise.

CAPT. CAPE. Whom you have so often encouraged to adore you.

MISS HARLOW. Pray Sir, don't touch my hand: it is now the property of another.

CAPT. CAPE. Can't you still break off with him?

MISS HARLOW. No Sir, I can't; I won't; I love him, and if you are a man of honour, you will speak to me no more; desist, Sir, for if you don't, my brother shall tell you of it, and tomorrow Mr. Clerimont shall tell you of it.

CAPT. CAPE. Mr. Clerimont, Madam, shall fight me for daring——

MISS HARLOW. And must I fight you too, most noble, valiant Captain?

CAPT. CAPE. Laughed at too!

MISS HARLOW. What a passion you are in!——I can't bear to see a man in such a passion. Oh! I have a happy riddance of you: the violence of your temper is dreadful. I won't stay a moment longer with you; you frighten me: you have your answer——and so your servant, Sir.

Exit.

CAPT. CAPE. Ay! She is gone off like a fury, and the furies catch her, say I. I will never put up with this: I will find out this Mr. Clerimont: he shall be accountable to me; Mr. Harlow too shall be accountable; and——

Enter MR. *and* MRS. HARLOW.

Mr. Harlow, I am used very ill here, by all of you, and Sir, let me tell you——

MR. HARLOW. Nay; don't be angry with me. I was not to marry you.

CAPT. CAPE. But Sir, I can't help being angry. I must be angry. and let me tell you, you don't behave like a gentleman.

MRS. HARLOW. How can Mr. Harlow help it, Sir, if my sister—

MR. HARLOW. You are too warm; you are indeed. Let us talk this matter over a bottle.

CAPT. CAPE. No, Sir: no bottle: over a cannon, if you will.

MRS. HARLOW. Mercy on me! I beg you won't talk in that terrible manner: you frighten me out of my wits.

MR. HARLOW. Be you quiet, my dear. Captain Cape, I beg you will just step into that room with me; and if, in the dispatching of one bottle, I don't acquit myself of all sinister dealing, why then—— come, come, be a little moderate: you shall step with me: I'll take it as a favour. Come, come, you must.

CAPT. CAPE. I always found you a gentleman, Mr. Harlow, and so with all my heart, I don't care if I do talk the matter over.

MR. HARLOW.[10] That's fair, and I am obliged to you. Come, I'll show you the way.

Exeunt.

_____

[10] 1786 wrongly assigns this speech to Miss Harlow.

MRS. HARLOW. Just as I foresaw: my sister was sure of him, and now is she going to break off for a young man, who will despise her in a little time. I wish she would have Captain Cape.

Enter MISS HARLOW.

MISS HARLOW. Is he gone, sister?

MRS. HARLOW. No; and here is the deuce and all to do. He is for fighting everybody: upon my word you are wrong: you don't behave genteelly in the affair.

MISS HARLOW. Genteelly! I like that notion prodigiously: an't I going to marry genteelly?

MRS. HARLOW. Well, follow your own inclinations. I won't intermeddle any more, I promise you. I'll step into the parlour, and see what they are about.

Exit.

MISS HARLOW. As you please, Ma'am. I see plainly the ill-natured thing can't bear my success. Heavens! Here comes Mr. Clerimont.

Enter MR. CLERIMONT.

MISS HARLOW. You are earlier than I expected, Sir.

CLERIMONT. I have flown, Madam, upon the wings of love. I have seen my uncle: he will be here within this half hour. Everything succeeds to my wishes. I hope there is no alteration here since I saw you.

MISS HARLOW. Nothing of moment, Sir.

CLERIMONT. You alarm me: Mr. Harlow has not changed his mind, I hope.

MISS HARLOW. No, he continues in the same opinion.

CLERIMONT. And your sister——I tremble with doubt and fear ——she does not surely recede from the sentiments she flattered me with.

MISS HARLOW. Why there, indeed, I can't say much. She seems to——

CLERIMONT. How!

MISS HARLOW. She——I don't know what to make of her.

CLERIMONT. I am on the rack: in pity, do not torture me.

MISS HARLOW. How tremblingly solicitous he is.——Oh! I have made a sure conquest. (*Aside*)——Why, she, Sir——

CLERIMONT. I am all attention, Madam. (*Disconcerted*)

MISS HARLOW. She does not seem entirely to approve.

CLERIMONT. You kill me with despair.

MISS HARLOW. Oh! he is deeply smitten. (*Aside*)——She thinks another match would suit better.

CLERIMONT. Another match!

MISS HARLOW. Yes, another; an India captain, who has made his proposals; but I shall take care to see him dismissed.

CLERIMONT. Will you?

MISS HARLOW. I promise you I will. Though he runs much in my sister's head, and she has taken great pains to bring the family over to her opinion.

CLERIMONT. How cruel! I could not have expected that from her. But has she fixed her heart upon a match with this other gentleman?

MISS HARLOW. Why, truly, I think she has: but my will in this affair ought, and shall be consulted.

CLERIMONT. It is highly proper, Madam. Your long acquaintance with the world——

MISS HARLOW.[11] Long acquaintance, Sir! I have a few years' experience only.

CLERIMONT. That is, your good sense, Ma'am.——Oh! confound my tongue! How that slipt from me. (*Aside*)——Your good sense ——your early good sense——and——and——inclination should be consulted.

MISS HARLOW.[11] And they shall, Sir. Hark! I hear her coming. I'll leave you this opportunity to speak to her once more, and try to win her over by persuasion. It will make things easy if you can. I am gone, Sir.

Curtsies affectedly and exit.

---

[11] 1786 wrongly assigns these speeches to Mrs. Harlow.

CLERIMONT. The happiness of my life will be owing to you, Madam. The woman is really better-natured than I thought. She comes, the lovely tyrant comes.

Enter MRS. HARLOW.

CLERIMONT. She triumphs in her cruelty, and I am ruined. (*Aside*)

MRS. HARLOW. You seem uneasy, Sir. I hope no misfortune——

CLERIMONT. The severest misfortune!——You have broke my heart.

MRS. HARLOW. I break your heart, Sir?

CLERIMONT. Yes, cruel fair, you——you have undone me.

MRS. HARLOW. How can that be, Sir?

CLERIMONT. And you seem unconscious of the mischief you have made.

MRS. HARLOW. Pray unriddle.

CLERIMONT. Your sister has told me all.

MRS. HARLOW. Ha! ha! What has she told you, Sir?

CLERIMONT. It may be sport to you, but to me 'tis death.

MRS. HARLOW. What is death?

CLERIMONT. The gentleman from India, Madam——I have heard it all——you can give him a preference; you can blast my hopes, my fond delighted hopes, which you yourself had cherished.

MRS. HARLOW. The gentleman is a very good sort of a man.

CLERIMONT. She loves him, I see.——(*Aside*)——Madam, I perceive my doom is fixed, and fixed by you.

MRS. HARLOW. How have I fixed your doom?——If I speak favourably of Captain Cape, it is no more than he deserves.

CLERIMONT. Distraction! I cannot bear this——(*Aside*)

MRS. HARLOW. I believe there is nobody that knows the gentleman but will give him his due praise.

CLERIMONT. Love! love! love! (*Aside*)

MRS. HARLOW. And besides, his claim is in fact prior to yours.

CLERIMONT. And must love be governed, like the business of

mechanics, by the laws of tyrant custom? Can you think so, Madam?

MRS. HARLOW. Why, Sir, you know I am not in love.

CLERIMONT. Confusion!——No, Madam, I see you are not.

MRS. HARLOW. And really, Sir, reasonably speaking, my sister is for treating Captain Cape very ill. He has been dancing attendance here these three years.

CLERIMONT. Yet that you knew when you were pleased to fan the rising flame that matchless beauty had kindled in my heart.

MRS. HARLOW. Matchless beauty!——Ha! ha!——I cannot but laugh at that. (*Aside*)

CLERIMONT. Laugh, Madam, if you will at the pangs you yourself occasion: yes, triumph, if you will: I am resigned to my fate, since you will have it so.

MRS. HARLOW. I have it so!——You seem to frighten yourself without cause. If I speak favourably of anybody else, what then? I am not to marry him, you know.

CLERIMONT. An't you?

MRS. HARLOW. I!——No, truly; thank Heaven!

CLERIMONT. She revives me. (*Aside*)

MRS. HARLOW. That must be as my sister pleases.

CLERIMONT. Must it?

MRS. HARLOW. Must it! To be sure it must.

CLERIMONT. And may I hope some interest in your heart?

MRS. HARLOW. My heart, Sir!

CLERIMONT. While it is divided, while another has possession of but part of it——

MRS. HARLOW. I don't understand him! Why, it has been given away long ago.

CLERIMONT. I pray you, do not tyrannize me thus with alternate doubts and fears. If you will but bless me with the least kind return——

MRS. HARLOW. Kind return! What, would you have me fall in love with you?

CLERIMONT. It will be generous to him who adores you.

MRS. HARLOW. Adore me!

CLERIMONT. Even to idolatry.

MRS. HARLOW. What can he mean? I thought my sister was the object of your adoration.

CLERIMONT. Your sister, Ma'am! I shall ever respect her as my friend on this occasion, but love——no——no——she is no object for that.

MRS. HARLOW. No!

CLERIMONT. She may have been handsome in her time, but that has been all over long ago.

MRS. HARLOW. Well! This is charming——I wish she heard him now, with her newfangled airs. (*Aside*) But let me understand you, Sir: adore me?

CLERIMONT. You!——You! and only you! By this fair hand—— (*Kisses it*)

MRS. HARLOW. Hold, hold. This is going too far. But pray, Sir, have you really conceived a passion for me?

CLERIMONT. You know I have; a passion of the tenderest nature.

MRS. HARLOW. And was that your drift in coming hither?

CLERIMONT. What else could induce me?

MRS. HARLOW. And introduced yourself here to have an opportunity of speaking to me?

CLERIMONT. My angel! Don't torment me thus.

MRS. HARLOW. Angel! And what do you suppose Mr. Harlow will say to this?

CLERIMONT. Oh! Ma'am——he! He approves my passion.

MRS. HARLOW. Does he really? I must speak to him about that.

CLERIMONT. Do so, Ma'am; you will find me a man of more honour than to deceive you.

MRS. HARLOW.[12] Well! It will be whimsical enough if he does. And my sister too, this will be a charming discovery for her. (*Aside*)——Ha! ha! Well! Really, Sir, this is mighty odd. I'll speak to Mr. Harlow about this matter, and you shall know his answer. (*Going*)

CLERIMONT. And may I then flatter myself?

---

[12] 1786 wrongly assigns this speech to Miss Harlow.

MRS. HARLOW. Oh! to be sure: such an honourable project! I'll step to him this moment; and then, Sister, I shall make such a piece of work for you.

Exit.

CLERIMONT. Very well, Ma'am, see Mr. Harlow: he will confirm it all. While there is life there is hope. To lose that matchless beauty, were the worst misery in the power of fortune to heap upon me.

Enter MISS HARLOW.

MISS HARLOW. I beg pardon for leaving you all this time.——Well, Sir, what says my sister?

CLERIMONT. She has given me some glimmering hopes.

MISS HARLOW. Don't be uneasy about her; it shall be as I please——

CLERIMONT. But with her own free consent it would be better: however, to you I am bound by every tie, and thus let me seal a vow——(*Kisses her hand*)

MISS HARLOW. He certainly is a very passionate lover. He is ready to eat my hand up with kisses. I wish my sister saw this. (*Aside*) Hush! I hear Captain Cape's voice. The hideous sea-monster! He is coming this way. I would not see him again for the world. I'll withdraw for a moment, Sir. You'll excuse me: (*Kisses her hand and curtsies very low*) your most obedient.——Oh! he is a charming man.

Curtsies and exit.

Enter CAPT. CAPE.

CAPT. CAPE. There she goes, the perfidious! Sir, I understand your name is Clerimont.

CLERIMONT. At your service, Sir.

CAPT. CAPE. Then, draw this moment.

CLERIMONT. Draw, Sir! For what?

CAPT. CAPE. No evasion, Sir.

CLERIMONT. Explain the cause.

CAPT. CAPE. The cause is too plain: your making love to that lady, who went out there this moment.

CLERIMONT. That lady! Not I upon my honour, Sir.

CAPT. CAPE. No shuffling, Sir, draw.

CLERIMONT. Sir, I can repel an injury like this: but your quarrel is groundless. And, Sir, if ever I made love to that lady, I will lay my bosom naked to your sword. That lady!——I resign all manner of pretension to her.

CAPT. CAPE. You resign her?

CLERIMONT. Entirely.

CAPT. CAPE. Then I am pacified. (*Puts up his sword*)

CLERIMONT. Upon my word, Sir, I never so much as thought of the lady.

Enter MR. HARLOW.

MR. HARLOW. So, Sir, fine doings you have been carrying on here!

CLERIMONT. Sir!

MR. HARLOW. You have been attempting my wife, I find.

CLERIMONT. Upon my word, Mr. Harlow——

MR. HARLOW. You have behaved in a very base manner, and I insist upon satisfaction. (*Draws his sword*)

CLERIMONT. This is the strangest accident! I assure you, Sir—— only give me leave.

MR. HARLOW. I will not give you leave——I insist——

CAPT. CAPE. Nay, Mr. Harlow. This is neither time or place: and besides, hear the gentleman; I have been overhasty, and he has satisfied me: only hear him.

MR. HARLOW. Sir, I will believe my own wife. Come on, Sir.

CLERIMONT. Without cause I cannot: I have no quarrel, Sir. You may believe me, Mr. Harlow, when I assure you, that I came into this house upon honourable principles: induced, Sir, by my regard for Miss Harlow.

CAPT. CAPE. For Miss Harlow!——Wounds! Draw this moment.

CLERIMONT. Again! This is downright madness: two upon me at once! You will murder me between you.

MR. HARLOW. There is one too many upon him sure enough: and so, Captain, put up your sword.

CAPT. CAPE. Resign your pretensions to Miss Harlow.

CLERIMONT. Resign Miss Harlow!——Not for the universe: in her cause, I can be as ready as any bravo of ye all. (*Draws his sword*)

MR. HARLOW. For heaven's sake, Captain Cape, moderate your anger; this is neither time nor place. I have been too rash myself: I beg you will be pacified. (*He puts up*)——Mr. Clerimont, sheath your sword.

CLERIMONT. I obey, Sir.

MR. HARLOW. Captain Cape, how can you? You promised me you would let things take their course. If my sister will marry the gentleman, how is he to blame?

CAPT. CAPE. Well argued, Sir: I have done:——she is a worthless woman, that's all.

CLERIMONT. A worthless woman, Sir!

CAPT. CAPE. Ay! worthless.

CLERIMONT. Damnation!——Draw, Sir!

MR. HARLOW. Nay, now, Mr. Clerimont, you are too warm; and there's a gentleman coming——this is your uncle, I suppose.

CLERIMONT. It is, and he comes opportunely.

Enter MR. HEARTWELL.

MR. HARLOW. (*Aside*) I'll wave all disputes now, that I may conclude my sister's marriage.

HEARTWELL. My nephew has informed me, Sir, of the honour you have done him, and I am come to ratify the treaty by my consent.

MR. HARLOW. I thought it necessary to have the advice of Mr. Clerimont's friends, as he is very young, and my sister not very handsome.

CLERIMONT. She is an angel, Sir.

HEARTWELL. Patience, Charles, patience. My nephew's estate will provide for his eldest born, and upon the younger branches of his marriage, I mean to settle my fortune.

MR. HARLOW. Generously spoken, Sir, and after that declaration, there is no occasion for delay. Who waits there?——Tell the ladies they are wanted.

HEARTWELL. I have ever loved my nephew, and since he tells me he has made a good choice, I shall be glad to see him happy.

CAPT. CAPE. But, Sir, let me tell you, that your nephew has used me basely, and Sir——

MR. HARLOW. Po! Captain Cape, now you are wrong again: everything was settled between us in the other room: recollect yourself; I beg you will.——Oh! Here come the ladies.

Enter MRS. HARLOW *and* MISS HARLOW.

MISS HARLOW. Now, Sister, you shall see that I have completed my conquest.

CLERIMONT. At length, I am happy indeed! My lovely, charming bride! Thus let me snatch thee to my heart, and thus, and thus—— (*Embraces Mrs. Harlow*)

MR. HARLOW. Death and distraction! Before my face—— (*Pushing him away*)

CLERIMONT. Prithee, indulge my transport: my life, my angel!

MR. HARLOW. I desire you will desist, Sir: these liberties may provoke me too far.

CLERIMONT. Nay, nay, prithee be quiet. My charming, charming wife!

MR. HARLOW. That lady is not your wife.

CLERIMONT. How my wife, not my wife!——Ecstasy and bliss!

MR. HARLOW. Come, come, Sir, this is too much: I desire——

CLERIMONT. Ha! ha! You are very pleasant, Sir.

MR. HARLOW. This is downright madness, but it shall not excuse you: that lady is my wife.

CLERIMONT. Sir!

MR. HARLOW. I say, Sir, that lady is my wife.

CAPT. CAPE. Ha! ha! I see through this: it is a comedy of errors, I believe. (*Sings*)

HEARTWELL. What does all this mean?

CLERIMONT. Your wife, Sir!

MR. HARLOW. Yes, my wife: and there is my sister, if you please to take her.

CLERIMONT. Sir!

MR. HARLOW. Sir, this is the lady whom you have desired in marriage.

CLERIMONT. Who I, Sir? I beg your pardon: that lady I took to be your wife (*Pointing to Miss Harlow*)——and that lady (*Pointing to Mrs. Harlow*) I took to be your sister.

CAPT. CAPE *and* MRS. HARLOW. Ha! ha! ha!——

MISS HARLOW. How! How is this? Have I been made a fool of all this time? Furies! torture! madness!

CAPT. CAPE. Ha! ha!——My lady fair is taken in, I think.

MRS. HARLOW. Sister, the men don't see with my eyes——ha! ha!

CAPT. CAPE. Ha! ha! The gentleman is no dangler, Ma'am.

MRS. HARLOW. This is a complete conquest my sister has made.

MISS HARLOW. I can't bear this.——Sir, I desire I may not be made a jest of.——Did not you solicit me? Importune me?

CLERIMONT. For your interest in that lady, whom I took for Miss Harlow. I beg pardon if I am mistaken: I hope there is no harm done.

MISS HARLOW. Yes, Sir, but there is harm done. I am made sport of; exposed to derision.——Oh! I cannot bear this——I cannot bear it—— (*Cries*)

MRS. HARLOW. Don't cry, Sister: some faces preserve their bloom longer than others you know——ha! ha!

CAPT. CAPE. Loll toll loll——

HEARTWELL. This is all a riddle to me: is that lady your wife, Sir?

MR. HARLOW. She is, Sir.

HEARTWELL. And pray, Nephew; you took that lady for Mr. Harlow's sister, I suppose.

CLERIMONT. I did, Sir. I beg pardon for the trouble I have given ——I am in such confusion, I can hardly——

HEARTWELL. Well, well! The thing is cleared up, and you have been proceeding upon a mistake. But you should have known what ground you went upon——ha! ha! I can't help laughing neither.

MR. HARLOW. Why faith, nor I——ha! ha!

CLERIMONT. Since matters have turned out so unexpectedly, I beg pardon for my mistake, and, Sir, I take my leave—— (*Going*)

MISS HARLOW. And will you treat me in this manner, Sir? Will you draw me into such a scrape, and not——

CLERIMONT. Madam, that gentleman would cut my throat: his claim is prior to mine; and I dare say, he will be very glad to be reconciled.

MISS HARLOW. You are a base man then, and I reject you. Captain Cape, I see my error, and I resign myself to you.

CAPT. CAPE. No, Madam, I beg to be excused. I have been a dangler too long. I ought to have been a brisker lover. I shall endeavour to survive it, Madam; I won't do myself a mischief: I have my answer, and I am off, Madam. Loll toll loll——

MRS. HARLOW. Ha! ha! I told you this, my dear sister.

CLERIMONT. Madam, I dare say the gentleman will think better of it. Mr. Harlow, I am sorry for all this confusion, and I beg pardon of the whole company for my mistake. Mrs. Harlow, I wish you all happiness, Ma'am.——Angelic creature! What a misfortune to lose her!

Bows and exit.

CAPT. CAPE. And I will follow his example.——Miss Harlow, I wish you all happiness. Angelic creature! What a misfortune to lose her!——Upon my soul I think you a most admirable jilt, and so now you may go and bewail your virginity in the mountains—— loll toll loll——

Exit.

MISS HARLOW. Oh! oh! I can't bear to be thus disgraced. I'll go and hide myself from the world for ever. The men are all savages, barbarians, monsters, and I hate the whole sex.

Exit.

MRS. HARLOW. My dear sister, with her beauty and her conquests, ha! ha!

MR. HARLOW. Ha! ha! Whimsical and ridiculous!

HEARTWELL. Sir, my nephew is young: I am sorry for this scene of errors, and I hope you'll ascribe the whole to his inexperience.

MR. HARLOW. I certainly shall, Sir.

MRS. HARLOW. I cautioned my sister sufficiently about this matter, but vanity got the better of her, and leaves her now a whimsical instance of folly and affectation.

> In vain the FADED TOAST her mirror tries,
> And counts the cruel murders of her eyes;
> For Ridicule, sly-peeping o'er her head,
> Will point the roses and the lillies dead;
> And while, fond soul! she weaves her myrtle chain,[13]
> She proves a subject of the comic strain.

---

[13] The ancients believed that the "myrtle" was sacred to the goddess of love.

THREE WEEKS AFTER MARRIAGE (1776)

IN 1763 Murphy wrote *What We Must All Come To*, a farce of two acts. The play was scheduled to open at Covent Garden Theatre on January 9, 1764. But Murphy's political enemies concerted to damn it. They had not forgotten his political periodical the *Auditor* (June 10, 1762-Feb. 8, 1763), which had supported John Stuart, third Earl of Bute, against William Pitt, first Earl of Chatham. In the course of the second act of the initial performance, during the renewed quarrel of Lady Rackett and Sir Charles Rackett, the hostile faction succeeded in stopping the performance of Murphy's best farce.

Three years later, James Hook composed musical airs for *What We Must All Come To*, and under the title *Marriage à-la-Mode, or Conjugal Douceurs*, it was performed at Drury Lane Theatre on April 22, 1767. This version was produced also in the provinces.

Then, in 1776, the actor William Thomas Lewis induced Murphy to change the title of *What We Must All Come To* to *Three Weeks after Marriage*. The rejuvenated farce opened at Covent Garden on March 30, 1776, with great success, and was performed fifteen times by June 1. This cast starred William Thomas Lewis as Sir Charles Rackett, John Quick as Drugget, Isabella Mattocks as Lady Rackett, and Jane Hippisley Green as Dimity. The play was produced at Covent Garden every year for the rest of the eighteenth century and held the stage as a stock piece until at least the middle of the nineteenth century. The famous Lady Racketts included Frances Abington and Dorothea Jordan.

The foremost merits of *Three Weeks after Marriage* are characterization and dialogue. Sir Charles Rackett and Lady Rackett represent Murphy's farcical characterization at its best. Farcical situation, farcical dramatic irony, and laughing satire blend with realistic dialogue. These married whist devotees of 1776 have many descendants among the married bridge adherents of today.

In 1764, the bookseller Paul Vaillant had published *What We Must All Come To* "upon Mr. Murphy's account." * Although there are numerous minor differences between this text and the 1763 manuscript in the Larpent Collection of the Huntington Library, which the Lord Chamberlain approved for the production in January, 1764, the noteworthy changes are few. Murphy eliminated in 1764 all mention of Fulham, then near London, as the specific site of Drugget's house. He improved clarity in nine passages and diction in two, deleted redundant words in two, and strikingly expanded two exit speeches.

Three Weeks after Marriage was printed for the bookseller G. Kearsley in 1776. The textual revisions from 1764 consist of the elimination of nine speeches, the cutting of thirteen passages, five transpositions, eight rewritten passages, fourteen expanded passages, one new speech, sixteen changes in diction, three corrections in grammar, and one change in staging. Three additions and one cut are due to the new title; in 1764 the time of the action was six weeks after marriage. One modification in the card game appears in three speeches. Murphy excises one sentimental sentence and one topical allusion. He achieves greater clarity in twelve places. But the totality of effect of both the 1764 and the 1776 texts does not suggest that the damning of 1764 was due to any other than political reasons.

Several years later the bookseller Paul Vaillant, who had published *What We Must All Come To* in 1764, utilized some leftover copies. He prepared a new undated title page bearing the two titles, that of 1776 and that of 1764; altered the "Advertisement" by correcting the word "object" to "subject" and by omitting the concluding sentence, concerning the damning of the play, and the year part of the date of the preface from "January 10, 1764"; and introduced a new dramatis personae. The text of this edition is

---

* Jessé Foot, *The Life of Arthur Murphy* (London, 1811), p. 308.

the same as that of 1764, with the indication of the time of action as six weeks after marriage and with the running title *What We Must All Come To* throughout. On the basis of the Covent Garden cast in this edition, the editor dates it approximately 1784. Charles Bonnor, who played Lovelace, first acted at Covent Garden Sept. 19, 1783, and was there as late as May 6, 1785, shortly after which he retired from the stage.

About 1785, the bookseller E. Johnson published an unauthorized edition of the 1776 text of *Three Weeks after Marriage*. The editor bases the date 1785 on the evidence of the Covent Garden dramatis personae in Johnson's edition. The limits are certain. Frances Abington, who played Lady Rackett, came to Covent Garden in 1782. Mrs. Wilson, who had the role of Dimity, died in 1786; she acted in the year of her death. Frances Abington appeared as Lady Rackett March 5, 1785. A Mr. Palmer is the Lovelace in Johnson's cast. A certain W. Palmer was at Covent Garden in 1785-86. But whether he and "Mr. Palmer" are one and the same is not known. The "Advertisement" or preface of the 1785 edition has two deliberate changes, both in connection with the act of Lewis in desiring a revival of the farce in 1776: "courage" becomes "good taste," and "in March last" is excised. There are no textual changes in the play proper, though there are six textual corruptions. There is no evidence that Murphy had any connection with this 1785 edition. In fact, for his *Works* of 1786, in the "Advertisement" of *Three Weeks after Marriage* he retained "Courage" and altered "in March last" to "in March 1776."

For his *Works* Murphy rewrote the 1776 version of *Three Weeks after Marriage*, but with fewer than habitual alterations. There is some rewriting of every named part. The new speeches, not including a few divisions of speeches from the 1776 edition, comprise seventeen for Lady Rackett, sixteen for Sir Charles Rackett, two for Mrs. Drugget, and two for Drugget. Murphy drops three speeches of Lady Rackett and one of Sir Charles Rackett. There are many revised passages, several expansions, a few transpositions, and one cut. A change in the card game is noteworthy in five speeches. Better exposition or better clarity is apparent in seven others. The editior reproduces this final text of Murphy.

Texts Collated

MS., LA, 231, Dec. 10, 1763. Larpent Collection, Huntington Library.

[Murphy, Arthur], *What We Must All Come To*. London: P. Vaillant, 1764. [Temple University]

——, *Three Weeks after Marriage*. London: G. Kearsley, 1776. [Harvard University; Haverford College]

——, *Three Weeks after Marriage; or, What We Must All Come To*. London: P. Vaillant, [1784?]. [Yale University; Library of Congress]

——, *Three Weeks after Marriage*. London: E. Johnson, [1785?]. [State University of Iowa]

The Works of Arthur Murphy, II, 359-434. London: T. Cadell, 1786. [University of Pennsylvania; Copy of Editor]

THREE WEEKS
AFTER MARRIAGE:

A

COMEDY,

In TWO ACTS.

Performed at the

THEATRE ROYAL

in

COVENT-GARDEN.

. . . Otium & oppidi

Laudat rura sui . . .

Hor.[1]

. . . Nugae seria ducent

In mala . . .

Hor.[2]

¹ Horace, *Odae* I.i.16-17. "He commends the tranquillity and ruralness of his own village."

² Horace, *Ars Poetica*, lines 451-452. "Trifles will lead to serious evils."

ADVERTISEMENT

THE following scenes were offered to the public in January 1764; but a party of that species of critics whom the love of mischief sometimes assembles at the theatre being unwilling to hear, the piece was damned.[3] Mr. Lewis, of Covent Garden Theatre, had the courage to revive it for his benefit in March 1776, with an alteration of the title,[3] and it has been since frequently repeated with success. A similar incident happened to Voltaire at Paris. That writer, in the year 1734, produced a tragedy entitled *Adélaïde du Guesclin*, which was hissed through every act. In 1765, Le Kain,[4] an actor of eminence, revived the play, which had lain for years under condemnation. Every scene was applauded. "What can I think," says Voltaire, "of these opposite judgments?" He relates the following anecdote. A banker at Paris had orders to get a new march composed for one of the regiments of Charles XII. He employed a man of talents for the purpose. The march was prepared, and a practice of it had at the banker's house before a numerous assembly. The music was found detestable. Mouret[5] (that was the composer's name) retired with his performance, and soon after inserted it in one of his operas. The banker and his friends went to the opera: the march was universally admired. "Ah," says the banker, "that's what we wanted: why did not you give us something in this taste?" "Sir," replied Mouret, "the march, which you now applaud, is the very same that you condemned before." [6]

---

[3] See "Introduction."
[4] Lekain (Henri-Louis Cain) (1728-78).
[5] Jean-Joseph Mouret (1682-1738).
[6] *Œuvres Complètes De Voltaire* (Paris: Garnier Frères, 1877), Nouvelle Édition, III.77-79.

DRAMATIS PERSONAE

Men

Sir Charles Rackett,	Mr. Lewis.
Drugget,	Mr. Quick.
Lovelace,	Mr. Booth.
Woodley,	Mr. Young.

Women

Lady Rackett,	Mrs. Mattocks.
Mrs. Drugget,	Mrs. Pitt.
Nancy,	Miss Dayes.
Dimity,	Mrs. Green.

THREE WEEKS AFTER MARRIAGE

ACT the FIRST
[SCENE I]

[A Room in the Drugget House]

Enter WOODLEY *and* DIMITY.

DIMITY. Po! po!——No such thing: I tell you, Mr. Woodley, you are a mere novice in these affairs.

WOODLEY. Nay, but listen to reason, Mrs. Dimity: has not your master, Mr. Drugget, invited me down to his country-seat? Has not he promised to give me his daughter Nancy in marriage? And with what pretence can he now break off?

DIMITY. What pretence!——You put a body out of all patience. Go on your own way, Sir; my advice is lost upon you.

WOODLEY. You do me injustice, Mrs. Dimity. Your advice has governed my whole conduct. Have not I fixed an interest in the young lady's heart?

DIMITY. An interest in a fiddlestick!——You ought to have made sure of the father and mother. What, do you think the way to get a wife, at this time of day, is by speaking fine things to the lady you have a fancy for? That was the practice, indeed; but things are altered now. You must address the old people, Sir; and never trouble your head about your mistress. None of your letters, and verses, and soft looks, and fine speeches——"Have compassion, thou angelic

293

creature, on a poor dying"——Pshaw! stuff! nonsense! All out of fashion. Go your ways to the old curmudgeon, humour his whims ——"I shall esteem it an honour, Sir, to be allied to a gentleman of your rank and taste." "Upon my word, he's a pretty young gentleman."——Then wheel about to the mother: "Your daughter, Ma'am, is the very model of you, and I shall adore her for your sake." "Here, come hither, Nancy; take this gentleman for better for worse." "La, Mama, I can never consent."—— "I should not have thought of your consent: the consent of your relations is enough: why, how now, hussy!" So away you go to church; the knot is tied; an agreeable honeymoon follows; the charm is then dissolved; you go to all the clubs in St. James's Street; [7] your lady goes to the coterie; and, in a little time you both go to Doctors' Commons; [8] the *Morning Post* displays you in black and white; *Poets' Corner* [9] treats you with a ballad or an epigram; your friends pity you; the town laughs at you; the lawyers abuse you; and if faults on both sides prevent a divorce, you quarrel like contrary elements all the rest of your lives: that's the way of the world now.

WOODLEY. But you know, my dear Dimity, the old couple have received every mark of attention from me.

DIMITY. Attention! To be sure you did not fall asleep in their company; but what then? You should have entered into their characters, play'd with their humours, and sacrificed to their absurdities.

WOODLEY. But if my temper is too frank——

DIMITY. Frank, indeed! Yes, you have been frank enough to ruin yourself. Have not you to do with a rich old shopkeeper, retired from business with an hundred thousand pounds in his pocket, to enjoy the dust of the London road, which he calls living in the country? And yet you must find fault with his situation! What if he has made a ridiculous gimcrack of his house and gardens? You

---

[7] The site of such clubs as White's and Almack's, notorious for gambling. Added in 1776.

[8] Doctors' Commons pertained first to the common dining hall and later to other buildings of the College of Doctors of Civil Law, London; the jurisdiction of these courts and offices included divorce. Added in 1776.

[9] Literally, an angle in the south transept of Westminster Abbey. Here, a section of a newspaper. Added in 1786.

know his heart is set upon it; and could not you have commended his taste? But you must be too frank! "Those walks and alleys are too regular; those evergreens should not be cut into such fantastic shapes."——And thus you advise a poor old mechanic, who delights in everything that's monstrous, to follow nature. Oh, you are likely to be a successful lover!

WOODLEY. But why should I not save a father-in-law from being a laughingstock?

DIMITY. Make him your father-in-law first.

WOODLEY. Why, he can't open his windows for the dust: he stands all day looking through a pane of glass at the carts and stage-coaches as they pass by, and he calls that living in the fresh air, and enjoying his own thoughts.

DIMITY. And could not you let him go on his own way? You have ruined yourself by talking sense to him; and all your nonsense to the daughter won't make amends for it. And then the mother; how have you played your cards in that quarter? She wants a tinsel man of fashion for her second daughter. "Don't you see (says she) how happy my eldest girl is made by her match with Sir Charles Rackett? She has been married three entire weeks, and not so much as one angry word has passed between them! Nancy shall have a man of quality too."

WOODLEY. And yet I know Sir Charles Rackett perfectly well.

DIMITY. Yes, so do I; and I know he'll make his Lady wretched at last. But what then? You should have humoured the old folks: you should have been a talking, empty fop to the good old lady; and to the old gentleman, an admirer of his taste in gardening. But you have lost him: he is grown fond of this beau Lovelace, who is here in the house with him: the coxcomb ingratiates himself by flattery, and you're undone by frankness.

WOODLEY. And yet, Dimity, I won't despair.

DIMITY. And yet you have reason to despair, a million of reasons: tomorrow is fixed for the wedding-day; Sir Charles and his Lady are to be here this very night; they are engaged, indeed, at a great rout [10] in town, but they take a bed here, notwithstanding. The

---

[10] A fashionable evening party.

family is sitting up for them; Mr. Drugget will keep you all in the next room there till they arrive; tomorrow the business is over; and yet you don't despair!——Hush! hold your tongue; here comes Lovelace, and Mr. Drugget with him; step in, and I'll devise something, I warrant you.

Exit.

WOODLEY. The old folks shall not have their own way. It is enough to vex a body, to see an old father and mother marrying their daughter as they please, in spite of my judgment, and all I can do.

Exit.

Enter DRUGGET *and* LOVELACE.

DRUGGET. And so you like my house and gardens, Mr. Lovelace.

LOVELACE. Oh! perfectly, Sir; they gratify my taste of all things. One sees villas where Nature reigns in a wild kind of simplicity: but then they have no appearance of art, no art at all.

DRUGGET. Very true, rightly distinguished: now mine is all art; no wild nature here; I did it all myself.

LOVELACE. Indeed! I thought you had some of the great proficients in gardening to assist you.

DRUGGET. Lackaday! no. Ha! ha! I understand these things. I love my garden. The front of my house, Mr. Lovelace, is not that very pretty?

LOVELACE. Elegant to a degree!

DRUGGET. Don't you like the sundial, placed just by my dining-room windows!

LOVELACE. A perfect beauty!

DRUGGET. I knew you'd like it: and the motto is so well adapted —*Tempus edax & index rerum.*[11] And I know the meaning of it. Time eateth and discovereth all things. Ha! ha! pretty, Mr. Lovelace! I have seen people so stare at it as they pass by! Ha! ha!

---

[11] Ovid, *Metamorphoses* 15.234 combined with "et index" of Ovid, *Artis Amatoriae* III.719. "Time devourer and informer of things."

LOVELACE. Why now, I don't believe there's a nobleman in the kingdom has such a thing.

DRUGGET. Oh no; they have got into a false taste. I bought that bit of ground on the other side of the road, and now it is a perfect beauty. I made a duck-pond there, for the sake of the prospect.

LOVELACE. Charmingly imagined!

DRUGGET. My leaden images are well!

LOVELACE. They exceed ancient statuary.

DRUGGET. I love to be surprised at the turning of a walk with an inanimate figure, that looks you full in the face, and can say nothing at all, while one is enjoying one's own thoughts. Ha! ha!——Mr. Lovelace, I'll point out a beauty to you. Just by the haw-haw,[12] at the end of my ground, there is a fine Dutch figure, with a scythe in his hand, and a pipe in his mouth. That's a jewel, Mr. Lovelace!

LOVELACE. That escaped me: a thousand thanks for pointing it out. I observe you have two very fine yew trees before the house.

DRUGGET. Lackaday, Sir! They look uncouth. I have a design about them. I intend——ha! ha! It will be very pretty, Mr. Lovelace——I intend to have them cut into the shape of the two giants at Guildhall! [13]

LOVELACE. Exquisite!——Why then they won't look like trees.

DRUGGET. No, no; not in the least; I won't have anything in my garden that looks like what it is.

LOVELACE. Nobody understands these things like you, Mr. Drugget.

DRUGGET. Lackaday! It's all my delight now. This is what I have been working for. I have a great improvement to make still: I propose to have my evergreens cut into fortifications; and then I shall have the Morro Castle,[14] and the Havana; [15] and then near it

---

[12] A sunken fence.

[13] The hall of the Corporation of the City of London. The two giants, Gog and Magog, were colossal wooden statues carved by Richard Saunders and set up in 1708.

[14] A fortress on the east side of the harbor of Havana, built by the Spaniards in the late sixteenth century.

[15] A weather vane in the shape of a woman on top of the watchtower of the fortress of La Fuerza, Havana.

shall be ships of myrtle, sailing upon seas of box to attack the town: won't that make my place look very rural, Mr. Lovelace?

LOVELACE. Why, you have the most fertile invention, Mr. Drugget.

DRUGGET. Ha! ha! This is what I have been working for. I love my garden. But I must beg your pardon for a few moments: I must step and speak with a famous nurseryman, who is come to offer me some choice rarities. Go and join the company, Mr. Lovelace: my daughter Rackett and Sir Charles will be here presently. I shan't go to bed till I see them. Ha! ha!——My place is prettily variegated. This is all I delight in now. I fined for sheriff [16] to enjoy these things——ha! ha!

Exit.

LOVELACE. Poor Mr. Drugget! Mynheer Van Thundertentrunck, in his little box at the side of a dike, has as much taste and elegance. However, if I can but carry off his daughter, if I can but rob his garden of that flower, why then I shall say, "This is what I have been working for."

Enter DIMITY.

DIMITY. Do lend us your assistance, Mr. Lovelace. You are a sweet gentleman, and love a good-natured action.

LOVELACE. Why, how now! What's the matter?

DIMITY. My master is going to cut the two yew trees into the shape of two devils, I believe; and my poor mistress is breaking her heart for it. Do, run and advise him against it. She is your friend, you know she is, Sir.

LOVELACE. Oh, if that's all, I'll make that matter easy directly.

DIMITY. My mistress will be for ever obliged to you; and you will marry her daughter in the morning.

LOVELACE. Oh, my rhetoric shall dissuade him.

DIMITY. And, Sir, put him against dealing with that nurseryman; Mrs. Drugget hates him.

---

[16] I paid to avoid serving as sheriff.

LOVELACE. Does she?

DIMITY. Mortally.

LOVELACE. Say no more; the business is done.

Exit.

DIMITY. If he says one word against the giants at Guildhall, he is undone. Old Drugget will never forgive him. My brain was at its last shift; but if this plot takes——so, here comes our Nancy.

Enter NANCY.

NANCY. Well, Dimity, what's to become of me?

DIMITY. My stars! What makes you up, Miss? I thought you were gone to bed.

NANCY. What should I go to bed for? Only to tumble and toss, and fret, and be uneasy. They are going to marry me, and I am frighted out of my wits.

DIMITY. Why then you are the only young lady within fifty miles round that would be frightened at such a thing.

NANCY. Ah! if they would let me choose for myself.

DIMITY. Don't you like Mr. Lovelace?

NANCY. My mama does, but I don't; I don't mind his being a man of fashion, not I.

DIMITY. And, pray, can you do better than to follow the fashion?

NANCY. Ah! I know there's a fashion for new bonnets, and a fashion for dressing the hair; but I never heard of a fashion for the heart.

DIMITY. Why then, my dear, the heart mostly follows the fashion now.

NANCY. Does it! Pray, who sets the fashion of the heart?

DIMITY. All the fine ladies in London, o'my conscience.

NANCY. And what's the last new fashion, pray?

DIMITY. Why, to marry any fop that has a few deceitful agreeable appearances about him; something of a pert phrase, a good operator [17] for the teeth, and tolerable tailor.

NANCY. And do they marry without loving?

---

[17] An operative dentist.

DIMITY. Oh! marrying for love has been a great while out of fashion.

NANCY. Why then I'll wait till that fashion comes up again.

DIMITY. And then, Mr. Lovelace, I reckon——

NANCY. Pshaw! I don't like him: he talks to me as if he was the most miserable man in the world, and the confident thing looks so pleased with himself all the while. I want to marry for love, and not for card-playing. I should not be able to bear the life my sister leads with Sir Charles Rackett. Shall I tell you a secret? I will forfeit my new cap if they don't quarrel soon.

DIMITY. Oh fie! no! They won't quarrel yet awhile. A quarrel in three weeks after marriage would be somewhat of the quickest. By and by we shall hear of their whims and their humours. Well, but if you don't like Mr. Lovelace, what say you to Mr. Woodley?

NANCY. Ah!——I don't know what to say——but I can sing something that will explain my mind.

SONG

I.

When first the dear youth passing by,
　　Disclos'd his fair form to my sight,
I gaz'd, but I could not tell why;
　　My heart it went throb with delight.

II.

As nearer he drew, those sweet eyes
　　Were with their dear meaning so bright,
I trembled, and, lost in surprise,
　　My heart it went throb with delight.

III.

When his lips their dear accents did try
　　The return of my love to excite,
I feign'd, yet began to guess why
　　My heart it went throb with delight.

IV.

We chang'd the stol'n glance, the fond smile,
    Which lovers alone read aright;
We look'd and we sigh'd, yet the while
    Our hearts they went throb with delight.

V.

Consent I soon blush'd, with a sigh
    My promise I ventur'd to plight;
Come, Hymen, we then shall know why
    Our hearts they go throb with delight.

Enter WOODLEY.

WOODLEY. My sweetest angel! I have heard it all, and my heart overflows with love and gratitude.

NANCY. Ah! but I did not know you was listening. You should not have betrayed me so, Dimity: I shall be angry with you.

DIMITY. Well, I'll take my chance for that. Run both into my room, and say all your pretty things to one another there, for here comes the old gentleman——make haste away.

Exeunt WOODLEY *and* NANCY.

Enter DRUGGET.

DRUGGET. A forward, presuming coxcomb! Dimity, do you step to Mrs. Drugget, and send her hither.

DIMITY. Yes, Sir;——it works upon him I see.

Exit.

DRUGGET. The yew trees ought not to be cut, because they'll help to keep off the dust, and I am too near the road already. A sorry, ignorant fop! When I am in so fine a situation, and can see every cart, wagon, and stagecoach that goes by. And then to abuse the nurseryman's rarities! A finer sucking pig in lavender, with sage growing in his belly, was never seen! And yet he wants me not to have it. But have it I will.——There's a fine tree of knowledge, with

Adam and Eve in juniper; Eve's nose not quite grown, but it's thought in the spring will be very forward: I'll have that too, with the serpent in ground ivy. Two poets in wormwood! I'll have them both. Ay; and there's a Lord Mayor's feast in honeysuckle; and the whole court of aldermen in hornbeam: and three modern beaux in jessamine, somewhat stunted: they all shall be in my garden, with the Dragon of Wantley [18] in box, all, all; I'll have them all, let my wife and Mr. Lovelace say what they will.

Enter MRS. DRUGGET.

MRS. DRUGGET. Did you send for me, lovey?

DRUGGET. The yew trees shall be cut into the giants at Guildhall, whether you will or not.

MRS. DRUGGET. Sure my own dear will do as he pleases.

DRUGGET. And the pond, though you praise the green banks, shall be walled round, and I'll have a little fat boy in marble, spouting up water in the middle.

MRS. DRUGGET. My sweet, who hinders you?

DRUGGET. Yes, and I'll buy the nurseryman's whole catalogue. Do you think, after retiring to live all the way here, almost four miles from London, that I won't do as I please in my own garden?

MRS. DRUGGET. My dear, but why are you in such a passion?

DRUGGET. I'll have the lavender pig, and the Adam and Eve, and the Dragon of Wantley, and all of 'em: and there shan't be a more romantic spot on the London road than mine.

MRS. DRUGGET. I'm sure it is as pretty as hands can make it.

DRUGGET. I did it all myself, and I'll do more. And Mr. Lovelace shan't have my daughter.

MRS. DRUGGET. No! What's the matter now, Mr. Drugget?

DRUGGET. He shall learn better manners than to abuse my house and gardens. You put him in the head of it, but I'll disappoint ye both. And so you may go and tell Mr. Lovelace that the match is quite off.

---

[18] A character in Henry Carey's very popular burlesque opera *The Dragon of Wantley* (1737).

MRS. DRUGGET. I can't comprehend all this, not I. But I'll tell him so, if you please, my dear. I am willing to give myself pain if it will give you pleasure: must I give myself pain? Don't ask me, pray don't; I can't support all this uneasiness.

DRUGGET. I am resolved, and it shall be so.

MRS. DRUGGET. Let it be so then. (*Cries*) Oh! oh! Cruel man! I shall break my heart if the match is broke off. If it is not concluded tomorrow, send for an undertaker, and bury me the next day.

DRUGGET. How! I don't want that neither.

MRS. DRUGGET. Oh! oh!

DRUGGET. I am your lord and master, my dear, but not your executioner. Before George,[19] it must never be said that my wife died of too much compliance. Cheer up, my love; and this affair shall be settled as soon as Sir Charles and Lady Rackett arrive.

MRS. DRUGGET. You bring me to life again. You know, my sweet, what an happy couple Sir Charles and his Lady are. Why should not we make our Nancy as happy?

Enter DIMITY.

DIMITY. Sir Charles and his Lady, Ma'am.

MRS. DRUGGET. Oh! charming! I'm transported with joy! Where are they? I long to see 'em.

Exit.

DIMITY. Well, Sir; the happy couple are arrived.

DRUGGET. Yes, they do live happy indeed.

DIMITY. But how long will it last?

DRUGGET. How long! Don't forebode any ill, you jade; don't, I say. It will last during their lives, I hope.

DIMITY. Well, mark the end of it. Sir Charles, I know, is gay and good-humoured; but he can't bear the least contradiction, no, not in the merest trifle.

DRUGGET. Hold your tongue; hold your tongue.

DIMITY. Yes, Sir, I have done; and yet there is in the composition

---

[19] An earlier form of "by George," used as a mild oath.

of Sir Charles a certain humour, which, like the flying gout,[20] gives no disturbance to the family till it settles in the head: when once it fixes there, mercy on everybody about him! But here he comes.

Exit.

Enter SIR CHARLES.

SIR CHARLES. My dear Sir, I kiss your hand. But why stand on ceremony? To find you up at this late hour mortifies me beyond expression.

DRUGGET. 'Tis but once in a way, Sir Charles.

SIR CHARLES. My obligations to you are inexpressible; you have given me the most amiable of girls; our tempers accord like unisons in music.

DRUGGET. Ah! that's what makes me happy in my old days; my children and my garden are all my care.

SIR CHARLES. And my friend Lovelace——he is to have our sister Nancy, I find.

DRUGGET. Why, my wife is so minded.

SIR CHARLES. Oh, by all means, let her be made happy. A very pretty fellow Lovelace; as to that Mr.——Woodley, I think you call him——he is but a plain, underbred, ill-fashioned sort of a—— nobody knows him; he is not one of us. Oh, by all means marry her to one of us.

DRUGGET. I believe it must be so. Would you take any refreshment?

SIR CHARLES. Nothing in nature: it is time to retire to rest.

DRUGGET. Well, well! Good night, Sir Charles. Ha! here comes my daughter. Good night, Sir Charles.

SIR CHARLES. *Bon repos.*

Enter LADY RACKETT.

LADY RACKETT. Dear Sir! I did not expect to see you up so late.

DRUGGET. My Lady Rackett, I am glad to hear how happy you

---

[20] Migratory gout.

are: I won't detain you now. There's your good man waiting for you: good night, my girl.

Exit.

SIR CHARLES. I must humour this old muckworm, in order to be remembered in his will. (*Aside*)

LADY RACKETT. O la! I am quite fatigued. I can hardly move. Why don't you help me, you barbarous man?

SIR CHARLES. There; take my arm——"Was ever thing so pretty made to walk?" [21]

LADY RACKETT. But I won't be laughed at. (*Looking tenderly at him*) I don't love you.

SIR CHARLES. Don't you?

LADY RACKETT. No. Dear me! This glove! Why don't you help me off with my glove? Pshaw! You awkward thing, let it alone; you an't fit to be about my person. I might as well not be married, for any use you are of. Reach me a chair. You have no compassion for me. I am so glad to sit down. Why do you drag me to routs? You know I hate them.

SIR CHARLES. Oh! there's no existing, no breathing, unless one does as other people of fashion do.

LADY RACKETT. But I am out of humour: I lost all my money.

SIR CHARLES. How much?

LADY RACKETT. Three hundred.

SIR CHARLES. Never fret for that. I don't value three hundred pounds to contribute to your happiness.

LADY RACKETT. Don't you?——Not value three hundred pounds to please me?

SIR CHARLES. You know I don't.

LADY RACKETT. Ah! you fond fool!——But I hate gaming: it almost metamorphoses a woman into a fury. Do you know that I was frighted at myself several times tonight? I had an huge oath at the very tip of my tongue.

SIR CHARLES. Had ye?

LADY RACKETT. I caught myself at it; but I bit my lips, and so I

---

[21] Altered from Edward Young, *Love of Fame, The Universal Passion* (1725-8), Satire II, line 170: "Was ever thing so pretty born to stand?"

did not disgrace myself. And then I was crammed up in a corner of the room with such a strange party at a whist-table, looking at black and red spots: did you mind them?

SIR CHARLES. You know I was busy elsewhere.

LADY RACKETT. There was that strange, unaccountable woman, Mrs. Nightshade: she behaved so fretfully to her husband, a poor, inoffensive, good-natured, good sort of a good-for-nothing kind of man: but she so teased him——"How could you play that card? Ah, you've a head, and so has a pin——you're a numskull, you know you are.——Ma'am, he has the poorest head in the world, he does not know what he is about; you know you don't.——Oh fie!——I'm ashamed of you!"

SIR CHARLES. She has served to divert you, I see.

LADY RACKETT. And to crown all, there was my Lady Clackit, who runs on with an eternal larum about nothing, out of all season, time, and place.——In the very midst of the game she begins, "Lard, Ma'am, I was apprehensive I should not be able to wait on your La'ship; my poor little dog, Pompey——the sweetest thing in the world——a spade led!——there's the knave——I was fetching a walk, Me'm, the other morning in the park; a fine frosty morning it was; I love frosty weather of all things. Let me look at the last trick.——And so, Me'm, little Pompey——oh! if your La'ship was to see the dear creature pinched with the frost, and mincing his steps along the Mall,[22] with his pretty innocent face——I vow I don't know what to play.——And so, Me'm, while I was talking to Captain Flimsey——your La'ship knows Captain Flimsey—— nothing but rubbish in my hand——I can't help it.——And so, Me'm, five odious frights of dogs beset my poor little Pompey——the dear creature has the heart of a lion, but who can resist five at once? And so Pompey barked for assistance. The hurt he received was upon his chest: the doctor would not advise him to venture out till the wound is healed, for fear of an inflammation.——Pray what's trumps?"

SIR CHARLES. My dear, you'd make a most excellent actress.

---

[22] The Mall was a fashionable sheltered promenade at the north side of St. James's Park, London.

LADY RACKETT. Why don't you hand me upstairs? Oh!——I am so tired: let us go to rest.

SIR CHARLES. (*Assisting her*) You complain, and yet raking is the delight of your little heart.

LADY RACKETT. (*Leaning on him as she walks away*) It is you that make a rake of me. Oh! Sir Charles, how shockingly you played that last rubber, when I stood looking over you!

SIR CHARLES. My love, I played the truth of the game.

LADY RACKETT. No, indeed, my dear, you played it wrong. Ah! Sir Charles, you have a head.

SIR CHARLES. Po! Nonsense! You don't understand it.

LADY RACKETT. I beg your pardon: I am allowed to play better than you.

SIR CHARLES. All conceit, my dear: I was perfectly right.

LADY RACKETT. No such thing, Sir Charles. How can you dispute it? The diamond was the play.

SIR CHARLES. Po! Ridiculous! The club was the card against the world.

LADY RACKETT. Oh, no, no, no, I say it was the diamond.

SIR CHARLES. Zounds! Madam, I say it was the club.

LADY RACKETT. What do you fly into such a passion for?

SIR CHARLES. Death and fury, do you think I don't know what I am about? I tell you once more, the club was the judgment of it.

LADY RACKETT. Maybe so. Have it your own way, Sir. (*Walks about and sings*)

SIR CHARLES. Vexation! You're the strangest woman that ever lived; there's no conversing with you. Look ye here, my Lady Rackett: it is the clearest case in the world: I'll make it plain to you in a moment.

LADY RACKETT. Very well, Sir. To be sure you must be right. (*With a sneering laugh*)

SIR CHARLES. Listen to me, Lady Rackett: I had four cards left. Trumps were out. The lead was mine. They were six——no, no, no, they were seven, and we nine; [23] then you know, the beauty of the play was to——

---

[23] In whist, ten points constituted a game.

LADY RACKETT. Well, now it's amazing to me, that you can't perceive: give me leave, Sir Charles. Your left-hand adversary had led his last trump, and he had before finessed the club,[24] and roughed the diamond: [25] now if you had led your diamond——

SIR CHARLES. Zoons! Madam, but we played for the odd trick.[26]

LADY RACKETT. And sure the play for the odd trick——

SIR CHARLES. Death and fury! Can't you hear me?

LADY RACKETT. And must not I be heard, Sir?

SIR CHARLES. Zoons, hear me, I say. Will you hear me?

LADY RACKETT. I never heard the like in my life. (*Hums a tune and walks about fretfully*)

SIR CHARLES. Why then you are enough to provoke the patience of a Stoic.——(*Looks at her; she walks about and laughs*) Very well, Madam; you know no more of the game than your father's leaden Hercules on the top of the house. You know no more of whist than he does of gardening.

LADY RACKETT. Go on your own way, Sir. (*Takes out a glass and settles her hair*)

SIR CHARLES. Why then, by all that's odious, you are the most perverse, obstinate, ignorant——

LADY RACKETT. Polite language, Sir!

SIR CHARLES. You are, Madam, the most perverse, the most obstinate——you are a vile woman!

LADY RACKETT. I am obliged to you, Sir.

SIR CHARLES. You are a vile woman, I tell you so, and I will never sleep another night under one roof with you.

LADY RACKETT. As you please.

SIR CHARLES. Madam, it shall be as I please. I'll order my chariot this moment. (*Going*) I know how the cards should be played as well as any man in England, that let me tell you. (*Going*)——And when your family were standing behind counters, measuring out

---

[24] Taken a trick with an inferior club while holding a higher club not in sequence.

[25] Trumped the diamond when unable to follow suit.

[26] The seventh trick of thirteen would score a point.

tape, and bartering for Whitechapel needles,[27] my ancestors, my ancestors, Madam, were squandering away whole estates at cards; whole estates, my Lady Rackett. (*She hums a tune, and he looks at her*) Why then, by all that's dear to me, I'll never exchange another word with you, good, bad, or indifferent. (*Goes and turns back*) Will you command your temper, and listen to me?

LADY RACKETT. Go on, Sir.

SIR CHARLES. Can't you be cool as I am?——Look ye, my Lady Rackett: thus it stood. The trumps being all out, it was then my business——

LADY RACKETT. To play the diamond to be sure.

SIR CHARLES. Damnation! I have done with you for ever; for ever, Madam, and so you may tell your father. (*Going*)

LADY RACKETT. What a passion the gentleman is in!

SIR CHARLES. Will you let me speak?

LADY RACKETT. Who hinders you, Sir?

SIR CHARLES. Once more then out of pure good nature——

LADY RACKETT. Oh, Sir, I am convinced of your good nature.

SIR CHARLES. That, and that only prevails with me to tell you, the club was the play.

LADY RACKETT. I am prodigiously obliged to you for the information. I am perfectly satisfied, Sir.

SIR CHARLES. It is the clearest point in the world. Only mind now. We were nine, and——

LADY RACKETT. And for that reason, the diamond was the play. Your adversary's club was the best in the house.

SIR CHARLES. Why then, such another fiend never existed. There is no reasoning with you. It is in vain to say a word. Good sense is thrown away upon you. I now see the malice of your heart. You are a base woman, and I part from you for ever. You may live here with your father, and admire his fantastical evergreens, till you become as fantastical yourself. I'll set out for London this moment. Your servant, Madam. (*Turns and looks at her*) The club was not the best in the house.

---

[27] Here, needles sold in second-rate shops in Whitechapel, an ungenteel section of London east of the City or commercial center.

LADY RACKETT. How calm you are!——Well, I'll go to bed. Will you come? You had better. Not come when I ask you?——Oh! Sir Charles. (*Going*)

SIR CHARLES. That ease is so provoking. I desire you will stay and hear me. Don't think to carry it in this manner. Madam, I must and will be heard.

LADY RACKETT. Oh! Lud! With that terrible countenance! You frighten me away. (*Runs in and shuts the door*)

SIR CHARLES. (*Following her*) You shall not fly me thus. Confusion!——Open the door——will you open it? This contempt is beyond enduring. (*Walks away*) I intended to have made it clear to her, but now let her continue in her absurdity. She is not worth my notice. My resolution is taken. She has touched my pride, and I now renounce her for ever; yes, for ever; not to return, though she were to request, beseech and implore on her very knees.

Exit.

LADY RACKETT. (*Peeping in*) Is he gone? (*Comes forward*) Bless me! What have I done?——I have carried this too far, I believe. I had better call him back. For the sake of peace I'll give up the point. What does it signify which was the best of the play?—— It is not worth quarrelling about.——How!——Here he comes again. ——I'll give up nothing to him. He shall never get the better of me: I am ruined for life if he does. I will conquer him, and I am resolved he shall see it. (*Runs in and shuts the door*)

SIR CHARLES. (*Looking in*) No; she won't open it. Headstrong and positive!——If she could but command her temper, the thing would be as clear as daylight. She has sense enough, if she would but make use of it. It were pity she should be lost. (*Advances towards the door*) All owing to that perverse spirit of contradiction.——I may reclaim her still.——(*Peeps through the keyhole*) Not so much as a glimpse of her. (*Taps on the door*) Lady Rackett ——Lady Rackett——

LADY RACKETT. (*Within*) What do you want?

SIR CHARLES. (*Laughing affectedly*) Come, you have been very pleasant. Open the door: I cannot help laughing at all this.——Come, no more foolery: have done now, and open the door.

LADY RACKETT. (*Within*) Don't be such a torment.

SIR CHARLES. Will you open it?

LADY RACKETT. (*Laughing*) No——no——ho! ho!

SIR CHARLES. Hell and confusion! What a puppy I make of myself! I'll bear this usage no longer. To be trifled with in this sort by a false, treacherous——(*Runs to the door and speaks through the keyhole*) The diamond was NOT the play. (*Walks away as fast as he can*) I know what I am about, (*Looks back in a violent rage*) and the club was NOT the best in the house.

Exit.

End of the FIRST ACT.

ACT the SECOND
[SCENE I]

[A Room in the Drugget House]

Enter DIMITY.

DIMITY. (*Laughing violently*) Oh! I shall die; I shall expire in a fit of laughing. This is the modish couple that were so happy! Such a quarrel as they have had; the whole house is in an uproar. Ho! ho! ho! A rare proof of the happiness they enjoy in high life. I shall never hear people of fashion mentioned again but I shall be ready to crack my sides. They were both——ho! ho! ho! This is three weeks after marriage, I think.

Enter DRUGGET.

DRUGGET. Hey! How! What's the matter, Dimity? What am I called downstairs for?

DIMITY. Why there's two people of fashion—— (*Stifles a laugh*)

DRUGGET. Why, you malapert hussy! Explain this moment.

DIMITY. The fond couple have been together by the ears this half hour. Are you satisfied now?

DRUGGET. Ay!——What, have they quarrelled? What was it about?

DIMITY. Something too nice and fine for my comprehension, and yours too, I believe. People in high life understand their own forms best. And here comes one that can unriddle the whole affair.

Exit.

Enter SIR CHARLES.

SIR CHARLES. (*To the people within*) I say, let the horses be put-to this moment. So, Mr. Drugget!

DRUGGET. Sir Charles, here's a terrible bustle. I did not expect this. What can be the matter?

SIR CHARLES. I have been used by your daughter in so base, so contemptuous, so vile a manner, that I am determined not to stay in this house tonight.

DRUGGET. This is a thunderbolt to me! After seeing how elegantly and fashionably you lived together, to find now all sunshine vanished! Do, Sir Charles, let me heal this breach if possible.

SIR CHARLES. Sir, it is impossible. I'll not live with her an hour longer.

DRUGGET. Nay, nay, don't be too hasty. Let me entreat you, go to bed and sleep upon it. In the morning, when you are cool——

SIR CHARLES. Oh, Sir, I am very cool, I assure you. Ha! ha!—— It is not in her power, Sir, to——a——a——to disturb the serenity of my temper. Don't imagine that I'm in a passion. I am not so easily ruffled as you imagine. But quietly and deliberately, I can repay the injury done me by a false, ungrateful, deceitful woman.

DRUGGET. The injuries done you by a false, ungrateful! My daughter I hope, Sir——

SIR CHARLES. Her character is now fully known to me. I understand her perfectly. She is a vile woman! That's all I have to say, Sir!

DRUGGET. Hey! How!——A vile woman! What has she done? I hope she is not capable——

SIR CHARLES. I shall enter into no detail, Mr. Drugget; the time and circumstances will not allow it at present. But depend upon it, I have done with her. A low, unpolished, uneducated, false, imposing——see if the horses are put-to.

DRUGGET. Mercy on me! In my old days to hear this.

Enter MRS. DRUGGET.

MRS. DRUGGET. Deliver me! I am all over in such a tremble. Sir Charles, I shall break my heart if there is anything amiss.

SIR CHARLES. Madam, I am very sorry, for your sake; but to live with her is impossible.

MRS. DRUGGET. My poor, dear girl! What can she have done?

SIR CHARLES. What all her sex can do: it needs no explanation: the very spirit of them all.

DRUGGET. Ay! I see how it is.——She is bringing foul disgrace upon us. This comes of her marrying a man of fashion.

SIR CHARLES. Fashion, Sir! That should have instructed her better. She might have been sensible of her happiness. Whatever you may think of the fortune you gave her, my rank in life claims respect; claims obedience, attention, truth, and love, from one raised in the world as she has been by an alliance with me.

DRUGGET. And, let me tell you, however you may estimate your quality, my daughter is dear to me.

SIR CHARLES. And, Sir, my character is dear to me. It shall never be in her power to expose me.

DRUGGET. Yet you must give me leave to tell you——

SIR CHARLES. I won't hear a word.

DRUGGET. Not in behalf of my own daughter?

SIR CHARLES. Nothing can excuse her. It is to no purpose. She has married above her; and if that circumstance makes the lady forget herself, she at least shall see that I can, and will support my own dignity.

DRUGGET. But, Sir, I have a right to ask——

MRS. DRUGGET. Patience, my dear, be a little calm.

DRUGGET. Mrs. Drugget, do you have patience. I must and will enquire.

MRS. DRUGGET. Don't be so hasty, my love; have some respect for Sir Charles's rank; don't be violent with a man of his fashion.

DRUGGET. Hold your tongue, woman, I say: hold your tongue. You are not a person of fashion at least. My daughter was ever a good girl.

SIR CHARLES. I have found her out.

DRUGGET. Oh! then it's all over, and it does not signify arguing about it.

MRS. DRUGGET. That ever I should live to see this hour! How the unfortunate girl could take such wickedness in her head, I can't imagine. I'll go and speak to the unhappy creature this moment.

Exit.

SIR CHARLES. She stands detected now: detected in her truest colours.

DRUGGET. Well, grievous as it may be, let me hear the circumstances of this unhappy business.

SIR CHARLES. Mr. Drugget, I have not leisure now. Her behaviour has been so exasperating that I shall make the best of my way to town. My mind is fixed. She sees me no more, and so, your servant, Sir.

Exit.

DRUGGET. What a calamity has here befallen us! A good girl, and so well-disposed! But the evil communication of high life, and fashionable vices, turned her heart to folly.

Enter LOVELACE.

LOVELACE. Joy! joy! Mr. Drugget, I give you joy.

DRUGGET. Don't insult me, Sir; I desire you won't.

LOVELACE. Insult you, Sir! Is there anything insulting, my dear Sir, if I take the liberty to congratulate you on the approaching——

DRUGGET. There! there! The manners of high life for you! He wishes me joy on the approaching ruin of my daughter. She is to be in the fashion! Mr. Lovelace, you shall have no daughter of mine.

LOVELACE. My dear Sir, never bear malice. I have reconsidered the thing, and curse catch me, if I don't think your notion of the Guildhall giants, and the court of aldermen in hornbeam——[28]

DRUGGET. Well! well! well! There may be people at the court end of the town in hornbeam too.[29]

LOVELACE. Yes, faith, so there may; and I believe I could help you to a tolerable collection. However, with your daughter I am ready to venture.

DRUGGET. But I am not ready. I'll not venture my girl with you. No more daughters of mine shall have their minds depraved by polite vices.

LOVELACE. Strike me stupid if I understand one word of all this.

Enter WOODLEY.

DRUGGET. Mr. Woodley, you shall have Nancy to your wife, as I promised you: take her tomorrow morning.

WOODLEY. Sir, I have not words to express——

LOVELACE. What the devil is the matter with the old haberdasher now?

DRUGGET. And hark ye, Mr. Woodley; I'll make you a present for your garden, of a coronation dinner in greens, with the champion riding on horseback, and the sword will be full-grown before April next.

WOODLEY. I shall receive it, Sir, as your favour.

DRUGGET. Ay, ay! I see my error in wanting an alliance with great folks. I had rather have you, Mr. Woodley, for my son-in-law than any courtly fop of 'em all. Is this man gone? Is Sir Charles Rackett gone?

---

[28] A small tree used in hedges.

[29] The main trunk of a stag's horn that bears the branches or antlers is a beam. The reference is to the horns of the cuckold.

WOODLEY. Not yet: he makes a bawling yonder for his horses. I'll step and call him to you.

Exit.

DRUGGET. Do so; do so, Mr. Woodley. I am out of all patience. I am out of my senses. I must see him once more. Mr. Lovelace, neither you nor any person of fashion, shall ruin another child of mine.

Exit.

LOVELACE. Droll this! Damn'd droll! And every syllable of it Greek to me. The queer old putt [30] is as whimsical in his notions of life as of gardening. If this be the case, I shall brush, and leave him to his exotics.

Exit.

Enter LADY RACKETT, MRS. DRUGGET, *and* DIMITY.

LADY RACKETT. A cruel, barbarous man! To quarrel in this unaccountable manner; to alarm the whole house, and to expose me and himself too.

MRS. DRUGGET. Oh! child! I never thought it would have come to this. Your shame will not end here; it will be all over St. James's parish by tomorrow morning.

LADY RACKETT. Well, if it must be so, there is one comfort still: the story will tell more to his disgrace than mine.

DIMITY. As I'm a sinner, and so it will, Madam. He deserves what he has met with.

MRS. DRUGGET. Dimity, don't you encourage her. You shock me to hear you speak so. I did not think you had been so hardened.

LADY RACKETT. Hardened, do you call it? I have lived in the world to very little purpose if such trifles as these are to disturb my rest.

MRS. DRUGGET. You wicked girl! Do you call it a trifle to be guilty of falsehood to your husband's bed?

LADY RACKET. How!——(*Turns short, and stares at her*)

---

[30] Bumpkin.

DIMITY. That! That's a mere trifle indeed. I have been in as good places as anybody, and not a creature minds it now.

MRS. DRUGGET. My Lady Rackett, my Lady Rackett, I never could think to see you come to this deplorable shame.

LADY RACKETT. Surely the base man has not been capable of laying anything of that sort to my charge? (*Aside*) All this is un-accountable to me——ha! ha!——It is ridiculous beyond measure.

DIMITY. That's right, Madam: laugh at it; you served him right.

MRS. DRUGGET. Charlotte! Charlotte! I'm astonished at your wickedness.

LADY RACKETT. Well, I protest and vow I don't comprehend all this. Has Sir Charles accused me of any impropriety in my conduct?

MRS. DRUGGET. Oh! too true, he has: he has found you out, and you have behaved basely, he says.

LADY RACKETT. Madam!

MRS. DRUGGET. You have fallen into frailty, like many others of your sex, he says; and he is resolved to come to a separation directly.

LADY RACKETT. Why then if he is so base a wretch as to dishonour me in that manner, his heart shall ache before I live with him again.

DIMITY. Hold to that, Ma'am, and let his head ache [31] into the bargain.

MRS. DRUGGET. Your poor father heard it as well as I.

LADY RACKETT. Then let your doors be open for him this very moment; let him return to London. If he does not, I'll lock myself up, and the false one shan't approach me, though he were to whine on his knees at my very door. A base, injurious man!

Exit.

MRS. DRUGGET. Dimity, do let us follow, and hear what she has to say for herself.

Exit.

DIMITY. She has excuse enough I warrant her. What a noise is here indeed! I have lived in polite families where there was no such bustle made about nothing.

Exit.

---

[31] Dimity refers to the horns of the cuckold.

Enter SIR CHARLES *and* DRUGGET.

SIR CHARLES. It is in vain, Sir, my resolution is taken.

DRUGGET. Well, but consider, I am her father. Indulge me only till we hear what the girl has to say in her defence.

SIR CHARLES. She can have nothing to say: no excuse can palliate such behaviour.

DRUGGET. Don't be too positive: there may be some mistake.

SIR CHARLES. No, Sir, no; there can be no mistake. Did not I see her, hear her myself?

DRUGGET. Lackaday! Then I am an unfortunate man!

SIR CHARLES. She will be unfortunate too: with all my heart. She may thank herself. She might have been happy, had she been so disposed.

DRUGGET. Why truly, I think she might.

Enter MRS. DRUGGET.

MRS. DRUGGET. I wish you would moderate your anger a little, and let us talk over this affair with temper. My daughter denies every tittle of your charge.

SIR CHARLES. Denies it! Denies it!

MRS. DRUGGET. She does indeed.

SIR CHARLES. And that aggravates her fault.

MRS. DRUGGET. She vows that you never found her out in anything that was wrong.

SIR CHARLES. She does not allow it to be wrong then! Madam, I tell you again, I know her thoroughly. I have found her out: I am now acquainted with her character. I am to be deceived no more.

MRS. DRUGGET. Then you are in opposite stories. She swears, my dear Mr. Drugget, the poor girl swears she never was guilty of the smallest infidelity to her husband in her born days.

SIR CHARLES. And what then? What if she does say so?

MRS. DRUGGET. And if she says truly, it is hard her character should be blown upon without just cause.

SIR CHARLES. And is she therefore to behave ill in other respects? I never charged her with infidelity to me, Madam: there I allow her innocent.

DRUGGET. And did not you charge her then?

SIR CHARLES. No, Sir, I never dreamt of such a thing.

DRUGGET. Why then, if she is innocent, let me tell you, you are a scandalous person.

MRS. DRUGGET. Prithee, my dear——

DRUGGET. Be quiet; though he is a man of quality, I will tell him of it. Did not I fine for sheriff?——Yes, you are a scandalous person to defame an honest man's daughter.

SIR CHARLES. What have you taken into your head now?

DRUGGET. You charged her with falsehood to your bed.

SIR CHARLES. No——never——never.

DRUGGET. I say you did.

SIR CHARLES. And I say no, no.

DRUGGET. But I say you did; you called yourself a cuckold. Did not he, wife?

MRS. DRUGGET. Yes, lovey, I am witness.

SIR CHARLES. Absurd! I said no such thing.

DRUGGET. But I aver you did.

MRS. DRUGGET. You did, indeed, Sir.

SIR CHARLES. But I tell you no, positively no.

DRUGGET *and* MRS. DRUGGET. And I say, yes, positively yes.

SIR CHARLES. 'Sdeath, this is all madness.

DRUGGET. You said that she followed the ways of most of her sex.

SIR CHARLES. I said so, and what then?

DRUGGET. There he owns it; owns that he called himself a cuckold, and without rhyme or reason into the bargain.

SIR CHARLES. I never owned any such thing.

DRUGGET. You owned it even now——now——now——now——

MRS. DRUGGET. This very moment.

SIR CHARLES. No, no; I tell you, no.

DRUGGET. This instant.——Prove it: make your words good: show me your horns, and if you can't, it is worse than suicide to call yourself a cuckold, without proof.

Enter DIMITY. (*In a fit of laughing*)

DIMITY. What do you think it was all about. Ha! ha! The whole secret is come out. Ha! ha! It was all about a game of cards.——Ho! ho! ho!

DRUGGET. A game of cards!

DIMITY. (*Laughing*) It was all about a club and a diamond. (*Runs out laughing*)

DRUGGET. And was that all, Sir Charles?

SIR CHARLES. And enough too, Sir.

DRUGGET. And was that what you found her out in?

SIR CHARLES. I can't bear to be contradicted, when I am clear that I am in the right.

DRUGGET. I never heard of such a heap of nonsense in all my life. Woodley shall marry Nancy.

MRS. DRUGGET. Don't be in a hurry, my love; this will all be made up.

DRUGGET. Why does he not go and beg her pardon then?

SIR CHARLES. I beg her pardon! I won't debase myself to any of you; I shan't forgive her, you may rest assured.

Exit.

DRUGGET. Now there, there's a pretty fellow for you.

MRS. DRUGGET. I'll step and prevail on my Lady Rackett to speak to him: all this will be set right.

Exit.

DRUGGET. A ridiculous fop! I am glad it is no worse, however.—— He must go and talk scandal of himself, as if the town did not abound with people ready enough to take that trouble off his hands.

Enter NANCY.

DRUGGET. So, Nancy——you seem in confusion, my girl!

NANCY. How can one help it, with all this noise in the house? And you are going to marry me as ill as my sister. I hate Mr. Lovelace.

DRUGGET. Why so, child?

NANCY. I know these people of quality despise us all out of pride, and would be glad to marry us out of avarice.

DRUGGET. The girl's right.

NANCY. They marry one woman, live with another, and love only themselves.

DRUGGET. And then quarrel about a card.

NANCY. I don't want to be a gay lady. I want to be happy.

DRUGGET. And so you shall: don't fright yourself, child. Step to your sister, bid her make herself easy: go, and comfort her, go.

NANCY. Yes, Sir.

Exit.

DRUGGET. I'll step and settle the matter with Mr. Woodley this moment.

Exit.

SCENE [II]

Another Apartment

SIR CHARLES, *with a Pack of Cards, at a Table.*

SIR CHARLES. Never was anything like her behaviour. I can pick out the very cards I had in my hand, and then 'tis as plain as the sun.——There——there——now——there——no——damn it——no ——there it was——now let me see.——They had four by honours [32] and we play'd for the odd trick.——Damnation! Honours were divided [33]——ay!——honours were divided and then a trump was led, and the other side had the—— Confusion!—— This preposterous woman has put it all out of my head. (*Puts the cards into his pocket*) Mighty well, Madam; I have done with you.

Enter MRS. DRUGGET.

---

[32] The four highest trumps would have counted four points.
[33] Honours count nothing when each side has two.

MRS. DRUGGET. Sir Charles, let me prevail. Come with me and speak to her.

SIR CHARLES. I don't desire to see her face.

MRS. DRUGGET. If you were to see her all bath'd in tears, I am sure it would melt your very heart.

SIR CHARLES. Madam, it shall be my fault if ever I am treated so again. I'll have nothing to say to her. (*Going, stops*) Does she give up the point?

MRS. DRUGGET. She does; she agrees to anything.

SIR CHARLES. Does she allow that the club was the play?

MRS. DRUGGET. Just as you please: she is all submission.

SIR CHARLES. Does she own that the club was not the best in the house?

MRS. DRUGGET. She does; she is willing to own it.

SIR CHARLES. Then I'll step and speak to her. I never was clearer in anything in my life.

Exit.

MRS. DRUGGET. Lord love 'em, they'll make it up now, and then they'll be as happy as ever.

Exit.

Enter NANCY.

NANCY. Well! They may talk what they will of taste, and genteel life; I don't think it's natural. Give me Mr. Woodley.——La! That odious thing coming this way.

Enter LOVELACE.

LOVELACE. My charming little innocent, I have not seen you these three hours.

NANCY. I have been very happy these three hours.

LOVELACE. My sweet angel, you seem disconcerted. And you neglect your pretty figure. No matter for the present; in a little time I shall make you appear as graceful and as genteel as your sister.

NANCY. That is not what employs my thoughts, Sir.

LOVELACE. Ay! but my pretty little dear, that should engage your attention. To set off and adorn the charms that nature has given you, should be the business of your life.

NANCY. But I have learnt a new song that contradicts what you say, and though I am not in a very good humour for singing, yet you shall hear it.

LOVELACE. By all means; don't check your fancy: I am all attention.

NANCY. It expresses my sentiments, and when you have heard them, you won't tease me any more.

SONG.

I.

To dance, and to dress, and to flaunt it about,
To run to park, play, to assembly and rout;
To wander for ever in whim's giddy maze,
And one poor hair torture a million of ways;
To put at the glass every feature to school,
And practise their art on each fop and each fool;
Of one thing to think, and another to tell,
These, these are the manners of each giddy belle.

II.

To smile, and to simper, white teeth to display;
The time in gay follies to trifle away;
Against ev'ry virtue the bosom to steel,
And only of dress the anxieties feel;
To be at Eve's ear the insidious decoy,
The pleasure ne'er taste, but the mischief enjoy;
To boast of soft raptures they never can know,
These, these are the manners of each giddy beau.

Exit.

LOVELACE. I must have her, notwithstanding this: for tho' I am not in love, I am most confoundedly in debt.

Enter DRUGGET.

DRUGGET. So, Mr. Lovelace! Any news from abovestairs? Is this absurd quarrel at an end? Have they made it up?

LOVELACE. Oh! a mere bagatelle, Sir: these little fracas among the better sort of people never last long: elegant trifles cause elegant disputes, and we come together elegantly again; as you see; for here they come, in perfect good humour.

Enter SIR CHARLES *and* LADY RACKETT.

SIR CHARLES. Mr. Drugget, I embrace you; you see me in the most perfect harmony of spirits.

DRUGGET. What, all reconciled again?

LADY RACKETT. All made up, Sir. I knew how to bring the gentle-man to a sense of his duty. This is the first difference, I think, we ever had, Sir Charles.

SIR CHARLES. And I'll be sworn it shall be the last.

DRUGGET. I am happy now, as happy as a fond father can wish. Sir Charles, I can spare you an image to put on the top of your house in London.

SIR CHARLES. Infinitely oblig'd to you.

DRUGGET. Well! well! It's time to retire: I am glad to see you reconciled; and now I wish you a good night, Sir Charles. Mr. Love-lace, this is your way. Fare ye well both. I am glad your quarrels are at an end. This way, Mr. Lovelace.

Exeunt DRUGGET *and* LOVELACE.

LADY RACKETT. Ah! you are a sad man, Sir Charles, to behave to me as you have done.

SIR CHARLES. My dear, I grant it: and such an absurd quarrel too ——ha! ha!

LADY RACKETT. Yes——ha! ha!——About such a trifle.

SIR CHARLES. It is pleasant how we could both fall into such an error. Ha! ha!——

LADY RACKETT. Ridiculous beyond expression! Ha! ha!

SIR CHARLES. And then the mistake your father and mother fell into!

LADY RACKETT. That too is a diverting part of the story. Ha! ha! ——But, Sir Charles, must I stay and live with my father till I grow as fantastical as his own evergreens?

SIR CHARLES. Nay, prithee don't remind me of my folly.

LADY RACKETT. Ah! my relations were all standing behind counters, selling Whitechapel needles, while your family were spending great estates.

SIR CHARLES. Spare my blushes: you see I am covered with confusion.

LADY RACKETT. How could you say so indelicate a thing? I don't love you.

SIR CHARLES. It was indelicate; I grant it.

LADY RACKETT. Am I a vile woman?

SIR CHARLES. How can you, my angel?

LADY RACKETT. I shan't forgive you! I'll have you on your knees for this. (*Sings and plays with him*) ——"Go, naughty man." [34] —— Ah! Sir Charles!

SIR CHARLES. The rest of my life shall aim at convincing you how sincerely I love you.

LADY RACKETT. (*Sings*) "Go, naughty man, I can't abide you." —— Well! come; let us go to rest. (*Going*) Ah, Sir Charles! Now it's all over, the diamond was the play.

SIR CHARLES. Oh, no, no, no; now that one may speak, it was the club indeed.

LADY RACKETT. Indeed, my love, you are mistaken.

SIR CHARLES. You make me laugh: but I was not mistaken: rely upon my judgment.

LADY RACKETT. You may rely upon mine: you was wrong.

SIR CHARLES. (*Laughing*) Po! No, no, no such thing.

LADY RACKETT. (*Laughing*) But I say, yes, yes, yes.

SIR CHARLES. Oh! no, no; it is too ridiculous; don't say any more about it, my love.

---

[34] Isaac Bickerstaffe, *Love in a Village* (1762), Act III, Scene X, Air xli, line 1. Thomas A. Arne composed this song for Bickerstaffe's comic opera.

LADY RACKETT. (*Toying with him*) Don't you say any more about it: you had better give it up, you had indeed.

Enter FOOTMAN.

FOOTMAN. Your honour's cap and slippers.

SIR CHARLES. Lay down my cap, and here take these shoes off. (*He takes 'em off, and leaves 'em at a distance*) Indeed, my Lady Rackett, you make me ready to expire with laughing. Ha! ha!

LADY RACKETT. You may laugh, but I am right notwithstanding.

SIR CHARLES. How can you say so?

LADY RACKETT. How can you say otherwise?

SIR CHARLES. Well now mind me, my Lady Rackett, we can now talk of this matter in good humour: we can discuss it coolly.

LADY RACKETT. So we can——and it is for that reason I venture to speak to you. Are these the ruffles I bought for you?

SIR CHARLES. They are, my dear.

LADY RACKETT. They are very pretty. But indeed you played the card wrong.

SIR CHARLES. Po, there is nothing so clear, if you will but hear me; only hear me.

LADY RACKETT. Ah! but do you hear me. The thing was thus. The adversary's club being the best in the house——

SIR CHARLES. No, no, listen to me: the affair was thus: Mr. Jenkins having never a club left——

LADY RACKETT. Mr. Jenkins finessed the club.

SIR CHARLES. (*Peevishly*) How can you?

LADY RACKETT. And trumps being all out——

SIR CHARLES. And we playing for the odd trick——

LADY RACKETT. If you had minded your game——

SIR CHARLES. And the club being the best——

LADY RACKETT. If you had led your diamond——

SIR CHARLES. Mr. Jenkins would of course put on a spade.

LADY RACKETT. And so the odd trick was sure.

Both speaking very fast and together

SIR CHARLES. Damnation! Will you let me speak?

LADY RACKETT. Well, to be sure, you are the strangest man.

SIR CHARLES. Plague and torture! There is no such thing as conversing with you.

LADY RACKETT. Very well, Sir, fly out again.

SIR CHARLES. Look here now: here is a pack of cards. Now you shall be convinced.

LADY RACKETT. You may talk till tomorrow, I know I am right. (*Walks about*)

SIR CHARLES. Why then, by all that's perverse, you are the most headstrong—— Can't you look here? Here are the very cards.

LADY RACKETT. Go on; you'll find it out at last.

SIR CHARLES. Will you hold your tongue, or not? Will you let me show you?——Po! It's all nonsense. (*Puts up the cards*) Come, let us go to bed. (*Going*) Only stay one moment. (*Takes out the cards*) Now command yourself, and you shall have demonstration.

LADY RACKETT. It does not signify, Sir. Your head will be clearer in the morning. I choose to go to bed.

SIR CHARLES. Stay and hear me, can't you?

LADY RACKETT. No; my head aches. I am tired of the subject.

SIR CHARLES. Why then, damn the cards. There, and there, and there. (*Throwing them about the room*) You may go to bed by yourself. Confusion seize me if I stay here to be tormented a moment longer. (*Putting on his shoes*)

Enter DIMITY.

DIMITY. Did you call, Sir?

SIR CHARLES. No; never, never, Madam.

DIMITY. (*In a fit of laughing*) At it again!

LADY RACKETT. Take your own way, Sir.

SIR CHARLES. Now then I tell you once more, you are a vile woman.

DIMITY. Law, Sir!——This is charming; I'll run and tell the old couple.

Exit.

SIR CHARLES. (*Still putting on his shoes*) You are the most malicious, positive, nonsensical——

LADY RACKETT. Don't make me laugh again, Sir Charles. (*Walks and sings*)

SIR CHARLES. Hell and the devil! Will you sit down quietly and let me convince you?

LADY RACKETT. I don't choose to hear any more about it.

SIR CHARLES. Why then I believe you are possessed. It is in vain to talk sense and reason to you.

LADY RACKETT. Thank you for your compliment, Sir.——Such a man! (*With a sneering laugh*) I never knew the like of this. (*Sits down*)

SIR CHARLES. I promise you, you shall repent of this usage, before you have a moment of my company again. It shan't be in a hurry you may depend, Madam.——Now see here——I can prove it to a demonstration. (*Sits down by her, she gets up*) Look ye there again now: the very devil must be in your temper. I wish I had never seen your face. I wish I was a thousand miles off. Sit down but one moment.

LADY RACKETT. I am dispos'd to walk, Sir.

SIR CHARLES. Why then may I perish if ever——a blockhead, an idiot I was to marry. (*Walks about*) Such provoking impertinence! (*She sits down*) Damnation! I am so clear in the thing. She is not worth my notice.——(*Sits down, turns his back, and looks uneasy*) I'll take no more pains about it. (*Pauses for some time; then looks at her*) Is it not very strange that you won't hear me?

LADY RACKETT. Sir, I am very ready to hear you.

SIR CHARLES. Very well then, very well; you remember how the game stood. (*Draws his chair near her*)

LADY RACKETT. I wish you would untie my necklace, it hurts me.

SIR CHARLES. Why can't you listen?

LADY RACKETT. I tell you it hurts me terribly.

SIR CHARLES. Death and confusion! (*Moves his chair away*) There is no bearing this. (*Looks at her angrily*) It won't take a moment, if you will but listen. (*Moves toward her*) Can't you see, that by forcing the adversary's hand, Mr. Jenkins would be obliged to——

LADY RACKETT. (*Moving her chair away from him*) Mr. Jenkins had the best club, and never a diamond left.

SIR CHARLES. (*Rising*) Distraction! Bedlam is not so mad. Be as wrong as you please, Madam. May I never hold four by honours, may I lose everything I play for, may fortune eternally forsake me, if I endeavour to set you right again.

Exit.

Enter MR. *and* MRS. DRUGGET, WOODLEY, LOVELACE, *and* NANCY.

MRS. DRUGGET. Gracious! What's the matter now?

LADY RACKETT. Such another man does not exist. I did not say a word to the gentleman, and yet he has been raving about the room, and storming like a whirlwind.

DRUGGET. And about a club again! I heard it all. Come hither, Nancy; Mr. Woodley, she is yours for life.

MRS. DRUGGET. My dear, how can you be so passionate?

DRUGGET. It shall be so. Take her for life, Mr. Woodley.

WOODLEY. My whole life shall be devoted to her happiness.

LOVELACE. The devil! And so I am to be left in the lurch in this manner, am I?

LADY RACKETT. Oh! This is only one of those polite disputes which people of quality, who have nothing else to differ about, must always be liable to. This will be made up tomorrow.

DRUGGET. Never tell me: it is too late now. Mr. Woodley, I recommend my girl to your care. I shall have nothing now to think of, but my greens, and my images, and my shrubbery. Though, mercy on all married folks, say I!——For these wranglings are, I am afraid, what they must all come to.

LADY RACKETT. (*Comes forward*)

What We Must All Come To? [35] What? Come to what?
Must broils and quarrels be the marriage lot?
If that's the wise, deep meaning of our poet,
The man's a fool! a blockhead! and I'll show it.

---

[35] See "Introduction."

What could induce him in an age so nice,
So fam'd for virtue, so refin'd from vice,
To form a plan so trivial, false, and low?
As if a belle could quarrel with a beau:
As if there were in these thrice happy days,
One who from nature, or from reason strays!
There's no cross husband now; no wrangling wife,
The man is downright ignorant of life.

'Tis the millennium this: devoid of guile,
Fair gentle Truth, and white rob'd Candour smile.
From every breast the sordid love of gold
Is banish'd quite; no boroughs now are sold!
Pray tell, Sirs——(For I don't know, I vow)
Pray, is there such a thing as gaming now?
Do peers make laws against that giant vice,
And then at Arthur's [36] break them in a trice?

No, no; our lives are virtuous all, austere and hard;
Pray, ladies——do you ever see a card?
Those empty boxes show you don't love plays;
The managers, poor souls! get nothing nowadays.
If here you come——by chance——but once a week,
The pit can witness that you never speak.
Pensive Attention sits with decent mien;
No paint, no naked shoulders to be seen!

And yet this grave, this moral, pious age,
May learn one useful lesson from the stage.
Shun strife, ye fair, and once a contest o'er,
Wake to a blaze the dying flame no more.
From fierce debate fly all the tender loves,
And Venus cries, "Coachman, put-to my doves."
The genial bed no blooming Grace prepares,
"And ev'ry day shall be a day of cares." [37]

---

[36] An exclusive gambling club on St. James's Street.
[37] Vaguely based on Pope, *The Iliad* VI.520-521.

KNOW YOUR OWN MIND (1777)

INTRODUCTION

As early as 1760 Murphy planned his best play, the five-act comedy of manners *Know Your Own Mind*. He virtually completed its composition in 1764, when he wrote the part of Lady Bell, his most delightful feminine creation, for the vivacious and talented actress Ann Elliott, his mistress. Repeatedly disgusted, however, by the difficulties that attended practical arrangements for a production by David Garrick at Drury Lane Theatre, Murphy withheld his masterpiece from the stage year after year, though in 1772, three years after the death of Ann Elliott, he reworked the role of Lady Bell for Ann Spranger Barry. Finally, after negotiating with Thomas Harris, one of the managers of Covent Garden Theatre, Murphy agreed to a production of his comedy, and *Know Your Own Mind* opened at Covent Garden February 22, 1777. Garrick, reconciled with Murphy, had written the epilogue.

At Covent Garden between February 22 and May 8, 1777, *Know Your Own Mind* was performed eighteen times. The original cast of fifteen included William Thomas Lewis as Millamour, Charles Lee Lewes as Dashwould, Richard Wroughton as Malvil, Isabella Mattocks as Lady Bell, and Elizabeth Hartley as Miss Neville. The comedy was first presented at Drury Lane on April 21, 1789, with Richard Wroughton as Millamour, John Bannister as Dashwould, Dorothea Jordan as Lady Bell, and Priscilla Kemble as Miss Neville. Although *Know Your Own Mind* remained a stock piece until the middle of the nineteenth century, its theatrical success was sometimes hampered by inadequate casting and by the low taste of the audience. But some of the other stars in it were Elizabeth Farren as Lady Bell; Harriot Mellon and Mary Ann

Orger as Lady Jane; Jane Pope as Mrs. Bromley; Charles Kemble and George Bartley as Captain Bygrove; Robert William Elliston and Benjamin Wrench as Millamour; Samuel Thomas Russell as Dashwould; and Edmund John Eyre as Malvil.

The editor invites the reader to compare *Know Your Own Mind* and Sheridan's *The School for Scandal*—without prejudice. The latter comedy opened at Drury Lane on May 8, 1777, three months after the appearance of the former. Murphy's Malvil influenced Sheridan's Joseph Surface and Mrs. Candour. Joseph resembles Malvil in hypocrisy, in glibness of (and the breaking of) moral sentiments, in pretended objection to scandal, and in persistent duplicity at the very end. Mrs. Candour follows Malvil in spreading scandal by seeming to object to it. Ernest Bernbaum comments that in comparison with Murphy's lively Lady Bell, "Sheridan's young women are tiresome." * In fact, Lady Bell belongs with Shakespeare's Beatrice and Congreve's Millamant. Bernbaum also observes that *The School for Scandal* "is decidedly not as free from sentimental tendencies" as *Know Your Own Mind.*† Murphy excels Sheridan in characterization and in the provocation of genuine laughter. Nor can one overlook the unsurpassed satiric wit of Murphy's Dashwould.

In May, 1778, the bookseller T. Becket brought out the first edition of *Know Your Own Mind*. It is interesting to note the improvements as one turns to this edition from the 1777 acting manuscript in the Larpent Collection of the Huntington Library. Act I of the manuscript opens with four servants of Millamour—Charles, William, Robert, and Richard; the 1778 edition opens with Sir John Millamour and Bygrove, and it eliminates William. Sir Harry Lizard of the manuscript becomes Sir Harry Lovewit in 1778. In Act I there are also transposed speeches, cuts, and additions. In Act II, Trinket, a servant of Mrs. Bromley, makes two brief appearances in the manuscript only. Near the end of this act Madame La Rouge exits in the manuscript just before the second

---

* *The Drama of Sensibility* (Cambridge: Harvard University Press, 1925), p. 256.

† *Ibid.*, p. 257.

re-entrance of Malvil; in the 1778 version she remains to talk with Malvil and mentions the apartment that he has rented from her. This exposition helps to prepare the audience for the last scene of the comedy. There is no noteworthy change in Act III. Near the end of Act IV of the manuscript, Lady Bell and Millamour are together; in 1778, Captain Bygrove is also on-stage, for the purpose of furthering the jealousy of Millamour. In Act V, Scene i, of the manuscript only, Trinket again appears. Here, Dashwould tricks Bygrove into mistaking Trinket, who is wearing a discarded dress of her mistress, for Mrs. Bromley and into making love to her. Throughout the version of 1778, there are many minor improvements.

For his *Works* in 1786, Murphy only very slightly revised *Know Your Own Mind*. This unwonted type of revision was due to the long period of composition of the comedy (from 1760 to 1778) before the publication of the first edition and to the relatively short span of time between the appearance of the first edition and the rewriting for the *Works*. The most pronounced changes are a deletion of twenty-four words from one of Bygrove's speeches in Act III and a rewriting of the last and Millamour's final speech of the play, preceded by two new speeches, of Millamour and Lady Bell, for a smoother conclusion. None of the other twenty-eight textual modifications concerns more than two words. The editor reproduces the 1786 text with assistance from that of 1778 for four textual corruptions, as indicated in the footnotes.

Texts Collated

MS., LA, 425, Feb., 1777. Larpent Collection, Huntington Library.

[Murphy, Arthur], *Know Your Own Mind*. London: T. Becket, 1778. [University of Pennsylvania; Copy of Editor]

The Works of Arthur Murphy, IV, 1-182. London: T. Cadell, 1786. [University of Pennsylvania; Copy of Editor]

KNOW YOUR OWN MIND:

A
COMEDY,

Performed at the
THEATRE ROYAL
in
COVENT-GARDEN.

. . . Pugnat sententia secum;
Quod petiit, spernit; repetit quod nuper omisit;
Aestuat, & vitae disconvenit ordine toto.
Hor.[1]

Ut callidum ejus ingenium, ita anxium judicium.
Tacit.[2]

¹ Horace, *Epistulae* I.i.97-99. "Judgement is at strife with itself, scorns what it craved, asks again for what it lately cast aside; when it shifts like a tide, and in the whole system of life is out of joint." [Loeb translation]

² Tacitus, *Annales*, I.LXXX.6-7. "Although his shrewd natural capacity, yet anxious judgment."

PROLOGUE,

Spoken by Mr. Lewis.

Through the wide tracts of life, in ev'ry trade,
What numbers toil with faculties decay'd?
Worn out, yet eager, in the race they run,
And never learn——when proper to have done.

What need of proofs? Ev'n authors do the same,
And rather than desist, decline in fame.
Like gamesters thrive at first; then bolder grow,
And hazard all upon one desp'rate throw.

This truth to feel, perhaps too much, inclin'd,
Our bard, long hackney'd, trembles there behind,
Lest he should prove——another vanish'd mind.
Long has his play lain hid, suppress'd by fears,
Beyond the critics' rule, above nine years!
And now he comes, 'tis the plain simple truth,
This night to answer for his sins of youth.

The piece, you'll say, should now perfection bear;
But who can reach it after all his care?
He paints no monsters for ill-judg'd applause:
Life he has view'd, and from that source he draws.
Here are no fools, the drama's standing jest!
And Welchmen now, North Britons too may rest.
Hibernia's sons shall here excite no wonder,
Nor shall St. Patrick blush to hear them blunder.

By other arts he strives your taste to hit,
Some plot, some character; he hopes, some wit.
And if this piece should please you like the past;
Ye Brother Bards! forgive him:——'tis his last.

Lost are the friends who lent their aid before;
Roscius retires,[3] and Barry is no more.[4]
Harmonious Barry! with what varied art
His grief, rage, tenderness assail'd the heart!
Of plaintive Otway now no more the boast!
And Shakespeare grieves for his Othello lost.
Oft on this spot the tuneful swan expir'd,
Warbling his grief; you listen'd and admir'd.
'Twas then but fancied woe; now ev'ry Muse,
Her lyre unstrung, with tears his urn bedews.

From this night's scenes e'n Woodward too is fled,
Stretch'd by pale sickness on his languid bed,
Nor can Thalia raise her favourite's head.[5]

For them our author lov'd the tale to weave;
He feels their loss, and now he takes his leave;
Sees new performers in succession spring,
And hopes new poets will expand their wing.
Beneath your smile his leaf of laurel grew;
Gladly he'd keep it;——for 'twas giv'n by you.
But if too weak his art, if wild his aim,
On favours past he builds no idle claim.
To you once more he boldly dares to trust;
Hear, and pronounce;——he knows you will be just.

---

[3] David Garrick had retired in 1776.

[4] Spranger Barry had died in 1777. Jaffeir, in Thomas Otway's *Venice Preserv'd* (1682), was one of Barry's leading roles.

[5] Murphy's footnote: Mr. Woodward was to have played the part of Dashwould: in his last illness he lamented to the author that he could not close his theatrical life with that character: he died a few weeks after the play appeared; for years the life of the comic scene, and in his end regretted as a worthy and an honest man.

DRAMATIS PERSONAE

Men

Millamour,	Mr. Lewis.
Dashwould,	Mr. Lee Lewes.
Malvil,	Mr. Wroughton.
Bygrove,	Mr. Aickin.
Captain Bygrove, his son,	Mr. Booth.
Sir John Millamour, father to Millamour,	Mr. Fearon.
Sir Harry Lovewit,	Mr. Whitfield.
Charles, servant to Millamour,	Mr. Wewitzer.
Footmen, etc.	

Women

Lady Bell,	Mrs. Mattocks.
Lady Jane,	Miss Dayes.
Mrs. Bromley,	Mrs. Jackson.
Miss Neville,	Mrs. Hartley.
Madame La Rouge,	Miss Ambrose.

KNOW YOUR OWN MIND

ACT the FIRST
SCENE [I]

The House of Sir John Millamour

Enter SIR JOHN *and* BYGROVE.

BYGROVE. Why then I'd marry again, and disinherit him.

SIR JOHN. Brother Bygrove, you think too severely in these matters.

BYGROVE. Severely, Sir John? If I had a mind that my son should marry, why should not he [6] do as I would have him?

SIR JOHN. Allowance must be made for inclination. The success of our children depends upon the manner in which we set them out in the world. They are like bowls which if delivered out of hand with a due regard to their bias, our aim is answer'd! If otherwise, they are short or wide of the mark in view, or perhaps rush wildly out of the green.

BYGROVE. Well argued, truly! He that should obey is to judge for himself, and you that are his governor, are to be directed by him.

SIR JOHN. Why, he is chiefly interested in the end, and the choice of the means may be fairly left to himself. I can't but be tender of

---

[6] 1778: "he not"; 1786: "not he." But the latter is Murphy's change, in his characteristic style.

George; a plant of my own rearing, and the tree will hereafter be known by its fruit.

BYGROVE. It is a tree that will bear nothing without grafting; and if I could not inoculate what will make it thrive and flourish, it should not incumber a foot of my land.

SIR JOHN. Your system, and mine, differ widely, Brother Bygrove. My son is of an enlarged and liberal understanding, and I a father of mild authority.

BYGROVE. Authority!——Your son's word is a law to you. Now there is my young graceless; he is in the Army, and why? Because I chose it. I had a mind he should serve; and so he went to be shot at. No arguing with me. If I see anything wrong, I accost him directly: "Look ye, Sir, do you think to go on in this fashion? Not during my life, I promise you: I will acknowledge you no longer than you prove worthy; and if you can't discern what is befitting you, I at least will judge what is proper on my part."

SIR JOHN. Well, George and I have lived together as friends. From a boy, I endeavoured to subject him rather to his reason than his fears. If any little irregularity happened, he was no sooner sensible of it than his cheek coloured, and the blush of youth not only looked decent, but expressed an ingenuous and well-disposed mind.

BYGROVE. But the consequence of all this? Has he a settled opinion? A fixed principle for a moment? He is grown up in caprice; his judgment has not vigour to be decisive upon the merest trifle; he is distracted by little things, and of course is perishing by little and little.

SIR JOHN. Oh! no; all from a good cause; his knowledge of life occasions quick reflection: quick reflection shows things in a variety of lights. I am not angry. He will settle in the world; you will see him married before long.

BYGROVE. In what a variety of lights his wife will appear to him!

SIR JOHN. I beg your pardon for a moment. I see a person there. Charles, Charles, this way.

Enter CHARLES.

SIR JOHN. Well, Charles, what is he about?

CHARLES. Very busy, Sir, a thousand things in hand.

BYGROVE. And all at the same time, I'll warrant.

CHARLES. We have a deal to employ us, Sir.

SIR JOHN. Have you sounded him in regard to what I mentioned last night?

CHARLES. That's what I wanted to tell your Honour. Last night, Sir, as he was going to bed, I touch'd upon the subject; dropt a hint or two, that it is now time to think of raising heirs to himself; enlarged upon the comforts of matrimony, and I think with no small degree of eloquence.

BYGROVE. The fellow is laughing at you.

SIR JOHN. Well, and how? What effect?

CHARLES. A very visible effect, Sir. This morning early, my master rings his bell. "Charles," says he, "I have been considering what you said last night: I shall pay a visit to the young ladies, and, I believe, I shall marry one of them."

SIR JOHN. There, Mr. Bygrove; I am for ever obliged to you, Charles. Well, go on.

CHARLES. I fly immediately to get him his things to dress, and return in an instant. "Charles," says he, then tossed himself back in his chair, beat the ground with his heel, and fell a reading. "Won't your Honour get ready to visit the young ladies?"——"The ladies? What ladies, you blockhead?"——"Lady Bell, and Lady Jane, your Honour, Mrs. Bromley's handsome nieces." "Po! you're a num-skull," says he, with an oblique kind of a smile; stretched his arms, yawned, talked to himself, and bade me go about my business.

BYGROVE. I knew it would end so. There is not a crane-neck carriage [7] in town can give a short turn with him. He will continue going on from one thing to another, and end in nothing at last.

SIR JOHN. This is provoking. Anybody with him this morning?

CHARLES. He has had a power of people with him, Sir——a com-mission-broker, to sell him a company in a marching regiment; the

---

[7] With crane-necked iron bars at the sides to facilitate movement of the front wheels.

mayor of a borough, about a seat in Parliament. And there are several with him now, Sir. There is Sir Harry Lovewit, and——

BYGROVE. Ay! Sir Harry! I am glad he is of age, and that I am no longer his guardian. He has not had a new idea in his head since he was five years old, and yet the blockhead affects to be lively. He runs after wits, who do nothing but laugh at him. He repeats scraps and sentences; all memory and no understanding; a mere retailer of what falls from other people, and with that stock he sets up for a wit.

CHARLES. He is with my master, Sir; and there is Mr. Malvil, and Mr. Dashwould, and——(*Bell rings*)—— He rings, Sir: you will pardon me; I must be gone, Sir.

Exit.

BYGROVE. And that fellow Dashwould; he is the ruin of your son, and of poor Sir Harry into the bargain. He is the merry-andrew of the town: honour has no restraint upon him; truth he sets at nought, and friendship he is ever ready to sacrifice to a joke.[8]

SIR JOHN. Po! Mere innocent pleasantry. Dashwould has no harm in him.

BYGROVE. No harm in him? I grant you the fellow has a quick sense of the ridiculous, and draws a character with a lucky hit. But everything is distorted by him. He has wit to ridicule you; invention to frame a story of you; humour to help it about; and when he has set the town a laughing, he puts on a familiar air, and shakes you by the hand.

Enter SIR HARRY, *laughing violently.*

SIR HARRY. Oh! ho! ho! I shall certainly expire one day in a fit of laughing.

SIR JOHN. What's the matter, Sir Harry?

BYGROVE. What fool's errand brings him hither?

SIR HARRY. That fellow, Dashwould, will be the death of me. The very spirit of whim, wit, humour, and raillery possess him.

---

[8] As was the dramatist Samuel Foote, the model for Dashwould.

BYGROVE. Ay! Wit and humour for the meridian of your understanding.

SIR HARRY. By the shade of Rabelais, he is the most entertaining creature! He has played off such a firework of wit. I'll tell you what he said this moment.

BYGROVE. No, Sir, no; if you are a pedlar in smart sayings, and brisk repartees, we don't desire you to unpack for us.

SIR HARRY. A plague on him for an agreeable devil! And then the rogue has so much ease.

BYGROVE. Yes, the ease of an executioner. He puts all to death without remorse. He laughs at everything, as if Heaven intended to make its own work ridiculous. He has no relish for beauty, natural or moral. He is in love with deformity, and never better pleased than when he has most reason to find fault.

SIR HARRY. There is a picture of as harsh features as any in Dashwould's whole collection.

BYGROVE. But the picture is true. No exaggeration in it.

SIR HARRY. He gave us a miniature of you, this morning, my dear guardian, and you shall have it. Dashwould has made a discovery, Sir John. What reason do you think he gives for Mr. Bygrove's railing for ever at your son's inconstancy of temper?

BYGROVE. Ay, now! Now!

SIR HARRY. You positively shall hear it. Mr. Bygrove's desires being all rusted to a point, looking directly toward the land of matrimony——

BYGROVE. Matrimony! Now gild the pill with humour, and down it goes.

SIR HARRY. Dashwould has found you out. Mr. Bygrove's desires being all collected and fixed on matrimony, he rails at the variety of my friend Millamour's whimsies, like Sir George Bumper, with chalkstones on his knuckles, as big as nutmegs, hobbling along and thanking Doctor Le Fevre that he has no small humours flying about him.

SIR JOHN. That's a discovery indeed.

BYGROVE. Sir John, can you mind what such a fellow as Dashwould says? Everything that passes through the medium of his fancy appears deformed, as the straightest stick looks crooked in troubled water.

SIR HARRY. Well dashed out, upon my soul, with tolerable spleen, and some vivacity.

BYGROVE. Po!——If you had taken my advice, Sir Harry, and renounced his acquaintance long ago, you had been now a young man coming into life, with some promise of a character. Continue in dissipation, Sir. For my part, it is a rule with me, neither to give, nor take a joke.

SIR HARRY. Ho! ho! ho! A pleasant rule, positively——ho! ho! ho! Dashwould shall have it this moment; do you take the consequence; and in the meantime I'll leave you to the practice of your social humour.

Exit.

BYGROVE. It is such coxcombs as that butterfly, that encourage him to fix his pasquinades upon every man's character. Matrimony! ——A licentious——no, Sir John, I still cherish the memory of your sister; she was the best of wives: 'sdeath, interrupted again by that——no, it's my friend Malvil; he is a man of true value.

SIR JOHN. Dashwould says he is a compound of false charity and real malice.

BYGROVE. And it is enough for you that Dashwould says it. Malvil is a man of honour, Sir; and an enemy to all scandal, though wit prove a palatable ingredient in the poison.

Enter MALVIL.

MALVIL. Intolerable! There is no being safe where he is. A licentious railer! All truth, all morality sacrificed to a jest: nothing sacred from his buffoonery.

BYGROVE. I told you, Sir John, how it is.

MALVIL. Oh! such indiscriminate satire!

BYGROVE. Yes, the fellow runs amuck, and nothing escapes him.

MALVIL. There is no enduring it. Ridicule is a very unfair weapon, Mr. Bygrove: it is by no means the test of truth, Sir John.

SIR JOHN. Nay, but you are too grave about this matter.

MALVIL. Too grave! Shall he wantonly stab the reputation of his neighbour, and then tell you it was in jest? For my part, I had rather throw a veil over the infirmities of my friend than seek a malicious pleasure in the detection. That's my way of thinking.

SIR JOHN. I fancy you are right. This son of mine does so perplex me. (*Walks aside*)

MALVIL. Pray, Mr. Bygrove, give me leave. I am sorry to hear certain whispers about a friend of ours.

BYGROVE. About whom? The widow, Mrs. Bromley?

MALVIL. Oh! no, no; I have a great respect for her: though I——pray don't you think she throws out the lure for a young husband?

BYGROVE. For a husband, yes; but not too young a one: you can serve my interest in that quarter.

MALVIL. I know it: rely upon my friendship. But have you heard nothing of an eminent Turkey merchant?

BYGROVE. Mr. Freeport?

MALVIL. I say nothing: I don't like the affair: have you really heard nothing?

BYGROVE. Not a syllable.

MALVIL. So much the better: though it is fit you should be put on your guard. Any money of yours in his hands?

BYGROVE. Po! As safe as the bank.

MALVIL. I may be mistaken. I hope I am: I was in company, the other night; several members of Parliament present; they did not speak plainly; hints and innuendoes only; you won't let it go any further. His seat in the house, they all agreed, is perfectly convenient at this juncture. I hope the cloud will blow over.——I shall remember you with the widow.

BYGROVE. One good turn deserves another: I shan't be unmindful of your interest.

MALVIL. There, now you hurt me: you know my delicacy: must friendship never act a disinterested part? I esteem you, Mr. Bygrove, and that's sufficient. Sir John, give me leave to say, the man who busies himself about other people's affairs, is a pragmatical character, and very dangerous in society.

BYGROVE. So I have been telling Sir John. But to laugh at everything is the fashion of the age. A pleasant good-for-nothing fellow is by most people preferred to modest merit. A man like Dashwould, who runs on——so! here comes scandal in folio.

Enter DASHWOULD.

DASHWOULD. Sir John, I rejoice to see you. Mr. Bygrove, I kiss your hand. Malvil, have you been uneasy for any friend since?

MALVIL. Po! Absurd! (*Walks away*)

DASHWOULD. I have been laughing with your son, Sir John. Pray, have I told you about Sir Richard Doriland?

BYGROVE. You may spare him, Sir; he is a very worthy man.

DASHWOULD. He is so: great good nature about him: I love Sir Richard. You know he was divorced from his wife; a good fine woman, but an invincible idiot.

MALVIL. Look ye there now, Mr. Bygrove!

BYGROVE. My Lady Doriland, Sir, was always counted a very sensible woman.

DASHWOULD. She was so; with too much spirit to be ever at ease, and a rage for pleasure, that broke the bubble, as she grasped it. She fainted away upon hearing that Mrs. All-Night had two card tables more than herself.

BYGROVE. Inveterate malice!

DASHWOULD. They waged war a whole winter, for the honour of having the greatest number of fools thinking of nothing but the odd trick. First, Mrs. All-Night kept Sundays; her Ladyship did the same: Mrs. All-Night had forty tables; her Ladyship rose to fifty. Then one added, then t'other; till every room in the house was cramm'd like the black hole at Calcutta,[9] and at last, upon casting up the account, Sir Richard sold off fifteen hundred acres, to clear incumbrances.

---

[9] The punishment cell of the barracks in Fort William, Calcutta, where Siraj-ud-daula, nawab of Bengal, confined 146 Europeans during the night of June 20, 1756; only 23 survived in the morning.

SIR JOHN. Ridiculous! And so they parted upon this?

DASHWOULD. Don't you know the history of that business?

MALVIL. Now mark him; now.

DASHWOULD. Tender of reputation, Malvil!——The story is well-known. She was detected with——the little foreign count——I call him the Salamander——I saw him five times in one winter upon the back of the fire at Bath, for cheating at cards.[10]

MALVIL. Go on, Sir, abuse everybody. My Lady was perfectly innocent. I know the whole affair: a mere contrivance to lay the foundation of a divorce.

DASHWOULD. So they gave out. Sir Richard did not care a ninepin for her while she was his. You know his way: he despises what is in his possession, and languishes for what is not. Her Ladyship was no sooner married to——what's his name?—— His father was a footman, and Madam Fortune, who every now and then loves a joke, sent him to the East Indies, and in a few years brought him back at the head of half a million, for the jest's sake.

MALVIL. Mr. Dashwould, upon my word, Sir.——Families to be run down in this manner!

DASHWOULD. Mushroom was his name: my Lady Doriland was no sooner married to him, but up to his eyes Sir Richard was in love with her. He dressed at her; sighed at her; danced at her; she is now libelled in the Commons, and Sir Richard has a *crim. con.* against him in the King's Bench.

MALVIL. Pshaw! I shall stay no longer to hear this strain of defamation.

Exit.

DASHWOULD. Malvil, must you leave us? A pleasant character this same Mr. Malvil.

BYGROVE. He has a proper regard for his friends, Sir.

DASHWOULD. Yes, but he is often present where their characters are canvassed, and is anxious about whispers which nobody has

---

[10] The count is the gambler Baron Newman. At piquet, an opponent thrust a fork through his hand to expose a concealed card. [*Biographia Dramatica* (London, 1812), II, 359.]

heard.[11] He knows the use of hypocrisy better than a court chaplain.

BYGROVE. There, call honesty by a burlesque name, and so pervert everything.

DASHWOULD. Things are more perverted, Mr. Bygrove, when such men as Malvil make their vices do their work, under a mask of goodness; and with that stroke we'll dismiss his character.

SIR JOHN. Ay, very right; my brother Bygrove has a regard for him, and so change the subject. My son, Mr. Dashwould, what does he intend?

DASHWOULD. Up to the eyes in love with Lady Bell, and determined to marry her.

SIR JOHN. I told you so, Mr. Bygrove; I told you, you would soon see him settled in the world. Mr. Dashwould, I thank you; I'll step and confirm George in his resolution.

Exit.

DASHWOULD. A good-natured man, Sir John, and does not want credulity.

BYGROVE. Ay! There, the moment his back is turned.

DASHWOULD. *Gulliver's Travels* is a true history to him. His son has strange flights. First, he was to be a lawyer; bought chambers in the Temple,[12] eat his commons,[13] and was called to the bar. Then the law is a damned dry municipal study; the Army is fitter for a gentleman; and as he was going to the War Office to take out his commission, he saw my Lord Chancellor's coach go by; in an instant back to the Temple, and no sooner there, "Po! Pox! Hang the law; better marry, and live like a gentleman." Now marriage is a galling yoke, and he does not know what he'll do. He calls his man, Charles; sends him away; walks about the room, sits down, asks a question; thinks of something else; talks to himself, sings, whistles, lively, pensive, pleasant, and melancholy in an

---

[11] Compare Mrs. Candour in *The School for Scandal*.

[12] An Inn of Court, a set of buildings for law students and lawyers.

[13] As a law student, he ate the required number of dinners a term at his Inn of Court.

instant. He approves, finds fault; he will, he will not; and in short, the man does not know his own mind for half a second. Here comes Sir John.

Enter SIR JOHN.

DASHWOULD. You find him disposed to marry, Sir John?

SIR JOHN. I hope so; he wavers a little; but still I——

BYGROVE. Po! I have no patience; my advice has been all lost upon you. I wish it may end well. A good morning, Sir John. (*Going*)

DASHWOULD. Mr. Bygrove, yours: Sir John will defend you in your absence.

BYGROVE. If you will forget your friends in their absence, it is the greatest favour you can bestow upon them.

Exit.

DASHWOULD. Did I ever tell you what happened to him last summer, at Tunbridge?

SIR JOHN. Excuse me for the present. This light young man! I must step and talk with my lawyer.

DASHWOULD. I'll walk part of the way with you. A strange medley this same Mr. Bygrove: with something like wit, he is always abusing wit.——You must know, last summer, at Tunbridge——

SIR JOHN. Another time, if you please.

Exit.

DASHWOULD. The story is worth your hearing: a party of us dined at the Sussex—— (*Following Sir John*)

Enter CHARLES.

CHARLES. Mr. Dashwould! Mr. Dashwould!

Re-enter DASHWOULD.

DASHWOULD. What's the matter, Charles?

CHARLES. My master desires you won't go.

Enter SIR HARRY.

SIR HARRY. Hey! What, going to leave us?

DASHWOULD. Only a step with Sir John. Strange vagaries in your master's head, Charles!——Sir Harry! Going to wait upon Miss Neville, I suppose. She has beauty, and you have a heart.

SIR HARRY. Pshaw! There you wrong me now! Why will you?

DASHWOULD. Very well; be it so; I can't see to be sure; but take my word for it, you will marry that girl. Come, I follow you.

SIR HARRY. I must not part with you: I had rather lose the whole College of Physicians.[14]

Exit.

DASHWOULD. March on, Sir Harry.——(*Turns to Charles*) Did you ever see such a baronet? This fellow, Charles, is as ridiculous himself as any of them.

Exit.

CHARLES. Now have I but one man in the house, and he will be fifty different men in a moment. Hurry! hurry! nothing but hurry! Get me this; get me that; get me t'other. Bring me the blue and silver. Scoundrel! what do you fetch me this for? Let me have the brown and gold.[15] A poor servant does not know which way to turn himself in this house.

Enter RICHARD.

CHARLES. Well, Richard, what are you about?

RICHARD. Why, a man in a whirlwind may as well tell what he is about. Going to order the coachman to put up. He intends to change his dress, and walk to the Temple.

Exit.

CHARLES. What does he mean by talking of the Temple again? I hope we are not going to take to our studies once more. I hate the law: there is not a footman in the Temple has a grain of taste. All mere lawyers! They have not an idea out of the profession.

Enter ROBERT.

---

[14] An English chartered body.
[15] Men's coats were brilliantly colored.

ROBERT. Richard! Richard! Where is he gone?

CHARLES. What's in the wind now?

ROBERT. The wind's in another quarter. He has been writing verses, as he calls them, ever since the company left him. He has torn a quire of paper, I believe, and now he wants the carriage directly.

Exit.

CHARLES. Run, and order it. I had rather be a country curate than go on in this manner. (*Bell rings*) What is he at now?

MILLAMOUR. (*Within*) Charles:——who answers there?

CHARLES. Ay; now for the old work.

Enter MILLAMOUR.

MILLAMOUR. Is the chariot ready?

CHARLES. At the door, Sir.

MILLAMOUR. Do you step to Mrs. Bromley's and——perhaps it would be better to——no, do you step, Charles, and——you need not mind it——another time will do as well.

Exit.

CHARLES. There again now: this is the way from morning to night.

MILLAMOUR. (*Entering*) The sooner, the better: I promised Sir John, and I will pay this visit. Lady Bell reigns sovereign of my heart. That vivacity of mind! "Quick as her eyes, and as unfix'd as those." [16]

CHARLES. She is far preferable to her sister, your Honour.

MILLAMOUR. Po! You are illiterate in these matters. The sober graces of Lady Jane!——Lady Bell advances like a conqueror, and demands your heart: Lady Jane seems unconscious of her charms, and yet enslaves you deeper.

CHARLES. Which of them does your Honour think——

MILLAMOUR. Which of 'em, Charles? (*Reads a paper*) "I look'd, and I sigh'd, and I wish'd I could speak." [17]

---

[16] Pope, *The Rape of the Lock* II.10.

[17] Slightly altered from the opening line of William Congreve, *Song*.

Enter ROBERT.

ROBERT. Captain Bygrove, Sir.

MILLAMOUR. That's unlucky. I am not at home; tell him I went out an hour ago.

Enter CAPTAIN BYGROVE.

MILLAMOUR. My dear Bygrove, I longed to see you. But why that pensive air? Still in love, I suppose.

Exeunt CHARLES *and* ROBERT.

CAPT. BYGROVE. My dear Millamour, you have guessed it. I am in love, and I glory in my chains.

MILLAMOUR. Shall I tell you a secret? I suspect myself, plaguily. Everything is not as quiet here as it used to be.

CAPT. BYGROVE. Indulge the happy passion. Let wits and libertines say what they will; there is no true happiness but in the married state.

MILLAMOUR. Why, I have thought much upon the subject of late; and with a certain refinement, I don't know but a man may fashion a complying girl to his taste of happiness. Virtuous himself, he confirms her in her virtue; constant, he secures her fidelity: and by continuing the lover, instead of commencing the tyrant husband, he wins from her the sweetest exertion of tenderness and love. I shall most positively marry. Who is your idol? My dear boy, impart.

CAPT. BYGROVE. There I beg to be excused. You know my father. I must not presume to think for myself. I must contrive some stratagem to make him propose the match. Were it to move first from me, I should be obliged to decamp from before the town at once.

MILLAMOUR. I wish you success. My resolution is taken, and with the most amiable of her sex. She romps about the room like one of the Graces; and deals about her wit with such a happy negligence——

CAPT. BYGROVE. An agreeable portrait, but mine is the very reverse. That equal serenity in all her ways! Wit she has, but without ostentation; and elegance itself seems the pure effect of nature.

MILLAMOUR. (*Aside*) I don't know whether that is not the true character for a wife. And pray, what progress have you made in her affections?

CAPT. BYGROVE. Enough to convince me that I am not quite unacceptable. My dear Millamour, I had rather fold that girl in my arms than kiss his Majesty's hand for the first regiment of guards.

MILLAMOUR. I am a lost man. I shall most positively marry. We will wonder at each other's felicity; and be the envy of all our acquaintance.

Enter DASHWOULD.

DASHWOULD. I am as good as my word, you see. Most noble Captain, your father was here this morning. A good, agreeable old gentleman, and about as pleasant as a nightmare. Millamour, whom do you think I met since I saw you?

MILLAMOUR. Whom?

DASHWOULD. Our friend Beverly, just imported from Paris, perfectly Frenchified, and abusing everything in this country——"Oh! there is no breathing their English atmosphere.——Roast beef and liberty will be the death of me."

MILLAMOUR. Ha! ha! Poor Beverly! I saw him, last summer, at Paris, dressed in the style of an English fox-hunter: he swore there was not a morsel to eat in their country; kept an opera-singer upon beefsteaks and oyster sauce; drove to his villa every Saturday in a phaeton, and returned on the Monday, like a young buck, just come upon town.

DASHWOULD. He has done his country great honour abroad.

CAPT. BYGROVE. He will settle at home now: he is going to be married.

DASHWOULD. Yes, I hear he is in love, and much good may it do him. I wish I may die, if I know so ridiculous a thing as love.—— "My life!——My soul!——Hybla [18] dwells upon her lips; ecstasy and

---

[18] Ancient Hybla, Sicily, was known for the honey produced on neighboring hills.

bliss!" Blank verse and pastoral nonsense! In a little time, the man wonders what bewitched him: an armchair after dinner, and a box and dice till five in the morning, make all the comforts of his life.

MILLAMOUR. Very true! Love is a ridiculous passion indeed.

CAPT. BYGROVE. Do you take up arms against me? But a moment since, just as you came in, he was acknowledging to me——

MILLAMOUR. No, not I, truly; I acknowledge nothing. Marriage is not to my taste, I promise you. The handsome wife!——She is all affectation; routs, drums, hurricanes,[19] and intrigue!

DASHWOULD. And the ugly! She makes it up with good sense; pronounces upon wit; and talks you dead with maxims, characters, and reflections.

MILLAMOUR. And the woman of high birth, she produces her pedigree as her patent for vice and folly. "Seven's the main," [20] and away goes your whole fortune.

CAPT. BYGROVE. Mere commonplace.

DASHWOULD. And the tender maukin! She dotes upon you. "Don't drink any more, my dear: you'll take cold near that window, my love; pray don't talk so much; you'll flurry your spirits."——And then kisses you before company.

MILLAMOUR. And the sick madam! She has the vapours, and finds that she has nerves.——"I wish I had none.——But it is too true that I have nerves, as slight as so many hairs."

DASHWOULD. Ha! ha! The whole sex is divided into so many classes of folly.

MILLAMOUR. Right! So it is. Ha! ha! ha! (*Both laugh*)

CAPT. BYGROVE. You play finely into one another's hands.

MILLAMOUR. Now mark the champion of the sex!——

DASHWOULD. Yes; he'll throw down the gauntlet for 'em.

Both laughing

CAPT. BYGROVE. Nay, decide it your own way. Since you won't hear, gentlemen, there is a clear stage for you.

Exit.

---

[19] Large private assemblies.

[20] In hazard, before throwing the dice, the caster called a main or number between five and nine.

DASHWOULD. Fare ye well, most noble Captain. A facetious companion! Did you ever hear him say anything?

MILLAMOUR. He is in for it; and my father would fain reduce me to the same condition with one of Mrs. Bromley's nieces. A good fine woman, Mrs. Bromley!

DASHWOULD. Has been! Were she now to rub her cheek with a white handkerchief, her roses and lillies would go to the clear starcher.

MILLAMOUR. Ha! ha! And yet she sets up for the rival of her nieces.

DASHWOULD. The young ladies are pretty well in their way too. Lady Bell has a brisk volubility of nothing, that she plays the pretty idiot with: and Lady Jane, a sly piece of formality, ready to go post for Scotland, with the first redcoat that asks her the question. We all dine at the Widow's to-day; are you to be with us?

MILLAMOUR. Yes, to meet you: the party will be diverting.

DASHWOULD. Observe old Bygrove. He pronounces with rigour upon the conduct of others, and hopes his own follies lie concealed. His whole struggle is to escape detection. He hoodwinks himself, and thinks he blinds you. Positive and dogmatical in his opinions, yet a dupe to the designs of others; and flattering himself that a peevish and censorious spirit hides every defect, he gives you the full ridicule of his character.

MILLAMOUR. I have marked him before now.

DASHWOULD. Mark him with the Widow: you will see him sighing for his deceased wife and Mrs. Bromley's charms at the same time. One eye shall weep for the dead, and other ogle the living.

MILLAMOUR. Ha! ha!——And then Malvil laying siege to Miss Neville!

DASHWOULD. Miss Neville is the best of them. Mrs. Bromley has taken her into her house as a poor relation whom she pities; and her pity is no more than the cruel art of tormenting an unhappy dependent upon her generosity.

MILLAMOUR. But she has generosity. She has promised Miss Neville a fortune of five thousand pounds.

DASHWOULD. And so the hook is baited for Malvil. The Widow flings out that snare to counteract Sir Harry.

MILLAMOUR. Sir Harry!

DASHWOULD. Yes; he is in love with Miss Neville; and the best of the story is, he is afraid I shall think him ridiculous. If I say the word, and promise not to laugh at him, he breaks his mind at once. Miss Neville sees clearly that he admires her, and of course will never listen to Malvil. The self-interested designs of that fellow shall be disappointed.

MILLAMOUR. Admirable! Thou art a whimsical fellow. Come, I attend you. A pleasant group they are all together. It is as you say,

> Our passions sicken, and our pleasures cloy;
> A fool to laugh at, is the height of joy.

Exeunt.

End of the FIRST ACT.

ACT the SECOND
SCENE [I]

At Mrs. Bromley's

Enter MRS. BROMLEY *and* MISS NEVILLE.

MRS. BROMLEY. Why, to be sure, Neville, there is something in what you say: one is so odd, and so I don't know how in a morning.

MISS NEVILLE. Certainly, Madam; and then people of your turn, whose wit overflows in conversation, are liable to a waste of spirits, and the alteration appears sooner in them.

MRS. BROMLEY. So it does: you observe very prettily upon things. Heigh-ho! I am as faded as an old lutestring today.

MISS NEVILLE. No indeed, Madam, you look very tolerably, considering.

MRS. BROMLEY. (*Aside*) Considering! She grows pert, I think.——
I am glad you think me not altogether intolerable.

MISS NEVILLE. Ma'am!

MRS. BROMLEY. Tolerably! She is Lady Bell's prime agent.
(*Aside*) Has Sir Harry given you hopes lately?

MISS NEVILLE. Sir Harry! I really don't understand why he is
mentioned.

MRS. BROMLEY. Do you think it will be a match? And have you
made up your quarrel with Lady Bell? (*Sits down*)

MISS NEVILLE. The sweetness of her disposition reconciles everything.

MRS. BROMLEY. And is Millamour reconciled to Lady Bell?

MISS NEVILLE. There was only a slight mistake, which I explained.

MRS. BROMLEY. Oh! you explained? That was prudently done; I
am glad to hear this: and do you think he loves her? Tell me; tell
me all. Why? Why do you think he loves her?

MISS NEVILLE. He cannot be insensible of her merit; and the
other day he asked me if you were likely to approve of his pro-
posing for Lady Bell.

MRS. BROMLEY. And you told him.——Well!——What did you tell
him?

MISS NEVILLE. That you, no doubt, would be ready to promote
the happiness of so amiable a young lady.

MRS. BROMLEY. You told him so? (*Rises, and walks about*) And
so you are turned matchmaker: you busy yourself in my family?
——Hey!——Mrs. Start-up! You are dizened out, I think: my wardrobe has supplied you.

MISS NEVILLE. Your pardon, Ma'am: I had these things in the
country, when you first showed so much goodness to me.

MRS. BROMLEY. What airs! You know I hate to see creatures give
themselves airs. Was not I obliged to provide you with everything?

MISS NEVILLE. You have been very kind; I always acknowledge it.

MRS. BROMLEY. Acknowledge it! Does not everybody know it?

MISS NEVILLE. Yes, Ma'am, I dare say everybody does know it.

MRS. BROMLEY. That's maliciously said: I can spy a sneer upon
that false face. You suppose I have made my brags. That's what

lurks in your ambiguous meaning. I deserve it: deliver me from poor relations.

MISS NEVILLE. (*Aside*) Now the storm begins! I am sure I have said nothing to offend you. I am helpless, it is true, but your relation, and by that tie a gentlewoman still.

MRS. BROMLEY. I made you a gentlewoman. Did not I take you up in the country, where you lived in the parsonage-house, you, and your sister, with no other company to converse with than the melancholy tombstones, where you read the high and mighty characters of John Hodge, and Deborah his wife? While your father's miserable horse, worn to a shadow with carrying double to the next market-town, limped about, with a dull alms-begging eye in quest of the wretched sustenance that grew thriftily between the graves? Did not I take you out of your misery?

MISS NEVILLE. You did, Ma'am. (*In a softened tone*)

MRS. BROMLEY. Did not I bring you home to the great house?

MISS NEVILLE. You did, Ma'am! (*Weeps aside*)

MRS. BROMLEY. And I am finely thanked for it. Warm the snake, and it will turn upon you.

MISS NEVILLE. I cannot bear to be insulted thus! (*Aside*)

MRS. BROMLEY. So! Your spirit is humbled, is it?

MISS NEVILLE. Give me leave to tell you, Madam, that when people of superior fortune, whom Providence has enabled to bestow obligations, claim a right, from the favours they confer, to tyrannize over the hopes and fears of a mind in distress, they exercise a cruelty more barbarous than any in the whole history of human malice.

MRS. BROMLEY. Is this your gratitude?

MISS NEVILLE. I could be thankful for happiness if you permitted me to enjoy it: but when I find myself, under colour of protection, made the sport of every sudden whim, I have a spirit, Madam, that can distinguish between real benevolence and the pride of riches.

MRS. BROMLEY. O brave! That is your spirit!

MISS NEVILLE. A spirit, give me leave to say, that would rather, in any obscure corner, submit to drudgery, for a slender pittance, than continue to be an unhappy subject for cruelty to try its experiments upon. (*Weeps*)

MRS. BROMLEY. I fancy I have been too violent. After all this sour, I must sweeten her a little. [*Aside*] Come, dry up your tears: you know I am good-natured in the main. I am only jealous that you don't seem to love me.

MISS NEVILLE. Were that left to my own heart, every principle there would attach me to you. But to be dunned for gratitude!——

MRS. BROMLEY. You are right; the observation is very just: I am in the wrong.——Come, let us be friends; I have a great regard for you, Neville. (*Walks aside*) The creature should visit with me, only she looks so well.——How! Did not I hear Mr. Malvil's voice? Yes, it is he; I am visible; I am at home; show him in. Walk in, Mr. Malvil.

Enter MALVIL.

MALVIL. To a person of sentiment, like you, Madam, a visit is paid with pleasure.

MRS. BROMLEY. You are very good to me. Neville, do you step and bring me the letter that lies upon my table. (*Exit Miss Neville*) I am obliged to go out this morning. (*Smiles at Malvil*) She looks mighty well: I have been speaking for you: our scheme will take. Sir Harry will not be able to rival you: she will be your reward for all your services to me.

MALVIL. Your generosity is above all praise, and so I was saying this moment to Mr. Bygrove: he is coming to wait on you.

MRS. BROMLEY. That's unlucky: I wanted to have some talk with you: well, have you seen Millamour?

MALVIL. Yes, and I find him apt: I have hopes of succeeding.

MRS. BROMLEY. Hush!——Not so loud!——You think me mad, I believe. May I hazard myself with that wild man?

MALVIL. Your virtue will reclaim him. I have a friendship for Millamour, and that is my reason for counteracting the designs of my friend Bygrove.——Mr. Bygrove has desired me to speak favourably of him to your ladyship.

MRS. BROMLEY. Oh! but he kept his last wife mew'd up in the country; I should certainly expire in the country.

MALVIL. Why, I can't say much for a country life: you are perfectly right. Rooks and crows about your house; foxhounds in full cry all the morning; the country 'squires as noisy at dinner as their own hounds; disputes about the game; commissioners of turnpikes, justices of the peace, and pedigrees of horses; "Oroonoko, brother to White Surry, got by Brisk Lightning, his dam by Bold Thunder." ——That's the whole of their conversation.

MRS. BROMLEY. Deliver me! It would be the death of me. But don't tell Mr. Bygrove: amuse him with hopes.

MALVIL. He is a very worthy man. I am sorry to see some oddities in him; but that is very common in life. Vices always border upon virtues. Dashwould says——but there is no believing his slander;—— he says Mr. Bygrove's sorrow for his deceased wife is all mere artifice, to weep himself into the good graces of another. But I don't believe it.

MRS. BROMLEY. I hear him coming. Do you go and take care of your interest with Neville.

MALVIL. I obey your commands. (*Going*)

MRS. BROMLEY. I shall make her fortune five thousand. Be sure you speak to Millamour. Go, go; success attend you.

Exit MALVIL.

Enter BYGROVE.

BYGROVE. (*Bowing*) Madam!

MRS. BROMLEY. This attention to one in my forlorn state is so obliging——

BYGROVE. It is a favour on your part to receive a lost, dejected, sprightless——

MRS. BROMLEY. I admire your sensibility, Mr. Bygrove. That tender look, which you are for ever casting back to a beloved but irrecoverable object, shows so amiable a sorrow! Oh! there is something exquisite in virtuous affection.

Enter MISS NEVILLE.

MISS NEVILLE. Is this the letter you want, Madam? (*Gives it her*)

MRS. BROMLEY. I thank you, Neville. Yes, there is a luxury in hankering after a valuable person who has been snatched away. I have found a pleasing indulgence in contemplations of that sort; have not I, Neville?

MISS NEVILLE. Ma'am!

MRS. BROMLEY. Ma'am! Are you deaf? Are you stupid? I was telling Mr. Bygrove, what a taking I was in, when poor, dear Mr. Bromley died.

MISS NEVILLE. I was not with you then, Ma'am.

MRS. BROMLEY. Was not with me! What memories some folks have!——Go, and try if you can recover your memory: leave the room.

MISS NEVILLE. Ungenerous, narrow-minded woman! [*Aside*]

Exit.

MRS. BROMLEY. Oh! you little know what a profusion of goodness I have lavished on that creature. She returns it all with sullenness, with ill humour; with aversion. She perfectly remembers the affliction I was in, when I lost the best of men.

BYGROVE. I have had my trials too. Heigh-ho!

MRS. BROMLEY. I beg your pardon: I am recalling your afflictions: you should not give way; you should struggle a little. Heaven knows how I have struggled. I have appeared, indeed, with an air, but it was all struggling. (*Looks and smiles*) I could divert you this morning. Do you know that your son is in love with Lady Jane?

BYGROVE. In love! Has he said anything?

MRS. BROMLEY. I don't know as to that; but I can see what is working in his heart. He is abovestairs now: I don't half like his choice: Lady Bell is the proper match for him, and her fortune is the best. An estate, you know, must come to her, by the family settlement. You should direct his choice.

BYGROVE. This comes of his presuming to think for himself. Has he declared himself?

MRS. BROMLEY. I fancy not; but he hinted something to me, about a match in my family.

BYGROVE. (*Looks at her and smiles*) Why, a match in your family has diverted me of late——Heigh-ho!——It is the only thing that has entertained me for a long time.

MRS. BROMLEY. I have had my fancies too. I should like to talk further, but I am engaged abroad, this morning. Can I set you down? Will you trust yourself with me?

BYGROVE. You encourage a smile, Madam.

MRS. BROMLEY. We shall be the town talk: but let them talk: what need we mind? I will just step and say a word to Neville.—— You should not be too solitary.

BYGROVE. So my friends tell me.

MRS. BROMLEY. I shall be with you in a moment. (*Returns*) Do you know that we are very like each other in our tempers? After all, that is the true foundation of lasting friendships. Poor, dear Mr. Bromley! (*Going, returns*) It was similitude of temper brought us together; and if ever I could be prevailed upon again, similitude of temper must do it. Well, you have diverted me this morning. Here comes your son; talk to him now.

Exit.

Enter CAPTAIN BYGROVE.

BYGROVE. Well, Sir, what brings you to this house?

CAPT. BYGROVE. A morning visit, Sir; merely to kill half an hour.

BYGROVE. There is nothing I hate so much as hypocrisy. I know your errand; you must pretend to be in love.

CAPT. BYGROVE. I, Sir!

BYGROVE. What have you been saying to Lady Jane? I thought I had cautioned you against presuming to think for yourself.

CAPT. BYGROVE. You have been very kind in that way.

BYGROVE. See what comes of your friend Millamour's being left to his own discretion. The ass in the fable, divided in his choice, and still doubting on, till it is too late to resolve,[21] gives but a faint image of him.

---

[21] In the Aesopic fable "The Ass and His Masters," the ass cannot decide on the choice of a master.

CAPT. BYGROVE. And if I, Sir, to avoid his irresolution——

BYGROVE. You are in the opposite extreme: he thinks too much, and never decides. You never think at all, and so resolve without judgment. Take the advice of your friends before you come here to play the antic tricks of love; to kneel, cringe, fawn, flatter, and make yourself ridiculous. Do you know enough of the world to judge for yourself? Can you tell what they are all doing in the gay sphere of life? The young are all bred up under the veterans of vice and folly. They see their mothers with autumnal faces, playing the agreeable, and forgetting that they are no longer young. The men are advanced beyond all former bounds, and the women press close after them. A club for the ladies! Intrepidity is now the female charm: to complete their career, there is nothing left but to build a turf coterie, at Newmarket, and ride their own matches, over the four-mile course.

CAPT. BYGROVE. An admirable picture, Sir: Dashwould could not colour it higher.

BYGROVE. Dashwould! An indiscriminate railer! I speak for your good, and remember, I tell you, you know nothing of the world. After all, Sir, Lady Bell is the person I wish to see you married to;——go, and pay your addresses to her. I will settle that matter for you: you may then marry the person to whom you have not degraded yourself, by pining, sighing, love verses, and I know not what.

CAPT. BYGROVE. This is all unaccountable to me, Sir. If you will but hear me——

Enter MALVIL.

BYGROVE. No, Sir, no; I won't allow you to fetch a single sigh till I say the word; when I give leave, you may then go and sigh till your heart is ready to break. I'll hear no more; no parleying with me. Leave the house, this moment.

CAPT. BYGROVE. I obey.

Exit.

MALVIL. I interrupt you.

BYGROVE. No, no; I am glad to see you. Well, have you had any opportunity with the Widow?

MALVIL. I have; she surprises me a little: she had dropt the mask. I did not think she had been so eager to marry. We had some talk about you. You know my heart: I am always true to my friends: I see but one difficulty: she will never agree to live in the country.

BYGROVE. The lover need not dispute that point, whatever the husband may do hereafter.

MALVIL. Very true; and besides, though I am not inclined, with the malicious part of the world, to suspect her virtue, yet this town has temptations. It grieves me to see the ways of this great city; fine women without principle; friends without sincerity: marriages today, divorces tomorrow; whole estates set upon the cast of a die; masquerades without wit or humour; new comedies that make you cry, and tragedies that put you to sleep. It grieves me to see all this. You are in the right to prefer good sense and tranquillity in the country.

Enter MRS. BROMLEY *and* MISS NEVILLE.

MRS. BROMLEY. I beg your pardon, gentlemen. Neville, mind what I say to you: don't let those giddy girls go out in my absence; to walk in the Green Park,[22] or run to hideous painters, under pretence of seeing odious pictures, that they may have an interview with more odious originals. Keep them at home; I will reward your pains. *Allons*, Mr. Bygrove. (*Exit Bygrove*) Come, Mr. Malvil.

MALVIL. Had not I better stay, and——

MRS. BROMLEY. No, no; come now; you may return to her.

Exit.

MALVIL. (*To Miss Neville*) You see that I am torn from you; but I shall return as soon as possible.

Exit.

MISS NEVILLE. Tyrannical woman! Some virtues she has; but they are overshadowed by their opposite qualities. Her love of praise

---

[22] Southwest of St. James's Street.

is a gross appetite of flattery. She oppresses with kindness, and her very civilities are sure to be disobliging. Oh! state of dependence! For mere support, to be subject every hour to caprice and arrogance!——Is it pride that makes me feel with this sensibility?——No, my heart can answer it is not. I can bow to the hand that relieves me; but I cannot stoop to the servile office of pampering vanity and ostentation, with low and fulsome flattery. What does Lady Bell mean by talking to me of Sir Harry? She does it——I know her goodness——she does it to soften affliction, and, if possible, divert a mind depressed with sorrow. Sir Harry never threw away a thought on me. He behaves, indeed, with marked civility; but I don't know what to think of him. I must not aspire too high: no, I have no pretensions.

Enter LADY JANE.

LADY JANE. Miss Neville, I am very angry with you. What is the matter? Has anything made you uneasy?

MISS NEVILLE. No; I am not remarkable for high spirits, you know.

LADY JANE. Why would not you give us your company? How can you be so cross? That sister of mine is the veriest madcap!

MISS NEVILLE. Lady Bell is rather lively to be sure.

LADY JANE. But when she once begins, she hazards everything, and talks sometimes like a very libertine.

MISS NEVILLE. The overflowing of gaiety, and good humour.

LADY JANE. I wish she would restrain herself a little. Madame La Rouge is with her: she has the sweetest point,[23] eyes ever beheld. I was endeavouring to cheapen it, but Lady Bell was so troublesome; she called me a thousand prudes, and will have it that nothing runs in my head but a lover.

MISS NEVILLE. I don't know but she may be right. We are apt to deceive ourselves. We talk of vapours, and fidgets, and retirement, but it is often artful, sly, insinuating man that lurks at the bottom.

---

[23] The comma following "point" is from the 1777 Larpent manuscript. Point is thread lace made with a needle.

LADY JANE. Well, I vow you'll make me hate you.

MISS NEVILLE. Has Captain Bygrove made no disturbance in your heart?

LADY JANE. How can you? You are as great a plague as my sister. As I live and breathe, the giddy romp is coming. You must take my part.

Enter LADY BELL.

LADY BELL. (*Repeating*)

"Yes, I'm in love, I own it now,
  And Caelia has undone me;
And yet, I swear, I can't tell how,
  The pleasing plague stole on me." [24]

What would I give to have some miserable swain talk in that style of me? "Belinda has undone me." Charming!

MISS NEVILLE. A lively imagination is a blessing, and you are happy, Lady Bell.

LADY BELL. I am so: but then I am not talked of: I am losing all my time.

LADY JANE. Why, you bold creature! I hate to hear you talk with so much intrepidity.

LADY BELL. Prudery! my dear sister, downright prudery! I am not for making mysteries of what all the world knows.

LADY JANE. And how do I make mysteries, pray?

LADY BELL. Why, you confident thing! I'll prove it against you.

LADY JANE. But what? What? What will you prove?

LADY BELL. That you are ready to jump out of your little wits for a husband, my demure, sober sister. Miss Neville, a poet is not more eager for the success of a new comedy, nor one of his brother poets more desirous to see it fail, than that girl is to throw herself into the arms of a man.

LADY JANE. All scandal, Sister.

---

[24] William Whitehead, "The Je Ne Sçay Quoi. A Song," lines 1-4, *The Museum*, May 10, 1746.

LADY BELL. Miss Neville shall be judge

LADY JANE. Your story is mere invention.

LADY BELL. Was there ever such a wrangler?

LADY JANE. You'll not make good your words.

LADY BELL. (*Pats her hand*) Hold your tongue, Miss, will you?

LADY JANE. Very well, go on.

LADY BELL. Will you have done? Now mind, Miss Neville. She does not want to be married, she says. The other night, my young madam, whose thoughts are always composed and even, went to sleep as soon as we got to bed, and then her busy imagination went to work with all the vivacity of an intriguing chambermaid.

LADY JANE. And how can you tell that, pray?

LADY BELL. Out of your own mouth you shall be judged. Miss Neville, she talked in her sleep, like a beauty in a side box, and then fell a singing,

> No, no; he is true, and I believe;
> He look'd, he sigh'd, he can't deceive;
> No, no; I have conquer'd; he is mine;
> My heart is touch'd, and I resign.

LADY JANE. Oh! you scurrilous creature.

MISS NEVILLE. Fairly caught, Lady Jane.

LADY JANE. All odious slander; you judge of me by yourself.

LADY BELL. I do so. I mean to be married, and am frank enough to own it. But you may let "concealment feed on your damask cheek." [25] My damask cheek, I hope, was made for other purposes.

LADY JANE. Gracious! There is no bearing this. What a mad girl you are!

LADY BELL. Not in the least. A natural character. One would not, to be sure, tell a hideous man that one loves him: but when one has encouraged him by degrees, and drawn him on, like a new glove, and perhaps done him a mischief in the doing it, why then one would draw him off again, and maybe ask a pretty fellow to help a body; and then the wretch looks so piteous, and kneels at your feet; then rises in a jealous fit. "I take my everlasting farewell;

---

[25] *Twelfth Night* II.iv.114-115.

never to return; no, never. What to her? Who encouraged me?" Encouraged him? "Who promised?" Broke her promise? "The treacherous, faithless, dear, deluding"——then returns in an instant; hands dangling; eyes imploring; tongue faltering; "Lady Bell—— Lady Bell——when you know that I adore you."——And I burst out into a fit of laughter in his face: oh! that's my joy, my triumph, my supreme delight.

LADY JANE. And is not there a kind of cruelty in all this?

LADY BELL. Oh! your very humble servant, my sweet Lady Graveairs. Cruelty! The difference between you and me, Sister, is this; you deny your love to your female friends, and own it to the man; now I deny it to him, but among ourselves, I fairly own that Miss Neville is not more impatient to be married to Sir Harry than I to——

MISS NEVILLE. Who, I? Spare me, I beg of you. Why Sir Harry?

LADY JANE. Now, now, your turn is come. Never spare her, Sister.

MISS NEVILLE. You must excuse me; I am not in spirits for all this raillery. (*Going*)

LADY JANE. You shan't leave us.

MISS NEVILLE. Give me leave; I beg you will. I'll go and talk to Madame La Rouge. Perhaps I may succeed for you.

Exit.

LADY JANE. Well, if you must go.——How you run on, Sister! And are you really in love?

LADY BELL. Over head and ears.

LADY JANE. With whom?

LADY BELL. Not with Captain Bygrove: how alarmed you are! With Millamour, Sister.

LADY JANE. Fix that roving temper if you can; he will be on his knees to you, and the first pair of black eyes that enters the room will be through his heart.

LADY BELL. As to that, I give myself very little trouble: but if I could once catch him paying his adoration to me, my Aunt Bromley does not raise and sink poor Miss Neville's spirits with such exquisite skill in the art of tormenting as I should his. I should use him as the men do their punch; a little more sweet; a little more sour; a little more spirit; more acid again; then perhaps say it's good for nothing, and then, perhaps——

LADY JANE. What?

LADY BELL. Sip it up at last, as you would do at first. You wicked girl, how could you ask me such a question? Law! what am I about? I have a thousand things to do.

Enter MISS NEVILLE and MADAME LA ROUGE.

LA ROUGE. Ah! my Lady! Always so gay; English climate no effect upon you. De *manières de Paris* for all de vorl. *En vérité, vous êtes charmante.*

LADY BELL. Oh! Madame La Rouge, you say such polite things; but you rob me of all my money. My sister is rich: you had better deal with her. Sister, you'll be married before me. (*Sings*)

No, no, he is true, and I believe, *&c.*

Exit.

LADY JANE. Was ever anything so crazy?

LA ROUGE. It is all *vivacité!* And, my Lady, you have ver great wit *en partage;* [26] *vous avez les grâces;* you have de grace; but you no deal vid me.

LADY JANE. I shall call at your house in Pall Mall. Miss Neville, you joined against me; I am very angry with you.

Exit.

LA ROUGE. Mademoiselle, I tell you; persuade my Lady to have de lace, and you come to my house, me give you ver pretty present.

MISS NEVILLE. Oh! you have a national talent for applying a little bribery.

LA ROUGE. *Diantre;* [27] 'tis false *délicatesse.* You not know de *manières* of the vorl.——Ah! Monsieur Malvil!

Enter MALVIL.

---

[26] "As your share."
[27] "The deuce."

MALVIL. Madame La Rouge, I did not expect this pleasure.

LA ROUGE. It is always pleasure to see *mes amis;* to see my friends; and I glad to see you here vid de lady. You have ver good choice. And I can tell you, make de dispatch: you have rival.

MALVIL. Rival!

LA ROUGE. You not know? Sir Harry have taste as well as you. Mademoiselle, you are ver great favourite.

MISS NEVILLE. A favourite! Keep your vivacity for some other subject; don't make me the town talk.

LA ROUGE. It is ver true: he come to my house in Pall Mall, and say ver fine ting of Mademoiselle Neville, and Monsieur Dash-would praise you ver much.

MALVIL. (*Aside*) Ay, his malice is at work.

LA ROUGE. Monsieur, you lose all your time.——(*Goes to him and speaks low*) You wait de fortune from Madam Bromley: Sir Harry vil take her vidout any money at all. Vat you slow for?

MALVIL. Are the apartments kept ready at your house?

LA ROUGE. De apartment it is ready. You take it two, tree week ago, and pay de rent for noting——I leave you vid de lady; and I go mind *mes affaires. Bon voyage.*

Exit.

MALVIL. I have disengaged myself, to have the honour of attending you.

MISS NEVILLE. Your attention is thrown away. Did not I hear Mr. Millamour's voice?

MALVIL. Yes; he came with me; he is gone into the next room to pay his compliments to Lady Jane. I am sorry to see him for ever distracted; always resolving, and yet every day beginning the world over again. You look chagrin'd; what has disturb'd you?

MISS NEVILLE. The old story; Mrs. Bromley's eternal whims.

MALVIL. She is not spoken of as I could wish. Good-natured and arrogant, generous and cruel, obliging and oppressive, at the same time.

MISS NEVILLE. There cannot, surely, be a more distressful situation than to remain under daily obligations and yet not be able to esteem our benefactress.

MALVIL. Your delicacy charms me: it has fixed me yours. I long for nothing so much as to see you out of her power. They have a strange report about town: people will be talking: the whisper goes that Mr. Bygrove, amidst all his grief, is slyly in a hurry for another wife. Mrs. Bromley, they say, encourages him; and at the same time has a design upon my friend Millamour.

MISS NEVILLE. The world is not always wrong.

MALVIL. Malice will be busy; and does not spare the young ladies.

MISS NEVILLE. If anything is said to their disadvantage, believe me, they do not deserve it.

MALVIL. I dare say not: I don't think they are too forward. I am sorry to see, in one of the papers, today, a character of Sir Harry, not at all favourable. His little follies, his whims, and caprices one does not mind: he may walk in Dashwould's train as long as he pleases; that only makes him ridiculous. But it grieves me to hear that perfidy stains his character, and, as I am told, the worst of perfidy: the ruin of beauty and innocence is his ruling passion.

MISS NEVILLE. This is very odd: somebody has been at the trouble of sending me an anonymous letter to that very effect: and why to me? I am not able to decipher.

MALVIL. I don't like anonymous letters. In general they aim at mischief, but this, perhaps, is meant as a caution to you: it must be a friend that sent it.

MISS NEVILLE. No; I can guess the quiver from whence that arrow comes.

MALVIL. Dashwould, perhaps?

MISS NEVILLE. I don't say that.

MALVIL. Nor I; I never charge anybody; but upon recollection, the letter in the newspaper is imputed to him. Mrs. Bromley, I know, has no opinion of Sir Harry. His designs, with regard to you, she does not think honourable. My heart interests me for you. You know I am all heart. The plan which Mrs. Bromley has pro-posed——hark! I think I hear Millamour coming. I'll follow you upstairs.

MISS NEVILLE. Oh! Sir! You have frighten'd me out of my wits.

Exit.

MALVIL. She loves Sir Harry, I see; and yet she shan't slip thro' my hands. I can set on Mrs. Bromley to lead her a weary life, and if I can prevail upon Millamour to renounce Lady Bell, and marry the Widow, my business is done. When Miss Neville is heartily tormented by Mrs. Bromley, affliction softens the mind, and I may then decoy her away, and stand upon terms with the family. But Dashwould's wit will fly about. No matter: he is a sad scoundrel, and does not mind how he murders reputations. So! Here comes Millamour. I must get clear of him, and talk further with Miss Neville.

Enter MILLAMOUR.

MILLAMOUR. From this moment I blot all other women from my memory. Malvil, wish me joy. The perplexity of choice is now at an end.

MALVIL. Why, what has happen'd?

MILLAMOUR. Lovely Lady Jane. "And yield her charms of mind with sweet delay." [28]——I can't stay to tell you now.

MALVIL. Nor will I stay to interrupt your raptures. You know, I wish you success.

Exit.

Enter LADY BELL.

LADY BELL. (*Reading*)

"Who yields too soon, must soon her lover lose,
  Would you restrain him long? then long refuse."

MILLAMOUR. (*Looks at her and smiles*) There is something commanding in that air of vivacity.

LADY BELL. (*Reads*)

---

[28] Edward Young, *Love of Fame, The Universal Passion* (1725-8) VI.110.

"Oft at your door let him for entrance wait,
    There let him"——[29]

How! Millamour here! How could you surprise me so? You
horrid thing! How long have you been here?

MILLAMOUR. Been, Madam?——I have been——I have been in
the next room, paying my respects to your sister.

LADY BELL. And never enquired for poor Lady Bell?

MILLAMOUR. Your Ladyship wrongs me. You do injustice to your
own charms: they can never be forgot.

LADY BELL. I see how it is: the other day you was listed in my
service, and now a deserter to my sister! You are right; you would
have been upon hard duty with me.

MILLAMOUR. Any duty but a forlorn hope would be——

LADY BELL. Hope!——Why sure, you would not have had the
intolerable assurance to entertain the smallest degree of hope?
My sister, I suppose, has given you some hope. Ay! that's her
way: she moves by settled rules, and shines with equal light. Now
I——I am a mere comet. I blaze of a sudden; dazzle for a while; then
wheel away, and am thought of no more.

MILLAMOUR. That gaiety of hers is charming. (*Aside*) The impression your Ladyship makes——

LADY BELL. Words; mere words.——No; I am a strange piece of
wild nature; never the same for two minutes together. Now, my
sister, she is a Prussian blue, holds her colour, and is always the
same.——I——I am a more changeable silk——I shift about, and display my wit and my folly so curiously blended that nobody can
tell where one begins or the other ends. I am not worth your notice.
(*Walks and hums a tune*)

MILLAMOUR. (*Looking at her*) She has described herself admirably; without variety, a woman is a downright piece of insipidity.

LADY BELL. Yes, I have my whims. Never the same for two
minutes together. Now I love to give a scope to folly, and the men
say, "Curse catch her, she pleases more when in the wrong than

---

[29] William Congreve's translation *Ovid's Art of Love* III.671-674.

other women when they are in the right." Then good sense is the
word; and the next moment I can't bear the fatigue of thinking;
why won't somebody write a comedy to divert me? Then all
spirit, and I long to lead up the ball.

> "Ladies, like variegated tulips show,
>   'Tis to their weakness all their charms they owe." [30]

(*Sings and walks about*)

MILLAMOUR. (*Aside*) Lady Jane is mere mediocrity compared
to her.

LADY BELL. Lord! I run on at a strange rate. Yours, Mr. Millamour: au revoir. (*Going*)

MILLAMOUR. A moment longer: you must not leave me. You
possess my heart: possess it without a rival.

LADY BELL. Hey! What's the matter now?

MILLAMOUR. Do not trifle with a passion sincere as mine. I
adore you, my Lady Bell; adore your matchless charms; thus on
my knees adore.

LADY BELL. Stay, stay; let me see what the poet says. (*Reads
quick*)

> "Oft at your door, let him for entrance wait,
>   There let him kneel, and threaten and entreat."

There, stay there; don't offer to stir. Now put up both your hands,
and pray, pray, have compassion, Lady Bell.

> *Exit laughing.*

MILLAMOUR.

> She flies disdainful from her lover's view,
> Yet looks and bids him, as she flies, pursue.[31]

End of the SECOND ACT.

---

[30] Altered from Pope, *Moral Essays* II.41-42.
[31] This passage is not a quotation, but compare Lewis Theobald's song
"The Bashful Lover," lines 37-38 [in *The Musical Miscellany* (London,
1729), I, 32].

ACT the THIRD
[SCENE I]

[At Mrs. Bromley's]

Enter LADY JANE *and* CAPT. BYGROVE.

LADY JANE. And laid his commands upon you to address my sister?

CAPT. BYGROVE. Most peremptorily.

LADY JANE. You have obey'd him, I hope.

CAPT. BYGROVE. You know your power too well; you know that I am devoted to you, and that my happiness depends upon the promise you have made me.

LADY JANE. There, that is always the way with you men: our smiles are sure marks of approbation; and every civil thing we say, is construed into a promise.

CAPT. BYGROVE. And have not you promised?

LADY JANE. (*Looks at him and smiles*) Need I answer that question? How easily frightened you are! But you have some reason to be alarmed. Millamour has been on his knees to me, breathing such raptures——

CAPT. BYGROVE. Ay!——Who has set him on?——What can be at the bottom of this?——And have you listened to him?——Here comes Dashwould; he perhaps can explain——

LADY JANE. He will only laugh at us; and so I'll make my escape. (*Going*)

CAPT. BYGROVE. Not to hear Millamour, again, I hope. (*Takes her hand*)

LADY JANE. Well, well, to purchase my liberty, you need not fear. I have received his vows, delivered with such ardour!——How terrified you look!——I have listened to him, to alarm my sister with an idea of Millamour's growing passion for me. If her jealousy is once touched, it may fix her resolution. At present, she is as volatile as Millamour himself.

Enter DASHWOULD.

DASHWOULD. As volatile as Millamour! What can that be? I never knew anything that would bear a comparison.

LADY JANE. What think you of my sister?

DASHWOULD. Lady Bell has her whims. I left her abovestairs, in close conference with Millamour; he has deserted your Ladyship already. Mrs. Bromley will be the next, I hope: your father, Captain, would grieve more for that than for his deceased wife.

LADY JANE. And then Miss Neville's turn may come.

DASHWOULD. Oh! no. To sport with her would be inhumanity. But a brisk widow is fair game.

CAPT. BYGROVE. Yes, and it may help to cure my father of his folly.

LADY JANE. It would be sport, but I despair of it. You know, Mr. Dashwould, you allow that Millamour has understanding.

DASHWOULD. But he does not act from his understanding. Fits and starts of passion govern him. If in any one pursuit of real use, he had half the alacrity of mind with which he runs on from one folly to another, he would be a man for the ladies to pull caps for. But he lives for ever in inconsistencies. One action of his life is the sure forerunner of the contrary. First Malvil is his favourite! Then arm in arm with me. Can any two things be more opposite? It is the same among the ladies! They all have him by turns, and the whim of one moment, is sure to find a ridiculous antithesis in the next.

LADY JANE. He sat for that picture, I'll swear.——Well there's a gentleman wants your advice, and so I'll leave you together.

Exit.

CAPT. BYGROVE. My dear Dashwould, you must assist me.

DASHWOULD. What distresses you?

CAPT. BYGROVE. My evil genius is at work. You know what my father has resolved upon. Lady Bell is the person he chooses for me.

DASHWOULD. I know all that business: a counterplot of the Widow's fertile brain, to disappoint Lady Bell, and wreak her malice on Millamour.

CAPT. BYGROVE. But the malice falls on me only. Why will not Millamour know his own mind? Lady Bell loves him, I know she does. I am thwarted in the tenderest point; what must be done?

DASHWOULD. Do as they would have you: you ensure success. Millamour's jealousy takes fire upon the first alarm, and while the passion holds, he will have vigour enough to act decisively.

CAPT. BYGROVE. May I hazard the experiment?

DASHWOULD. It's a sure card. Take my advice.

Enter MISS NEVILLE.

MISS NEVILLE. Mrs. Bromley's coach has just stopp'd at the door: had not you better step upstairs, gentlemen?

Enter SIR HARRY.

SIR HARRY. Dashwould, you are absent too long. They are all as dull as a funeral, abovestairs.

DASHWOULD. (*Aside to Capt. Bygrove*) How the Baronet follows Miss Neville from room to room!——Come, Captain, I'll play a game of piquet with you before dinner.——*Allons!*

Exit with CAPT. BYGROVE.

SIR HARRY. If I might have the liberty, Ma'am, to——

MISS NEVILLE. Another time, if you please, Sir Harry. Mrs. Bromley is coming: I hear her voice.

SIR HARRY. And you promise me the hearing?

MISS NEVILLE. You are entitled to it, Sir. I beg you'll leave me now.

SIR HARRY. I obey your commands; I am gone; you'll remember.

Exit.

MISS NEVILLE. Here she comes; and I think in good humour.

Enter MRS. BROMLEY.

MRS. BROMLEY. Oh! I am heartily tired. I have been paying visits to people who have never been let into my house, and who, I hope, will never be at home for me. I hate them all, but out of civility, we must keep up an acquaintance. Where are the girls? Has anybody been here?

MISS NEVILLE. Mr. Millamour, Ma'am, and the rest of the gentlemen that dine here: they are all abovestairs.

MRS. BROMLEY. Stupidity! Did not I give orders——how long has Millamour been here?

MISS NEVILLE. About an hour.

MRS. BROMLEY. With Lady Bell, I suppose.——Thou base ingratitude! And Sir Harry is here too, I reckon. Does your match go on? You shall go back to the country, I promise you. You'll be the ruin of those girls. They shall have no visitors when my back is turned. I'll give orders to all the servants this very moment. (*Going*)

Enter SIR JOHN MILLAMOUR.

SIR JOHN. To see Mrs. Bromley looking so well——

MRS. BROMLEY. You are very polite, Sir. Business calls me now, Sir John; I beg your pardon.

Exit.

SIR JOHN. Has my son been here today?

MISS NEVILLE. He is abovestairs with Lady Bell, Sir.

MRS. BROMLEY. (*Within*) Miss Neville, Neville, I say.

MISS NEVILLE. You'll excuse me, Sir John; what can she want?

Exit.

SIR JOHN. This visit portends some good, I hope. I shall be happy if he has declared himself. I'll step and see what he is about. (*Going*)

Enter MILLAMOUR.

MILLAMOUR. Exquisite! lovely angel!

SIR JOHN. Well!——How!——What!

MILLAMOUR. I beg your pardon, Sir; I am not at leisure; I am in the third region;[32] and can't descend to the language of the nether world.

SIR JOHN. Then you are in love, George.

MILLAMOUR. She is a sister of the Graces, and surpasses the other three. I am fixed; unalterably fixed; and am going about the marriage articles directly.

SIR JOHN. They are at my lawyer's ready engrossed; and only wait for the lady's name, to fill up the blanks.

MILLAMOUR. I know it, Sir: I must step for them; I have it through my heart: I feel it here: I am your humble servant, Sir. (*Going*)

SIR JOHN. No, no; do you stay here; I'll step for Mr. Copyhold. The writings shall be here in ten minutes.

Exit.

MILLAMOUR. The sooner the better, Sir.

"Let those love now, who never lov'd before;
    Let those who always lov'd, now love the more."[33]

(*Sings*) Loll, toll, loll.

Enter MALVIL.

MALVIL. Bravo! You seem in prodigious spirits.

MILLAMOUR. I am so: I am happy in myself, and happy in my friends, and happy in every circumstance, and in tiptop spirits, and——my dear Malvil, yours down to the ground.

MALVIL. Methinks I sympathize with you. When our friends are happy, the sensation is well called a fellow feeling.

MILLAMOUR. Malvil, I thank you; your turn of mind is formed for lasting friendships. With Dashwould it is all dissipation, and giddy mirth, the mere bubble of pleasure. To you, I may talk

---

[32] The air was divided into Upper Air, Middle Air, and Lower Air. Here, the Upper Air is thought of as heaven.

[33] The refrain of Thomas Parnell's *The Vigil of Venus*, a translation of the anonymous *Pervigilium Veneris*.

seriously. The topic of the day is enough for Dashwould. I can now tell you that I shall be happy for life. But for Dashwould, I should have been settled long ago. That fellow has led me into a thousand errors.

MALVIL. He has his admirers, and not without reason. He thinks me his enemy, but he is mistaken. I never harbour resentment.

MILLAMOUR. You are growing grave, and I am a flight above common sense at present.

MALVIL. Dashwould, notwithstanding all his faults, does hit the mark sometimes. I don't usually laugh at his pleasantry; I don't like to encourage him too much; but it must be owned, he is often right. Behind his back I cannot help being diverted by him. He has a quick insight into characters.

MILLAMOUR. No want of penetration there.

MALVIL. No, no; he says, and perhaps rightly, your lively ladies often want common prudence; and giddy in the pursuit of pleasure, they are frequently miserable in the end.

MILLAMOUR. But Lady Bell's good sense, that refinement of understanding——

MALVIL. There are false refinements; the shadow for the substance. Who is it that observes, we all discover early symptoms of the disease by which our minds and bodies go to ruin?

MILLAMOUR. Po! With Lady Bell there can be no risk.

MALVIL. I don't know whether Dashwould is good authority.—— You know him best. He says——

MILLAMOUR. Well!

MALVIL. He is a shrewd observer.

MILLAMOUR. Nobody more so.

MALVIL. If he has a regard for anybody, it is for you. You are the only man I never heard him speak ill of. A match with Lady Bell is not to his mind. He talked seriously on the subject. Has not he told you?

MILLAMOUR. Not a syllable.

MALVIL. I wonder at that. Lady Bell, he says, show'd herself early. Impatient of advice, attentive to nothing but her beauty! Whole days at her looking glass——I repeat his very words——he seemed to speak out of downright regard for you.——At her toilette every feature had its instructions how to look; but no instruction for the mind. And then, says he, that terrible love of gaming!

MILLAMOUR. Gaming!

MALVIL. Don't you know it? I can't say I ever saw it myself. Time will determine her character.

MILLAMOUR. If she loves gaming, it is pretty well determined already.

MALVIL. Perhaps not: I still hope for the best.

MILLAMOUR. Why yes; a man of sense may form her mind, and then the gentler affections may take their turn.

MALVIL. The very thing I said.——But our pleasant friend had an answer ready.——"Gentle affections!" says he. "Don't you see that it is with people that once love play as with persons addicted to strong cordials? They never return to cooler liquors."

MILLAMOUR. There is some truth in that. I am for ever obliged to you. It is ingenuous, it is friendly of you to convey the hint.

MALVIL. Don't build too much upon it. I have told you my author; and you know his way: he may deny it all.

MILLAMOUR. Shall I talk to him?

MALVIL. I don't know what to say to that. In his vein of pleasantry, he may give it another turn.

MILLAMOUR. He may so. I am glad to know all this. But my Lady Jane, there's a model for her sex to imitate.

MALVIL. Have you watched her well? People should appear what they really are. Let a precipice look like a precipice. When covered over with flowers, it only serves to deceive the unwary. Mrs. Bromley has been very communicative about Lady Jane.

MILLAMOUR. You alarm me. My dear friend, explain.

MALVIL. To do Lady Bell justice, she is above disguise. And tho' she has her faults, I have seen her please by those very faults.

MILLAMOUR. (*Smiling*) And so have I. Her very blemishes are beauty spots.

MALVIL. No frankness about the youngest girl. It is friendship for you that makes me speak. Her character is all forced, studied, put on with her rouge.

MILLAMOUR. Does she paint?

MALVIL. A little; the prudent touch. I am sorry for her. When she is settled in the world, many qualities, which now lie concealed, will break out into open daylight.

MILLAMOUR. What a masked battery there will be to play off upon a husband!

MALVIL. Their aunt told me all in confidence. You may judge how painful it is to her. I have known the family for some time. I can't but be sorry for the young ladies.

MILLAMOUR. And since this is the case, I don't care how little I know of them, or their family.

MALVIL. No occasion to quarrel with the family. Great merit about Mrs. Bromley. She made an admirable wife, and that at an early period. She was but seventeen when she married.

MILLAMOUR. No more?

MALVIL. Not an hour: she is not thirty: an estate in her own right, and the command of half a borough. No opposition there; the old houses have the votes. A man may get a seat without trouble. Does not Sir John want to see you in Parliament?

MILLAMOUR. Yes. It would give him pleasure.

MALVIL. Well, you will judge for yourself. Were I as you, I should know what course to take. Here she comes! A good, fine woman! A man may there sit down to his happiness at once.

Enter MRS. BROMLEY.

MRS. BROMLEY. Mr. Millamour. (*Curtsies*) Mr. Malvil, what have you done with Mr. Bygrove?

MALVIL. I parted with him where you set us down. (*Speaks to her aside*) I have talked to Millamour, and I think it will do.

MRS. BROMLEY. Go you upstairs. (*Aside to Malvil*)

MALVIL. How charmingly you look! Like Lady Bell's eldest sister!

MRS. BROMLEY. Po! you are laughing at me.

MALVIL. Not I truly: I appeal to Millamour. I'll take the liberty to join the company above. (*Aside to Millamour*) She is the best of the family.

Exit.

MRS. BROMLEY. A valuable man Mr. Malvil is! He has a great esteem for you, Sir. His sincerity is unequall'd. You seem thoughtful, Mr. Millamour.

MILLAMOUR. Thoughtful, Ma'am!——There are certain subjects that——what Malvil says is true——a man may marry her and sit down to his happiness at once. (*Aside*)

MRS. BROMLEY. Sir John has been saying a great deal to me about you.

MILLAMOUR. Has he, Ma'am?——There is a circumstance, which he is as yet a stranger to——a circumstance, which to communicate, will perhaps——it is what I have long wished, and——

MRS. BROMLEY. Faltering! Hesitating! (*Aside*) I interrupt you.

MILLAMOUR. There is a circumstance, Ma'am——the affair is—— my father for a long time——Sir John, for a long time——Sir John has wished——

MRS. BROMLEY. To see you married?

MILLAMOUR. To see me married, Ma'am.——And——he has—— he has wished it much.——And a settlement, by way of jointure ——long ready for the lady's name——that is——any lady, who shall honour me with her affection——and——

MRS. BROMLEY. No lady can be insensible of your pretensions.

MILLAMOUR. You are very good, Ma'am; and after long observation, and a lasting passion grafted on it, which, tho' silent hitherto, ——yet working secretly——when disclosed at length——may to the person in the world——who already formed by experience, may in every respect——and if without presuming too far——

MRS. BROMLEY. What a delicate confusion he is in. (*Aside*)

MILLAMOUR. And if this paper, Ma'am——

MRS. BROMLEY. (*Taking the paper*) When given by you, Sir,——

Enter BYGROVE.

MRS. BROMLEY. Perverse and cruel! (*Walks aside*)

BYGROVE. You both look grave; nothing amiss, I hope.

MRS. BROMLEY. Everything is as it should be, Sir.

MILLAMOUR. (*Aside*) Not if he knew all.

BYGROVE. Sir John has been complaining——

MRS. BROMLEY. Pass that by; advise your own son; had not you better step upstairs? Mr. Millamour will do what is right. (*Smiling at him*) You may leave it all to him; trust to his judgment.

Enter SIR HARRY.

SIR HARRY. Millamour, I have such a story for you: Malvil and Dashwould have been quarrelling about you, and——

BYGROVE. Po! And here they all come; I knew the substance could not be far off when the shadow projected before it.

Enter LADY BELL, DASHWOULD, *and* MALVIL.

LADY BELL. Mr. Dashwould, do you think I'll bear this? What liberty will you take next? You think, because I laugh, that I am not offended.——Aunt, I received a letter, and he has attempted to snatch it from me.

DASHWOULD. Why, it brings a little cargo of ridicule from the country, and my friend Malvil sees no joke in it.

MALVIL. When my friend's name is brought in question, Sir——

LADY BELL. It is diverting notwithstanding.——Aunt, what do you think? My cousin Cynthia, you know, was to be married to Sir George Squanderstock; [34] her mother opposed it, and broke off the match, and now it's come out that she was all the time the clandestine rival of her own daughter.

MILLAMOUR. Not inapplicable to the present business. (*Aside*)

MRS. BROMLEY. Go, you giddy girl, no such thing!

MILLAMOUR. (*Aside*) She charms by her very faults.

SIR HARRY. (*Goes up to Bygrove*) And Dashwould has been saying——

BYGROVE. Po! Repeat none of his sayings to me.

---

[34] Charles James Fox (Dunbar, *op. cit.*, p. 279). Fox had notorious gambling losses, and in 1778 his means were at their lowest ebb.

LADY BELL. Did you say anything Mr. Dashwould? What was it?

DASHWOULD. Oh! nothing. Sir George Squanderstock is my very good friend.

MALVIL. And for that reason, you might spare him. No man is without his faults.

DASHWOULD. Ay, allow him faults, out of tenderness.

BYGROVE. Sir George is a valuable man, Sir, and represents his county to great advantage.

DASHWOULD. He does so; takes a world of pains; nothing can escape him. Manila ransom not paid; [35] there must be a motion about that matter: he knots his handkerchief to remember it.——Scarcity of corn! Another knot.——Triennial parliaments.[36]——(*Knots*) Juries judges of law as well as fact. (*Knots*) National debt. (*Knots*) Bail in criminal cases. (*Knots*) And so on he goes, till his handkerchief is twisted into questions of state; the liberties and fortunes of all posterity dangling like a bederoll; he puts it in his pocket, drives to the gaming table, and the next morning his handkerchief goes to the wash, and his country and the minority are both left in the suds.

LADY BELL. What a description! | *Both*
SIR HARRY. Hey! lively Lady Bell! | *laugh*

MILLAMOUR. Ho! ho! I thank you, Dashwould.

MRS. BROMLEY. (*Aside to Millamour*) How can you encourage him? Let us leave 'em to themselves.

MALVIL. You see, Mr. Bygrove——

BYGROVE. Ay! Thus he gets a story to graft his malice upon, and then he sets the table in a roar at the next tavern.

SIR HARRY. Never be out of humour with Dashwould, Mr.

---

[35] When the English captured Manila from the Spaniards on October 6, 1762, "the private property of the inhabitants was saved from plunder on the condition of a payment of a ransom of a million sterling, one-half of which was paid in money and the other half in bills upon the Spanish Treasury. These bills the Spaniards afterwards refused to honour, and the English Government was never able to obtain their payment." [W. E. H. Lecky, *A History of England in the Eighteenth Century* (London, 1921), III, 204, 213.]

[36] Favored by Charles James Fox.

Bygrove; he keeps me alive; he has been exhibiting pictures of this sort all the morning, as we rambled about the town.

DASHWOULD. Oh! no; no pictures; I have shown him real life.

SIR HARRY. Very true, Dashwould: and now mind him; he will touch them off to the life for you.

MRS. BROMLEY. Millamour so close with Lady Bell! The forward importunity of that girl. (*Aside, and goes to Millamour*)

DASHWOULD. There is positively no such thing as going about this town without seeing enough to split your sides with laughing. We called upon my friend Sir Volatile Vainlove: he, you know, shines in all polite assemblies, and is, if you believe himself, of the first character for intrigue. We found him drinking valerian tea for his breakfast, and putting on false calves.

SIR HARRY. And the confusion he was in, when we entered the room!

DASHWOULD. In the next street, we found Jack Spinbrain, a celebrated poet, with a kept mistress at his elbow, writing lampoons for the newspaper; one moment murdering the reputation of his neighbours, and the next a suicide of his own.——We saw a young heir, not yet of age, granting annuity bonds, and five Jews, and three Christians, duped by their avarice to lend money upon them. A lawyer——

SIR HARRY. Hear, hear; it is all true. I was with him.

DASHWOULD. A lawyer taking notes upon Shakespeare; a deaf nabob ravished with music, and a blind one buying pictures. Men without talents, rising to preferment, and real genius going to a jail.——An officer in a marching regiment with a black-eye, and a French hairdresser wounded in the sword arm.

SIR HARRY. Oh! ho! ho! By this light I can vouch for every word.

BYGROVE. Go on, Sir Harry, ape your friend in all his follies; be the nimble marmoset, to grin at his tricks, and try to play them over again yourself.

SIR HARRY. Well now, that is too severe: Dashwould, defend me from his wit. You know I hoard up all your good things.

DASHWOULD. You never pay me in my own coin, Sir Harry: try now; who knows but you will say something.

MALVIL. Friend or foe it is all alike.

LADY BELL. (*Coming forward*) And where is the mighty harm? I like pulling to pieces of all things.

MILLAMOUR. (*Following Lady Bell*) To be sure it is the life of conversation. Does your Ladyship know Sir George Squander-stock's sister? [37]

LADY BELL. I have seen her.

MILLAMOUR. She is a politician in petticoats; a fierce republican; she talks of the dagger of Brutus while she settles a pin in her tucker; and says more about ship-money than pin-money.

BYGROVE. And now you must turn buffoon?

DASHWOULD. I know the lady; she scolds at the loyalists,[38] gossips against the act of settlement,[39] and has the fidgets for Magna Charta.

MILLAMOUR. She encourages a wrinkle against bribery; flirts her fan at the ministry, and bites her lips at taxes and a standing army.

MALVIL. Mr. Bygrove, will you bear all this?

Enter MISS NEVILLE, *and whispers* MRS. BROMLEY.

MRS. BROMLEY. Very well, Neville, I'll come presently.

Exit MISS NEVILLE.

MALVIL. (*Looking at Miss Neville*) I shall stay no longer. Mr. Bygrove, will you walk?

Exit.

BYGROVE. No, Sir, I shall not leave the enemy in this room behind me: a bad translator of an ancient poet, is not so sure to deface his original, as his licentious strain to disparage every character.

DASHWOULD. Sir Harry, he will neither give, nor take a joke.

SIR HARRY. No, I told you so.

BYGROVE. Let me tell you once for all, Sir——

---

[37] Mrs. Catharine Macaulay (1731-1791). [James Boaden, *Memoirs of Mrs. Siddons* (London, 1896), p. 60.]

[38] Americans opposed to separation from Great Britain during the American Revolution.

[39] The Act of Settlement of June, 1701, secured the succession after Anne for Protestant members of the House of Hanover.

DASHWOULD. I wish you would.

BYGROVE. Why interrupt? Do you know what I was going to say?

DASHWOULD. No, do you?

MILLAMOUR. I'll leave 'em all to themselves.

Steals out.

MRS. BROMLEY. (*Aside*) Millamour gone!

Exit.

BYGROVE. And what does all this mighty wit amount to? The wit in vogue, exposes one man; makes another expose himself; gets into the secrets of an intimate acquaintance, and publishes a story to the world; belies a friend; puts an anecdote, a letter, an epigram into the newspaper; and that is the whole amount of modern wit.

DASHWOULD. A strain of morose invective is more diverting, to be sure.

BYGROVE. (*Looking about for Mrs. Bromley*) Well, Sir, we'll adjourn the debate. You may go on; misrepresent everything; if there is nothing ridiculous, invent a story: and when you have done it, it is but a cheap and frivolous talent. Has a lady a good natural bloom? Her paint must be an expensive article. Does she look grave? She will sin the deeper. Is she gay and affable? Her true character will come out at the Commons.[40] That is the whole of your art, and I leave you to the practice of it. (*Going*)

DASHWOULD. Satirical Bygrove! Now the Widow has him in tow.

BYGROVE. (*Turning back*) Could not you stay till my back was fairly turned?

Exit.

DASHWOULD. What a look there was!

LADY BELL. At what a rate you run on! You keep the field against them all.

DASHWOULD. Sir Harry, step up, and watch him with the Widow.

SIR HARRY. I will; don't stay too long.

DASHWOULD. I'll follow you: and hark, make your party good with Miss Neville.

---

[40] The ecclesiastical court, which had jurisdiction of divorces, met in Doctors' Commons, the buildings of the College of Doctors of Civil Law near St. Paul's Churchyard.

SIR HARRY. You see, Lady Bell, a fling at everybody.

Exit.

DASHWOULD. The Baronet does not want parts; that is to say, he has very good materials to play the fool with. I shall get him to marry Miss Neville.

LADY BELL. Bring that about, and you will for once do a serious action for which everybody will honour you.

DASHWOULD. In the meantime, do you watch your Aunt Bromley: she is your rival.

LADY BELL. Rival? That would be charming.

DASHWOULD. It is even so. Now Millamour's understanding is good, but his passion's quick: if you play your cards right——

LADY BELL. Are you going to teach me how to manage a man?

DASHWOULD. Coquetry will never succeed with him. A quicksand does not shift so often as his temper. You must take him at his word, and never give him time to change and veer about.

LADY BELL. Totally out of nature.

DASHWOULD. Oh! very well. I give up the point.

Exit.

LADY BELL. You may leave the man to my management. My Aunt Bromley rival me! That would be delightful.

Enter LADY JANE.

LADY BELL. Well, Sister!

LADY JANE. Can you be serious for a moment?

LADY BELL. Well, the solemnity of that look! Must I set my face by yours, and contract a wrinkle by a formal economy of features, which you, like the rest of the world, mistake for wisdom?

LADY JANE. Will you hear me? They are hurrying this match too fast, I think. Sir John is come, and his lawyer is expected every moment. He wants to conclude the affair this day, and my aunt does not oppose it. But I don't like all this hurry.

LADY BELL. And why need you be concerned about it?

LADY JANE. Do you think Millamour capable of love?

LADY BELL. For the moment. It will be difficult to fix him.

LADY JANE. What would you have me do?

LADY BELL. Do?——Nothing.

LADY JANE. How silly! You know it is not my seeking.

LADY BELL. What are you about? Talking in your sleep again? Lady Jane, wake yourself. What have you taken into your head?

LADY JANE. Why since Mr. Millamour has prevailed with me——

LADY BELL. His affections then are fixed upon you?——Why the man has been dying at my feet, with a face as rueful as a love elegy.

LADY JANE. You will permit me to laugh in my turn.

LADY BELL. Oh! I can laugh with you, and at you, and at him too. This gives spirit to the business: here are difficulties, and difficulties enhance victory, and victory is triumph.

LADY JANE. Very well! Oh! brave! Laugh away! You will be undeceived presently.——If this does not take, I am at the end of my line. [*Aside*]

Exit.

LADY BELL. What does all this mean? Rivall'd, outwitted by my sister! Insupportable! This begins to grow serious.

Enter MILLAMOUR.

MILLAMOUR. 'Sdeath! She here! Sir John is quite impatient, and I am going for his attorney.

LADY BELL. And Lady Jane is impatient too: she is the object of your choice.

MILLAMOUR. Lady Jane! You are pleasant, very pleasant.

LADY BELL. She has told me with inflexible gravity!

MILLAMOUR. She is a great wit; and great wits have great quickness of invention; and so a story is easily dressed up. I could crack my sides with laughing. If trifling civilities have been received as a declaration of love——

LADY BELL. And is that the case? Very whimsical indeed.

MILLAMOUR. Yes, very whimsical! I am eternally yours, Ma'am, and I am on the wing, and your Ladyship's adorer. (*Going*)

Enter LADY JANE.

LADY JANE. (*Aside*) Now to plague 'em both.——Sister, you may hear it from himself.

MILLAMOUR. Confusion!

LADY BELL. That lady, Sir, has the strangest notion.——

LADY JANE. You will be so good as to explain all to my sister.

MILLAMOUR. (*Aside*) Both upon me at once.——I have explained, Madam, and all further talk about it is unnecessary.

LADY BELL. Only to satisfy her curiosity.

LADY JANE. To show my sister her mistake.

MILLAMOUR. (*To Lady Jane*) I have made everything clear, Ma'am.——(*To Lady Bell*) Have not I, Lady Bell? And a—— (*Turns to Lady Jane*) Everything now is upon a proper footing.

LADY JANE. Very well; only give her to understand——

MILLAMOUR. Your understanding is admirable. (*Turns to Lady Bell*) I told you she would talk in this style. (*Turns to Lady Jane*) You are perfectly right, and nobody understands things better. (*Turns to Lady Bell*) Nobody whatever. (*Looks and laughs at both by turns*)

LADY BELL. But give me leave. You must speak out, Sir.

MILLAMOUR. (*Aside to Lady Bell*) Never argue about it; it is not worth your while.

LADY JANE. There is some mystery in all this.

MILLAMOUR. No; all very clear: (*To Lady Jane*) drop it for the present.

LADY BELL. But I desire no doubt may remain. ⎫ *Pulling him*
LADY JANE. And I don't like to be kept in suspense.⎰ *by the arm*

MILLAMOUR. Distraction! I am like a lawyer that has taken fees on both sides. [*Aside*] You do me honour, ladies; but upon my soul, I can't help laughing. It will divert us some day or other, this will. Oh! ho! ho! I shall die with laughing. (*Breaks from them*)

Enter MRS. BROMLEY *and* SIR JOHN.

MRS. BROMLEY. What is all this uproar for?

MILLAMOUR. Another witness of my folly! (*Runs to the other side*)

Enter DASHWOULD.

DASHWOULD. Millamour, I give you joy. Mr. Copyhold, your attorney, is come with the deeds. What's the matter?

MILLAMOUR. The strangest adventure! I can't stay now. The ladies have been very pleasant. You love humour, and they have an infinite deal. I'll come to you in a moment.

Exit.

SIR JOHN. George, don't run away: let us finish the business.

DASHWOULD. If he says he'll marry, you may depend upon him. A poet determined to write no more, or a gamester forswearing play, is not so sure to keep his word. I wish I may die if I don't think him as much to be relied upon as a prime minister.

LADY BELL. Aunt? Would you believe it? The demure Lady Jane—— (*Bursts into a laugh*) She has taken such a fancy into her head! Millamour she thinks is up to the eyes in love with her.

MRS. BROMLEY. Ha! ha! ha! Poor Lady Jane!

LADY JANE. And my sister's pride is hurt. She carries it with an air, as if she had made a complete conquest.

MRS. BROMLEY. How ridiculous the girls are! Your son has open'd his mind to you, Sir John?

SIR JOHN. He has, and I approve of his choice. I hope it is as agreeable to you as to his father.

MRS. BROMLEY. I don't know how to refuse my consent.

Enter BYGROVE, *listening.*

BYGROVE. What does all this mean?

DASHWOULD. [*Aside*] As I could wish. There he is. (*Seeing Bygrove*)

MRS. BROMLEY. Since it has your approbation, Sir John, I believe I must yield my consent. I never thought to marry again, but since you will have it so——

SIR JOHN. Lady Bell, I understand, is willing to do me the honour of being my daughter-in-law.

LADY BELL. Oh! ho! ho! ho! This makes amends for all. My dear Aunt Bromley, you are imposed upon? Did you listen to the traitor's vows?——The dear, perfidious! (*Laughs violently*)

DASHWOULD. He will soon be settled, Sir John, since there are now three rival goddesses contending for him. Mr. Bygrove, you are come in good time.

BYGROVE. What fool's part are you to play now? (*Coming forwards*)

MRS. BROMLEY. Sir John, I desire I may not be made your sport. Have not I here, under his hand, a declaration of his mind; here, in this copy of verses, given to me by himself, an earnest of his affection?

LADY BELL. Verses! Aunt?

LADY JANE. Verses to you?

MRS. BROMLEY. Verses to me: only hear, Sir John. (*Reads*)

"I look'd, and I sigh'd, and I wish'd I could speak,
   And fain would have paid adoration."

LADY BELL. Stay, stay; mine begin the same way. (*Takes out a paper*)

LADY JANE. The very words of mine. (*Takes out a paper*)

MRS. BROMLEY. Will those girls have done? (*Reads*)

"But when I endeavour'd the matter to break,"

LADY BELL. (*Reads*)

"Still then I said least of my passion."

MRS. BROMLEY. Will you be quiet? (*Reads*)

"Still then I said least of my passion.
   I swore to myself"——

LADY BELL. (*Reads fast*)

"And resolv'd I would try,"

MRS. BROMLEY *and* LADY BELL. (*Reading together*)

"Some way my poor heart to recover."

LADY JANE, LADY BELL, *and* MRS. BROMLEY. (*Reading eagerly together*)

"But that was all vain, for I sooner could die,
  Than live with forbearing to love her." [41]

LADY BELL. Oh! ho! ho! ho! Mr. Dashwould, what a piece of work has he made?

DASHWOULD. And the verses copied from Congreve.

LADY BELL. Copied from Congreve! (*Laughs heartily*)

MRS. BROMLEY. There, Sir John, there is your son's behaviour!

DASHWOULD. There, Mr. Bygrove, there is the Widow's behaviour.

BYGROVE. And now, Mr. Dashwould, now for your wit.

MRS. BROMLEY. (*To Sir John*) I am not disappointed in the least, Sir.

SIR JOHN. I never was so cover'd with confusion!

LADY BELL. I never was so diverted in all my days.

DASHWOULD. He has acted with great propriety upon this occasion.

MRS. BROMLEY. He has made himself very ridiculous. He has exposed nobody but himself. Contempt is the only passion he can excite. A crazy, mad, absurd—— (*Tearing the paper*)

LADY JANE. An inconstant, wild, irresolute—— (*Tears the paper*)

LADY BELL. Ha! ha! ha! So whimsical a character. (*Kisses the paper*)

MRS. BROMLEY. (*Throwing the fragments about*) This behaviour will give him prodigious lustre. He will shine after this. I hope his visits will cease at this house.

BYGROVE. (*Going up to Mrs. Bromley*) If ever you marry again, similitude of temper must do it.

MRS. BROMLEY. Distraction! Must you plague me too?

BYGROVE. You have appear'd with an air, but it was all struggling.

MRS. BROMLEY. I cannot bear this.

BYGROVE. Heaven knows how you have struggled!

MRS. BROMLEY. And you too? (*Mimics him*) "A match in your

---

[41] Altered from the first two stanzas of William Congreve, *Song.*

family has diverted me of late." I renounce you all. Come, Lady
Bell, Lady Jane, and let us leave them to themselves.

Exit.

LADY JANE. You would not believe me, Sister.

Exit.

LADY BELL. Oh! this to me is as good as a comedy.

Exit.

DASHWOULD. (*To Bygrove*) What shall I give you for your
chance?

BYGROVE. More than I'll give you for your wit. And there's your
answer.

Exit.

DASHWOULD. The old pike is hooked, and struggles still at the end
of her line.

SIR JOHN. Mr. Dashwould, speak to this silly young man. You
have influence over him. Keep him to dinner. You will for ever
oblige me. I must go and pacify the ladies.

Exit.

DASHWOULD. Poor Millamour! Dryden has painted him to a hair.

    "Blest madman, who can ev'ry hour employ,
     With something new to wish, or to enjoy." [42]

End of the THIRD ACT.

ACT the FOURTH
[SCENE I]

[At Mrs. Bromley's]

Enter DASHWOULD *and* SIR HARRY.

DASHWOULD. This way, Sir Harry. While they are all engaged in
the pleasures of the table, I want a word with you in private.

------

[42] John Dryden, *Absalom and Achitophel* I.553-554.

SIR HARRY. With that face of importance! What is coming now?

DASHWOULD. Listen to me: know a little of the subject before you give your opinion.

SIR HARRY. I am all attention.

DASHWOULD. Did you mark Miss Neville, at dinner?

SIR HARRY. You know I did. And when Mrs. Bromley railed at her——

DASHWOULD. She railed at her with a littleness of spirit, that disgraced wealth and affluence, and gave to poverty the superior character. You must have seen in the behaviour of that girl, though treated with pride and arrogance, a propriety that was elegant, and went even further; it interested every heart for her. She is the best of the group. Were I, at the head of such a fortune as yours, to choose a wife, she should be the object of my affection.

SIR HARRY. You have some scheme in all this.

DASHWOULD. I have; to serve you. I should mortify the pride of Mrs. Bromley, by placing a valuable, but helpless, young lady upon a level with her at once.

SIR HARRY. (*Bursts into a laugh*) This is to end in some joke.

DASHWOULD. Wait for the wit before you laugh. I am in serious earnest. Her understanding is the best among them. The others are all artificial; she is a natural character; and if I am not mistaken, has a heart. If I wanted heirs to my estate, she should be the mother of my children.

SIR HARRY. Were I to be the dupe of all this, how you would laugh at me! Ha! ha! ha! I know you too well.

DASHWOULD. Again! Laughing without the provocation of a joke. Don't be the dupe of your own cunning. I know you love her; and will it not be a generosity worthy of you, to extricate merit out of distress? Nay, the merit which you admire? The merit which would do honour to the choice of any man in England?

SIR HARRY. Well, I cannot contain. (*Laughs heartily*)

DASHWOULD. What's the matter?

SIR HARRY. The scrape in which you involved Millamour with the Widow!

DASHWOULD. Foolish! That was Malvil's doing. You'll hear more of it by and by. There is an underplot in all his actions. I advise you for the best. Here is a lady in question, untainted by the fashions of the age. Make her your own. She has no fortune; what then? Show yourself superior to the sordid views that govern the little mercenary spirits of the world.

SIR HARRY. (*Laughs*) I have just recollected what you said of Jack Invoice, upon his marriage.

DASHWOULD. Jack Invoice? He never was intended for anything but to be laughed at. Upon the death of a rich uncle in the city, he comes to the West End of the town, with a plumb [43] in his pocket, and not an idea in his head; marries a fantastical woman of rank, and with a sovereign contempt of all his former acquaintance, mixes with lords and people of quality, who win his money, and throw his wig in the fire to divert themselves. He laughs at their wit, and thinks himself in good company.

SIR HARRY. Admirable! You have him to a hair. (*Laughing heartily*)

DASHWOULD. (*Laughing*) Hey! The picture is like.——(*Laughs*) Pretty well, is not it?

SIR HARRY. Oh! ho! ho! The very thing! Poor Jack Invoice! You have hunted him down.

DASHWOULD. Have I? (*Laughs*) Yes, I think I have been pleasant upon him. But come; to our point: in marrying Miss Neville, there is nothing ridiculous. You like her, that's clear.

SIR HARRY. But she does not like me, and that's as clear. Somebody has done me a prejudice there. She received this letter, and gave it me to read.

DASHWOULD. (*Reads*) "To Miss Neville"—— (*Opens it*) Without a name?

SIR HARRY. A poison'd arrow in the dark.

DASHWOULD. (*Reads*) "Anonymous letters are generally the effect of clandestine malice; this comes from a friend. If your honour, your virtue, and your peace of mind, are worth your care, avoid the acquaintance of Sir Harry. He is the deceiver of innocence, and

---

[43] £100,000.

means to add your name to the list of those whom his treachery has already ruined. Make use of this hint, and act accordingly." A pretty epistle—— (*Pauses*) Don't I know this hand?——So, so! I understand it: I can trace this: say no more, Sir Harry: pursue Miss Neville the closer for this. Will you let such a fellow as Malvil, rob you of a treasure?

SIR HARRY. You don't suspect him?

DASHWOULD. Leave it all to me. Assure Miss Neville that this shall be cleared up. Hush! we are interrupted: go and join the company.

Enter MALVIL.

SIR HARRY. Pshaw! Pox! The company without you——

DASHWOULD. Very well; leave me now. (*Exit Sir Harry*) What's the matter, Malvil?

MALVIL. It will be over presently: a sudden sensation; I can't bear to see others made unhappy. Mrs. Bromley is a very valuable woman, but at times rather violent.

DASHWOULD. And that's much to be lamented, is not it?

MALVIL. You may laugh at it, Sir, but I think it a serious matter. I left poor Miss Neville in a flood of tears; and——here she comes.

Enter MISS NEVILLE.

DASHWOULD. Not rising from table so soon?

MISS NEVILLE. Excuse me, Sir, I had rather not stay.

DASHWOULD. Never mind Mrs. Bromley's humours; come, we will all take your part.

MISS NEVILLE. I am not fit for company, Sir.

DASHWOULD. I am sorry to lose you: I'll leave you with my worthy friend; he will administer consolation.

Exit.

MISS NEVILLE. Was there ever such inhuman tyranny? Insulted before the whole company!

MALVIL. It hurts me to the quick. I could not have believed her capable of such violence.

MISS NEVILLE. You saw that I gave her no provocation.

MALVIL. It pains me to see what I do.

MISS NEVILLE. She breaks out in such passionate onsets, and never considers that an overbearing pride is the worst of cruelty to an ingenuous mind.

MALVIL. There are few who know how to confer an obligation. A disinterested action gives such moments of inward pleasure! Oh! there are moments of the heart worth all the giddy pleasures of life. One benevolent action pays so amply, and yields such exquisite interest, that I wonder people are not fond of laying out their money in that way.

MISS NEVILLE. During the whole time of dinner, it was one continued invective against me.

MALVIL. Millamour's behaviour had disconcerted her. But that is no excuse. Goodness by fits, and generosity out of mere whim, can never constitute a valuable character. I am sorry to see you so afflicted.

MISS NEVILLE. You are very good, Sir.

MALVIL. No, I have no merit in it; the instincts of my nature leave me no choice. I have studied myself, and I find I am only good by instinct. I am strangely interested for you. I have thought much of your situation: our time is short; they will be all rising from table presently. Attend to what I say: since Mrs. Bromley is so incessant in her tyranny, do as I already hinted to you. Withdraw from this house at once. Madame La Rouge has an apartment ready for you. You may there remain concealed. In the meantime I shall be at work for you. I shall prevail upon Mrs. Bromley to keep her word, about the five thousand pounds. That added to what is in my power, will make a handsome settlement for you.

MISS NEVILLE. You heard what she said to Sir Harry.

MALVIL. She wants to drive you to some act of despair; perhaps to give you up a sacrifice to Sir Harry's loose desires.

MISS NEVILLE. Are you so clear about Sir Harry?

MALVIL. (*Aside*) 'Sdeath! I see she loves him.——Hereafter, I will open a scene to astonish you. (*Pauses, and looks at her*) You can never be happy under this roof. Mrs. Bromley will make this quarrel up, I know she will. The whole of her virtue consists in repentance, but what kind of repentance? A specious promise to reform her conduct, and a certain return of the same vices.

MISS NEVILLE. She has made me desperate. I can stay here no longer. I'll go back to the country. I shall there be at peace.

MALVIL. You will be there too much out of the way. When you are settled at Madame La Rouge's, the haughty Mrs. Bromley will see to what she has driven you, and for the sake of her character, will begin to relent. Sir Harry must not know where you are. He means your ruin; I am sorry to say it, but I can give you such convincing proof——

Enter MRS. BROMLEY.

MRS. BROMLEY. Do you go to your room, Madam; let me see you no more today.

MALVIL. It was a mere unguarded word that fell from Miss Neville. (*Speaks to Mrs. Bromley aside*) Millamour is ashamed of his conduct. He is under my influence still: I shall mould him to your wishes.

MRS. BROMLEY. (*Aside to him*) I am a fool to think any more about him. Go to him; watch him all day; you will not find me ungrateful. (*Loud*) And pray tell those girls to come upstairs. (*Exit Malvil*) Mighty well, Madam. (*To Miss Neville*) You must sit next to Sir Harry: you have pretensions, have you? And you must vouch for Lady Bell too? She does not love gaming; that story is all calumny: bespeak yourself a place in the stagecoach; you shall quit this house, I promise you.

MISS NEVILLE. It will be the last time I shall receive those orders, Madam. Your favours are so embittered; there is such a leaven of pride, even in your acts of bounty, that I cannot wish to be under any further obligations. If doing justice to Lady Bell, if avowing my sentiments in the cause of so amiable a friend, can give you umbrage, I am not fit to remain in this house.

Exit.

MRS. BROMLEY. O brave! You shall travel. Give her a fortune! No, let Lady Bell reward her. How!——Millamour, as I live.

Enter MILLAMOUR.

MILLAMOUR. Deliver me, fate! She here:——Madam——I——I——I——you are not going to leave us, I hope.

Enter SIR JOHN.

MRS. BROMLEY. (*Smiling at Millamour*) And how can you look me in the face?

MILLAMOUR. (*Seeing Sir John*) I am glad you are come, Sir, I wanted to——

MRS. BROMLEY. Perverse! What brings Sir John! (*Aside*) ——I shall expect you abovestairs, gentlemen. I must try once more to fix that irresolute, inconstant man.

Exit.

SIR JOHN. What a day's work have you made here?

MILLAMOUR. Sir!

SIR JOHN. Can you expect any good from all this? For ever doing and undoing! These proceedings are terrible to your father.

MILLAMOUR. You know, Sir, that to gratify you is the height of my ambition.

SIR JOHN. For shame! Don't imagine that you can deceive me any longer. Are you to be for ever in suspense? Always resolving, and yet never decided? Never knowing your own mind for five minutes?

MILLAMOUR. I have not been hasty to determine.

SIR JOHN. My indulgence has made me too ridiculous. You will force me to tell you my mind in harsher terms than I ever thought I should have occasion to do.

MILLAMOUR. What has happened today was but a mere frolic, and it has all passed off in a little raillery.

SIR JOHN. And do you think that sufficient? While you remain insensible of your folly; transferring your inclinations from one object to another; hurried away by every casualty, you will prove the jest of all your acquaintance. You will cease to live before you have begun.

MILLAMOUR. This is rather too much, Sir. If I have, in a few instances, departed from a resolution that seemed fixed, you know very well, it is not uncommon; and when a person means an extraordinary leap, he retires back, to take advantage of the ground, and spring forward with greater vigour.

SIR JOHN. And thus you amuse yourself, compounding upon easy terms, for the folly of every hour. There is no relying upon you.

MILLAMOUR. After all, Sir, it is the prudent part to consider everything. The ladies were rather hasty in their conclusion. In our moments of reflection, as objects pass before us, opinion will wear different colours.

SIR JOHN. The very chameleon has that merit: but is there to be nothing inward? No self-governing principle? A ship without a pilot, without rudder, or compass, is as likely to avoid rocks, and quicksands, as you to steer clear of ruin.

MILLAMOUR. You seem exasperated, but I really don't see the cause.

SIR JOHN. No?——Can't you feel how absurd it is to be always beginning the world? For ever in a doubt? Day after day embarking in new projects, nay, twenty different projects in one day, and often in an hour?

MILLAMOUR. Spare my confusion: I feel my folly; I feel it all; and let my future conduct——

SIR JOHN. George, can I take your word? I know you have been at the gaming-table.

MILLAMOUR. The gaming-table!

SIR JOHN. Say no more: I know it all: after the indulgence I have shown you, I now see that my hopes are all to be disappointed. If you have a mind to atone for what is past, pursue one certain plan, and be somebody. The time now opens a new scene, and calls for other manners. Reform your conduct, and I shall be happy. But

I am tired of this eternal levity: my patience is wore out. I shall stay no longer in this house to be a witness of your absurdity.

Exit.

MILLAMOUR. I have made myself very ridiculous here. I can't show my face any more in this family. I'll go back to the Temple, and not marry these ten years. The law leads to great things: a seat in Parliament, a vote or two against your conscience, a silk gown, and a judge; that's the course of things. I'll pursue my ambition.——Honest friend, (*Calls to a servant*) hist! Honest friend, will you be so good as just to get my hat?

Enter DASHWOULD.

DASHWOULD. No, I bar hats. What, going to desert us? The sport is but just beginning. Bygrove has been lecturing his son, and quarrelling with Malvil. The integrity of that honest gentleman is suspected at last. He was the worthiest man in the world this morning, as good a creature as ever was born, but now he has sold himself to the Widow. Lady Bell has been lively upon the occasion; and Malvil, to support his spirits, has plied the Burgundy, till he looks the very picture of hypocrisy, with a ruddy complexion, and a sparkling eye.

MILLAMOUR. You may divert yourself, Sir; I have done with them all.

DASHWOULD. But I can't part with you: you shall join us; Malvil shall have no quarter: he will stick to his glass till his charity for his neighbour begins to stagger; then off drops the mask: he will have courage enough to rail at mankind, and his true character will come forth, like letters in lemon juice before the fire.

MILLAMOUR. Po! Absurd! I am on the rack. Why did you force me to stay dinner? I have been so weak, so frivolous.

DASHWOULD. How so? Because you chang'd your mind? There is nothing more natural. Don't you see men doing the same thing every day? Down goes the old mansion; a new one rises; exotic trees smile on the landscape, and enjoy the northern air; and when the whole is finished, in less than a twelvemonth, the auctioneer mounts his pulpit. "Pleasing contiguity"——"Beautiful, and picturesque scene"——"Delectably featured by Nature"——"Shall I say twenty thousand?"——Down it goes to the highest bidder, who pays his money, and runs away the next morning with an opera singer to Italy.

MILLAMOUR. (*Laughing*) Why, yes, we see these things every day.

DASHWOULD. No doubt; men are fickle, and inconstant.

MILLAMOUR. Very true; it is the way through life; in the lowest rank as well as the highest. You shan't see a journeyman weaver but he has his disgust, like a lord, and changes his lodging, his house of call,[44] his barber, and his field preacher.

DASHWOULD. Certainly; and then there is a real charm in variety. Besides, what you did today was a mere frolic.

MILLAMOUR. Nothing more: and that fellow Malvil was the occasion of it. My heart never rightly warmed to that man. I shall never consult him again. Affairs were in a right train if he had not interposed.

DASHWOULD. You shall have your revenge. I have a mine to spring will blow him up.——(*Laughs*) His advice today has served to produce the Widow's character.

MILLAMOUR. Yes, it has given a display of her. (*Laughs*) How could she think me in earnest? Marry her! I would go into the Army sooner.

DASHWOULD. A good pretty trade, the Army: if you are killed in battle, it is your affair; if you conquer, you may retire, and live very prettily upon half pay.

MILLAMOUR. Very true: the law is a more certain road.

DASHWOULD. A good agreeable life the law is: for ever entangled in the cobwebs of Westminster Hall; and you help to spin them yourself into the bargain.

MILLAMOUR. And at the end of twenty years, you are thought a good promising young man.

---

[44] A house at which journeymen of one trade met and through which they could be found.

DASHWOULD. In the meantime you are constantly hiring out your lungs, and ever in a passion about other people's affairs.

MILLAMOUR. And travelling circuits, in hopes of finding each county distracted: with a barbarous, bloody murder in every jail, and so live upon the calamities of mankind.

DASHWOULD. Like physicians, when a northeast wind, a Lord Mayor's feast, or a jail distemper, has made a good sickly time of it. (*Both laugh*)

Enter LADY BELL *and* LADY JANE.

LADY BELL. Come, Sister, leave the men to themselves. Mr. Dashwould, has their wit frightened you away?

MILLAMOUR. (*Looking at her*) "Look in her face, and you forget them all." [45]

DASHWOULD. Won't your Ladyship have compassion on that gentleman?

LADY BELL. Compassion!——My sister and I, we hope for his protection.

Enter CAPT. BYGROVE.

CAPT. BYGROVE. When you go away from company, Lady Bell, you draw everybody in your train.

LADY BELL. Oh! you have so overpowered me with civil and tender things!

MILLAMOUR. (*Aside*) What does he follow her for?

LADY BELL. A *l'honneur*, gentlemen. [46] (*Goes up to Millamour*) Uncle! Uncle Millamour, when you are married to my aunt, I hope you will be kind to us both. (*Curtsies*)

MILLAMOUR. (*Turning away*) Confusion! Daggers! daggers!

LADY JANE. (*Curtsying*) May I salute you, Uncle?

MILLAMOUR. Po! This foolery! (*Walks away*)

---

[45] Pope, *The Rape of the Lock* II.18.
[46] 1778: "gentleman"; 1786: "gentlemen."

LADY BELL. Let us give him all his titles!——Brother——when you marry my sister.——(*Makes a low curtsy*)

MILLAMOUR. How can you, Lady Bell?

LADY JANE. Uncle!——Brother! ⎤ *Both*

LADY BELL. And Brother Uncle! ⎦ *laugh*

MILLAMOUR. (*Breaking away from them*) This is too much—— no patience can endure it. (*Turns to Lady Bell*) Madam, this usage —— (*Lady Bell and Lady Jane both laugh loud*)

LADY JANE. Come, Sister, let us leave him.

Exit.

LADY BELL. Oh! ho! ho! I shall expire. (*Going*)

MILLAMOUR. Why will you torment me thus? (*Takes her by the hand*) Am I to be for ever made your sport?

LADY BELL. Oh! you would not have me laugh. To be sure, when one considers, it is a serious matter. And though Captain Bygrove (*Pointing to him*) has orders to be in love with me; and though he has declared himself in the warmest terms——

MILLAMOUR. And could you listen to him?

LADY BELL. And yet, after all your promises, when you had touched my heart—— (*In a softened tone*)

MILLAMOUR. Jealous of me by this light. (*Aside*)

LADY BELL. After all your faithless vows, to break them as you have done, like a Turk, or a Jew, or a Mahometan, (*Crying*) and leave me, like Dido and Aeneas, it is enough to break a young girl's heart. (*Crying bitterly*) So it is, it is——there, will that please you? (*Bursts into a laugh*) Adieu, Uncle! My compliments to my aunt——

Exit.

MILLAMOUR. Damnation!

Enter SIR HARRY.

SIR HARRY. Did not I hear somebody crying?

MILLAMOUR. Yes, and laughing too. Captain Bygrove, you said something to Lady Bell; what was it, Sir?

CAPT. BYGROVE. What I desire the world to know; I love her, I adore her. My father has ordered it, Mrs. Bromley approves; Lady Bell encourages me; and I shall be the happiest of mankind.

MILLAMOUR. You and I must talk apart, Sir. You know my prior claim. Attempt my life rather than my love. You must think no more of her, Sir; she is mine by every tie, and so I shall tell her, this moment.

Exit.

DASHWOULD. Now hold that resolution, if you can.

CAPT. BYGROVE. I have managed it well.

DASHWOULD. Admirably!

SIR HARRY. What does all this mean? Dashwould, you are wanted in the next room. Malvil is in for it: he sits toasting Miss Neville, while every idea fades away from his countenance, all going out one by one, and his eye sinks into the dim vacuity of a brisk no meaning at all.

DASHWOULD. I'll look in upon 'em.——Bygrove, I see Miss Neville: let us give Sir Harry his opportunity.

Enter MISS NEVILLE.

MISS NEVILLE. I thought Lady Bell was here: I beg your pardon, gentlemen.

DASHWOULD. Your company is always agreeable, is not it, Sir Harry? The gentleman will speak for himself. Come, Bygrove; I have occasion for you.

Exit with CAPT. BYGROVE.

SIR HARRY. May I now presume, Madam——

MISS NEVILLE. You choose your time but ill, Sir Harry. I have so many things to distract me, I cannot listen to you now.

SIR HARRY. (*Takes her hand*) But you promised to hear me; I have long beheld your sufferings.

MISS NEVILLE. They do not warrant improper liberties. I can be humble as becomes my situation. I hope you will not oblige me to show that spirit which virtue is as much entitled to as the proudest fortune in the kingdom.

SIR HARRY. I mean you no disrespect. That letter is a black artifice to traduce my character: the fraud shall be brought to light; you may rely upon it; nor will you be so ungenerous as to believe the dark assassin of my honour.

MISS NEVILLE. I know not what foundation there is for it, nor is it for me to charge you with anything. I have no right to take that liberty.

SIR HARRY. Why harbour suspicions unworthy of you? In me, you behold a warm admirer, who aspires at the possession of what he loves, and trembles for the event.

MISS NEVILLE. I must take the liberty to doubt your sincerity. I know my own deficiencies, and I beg leave to withdraw.

SIR HARRY. By all that's amiable in your mind and person, my views are honourable as ever yet inspired a lover's heart.

MISS NEVILLE. I would fain express my gratitude. (*Weeps*)

SIR HARRY. Why those tears?

MISS NEVILLE. Your character, I dare say, Sir, will come out clear and unsullied. You will permit me to take care of mine. It is all I have to value. I shall not continue any longer in this house. Mrs. Bromley has made it impossible; I wish you all happiness, Sir.

SIR HARRY. That resolution I approve of: let me provide you a retreat, and in a few days——

MISS NEVILLE. I must beg to be excused: that I can never think of.

SIR HARRY. By Heaven, I mean to raise you to that independence which your merit deserves. I would place you in that splendour which Mrs. Bromley may envy.

MISS NEVILLE. I can only return my thanks. Lady Bell will know where I am. I feel no ambition: I do not want to give pain to Mrs. Bromley: I seek humble content, and ask no more.

SIR HARRY. You do injustice to yourself and to me.——Hey! All breaking up from table!

MISS NEVILLE. You must not detain me now, Sir Harry. I humbly take my leave.

Exit.

SIR HARRY. I wonder what Dashwould will say to all this. I shall like to hear him: he will turn it to a joke, I warrant him. No end of his pleasantry.

Enter MALVIL *in liquor,* BYGROVE, *and* DASHWOULD.

MALVIL. Very well; make the most of it. Since you force me to speak, I say her character is a vile one.

BYGROVE. Here is a fellow whom wine only inspires with malice.

DASHWOULD. Po! malice! Malvil has no harm in him.

MALVIL. You may talk of Mrs. Bromley, but she is as vile a character as pride, and insolence, and avarice, and vanity, and fashionable airs, and decayed beauty can jumble together.

BYGROVE. Here's a return for her hospitality!

MALVIL. Marry her, I say; marry her, and try.

BYGROVE. You shall not have a shilling with Miss Neville.

MALVIL. There, the secret's out: you want to marry her, and make her break her word. Mankind's a villain! A medley of false friends, eloping wives, stockjobbers, and usurers. Wits that won't write, and fools that will. (*Sings*)

BYGROVE. Dashwould, you are a panegyrist compared to this man.

SIR HARRY. Yes, he takes your trade out of your hands.

MALVIL. She is Mrs. Bromley, the widow, and you are Mr. Bygrove, the widower; and so, bite the biter, that's all.

BYGROVE. His wit soars above you, Mr. Dashwould.

MALVIL. Wit is a bad trade. Letters have no friend left in these degenerate times. Show a man of letters to the first of your nobility, and they will leave him to starve in a garret. Introduce a fellow who can sing a catch, write a dull political pamphlet, or remarks upon a Dutch memorial, or play off fireworks, and he shall pass six months in the country, by invitation. Maecenas died two thousand years ago, and you are not historian enough to know it.

SIR HARRY. Dashwould, he makes a bankrupt of you.

BYGROVE. I have found him out: I know him now: a pretended friend, that he may more surely betray you. Go, and get some coffee, to settle your head.

Exit.

MALVIL. Mrs. Bromley will settle your head.

DASHWOULD. Let us take him upstairs; he'll tumble over the tea-table, to show his politeness.

SIR HARRY. (*Taking him by the arm*) Come, the ladies wait for us.

MALVIL. Mankind, I say, is a villain! (*Sings*)

Enter LADY BELL.

LADY BELL. Bless me, Mr. Malvil!

MALVIL. All Dashwould's doing to expose a body. Do you look to Millamour, that's what I say to you.

DASHWOULD. He shan't stay to plague your Ladyship.——Come, Malvil; let us go and be tender of reputation abovestairs.

MALVIL. I'm always tender, and you are scurrilous. (*Sings, and exit, led by Dashwould and Sir Harry*)

LADY BELL. How Millamour follows me up and down! Charming! Here he comes.

Enter MILLAMOUR.

MILLAMOUR. Lady Bell, allow me but one serious moment.

LADY BELL. This bracelet is always coming off. (*Fiddles with it*)

MILLAMOUR. Whatever appearances may have been, I burn with as true a passion as ever penetrated a faithful heart.

LADY BELL. (*Aside, and smiling*) I know he is mine.——This silly, obstinate bauble! What were you saying? Oh! making love again.

MILLAMOUR. By this dear hand I swear——

LADY BELL. Hold, hold, no violence. Give me my liberty, and thus I make use of it. (*Runs away from him*)

Enter CAPT. BYGROVE.

LADY BELL. (*Meeting him*) Oh! I have been wishing for you. How could you stay so long?

CAPT. BYGROVE. They detained me against my will. But you see, I am true to my appointment.

MILLAMOUR. (*Aside to Bygrove*) Are you so? You shall keep an appointment with me.

LADY BELL. I was surrounded with darts, and flames. That gentleman was for renewing the old story, but it is so ridiculous! (*Walks up the stage with Captain Bygrove*)

MILLAMOUR. Distraction! To be insulted thus!

LADY BELL. (*As she walks up*) You have prevailed upon me to be in earnest at last. Since your father has proposed it, and since you have declared yourself, why, if I must speak, get my aunt's consent, and mine follows of course.

MILLAMOUR. (*Listening*) If ever I forgive this.

CAPT. BYGROVE. Mrs. Bromley has consented. (*Then aside to Lady Bell*) He has it; this will gall his pride.

MILLAMOUR. No end of her folly. I was bent on marriage, but now it's all her own fault. And yet she knows my heart is fixed upon her.

LADY BELL. (*Walking down with Captain Bygrove*) You are so obliging, and I have so many things to say to you; but if people will not perceive when they interrupt private conversation.

MILLAMOUR. If ever I enter these doors again, may the scorn of the whole sex pursue me.

Exit.

CAPT. BYGROVE. We have carried this too far.

LADY BELL. The barbarous man, when he should have taken no denial, but have lain on the ground, imploring, beseeching.—— Delightful! Here he comes again. (*Goes to Captain Bygrove*)

Enter MILLAMOUR.

MILLAMOUR. (*Walking up to Lady Bell*) Is it not strange that you can't know your own mind for two minutes together?

LADY BELL. Ho! ho! The assurance of that reproach! (*Walks away*)

MILLAMOUR. (*To Bygrove*) Appoint your time and place: I must have satisfaction for this.

CAPT. BYGROVE. Tomorrow morning, when the marriage ceremony is over.

MILLAMOUR. I shall expect you, Sir. (*Going*)

Enter LADY JANE.

MILLAMOUR. This is lucky. I was in quest of your Ladyship.

LADY JANE. In quest of me, Sir?

MILLAMOUR. In quest of you, Ma'am. I have been waiting for an opportunity, and, if the sincerest sorrow can expiate past offences ——here's a chair, Ma'am. (*Hands a chair*)

CAPT. BYGROVE. (*To Lady Bell*) We may drive him to extremities with Lady Jane: I'll leave you to recover your wanderer.

Exit.

MILLAMOUR. (*Sitting down*) If you will permit me to assure you——

LADY JANE. But while my sister is my rival——

MILLAMOUR. Your sister's charms carry their own antidote with them. If there is faith in man, I mean to atone for what is past.

LADY BELL. (*Coming forward*) So, so; with what pleasure she hears him! Did you speak to me, Mr. Millamour?

MILLAMOUR. There was a time, Ma'am!——(*Turns to Lady Jane*) Now she wants to interrupt us: don't let us mind her, and she'll withdraw.

LADY BELL. Wear the willow, Lady Bell?——Not a word, Sir? You are in the right: my spirits are too violent for you; and though what I say is not absolutely wit—— Do you like wit? I am sure your ought; for it is undefinable, like yourself.

MILLAMOUR. (*Smiling*) That is not ill said.

LADY BELL. (*Sits at a distance*) Horrid! I shall be vapour'd up to my eyes. I'll try my song, to banish melancholy. Where is that foolish guitar? (*Goes for it*)

MILLAMOUR. Now her jealousy is at work. I knew she would be mortified. Let us agree to pique her pride, and probe her to the quick.

LADY BELL. Though I can't sing, it diverts a body to try. (*Sits down, and sings*)

Sabrina, with that sober mien,
The converse sweet, the look serene;

Those eyes that beam the gentlest ray,
And though she loves, that sweet delay;
Unconscious, seems each heart to take,
And conquers for her subject's sake!

MILLAMOUR. Vastly well! (*Listens, smiles, looks at her, draws his chair near her, and beats time on her knee*)

LADY BELL. (*Sings*)

The tyrant Cynthia wings the dart,
Coquetting with a bleeding heart;
Has cruelty, which all adore,
Flights that torment, yet please the more:
Her lover strives to break his chain,
But can't, such pleasure's in the pain.

MILLAMOUR. Oh! charming! charming! (*Kisses her hand*)

LADY BELL. What are you about, you wretch? Only look, Sister: I suppose, Sir, when you have done, you will give me my hand again.

LADY JANE. I promise you, Sister, your triumph will be short.
Exit.

LADY BELL. How she flung out of the room! (*Rises, and walks about*)

MILLAMOUR. You know, Lady Bell, that I am yours by conquest. I adore you still, and burn with a lover's faithful fires.

LADY BELL. Come, and have a dish of tea to cool you.

MILLAMOUR. Hear me but a moment. It is now time you should be tired of this eternal display of your power. Your power is sufficiently acknowledged and felt by all. You may triumph over adoring crowds, but one lover treated with generosity, will be more to your honour and your happiness.

LADY BELL. Pretty, very pretty! I have read all that in one of the poets. (*Repeats*)

"By our distress, you nothing gain,
   Unless you love, you please in vain."

Come upstairs, and I'll show you the whole poem.

"And one adorer kindly us'd,
  Gives more delight than crowds refus'd." [47]

Will you come? (*Beckons him*) Won't you? Well, consider of it,
and when you know your own mind, you may change it again.

Exit.

MILLAMOUR. There now! Everything by turns, and nothing
long. Fickle do they call me? A man must be fickle who pursues
her through all the whimsies of her temper. Admire her in one
shape, and she takes another in a moment.

One charm display'd, another strikes our view,
In quick variety for ever new.

End of the FOURTH ACT.

ACT the FIFTH
[SCENE I]

[At Mrs. Bromley's]

Enter MILLAMOUR *and* DASHWOULD.

MILLAMOUR. Am I to be sacrificed to your humour?
DASHWOULD. Am I to be sacrificed to your absurdity?
MILLAMOUR. When pleasantry is out of all time and place——
DASHWOULD. Why then I shall be tired of all time and place.
MILLAMOUR. Look ye, Mr. Dashwould, it is time to be serious.
The wit that wounds the breast of a friend is the pest of society.
DASHWOULD. The passion, Mr. Millamour, that runs headlong
without cause, and will not hearken to reason, is a greater pest of

---

[47] Altered from John Sheffield, Duke of Buckinghamshire, "To a Coquet
Beauty" (1701), lines 23-24, 29-30.

society than all the little wit that has been in the world. What does all this mean, Sir? What is it about?

MILLAMOUR. If I lost money at play, was it for you to carry the tale to my father? For you to subject me to his reproaches?

DASHWOULD. I don't know by what fatality it happens, but that generally comes last which ought to be mentioned first. I repeated nothing to Sir John.—— Who did? Do you ask that question? Malvil, Sir, with his usual duplicity.

MILLAMOUR. Malvil? He has this moment told me how pleasant you were upon the subject, and at my expense.

DASHWOULD. Yes; when he had revealed the whole, and with false tenderness lamented your folly.

MILLAMOUR. 'Sdeath! I understand it now. I have been absurd here.

DASHWOULD. I don't dislike you for your absurdity: that serves to divert one: Malvil excites other feelings. You know the character he gave you of Lady Bell?

MILLAMOUR. Yes, and all slander.

DASHWOULD. I left him but now, representing you to Lady Bell in the same colours——and here——(*Shows a letter*) here I have him fast. An anonymous letter against Sir Harry, sent for his own purposes, to Miss Neville. All his contrivance, dictated by himself, and written at an attorney's desk. You know old Copyhold?

MILLAMOUR. Did he pen the letter?

DASHWOULD. One of his clerks was the scribe. The young man is now in the house, at my request, and ready to prove Malvil the author. Here he comes——things are not ripe as yet. Say nothing now.

Enter MALVIL.

MILLAMOUR. Walk in; you come opportunely.

MALVIL. If I can be of any service——

MILLAMOUR. To be of disservice, is your province; and when you have done the mischief, you can transfer the blame to others.

MALVIL. I have been rather off my guard today. I am not used to be overtaken in that manner; my head is not quite clear.

MILLAMOUR. Then this business may sober you. What was your whisper to me about that gentleman?

MALVIL. That he treated with wanton pleasantry what I thought a serious matter. I may mistake the means, but the end of my actions I can always answer for. Sir John might hear of the affair from another quarter, and so to soften his resentment——

MILLAMOUR. You took care to excite it.

MALVIL. I——I——I am apt to carry my heart at my tongue's end.

DASHWOULD. I knew his heart was not in the right place.

MALVIL. I did not address myself to you, Sir.

MILLAMOUR. I know you have the grimace of character, Mr. Malvil, arm'd at all points with plausible maxims. But which of your maxims can justify the treachery of betraying the secret of a friend? Who does it is a destroyer of all confidence; and when he attempts to varnish his conduct, with the specious name of friendship, the malignity strikes the deeper: artful, smiling malignity.

MALVIL. I deserve all this. Friendship in excess is a fault. There are bounds and limits even to virtue. It would be well if a man could always hit the exact point. There is however something voluptuous in meaning well.

DASHWOULD. Well-expressed, Malvil! Ha! ha! You are right.

MILLAMOUR. No more of your musty sentences.

MALVIL. Morals are not capable of mathematical demonstration. And——now I recollect myself——it did not occur at first——it was Madame La Rouge told the affair to Sir John. This gentleman here——I suppose you will take his word——he says she hears everything, tells everything, and he calls her a walking newspaper: not that she means any harm——I only mean to say——

DASHWOULD. Oh! fie, don't be too severe upon her.

MALVIL. She said at the same time——you know her manner——she told Sir John that you are in love with half a dozen, and will deceive them all, and Lady Bell into the bargain.

MILLAMOUR. Distraction! She dare not say it. This is another of your subterfuges.——You know, Sir, how you traduced Lady Bell, and made that gentleman the author of your own malevolence. At any other time and place, this sword should read you a lecture of morality.

MALVIL. You are too warm: and since I see it is so, to avoid contention, I shall adjourn the debate.

Exit.

MILLAMOUR. Deceive Lady Bell!——Whoever has dared to say it——Madame La Rouge lives but a little way off. I'll bring her this moment, to confront this arch impostor. (*Going*)

DASHWOULD. You'll be sure to return.

MILLAMOUR. This very night shall unmask him.

Exit.

DASHWOULD. I shall depend upon you. Malvil shall answer to Sir Harry: all his artifices shall be fairly laid open.

Enter BYGROVE.

BYGROVE. Mr. Dashwould, we are now good friends. I have reposed a confidence in you. You know everything between me and Mrs. Bromley, but you see how she goes on.

DASHWOULD. And I see how you go on. You are the dupe of your own policy.

BYGROVE. How so?

DASHWOULD. The Widow's schemes are seconded by your own imprudence. Can't you see, that if Millamour were once married out of your way, Mrs. Bromley would then be at her last stake, and you might have some chance? And yet your son has it in command to defeat my friend Millamour with Lady Bell.

BYGROVE. How! Light breaks in upon me. Gull that I was! My son shall marry Lady Jane directly.

DASHWOULD. To be sure; and the consequence is, that Lady Bell declares for Millamour.

BYGROVE. Right: I am for ever obliged to you: I'll go, and speak to my son, this moment: Lady Jane shall be his, without delay.

Exit.

DASHWOULD. So much for my friend, the Captain: I have settled his business.

Enter MRS. BROMLEY.

MRS. BROMLEY. Mr. Dashwould, I am so distracted——a terrible business has happened.

DASHWOULD. What's the matter?

MRS. BROMLEY. Miss Neville, I can't think what is become [48] of her——she is not to be found, high or low. We have searched everywhere for her. What can be the meaning of this?

DASHWOULD. Is Malvil gone?

MRS. BROMLEY. This very moment: he has no hand in it. He sees, and pities my distress. He is gone to make enquiry. A girl that I was so fond of, and never said an angry word to.

DASHWOULD. You have been remarkably mild.

MRS. BROMLEY. You know how tender I have been of her.—— What can have put this into her head? How long has Millamour been gone?——I understand it now. This is his exploit.

DASHWOULD. You wrong him——I will undertake to discover this plot for you.

Enter BYGROVE.

DASHWOULD. You can comfort the Lady, Sir; I shall return immediately.

Exit.

BYGROVE. May I take the liberty, Madam——

MRS. BROMLEY. Why torment me thus? You are all in a plot against me.

Enter LADY BELL, LADY JANE, *and* CAPT. BYGROVE.

MRS. BROMLEY. There, Lady Bell, there is your lover run away with your cousin.

---

[48] 1778: "become"; 1786: "come."

LADY BELL. I can depend upon her. I can still venture to answer for her honour.

BYGROVE. She will come back; you need not alarm yourself.

MRS. BROMLEY. You have seduced her, for anything I know. I am distracted by you all, and will hear no more.

Exit.

BYGROVE. Mrs. Bromley, permit me to say a word.

Exit.

LADY BELL. I hope there is nothing amiss. I can rely upon Miss Neville's discretion; I think I can. Come, Sister, let us go and enquire. (*Going, looks back*) Hey! You two are staying, to say delicate things to each other.

CAPT. BYGROVE. Our difficulties, you know, are at an end. I have my father's orders to follow my inclination. Had Millamour stayed, I have a plot would have fixed him your Ladyship's for ever.

LADY JANE. And we shan't see him again this month, perhaps.

LADY BELL. Let him take his own way. I am only uneasy about Miss Neville at present.

Enter DASHWOULD. (*With a letter in his hand*)

DASHWOULD. This way, you are wanted: I have a letter here that discovers all.

Exit.

LADY BELL. But what does it say? Let us go and hear it directly.

Exeunt.

SCENE [II]

An Apartment at Madame La Rouge's

Enter MILLAMOUR *and* LA ROUGE.

MILLAMOUR. Have you sent to Dashwould?

LA ROUGE. Yes, I have sent him letter.

MILLAMOUR. Miss Neville here you say?

LA ROUGE. She come an hour ago, all in tear.

MILLAMOUR. Then she is safe.——You are sure you never said anything to Sir John about the gaming business?

LA ROUGE. *Sur mon honneur.* What I tell? I know noting. And I not see Sir John in my house, it is two, tree months.

MILLAMOUR. You shall come and confront Malvil, at Mrs. Bromley's.

LA ROUGE. Bagatelle! What you go dere for?——Bo, dis is all put me off——pay your little bill. Vat is money to you? I so poor, you so rich.

MILLAMOUR. You did not say that I should deceive Lady Bell?

LA ROUGE. Monsieur Malvil, he tell you so?

MILLAMOUR. Yes, and I tremble for the consequence.

LA ROUGE. It is one great villain——I great respect for you. *Vous êtes aimable.* Monsieur Malvil, he is great *fripon*.[49] And I ver sorry he be marry to Mademoiselle Neville.

MILLAMOUR. Married to her?

LA ROUGE. You not know it?——He is marry to her dis day. He take my apartment tree week ago. He not have it known dat he is marry for five, six day; write letter to me dis afternoon; he must be let in ver private; de servant not to see him; go up de back stairs to her room, and so *l'affaire est faite.*

MILLAMOUR. And thus he has seduced her from her relations? Let me see the letter. (*Reads aside*)

LA ROUGE. I not tink him so bad to talk of me, and tell such parcel of story, vid not one word of true.

MILLAMOUR. So; here he is in black and white. To come privately, is he? If I could detain him here, and prevent all means of his escaping——

LA ROUGE. Escape? Up back stairs, he must come thro' dat apartment. (*Pointing to a door in the back scene*) I turn de key in de back door: *voilà votre prisonnier;* he is prisoner.

MILLAMOUR. Exquisite woman! I'll lock this door, and secure

---

[49] Rogue.

the key. (*Locks the door in the back scene*) Hush! (*A rap at the street door*)

LA ROUGE. *Le voilà:* he come now.

MILLAMOUR. Fly, let him in; send once more to Dashwould; I want him this instant; fly, dispatch.

LA ROUGE. I do all vat you bid me.

Exit.

MILLAMOUR. It is honest of her to make this discovery. If this be Malvil——a soft whisper that—— (*Listens*) 'Tis he, I hear his voice——I shall have the merit of defeating villainy, and protecting innocence.——Don't I hear Miss Neville? (*Goes to a room door*) Miss Neville!

MISS NEVILLE. (*Entering*) Madame La Rouge!——Oh, Sir! What brings you hither?

MILLAMOUR. It is your interest to hear me; your happiness depends upon it.

MISS NEVILLE. Alas! I fear I have been too rash.

MILLAMOUR. Command your attention, and listen to me: Malvil has planned your ruin.

MISS NEVILLE. Impossible: he has too much honour: why will you alarm me thus? I am unfortunate, and you, Sir, need not add to my afflictions.

MILLAMOUR. You have trusted yourself to a villain: he means, at midnight, to gain access to your person; to triumph over your honour, and then leave you to remorse, to shame, and misery. Read that letter. (*Gives it her, and she reads it to herself*) She's an amiable girl, and I dare say, will make an admirable wife.—— Hark! I hear him in yonder room. Suppress each wild emotion of surprise, and wait the event.

MISS NEVILLE. I can scarce believe what I read. What have I done? (*Weeps*) You have led me into a maze of doubts and fears, and there I wander, distracted, lost; without a clue to guide me.

MILLAMOUR. I will direct you: rely upon me.

Enter DASHWOULD, LADY BELL, *and* LADY JANE.

DASHWOULD. La Rouge has told us the whole story.

MILLAMOUR. Hush! No noise.

LADY BELL. My sweet girl, how could you frighten me so?

MISS NEVILLE. I blush for what I have done. But Mrs. Bromley's cruelty drove me to despair.

LADY JANE. My dear, all will be well: don't flurry yourself.

LADY BELL. Tho' my aunt vexed you, why run away from me?

Enter MRS. BROMLEY, BYGROVE, SIR HARRY, *and* CAPT. BYGROVE.

MRS. BROMLEY. Where is this unhappy girl?

MILLAMOUR. A moment's patience.

Enter LA ROUGE.

MILLAMOUR. Is he safe?

LA ROUGE. He is dere in the room as safe as in Bastille.

MILLAMOUR. Speak to him thro' the door: now all be silent.

LA ROUGE. Monsieur Malvil, open de door.

MALVIL. (*Within*) Do you open it, you have the key.

LA ROUGE. De key, it is dere: Miss Neville, it is gone to bed; all de house asleep: I in de dark; now is your time.

MILLAMOUR. (*To La Rouge*) Hush! Here is the key. (*Takes away the lights*)

MALVIL. Will you dispatch?

LA ROUGE. *Attendez:* here is de key: I let you out. (*Unlocks the door*)

MALVIL. (*Entering*) All in darkness. Is she gone to bed?

LA ROUGE. (*Leading him*) She wait for you: vere was you marry?

MALVIL. St. James's parish: Sir Harry has not succeeded: she prefers me. Say nothing of it yet awhile.

LA ROUGE. No; not a vord: *tenez*, I get light for you.

Exit.

MALVIL. So; I have carried my point. The family will be glad to patch up the affair, to avoid the disgrace.

LA ROUGE. (*Entering*) Ah! you look *en cavalier;* ver good apartment for you; and dere is good picture. It is Tarquin and Lucrece; [50] Tarquin go to ravish de lady in de night. It was villain, was it not?

MALVIL. A terrible fellow!

LA ROUGE. And dis room it is velle furnish: look about you; more picture, and all original. (*Turns him to the company*)

OMNES. Ha! ha! ha! Your servant Mr. Malvil!

MALVIL. Hell and confusion!

MILLAMOUR. (*Taking him by the arm*) There are bounds and limits even to virtue.

DASHWOULD. (*At his other arm*) Morals are capable of mathematical demonstration.

LADY BELL. (*To Miss Neville*) Let us withdraw from all this bustle. Sir Harry, step this way; I want you.

Exit with MISS NEVILLE, LADY JANE, *and* SIR HARRY.

DASHWOULD. This is all according to the fitness of things.

MILLAMOUR. Something voluptuous in meaning well.

BYGROVE. Dashwould, your ridicule is now in season to expose such a character. He is fair game, and hunt him down as you please.

LA ROUGE. Ah! Monsieur Tartuffe.

Exit laughing.

MALVIL. The fiends about me!——Mr. Bygrove, you are a thinking man; I appeal to you.

MILLAMOUR. I appeal to this letter, Sir. (*Reads*)

"Madame La Rouge,

Miss Neville has this day given me her hand in marriage. I would not have it known for some time. Conduct me to her apartment, unknown to your servants. The way up the back stairs will be best. Your secrecy shall be rewarded by

Martin Malvil."

OMNES. Ha! ha! ha!

MALVIL. The letter is forged——let me see it. (*Snatches at it*)

DASHWOULD. And I have another proof! This anonymous scroll, written by your direction, and sent to Miss Neville, to give a stab

---

[50] The reference is probably to an engraving of the painting *Lucretia and Tarquin* by Guido Cagnacci rather than by Titian or Luca Giordano.

to the character of Sir Harry. Do you deny it, Sir? Your secretary is now in the house; I brought him with me; he is ready to prove you the author of this mean, clandestine mischief.

MALVIL. All false; all a forgery. Where is this French impostor? Where is your witness, Sir? (*To Dashwould*) I'll put them both to the proof, this moment.

Exit.

DASHWOULD. No private parleying.

Exit.

BYGROVE. No; we must all hear.

Exit.

MRS. BROMLEY. Yes; all must hear.

Exit.

MILLAMOUR. My presence may be necessary. (*Going*)

CAPT. BYGROVE. Millamour, stay and give me joy.

MILLAMOUR. Of what?

CAPT. BYGROVE. The idol of my heart! Tomorrow makes her mine.

MILLAMOUR. Well, I give you joy. Who is she?

CAPT. BYGROVE. My Lady Bell, thou dear fellow: come, let us go and see what they are about.

MILLAMOUR. Let us go and see who shall cut the other's throat.

CAPT. BYGROVE. A pleasant employment.

MILLAMOUR. You shall tear this heart out before you tear Lady Bell from me.

CAPT. BYGROVE. Very well; have your frolic.——This works as I could wish. [*Aside*]

Exit.

MILLAMOUR. Despair and phrensy! If she is capable of a treachery like this——

Enter LADY BELL.

LADY BELL. You have done some good at last, Mr. Millamour.

MILLAMOUR. Lady Bell! (*Pauses and looks at her*) I once thought ——but you will break my heart.

LADY BELL. It will bend a little, but never break.

MILLAMOUR. Will you listen to me? There is a tyrant fair, and you have interest with her; you can serve me; all the joys of life are center'd there.

LADY BELL. (*Smiles aside*) He is mine against the world. And so you want my interest? That's lucky, for I have a favour to request of you.

MILLAMOUR. Is there a favour in the power of man, you may not command at my hands?

LADY BELL. You are very good, Sir; there is a person, but the levity of his temper——

MILLAMOUR. (*Aside*) She means me—— Your beauty will reclaim him.

LADY BELL. (*Smiles at him*) May I rely upon you?

MILLAMOUR. What an angel look there was. And do you ask the question.

LADY BELL. When sincere affection——

MILLAMOUR. It is generous to own it.

LADY BELL. And since the impression made by——

MILLAMOUR. Do not hesitate.

LADY BELL. Made by Captain Bygrove——

MILLAMOUR. Made by Captain Bygrove! (*Turns away*)

LADY BELL. That wounds deep——and if you will assist my fond, fond hopes——it will be generous indeed.

MILLAMOUR. This is a blow I never looked for—— Yes, Ma'am, it will be generous——and in return, if you will intercede for me with Lady Bell——po! with a——with Lady Jane, I say——I say if you will intercede for me with Lady Jane——

LADY BELL. Oh! by all means. And as I approve of your choice, (*He walks away, she follows him*) I hope you will approve of mine; and by mutual acts of friendship, we may promote each other's happiness.

Enter DASHWOULD.

DASHWOULD. Malvil is detected.

LADY BELL. And Sir Harry has settled everything with Miss Neville. Go and wish him joy. (*Exit Dashwould*) My sweet friend will be happy at last. (*Going*)

MILLAMOUR. (*Taking her hand*) But you won't marry the Captain?

LADY BELL. Will you make interest for me?

MILLAMOUR. How can you torment me thus?

LADY BELL. You have done some service, and you may now entertain a degree of hope. (*Smiling at him*) But have you another copy of verses for my aunt?

MILLAMOUR. How can you? (*Kisses her hand; exit Lady Bell*)—— She yields, and I am blessed indeed.

Enter BYGROVE, MALVIL, *and* CAPT. BYGROVE.

BYGROVE. The fact is too clear, Mr. Malvil.

MALVIL. And shall the word of that French impostor——

MILLAMOUR. She has acted fairly, Sir; what reparation can you make the lady whose ruin you have attempted?

MALVIL. Mrs. Bromley promised her a fortune, and I have promised her marriage.

Enter DASHWOULD.

DASHWOULD. And I forbid the banns. Sir Harry has concluded a match with Miss Neville: I should have thought him ridiculous if he had not.

MALVIL. That you will do, whether he deserves it or not.

MILLAMOUR. You, Sir, deserve something worse than ridicule. You are thoroughly understood. Your tenderness for your neighbour, is malignant curiosity; your half hints, that hesitate slander, speak the louder; and your silence, that affects to suppress what you know, is a mute that strangles.

MALVIL. The probity of my character, Sir——

DASHWOULD. Ay, probity is the word. He has had pretty perquisites from his probity; legacies, trust money, and the confidence of families. For aught I see, probity is as good a trade as any a going.

OMNES. Ha! ha! ha!

MALVIL. The still voice of truth is lost: you are all in a combination.

BYGROVE. And you have forced me to be of the number.

Enter MRS. BROMLEY.

MALVIL. Mrs. Bromley! You will judge with candour.

MRS. BROMLEY. Oh! Sir, it is all too plain.

MALVIL. It is in vain to contend: I shall be cautious what I say of any of you: my heart is with you all.

Exit.

BYGROVE. Farewell, hypocrite!

OMNES. Ha! ha! ha!

Enter LADY BELL, MISS NEVILLE, SIR HARRY, *and* LADY JANE.

LADY BELL. Here, Sir Harry, in the presence of this company, I give you, in this friend of mine, truth, good sense, and virtue. Take her, Sir, and now you have got a treasure.

SIR HARRY. (*To Miss Neville*) It shall be my pride to raise you to that sphere of life which you merit, and your sufferings from—— (*Looks at Mrs. Bromley*)

MRS. BROMLEY. Why fix on me, Sir?

SIR HARRY. They are much mistaken who can find no way of showing their superior rank but by letting their weight fall on those whom fortune has placed beneath them.

DASHWOULD. And that sentiment, however I may rattle, I wish impressed upon all the patrons of poor relations, throughout his Majesty's dominions.

MISS NEVILLE. Mrs. Bromley, I have much to say to you. My obligations to you, I shall never forget. I am not ashamed, even in the presence of Sir Harry, to own the distress in which you found me. If at any time I have given offence, if under your displeasure, I have been impatient, you will allow for an education that raised me much above my circumstances. That education shall teach me to act as becomes Sir Harry's lady, with affection, with duty to him; and to you, Madam, with gratitude for that bounty which saved me from calamity and ruin.

MRS. BROMLEY. Your words overpower me. I feel that I have done wrong. I now see that to demand in return for favours conferred, an abject spirit, and mean compliance, is the worst usury society knows of. I rejoice at your good fortune: your merit deserves it. (*They embrace*)

DASHWOULD. Why this is as it should be.——Mr. Bygrove, I hope soon to wish you joy.

BYGROVE. Compared to Malvil, thou art an honest fellow, and I thank you.

DASHWOULD. Millamour, is there no recompence for your virtue? In a modern comedy, you would be rewarded with a wife.

MILLAMOUR. Lady Bell has more than poetical justice in her power. I wish Sir John were here: he would now see me reclaimed from every folly, by that lady.

MRS. BROMLEY. If it is so, I can now congratulate you both.

LADY BELL. It is even so, Aunt; the whim of the present moment. Mr. Millamour has served my amiable friend, and I have promised him my hand——and so (*Holds up both hands*) which will you have? Puzzle about it, and know your own mind if you can.

MILLAMOUR. With rapture thus I snatch it to my heart.

LADY BELL. Sister, what nunnery will you go to? Mr. Bygrove, command your son to take her.

CAPT. BYGROVE. That command I have obeyed already.

LADY JANE. Since the truth must out, we made use of a stratagem to fix my sister, and that gentleman.

LADY BELL. To fix yourself, if you please. I knew you would be married before me.

MILLAMOUR. Dashwould, give me your hand. Your wit shall enliven our social hours, and while I laugh with you at the events of life, you shall see me endeavour to weed out of my own mind every folly.

DASHWOULD. You do me honour, Sir. And, if Mr. Bygrove will now and then give and take a joke——

BYGROVE. As often as you please: but take my advice, and don't lose your friend for your joke.

DASHWOULD. By no means, Mr. Bygrove;——except now and then, when the friend is the worst of the two.[51]

MILLAMOUR. Well, there is some weight in Mr. Bygrove's observation:——and yet, as Dashwould says, conversation without a zest of wit, may flatten into a sort of insipidity, and——

LADY BELL. Oh! to be sure: change your mind about it.

MILLAMOUR. There is one subject, Lady Bell, upon which my mind will never change. The varieties of life, till now distracted my attention.

But when our hearts victorious beauty draws,
We feel its pow'r, and own its sov'reign laws;
To that subservient all our passions move,
And ev'n my constancy shall spring from love.

EPILOGUE,

Written by Mr. Garrick.

Spoken by Mrs. Mattocks.

If after tragedy 'tis made a rule,
To jest no more, I'll be no titt'ring fool,
To jog you with a joke in tragic doze,
And shake the dewdrops from the weeping rose.

Prudes of each sex affirm, and who denies?
That in each tear a whimp'ring Cupid lies.

---

[51] Again, this is a characteristic of Samuel Foote, the model for Dashwould.

To such wise, formal folk, my answer's simple;
A thousand Cupids revel in a dimple!
From those soft nests, with laughter, out they rush,
Perch'd on your heads, like small birds in a bush.
Beauty resistless in each smile appears:
Are you for dimples, ladies, or for tears?
Dare they in comedy our mirth abridge?
Let us stand up for giggling privilege;
Assert our rights, that laughter is no sin,
From the screw'd simper, to the broad-fac'd grin.

So much for self; now turn we to the poet:
"KNOW YOUR OWN MIND."——Are any here who know it?
To know one's mind is a hard task indeed,
And harder still for us, by all agreed.
Cards, balls, beaux, feathers, round the eddy whirling,
Change every moment, while the hair is curling.
The Greeks say——"Know Thyself" [52]——I'm sure I find,
I know myself that I don't know my mind.

Know you your minds, wise men?——Come, let us try.
I have a worthy cit there in my eye; (*Looking up*)
Tho' he to sneer at us takes much delight,
He cannot fix where he shall go tonight:
His pleasure and his peace are now at strife,
He loves his bottle, and he fears his wife.
He'll quit this house, not knowing what to do;
The Shakespeare's Head [53] first gives a pull or two,
But with a sideling struggle he gets through.
Darts across Russel Street: then with new charms,
The Siren Luxury his bosom warms,
And draws him in the vortex of the Bedford Arms.[54]

---

[52] The inscription over the portico of the temple of Apollo at Delphi—a maxim of Solon.

[53] A tavern under "The Piazza" or decorative arcades of Covent Garden.

[54] A more fashionable tavern at Covent Garden, not to be confused with the Bedford Coffeehouse, near Covent Garden Theatre.

Happy this night!——But when comes wife and sorrow?
"Tomorrow, and tomorrow, and tomorrow." [55]

I see some laughers here; pray which of you
Know your own minds?——in all this house but few!
Wits never know their minds;——our minor bards,
Changing from bad to worse, now spin charades.
O'er law and physic we will draw a curtain;
There nothing but uncertainty is certain:
Grave looks, wigs, coats——the doctors now relinquish 'em,
They're right——from undertakers to distinguish 'em.

The courtiers, do 'em justice, never doubt,
Whether 'tis better to be in or out.
Some patriots too, know their own mind and plan;
They're firmly fix'd, to get in when they can;
Gamesters don't waver; they all hazards [56] run,
For some must cheat, and more must be undone.
Great statesmen know their minds, but ne'er reveal 'em;
We never know [57] their secrets 'till we feel 'em.

Grant me a favour, critics, don't say nay;
Be of one mind with me, and like this play;
Thence will two wonders rise: wits will be kind,
Nay more——behold, a woman knows her mind!

---

[55] *Macbeth* V.v.19.
[56] There is a pun since *hazard* is a dice game.
[57] 1778: "know"; 1786: "knew."